HOGARTH and EUROPE

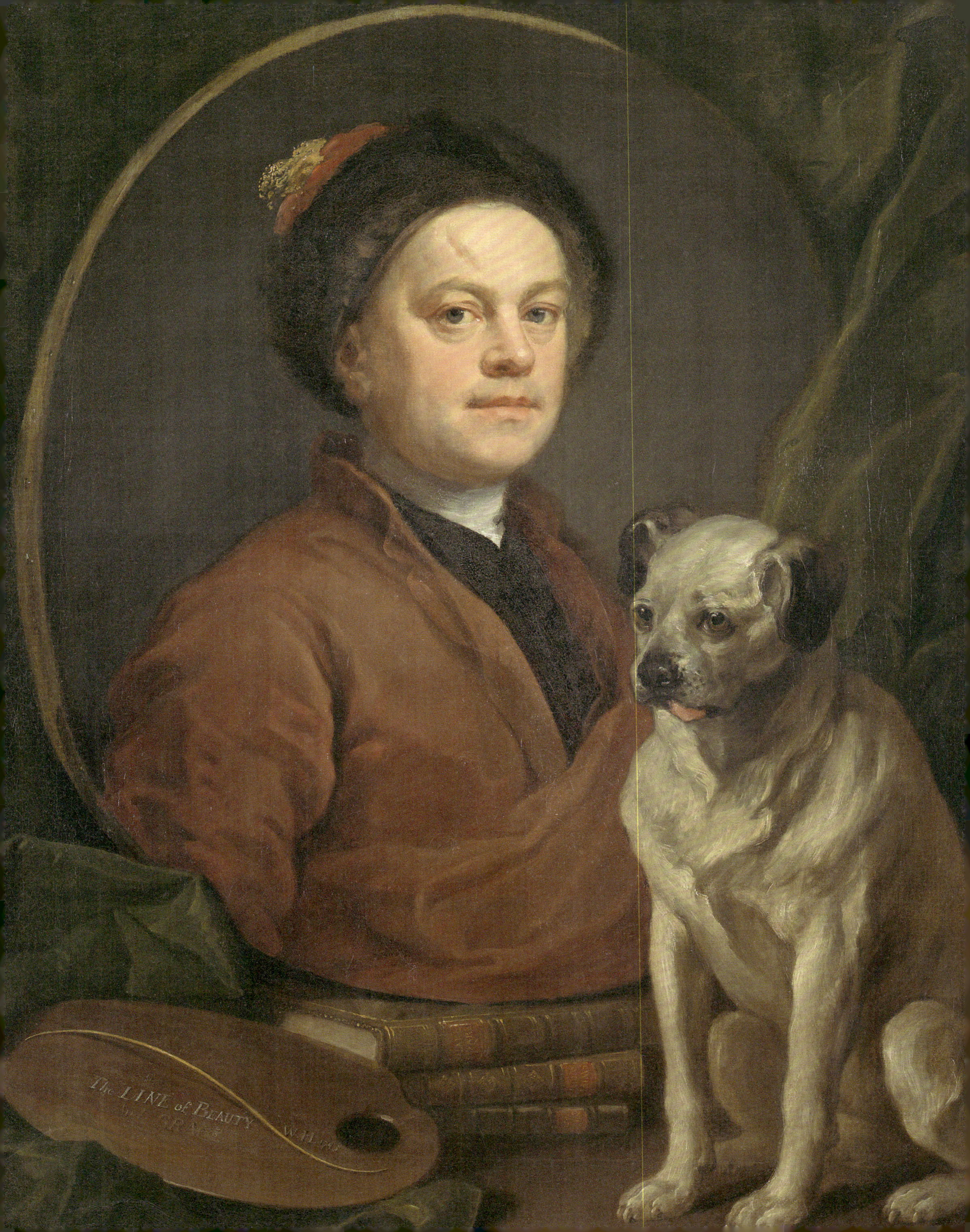

The LINE of BEAUTY
W. H. 1745

HOGARTH

AND

EUROPE

EDITED BY

ALICE INSLEY AND MARTIN MYRONE

CONTRIBUTIONS BY

SONIA E. BARRETT, JOSEPHINA DE FOUW,
MEREDITH GAMER, CORA GILROY-WARE,
LUBAINA HIMID, ALICE INSLEY,
PAUL KNOLLE, GERHARD DE KOK,
MARTIN MYRONE, TEMI ODUMOSU,
STACEY SLOBODA, LARS THARP,
HANNAH WILLIAMS AND JONNY YARKER

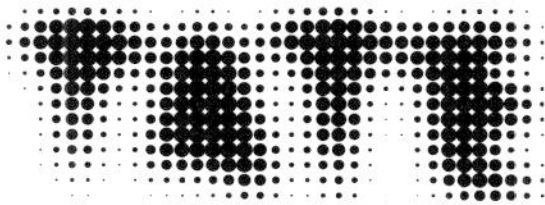

First published 2021 by order of the
Tate Trustees
by Tate Publishing, a division of
Tate Enterprises Ltd,
Millbank, London SW1P 4RG
www.tate.org.uk/publishing

on the occasion of the exhibition

Hogarth and Europe

Tate Britain
3 November 2021 – 20 March 2022

Supported by

Mala Gaonkar

With additional support from Tate
Americas Foundation and Tate Patrons

A catalogue record for this book
is available from the British Library

ISBN 978 1 84976 768 2

Distributed in the United States
and Canada by ABRAMS, New York
Library of Congress Control Number
applied for

Senior Editor: Nicola Bion
Production: Juliette Dupire
Picture Researcher: Emma O'Neill
Design: Wolfe Hall

'"The Dutch Hogarth": Cornelis Troost',
by Josephina de Fouw, translated by
Lynne & Paul Richards
'Amsterdam', by Paul Knolle,
translated by Ted Alkins

Colour reproduction
by DL Imaging, London
Printed and bound in Italy
by Graphicom
Typeset in Castling by Souvenir Typefaces
and Baskerville Original by Storm
Type Foundry

Cover: WILLIAM HOGARTH, *O the Roast Beef
of Old England ('The Gate of Calais')* 1748
(detail, see p.57)
Frontispiece: WILLIAM HOGARTH,
The Painter and his Pug (detail, see p.58)

Measurements of artworks are given
in centimetres, height before width
and depth

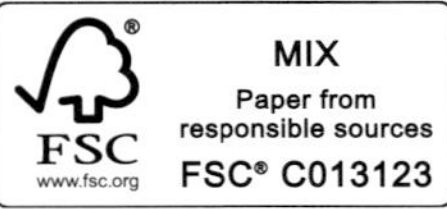

FOREWORD

The celebrated double-act of Hogarth and his dog Trump captured in the familiar self-portrait in Tate's collection has often been cast as signalling a definite sense of national character: Hogarth the true Brit, creative but down to earth, an intellectual, but cheeky and irreverent, an underdog, surely. In the hardly less famous painting *O The Roast Beef of Old England*, Hogarth appears sketching the fortifications at Calais and at the very moment of being mistakenly arrested as a spy in 1748. Here, a spectrum of moral and personal failings projected onto the French are embodied, in the unflatteringly portrayed women resembling the fish they sell, the scrawny and ragged soldiers barely sustained by watery soup, and the greedy friar, reportedly modelled on Hogarth's friend, the engraver John Pine. The 'Old England' – symbolised by the beef – is, Hogarth implies, prosperous and plentiful, its citizens free, and free to fill their bellies with simple, hearty fare.

Such patriotic overtones, to the point of xenophobia (here, drawing on already popular sentiments and not sparing the Irish, Scottish or Catholics either), have come to typify Hogarth as the 'true Brit' and, for some, the 'father' of English painting. But as this exhibition sets out to demonstrate, such paintings as *The Painter and his Pug* and *Roast Beef* can also be located within European contexts, and those European contexts might also point to wider, global networks as well. The self-portrait certainly had origins in European examples and was closely paralleled in the Dutch artist Cornelis Troost's self-imaging. Meanwhile, the dog would have been thought of as a Dutch breed, but also potentially as originating in China. In the luscious still-life details, Hogarth's *O The Roast Beef* seems indebted to Chardin, whose work he had recently seen in Paris. The recognisable locale and framing archway associate it with *vedute* or city views, made increasingly popular by Canaletto's presence in London from 1746. The anti-French imagery itself, recent scholarship has suggested, drew upon ideas and perceptions rooted in the accounts of the large Huguenot (French Protestant refugee) community in London, which Hogarth was closely connected to, including in his friendship with the Swiss miniaturist André Rouquet, who promoted his art across the channel. Additionally, *Roast Beef* was soon engraved and widely circulated, Hogarth's profile was lifted and widely copied including as trade cards and shop signs, and the whole scene appears on ceramics, notably punchbowls and vases painted in China for the English market. It is not long, then, before the overt nationalism of Hogarth's paintings is unsettled and complicated.

Previous Tate shows have helped establish Hogarth as a major figure in eighteenth-century culture. The last major Tate exhibition in 2007, curated by Mark Hallett and Christine Riding, drew on the full range of recent scholarship, presenting a comprehensive and multi-faceted view of Hogarth's modernity and the complex urban contexts of his art. Meanwhile, exhibitions elsewhere have looked at his printmaking, individual narrative series, or the display and reception of his work, further enriching our understanding of the artist and deepening the appreciation of his achievements, including most recently *Hogarth: Place and Progress* at Sir John Soane's Museum, London, in the winter of 2019–20.

This exhibition takes a different view of Hogarth. The English artist's major works appear in force, but rather than set out a biographical narrative or a series of contexts for aspects of Hogarth's art, the show offers a more fragmentary presentation of his work, connecting it with works by artists operating in Paris, Amsterdam, Venice and elsewhere to expose parallels, continuities, connections and contrasts. Such moments of correspondence or divergence might be in the social, secular and urban concerns expressed, the observational comedy and irreverence, or, to differing degrees, the development of new genres and styles. Alongside some of the canonical European artists featured, we hope that the quality and interest of perhaps less familiar figures will become clear, and that together these works will fruitfully give a sense of the changing times of eighteenth-century Europe: shifting ideas about who artists are and what role they play in society, the growth of cities as spaces of cultural production, and the new ideas about personal identity and behaviour that might be both liberating and constraining. The exhibition benefits enormously from the contributions of our invited authors, who bring a range of perspectives including that of practising artists, creative writers, historians and curators as well as art historians and make for a more expansive set of engagements with Hogarth and the worlds of eighteenth-century art than the co-curators alone could provide. This has been coupled with the generous support and contribution of Esther Chadwick, David Dibosa and Raimi Gbadamosi, who have brought their critical expertise and nuanced commentary to bear in shaping this publication and exhibition in its final stages.

As the curators note in their preface, the show has roots in a workshop organised in 2014 by the Paul Mellon Centre, and we would like to thank Mark Hallett, Director of Studies, for his ongoing support of the event and his participation, along with everyone who attended. Alongside this, I would like to warmly thank Martin Myrone, a former Tate colleague and now Convenor of the British Art Network at the Paul Mellon Centre, for developing and curating this exhibition with Alice Insley, Assistant Curator, Historic British Art, alongside Tim Batchelor, Assistant Curator, British Art 1550–1750, and Kiko Noda, Exhibitions Registrar. I also join the curators in thanking the numerous colleagues at Tate and the many curators, conservators and scholars who contributed to the making of this exhibition and catalogue.

At a time when we have all felt the impact and ongoing challenges of the pandemic, we would like to express our deepest thanks to all the lenders who have nonetheless made this exhibition possible. We are extraordinarily grateful not only for their enthusiasm and generous support of the show, but also for the collegiality, flexibility and understanding that we have been met with throughout, even in the face of such unprecedented disruptions, anxieties and uncertainties. We are delighted to be able to represent Hogarth and his European contemporaries in such force, and special thanks go to Gabriele Finaldi and the National Gallery for lending *Marriage A-la-Mode*, and to Bruce Boucher and Sir John Soane's Museum for parting with *A Rake's Progress*, as well as for their ongoing collaboration in conservation research. The show has also presented a unique opportunity to share artworks very rarely seen in the UK with our visitors and we are thrilled to be including Hogarth's *Miss Mary Edwards*, on display in London for the first time in over a century, and *Southwark Fair*, last exhibited in London in 1972. Thanks to Ian Wardropper and the Frick Collection, and to Cameron Kitchin and the Cincinnati Art Museum respectively, for supporting these exceptional loans. We would also like to thank especially Brent R. Benjamin and the Saint Louis Art Museum for making available John Greenwood's extraordinary, iconic and challenging painting, *Sea Captains Carousing in Surinam*, which is travelling to the UK for the first time since 1976. Last but by no means least, we are equally indebted to the private lenders who have kindly parted with artworks from their collections, including Andrew Edmunds for his continued support of Tate.

We are grateful to Mala Gaonkar for leading the support of the *Hogarth and Europe* exhibition, as well as Tate Americas Foundation and Tate Patrons. It has been made possible by the provision of insurance through the Government Indemnity Scheme. Tate Britain would like to thank HM Government for providing Government Indemnity and the Department for Digital, Culture, Media and Sport and Arts Council England for arranging this indemnity.

Alex Farquharson
Director, Tate Britain

ACKNOWLEDGEMENTS

Hogarth and Europe has been a long time in the making. Both have greatly benefited from the contributions of more people than we can do justice to here. Further to the acknowledgements made by Alex Farquharson in his foreword, we would like to add our thanks for the outstanding generosity of all our lenders, both institutional and private. For willingly sharing their knowledge and for their assistance in preparing works for loan, we would like to thank all the scholars, curators, registrars, conservators and collections managers involved at various stages of this project. Particular thanks to Mikael Ahlund, Sébastien Allard, Peter Bell, David Bindman, Giorgia Bottinelli, Emerson Bowyer, Duncan Bull, Werner Busch, Caroline Campbell, Vicky Carroll, John Chu, Alberto Craievich, India Dial, Simon Dickinson, Helen Dorey, Andrew Edmunds, Guillaume Faroult, Josephina de Fouw, Kate Grandjouan, Frans Grijzenhout, Tom Harper, Colin Harrison, Kate Heard, Helen Hillyard, Annelise Hone, Caro Howell, Julia Jones, Rica Jones, Paul Knolle, Sophy Lin, Becky MacGuire, Jane Munro, Arnould Odding, Frédéric Ogée, Amy Orrock, Carleigh Queenth, Thijs de Raedt, Jenny Reynaerts, Aileen Ribeiro, Christine Riding, James Roundell, Xavier Salomon, Camilla Smith, David Taylor, Jo Tinsworth, Amy Torbert, Robert Wenley and Melissa Wolfe. We would also like to warmly acknowledge the scholarship of Elizabeth Einberg, which forms the foundation of Hogarth studies now.

Like all exhibitions this has been a true team effort and we are deeply grateful to all those from whose expertise, encouragement and support we have benefitted. Particular thanks to Alex Farquharson, Andrea Schlieker and Carolyn Kerr for their support of the show; to Tim Batchelor and Kiko Noda, for their invaluable help at every stage. Many thanks to the catalogue authors, Sonia Barrett, Josephina de Fouw, Meredith Gamer, Cora Gilroy-Ware, Lubaina Himid, Paul Knolle, Gerhard de Kok, Temi Odumosu, Stacey Sloboda, Lars Tharp, Hannah Williams and Jonny Yarker, for their fascinating contributions; to Wolfe Hall for their wonderful book design; and to the Tate Publishing team – Nicola Bion, Juliette Dupire and Emma O'Neill. We are also truly grateful for the insights, collegial support and advice of Sayyeda Abir Khaja, Dina Amuah, Tabitha Barber, David Brown, Esther Chadwick, Amy Concannon, Caroline Corbeau-Parsons, David Dibosa, Mels Evers, James Finch, Raimi Gbadamosi, Carol Jacobi, Daniella Rose King and Mark Miller. Within the Tate project team, we would also like to thank Andy Shiel, Juleigh Gordon-Orr, Liam Tebbs and the art handling team; all our colleagues in conservation, including Jane McCree, Amy Griffin, Gabriella Macaro, Camille Polkownik and Joyce Townshend, for all their work on the technical analysis of Hogarth's paintings; Alessia Arcuri, Soraya Chumroo, Rosie Marshall and Adriana Rojas-Viquez in Design; Kirsteen McSwein, Gillian Wilson and Elliott Higgs in Interpretation; Kitty Malton, Eleanor Costello, La Kingsbeer and Kathy Maniura in the Press and Marketing teams; and Emma Garrett, Federica Cinardo and Michaela Moores in Visitor Experience.

Alice Insley and Martin Myrone

PREFACE

This book and exhibition appear in a context quite different from the one in which they were first conceived. In the most immediate and practical sense, the project originated in conversations with Paul Knolle of the Rijksmuseum Twenthe, Enschede, in 2012, when the displays there were enriched with eighteenth-century Dutch art from the Rijksmuseum Amsterdam and a loan exhibition of 'Golden Age' British painting from Tate. Ensuing discussions around 2013 with the then-director of Tate Britain, Penelope Curtis, led to a workshop supported by Mark Hallett and the Paul Mellon Centre for Studies in British Art in 2014. Prompted by various scholarly efforts to see Hogarth as a European figure, especially Robin Simon's important book on Hogarth and France, and reflecting the success of the 2007 Hogarth exhibition at Tate Britain (which toured to the Louvre, Paris, and La Caixa, Barcelona), this workshop brought together art historians and curators from Britain, Germany, Italy, the Netherlands and Scandinavia, with expertise across European art.[1] Together we reflected on the parallels and connections between European artists at the mid-eighteenth century working in what was broadly conceived as a 'Hogarthian' mode – producing, that is, paintings and prints of modern life with a comical or social-critical dimension. From that conversation it became clear that there were several exhibition projects, rather than just one, that could be developed, focusing variously on: the circulation of print around Europe and the transmission of ideas and images; the emergence of the 'Hogarthian' as a recognisable genre, and the knowing emulation of the English artist in different European contexts and at different times; Hogarth's direct contact with European peers, or the intriguing parallels between the English painter and his European contemporaries in portraiture, narrative painting and urban themes only sometimes – certainly not inevitably – supported by evidence of their direct knowledge of the others' work.

There is no escaping the fact that the world changed dramatically in the months and years after that workshop. In 2014 the 'Brexit' referendum was a Conservative party manifesto pledge, not yet a reality (the term itself existed but was not in everyday use). A quick online search tells us that the press at that time could report that 'Britain is dangerously unprepared for a flu pandemic that could kill as many as 315,000 people', but such a situation, let alone the emergence of a novel coronavirus of the damaging proportions we are experiencing now, still seemed a matter for apocalyptic speculation. The highly publicised deaths of three African-Americans, Eric Garner, Michael Brown and Tamir Rice in the same year, exposed yet again the realities of anti-Black racism, although these realities have been foregrounded in the mainstream press and media far more emphatically in 2020–21. And if the reality of economic uncertainty was increasingly felt and understood within cultural institutions as much as anywhere else in 2014, who could possibly have imagined what we, in 2021, live with and the practical constraints that have resulted?

This project inevitably bears the imprint of these various large historical forces. But it addresses a long-standing aspect of scholarship on William Hogarth, notably his reframing by the émigré scholars Francis Klingender and Frederick Antal.[2] Klingender, a German-born Marxist exiled in Britain where he worked extensively in adult education, saw in Hogarth a populist critic of class relations whose contributions to the art of political caricature belonged to wider historical processes. Antal, an Austrian-Hungarian Jewish émigré whose flight from Nazi persecution took him to London and the Courtauld Institute of Art, developed comprehensive models for the social history of art that were grounded in Marxism and sociology, and which promised to co-ordinate stylistic developments with class struggle and historical change. His book on Hogarth, published posthumously in 1962, established the English artist as deeply informed by, and contributing to, European art, and expressing a new bourgeois outlook.

Antal died in 1954, Klingender in 1955. The years that followed saw the scholarly literature on Hogarth grow and his canonisation as a major figure in British art history with the Tate Gallery exhibition of 1971.[3] If knowledge of Hogarth's biography and reception, his artistic output and literary productions grew profoundly, it was also arguably the case that Hogarth became a kind of heritage figure, a paradoxically comforting sort of social critic. The spark of critical art history was reignited with the more theoretically informed approach of the American literary historian Ronald Paulson,[4] and then with the Marxist and feminist critique and the developing post-colonial academic perspective apparent in the 'New Art History' of the 1980s and 1990s. David Bindman's work embedded Hogarth within the social fabric of the city and opened a multitude of new routes into his art; David Solkin's seminal publication on eighteenth-century politeness placed Hogarth within a transforming cultural context, ambiguously engaging with low and high culture as social formations gained definition. The literary and intellectual contexts of Hogarth's thinking were opened up by Frédéric Ogée, and the material culture aspects of his art explored by Marcia Pointon. The poet and scholar David Dabydeen's studies of Hogarth's treatment of commercial society and, especially, the Black figures in his art pointed to what has developed in only the last decade as a major focus of Hogarth studies: the intersection of aesthetics and empire and the possibilities for social protest in the emerging modern society.[5] Crucially, too, artists including Paula Rego, Yinka Shonibare and Lubaina Himid, who writes below, have engaged critically with Hogarth's work, exploring especially the potential for unsettling the psychological and social critique embedded in his work. This book and exhibition cannot but be richer for this varied heritage of reflection, research and engagement, and the various, sometimes challenging, perspectives it opens up.

But whereas such critical perspectives to other historical British artists, Constable or Gainsborough or Richard Wilson, sent shockwaves that sometimes spread beyond the world of art historians and curators into the public realm, Hogarth's status as a social critic has, paradoxically, insulated him to a degree. While the academic scholarship has exposed the ambiguities in the aesthetic and political dimensions of his art, his popular reputation has endured among both political Left and political Right. His apparent irreverence is sometimes cherished as an assault on lefty-liberal 'political correctness' and sometimes as fierce critique of imperialism or the social elite. Hogarth's freedom of opinion, his critical freedom, the freedom of his characters in fighting and drinking, lusting and lampooning, might seem to be something always to defend and which ought never to be lost. In this respect, Hogarth connects ostensibly opposed political radicalisms in ways which, since 2016 at least, we may be more alert to, with forms of populism that over-ride familiar distinctions between Left and Right, conservative and progressive. Recognising that unnerving historical possibility within Hogarth's art entails not idealising his social-critical dimensions, as appealing as they may continue to be, but emphasising the compromised and conflicted aspects of his art as well, the ways in which his social criticism served insidiously to sustain the status quo.

Like any substantial institutional enterprise, the exhibition project that this publication accompanies has several starting-points and has undergone an extended genesis. It responds to the cyclical impulse within major cultural institutions which leads to established art-historical figures being periodically revisited: as noted above, the last big Hogarth show at Tate Britain was in 2007. The present exhibition can be set within the history of Tate Britain, as a gallery committed to renewing and expanding our understanding of British art. The show manifests the co-curators' training within the discipline of art history and our different engagements with eighteenth-century art. It surfaces, too, and surely in many ways we are not cognizant of, the shifting political, economic and cultural contexts of our time. Most obviously, the title of the show and its basic premise inevitably seems to respond to Brexit, probably, it may be assumed, as an assertion of a cosmopolitan, outward-looking version of an artist often viewed as an insular patriot, xenophobe, or trailblazer of blunt nationalism.

Perhaps initially that was the intention. But this seems less certain now for several reasons. Firstly, the interplay of insular and outward-looking aspects in Hogarth's art and thought have proved to be highly complex, while the practical connections between the artist and his European peers remain incompletely documented. These matters are perhaps better dealt with, as far as they can be, in the context of academic research rather than in an exhibition. Instead, the show seeks to do the art history on the walls, in a less determined and definite way. The connections, resonances, echoes or repudiations which may emerge when Hogarth, Longhi, Chardin, Troost, Crespi, Lancret, and so on, are put together in the same gallery spaces are, we think, not wholly predictable. Nor do they depend upon the kinds of exacting art-historical narratives which can be set out in textual form. The selection and sequencing of works provides a definite framework for these juxtapositions, and we are authors of that. But there are multiple narratives and emphases to be brought into play, and to that end this publication is a collective effort with contributions by art historians, curators, artists and specialists with a range of experiences, expertise and commitments.

Meanwhile, crucially, we are seeing profound and ongoing shifts within art-historical understanding towards what is designated as the 'global' or 'transnational' and efforts towards 'decolonising' art history as a discipline, and of cultural institutions especially.[6] There are responses to these changes apparent here, in our own essay and in several different ways across the written pieces which punctuate the book. While we hope to acknowledge and confront the implicit, and sometimes explicit, prejudices and exclusions of eighteenth-century European culture, and of Hogarth's art particularly, and to highlight that to speak to a 'European' culture is also to speak to global networks, movements (of ideas, resources and people), and exclusions, this is not and cannot be a 'de-centred' or 'globalised' approach. The co-curators are White, educated within British art history and occupy institutional roles in the London art world. Almost all the artworks on display in the exhibition are made by western European, conspicuously all male, artists. All are now in European, British and American collections. This should, rightly, cast doubt on the possibility of offering an account external to the heritage of colonialism. Indeed, as a Eurocentric project, rooted even more narrowly in the perspective provided by the traditions of British art history, it can hardly escape being complicit with the ideas and forces that have shaped and defined 'Europeanness'. There have, accordingly, been challenges issued to us while developing this project by some of the many different people we have talked to or more formally consulted with, which we have not in the event been able to answer.

As the authors of the framing narratives and the organisers of the sequences of works reflected here, we have to acknowledge these occluded perspectives and the possibility for other, more radical, decentring perspectives that would represent more fully the agencies of those subject to colonial violence, or who sat outside European colonialism and beyond the purview of a normative western scholastic outlook. At the same time, we hope that the Eurocentric viewpoint, insofar as it attends to a pivotal narrative about the shifting status of the artist in western society in the mid-eighteenth century and the idea of creative, political and personal freedom that the figure of the creative individual came to embody, also forcibly brings the art into connection with the story of advancing capitalism and urbanism, of the rise of bourgeois society and of imperialism, and to the revolutions – in America, France and Haiti – which promised to undo these. Additionally, at each turn we find that the makers, materials, ideas, characters and narratives projected in the artworks included here, always already, incorporate something beyond, and that the bolstering of a European identity depends upon props and peoples drawn from outside Europe or European cultures.

Alice Insley and Martin Myrone

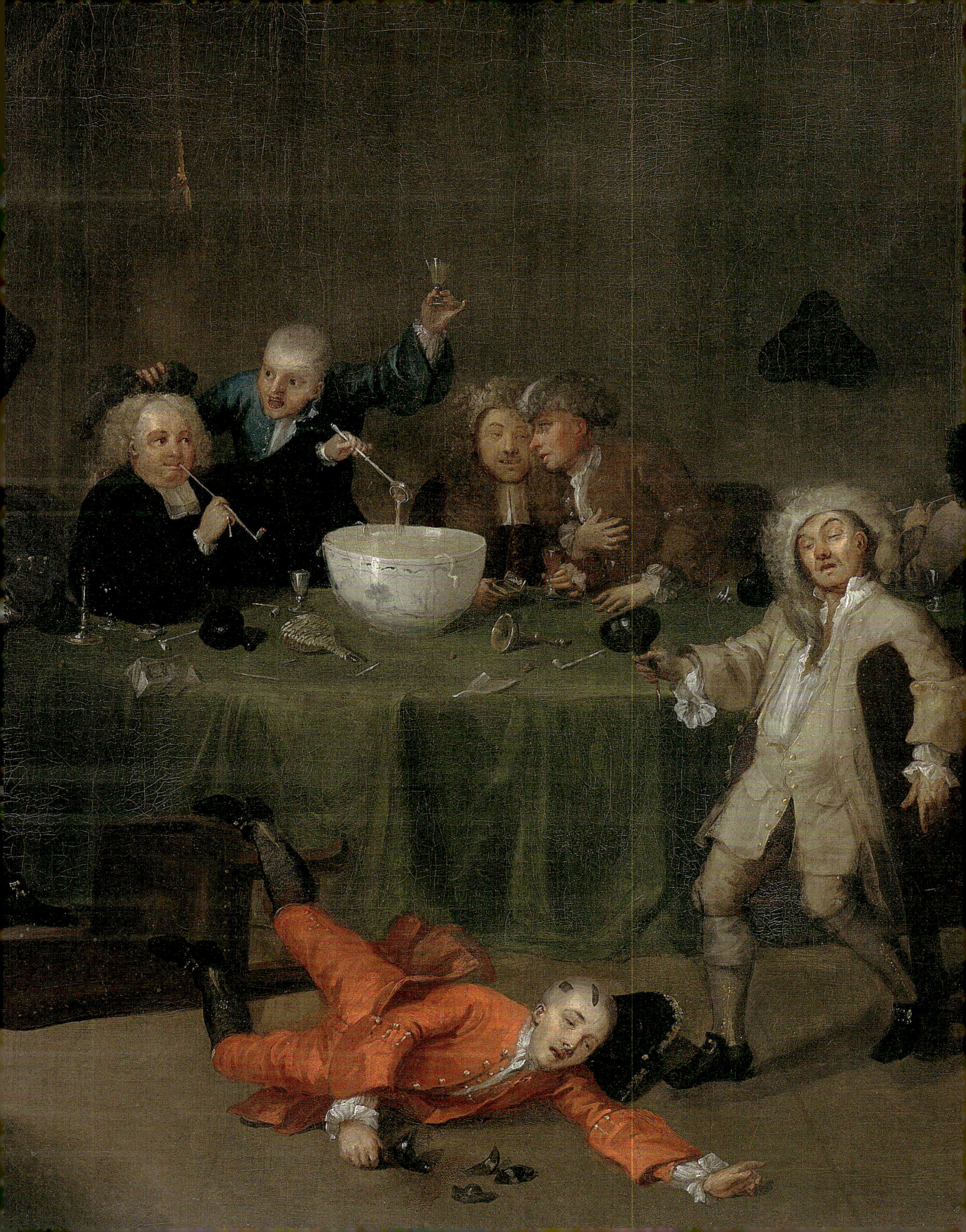

PAINTING MODERN LIFE, MAKING THE MODERN WORLD

ALICE INSLEY AND MARTIN MYRONE

The precise circumstances behind the production of John Greenwood's painting of a tavern scene in the Dutch slave colony of Suriname, on the northern coast of South America, remain obscure (pp.15, 126–7). We know about the commercial and colonial links that brought these men together, as detailed by Gerhard de Kok in his contribution below. We also know that Greenwood moved from Boston to Suriname in 1752, producing likenesses of planters and traders that would presumably have shown their subjects with a degree of dignity, perhaps outright flattery. His treatment of the White American sea captains in his tavern scene is quite different. They knock back drinks, gulp directly from punchbowls, suck on clay pipes, keel over and slump in a stupor. One vomits into another man's coat pocket, unaware that his own coat has been set alight by a candle, while another pisses in the doorway. There is conversation, some card-play, a wobbling attempt at a dance, booze and tobacco, a toppled chair and misplaced hats. The feeling of woozy tavern-room conviviality is insistent and claustrophobic.

The four Black figures in the scene wear only loincloths and are rendered as diminutive, childlike, androgynous: they are presumably enslaved individuals. Two of the figures serve; two more are asleep in a dark corner. Such is the generic character of their treatment, not to mention the nature of the archive relating to displaced and disenfranchised Africans in the eighteenth century, that these Black figures seem unlikely ever to be identified individually, even if they were intended as individuals originally. Yet they have a vital role in the picture: Greenwood's surviving drawings show he put some

efforts into setting out the perspective and establishing consistent light sources, but their presence disrupts the picture's perspectival logic.[1]

The scene derives from a composition by the English artist William Hogarth, *A Midnight Modern Conversation*. That painting – and, more importantly, the multiple painted derivations (pp.12, 124–5) and printed reproductions or versions of it – had a prolific existence: Greenwood would doubtless have encountered one of the prints in America. Subverting the visual convention of the conversation piece (grouped portrait figures engaged in polite dialogue or genteel communal activity), Hogarth's painting shows the participants boozing, smoking, falling over spectacularly. In its European context, Hogarth's composition can be taken as a satirical exposure of the underside of eighteenth-century polite society, the immorality and damaging behaviour that could arise among men when their access to alcohol and tobacco was not tempered by self-control (as cultivated, particularly, by the supposedly softening presence of women and children). But the image is also comical, and it is possible to interpret it as queasily celebrating such manly misdemeanours – what we might today call 'laddishness'.

The same questions of intention – whether the picture is a moralising effort or a dubious celebration of masculine bad behaviour – have hovered over Greenwood's painting. Arguably, such questions will always endure; eighteenth-century European and European colonial societies were sufficiently patriarchal and politically stable enough for the contradictions of the economically and socially dominant class of White men to be paraded openly without unduly compromising their authority.

Greenwood's technical limitations, and the constraining circumstances of working as an oil painter in a tropical colonial context, may play a role here as well. With its oddities of scale and perspective, and painted on bed ticking rather than standard artist's canvas, the painting has an improvised air. In Hogarth's more obviously refined paintings, the presence of servants in the corners of compositions could serve an eloquent narrative effect. If these figures can be idealised as vehicles of social criticism indicting White privilege, pointing out comic details or smirking tellingly, they might also be interpreted as objectified and demeaned.[2] Greenwood's Black figures are more definitely anonymised and diminished, near-naked in contrast to the White men, and androgynous (though presumably male, as they are being ignored). Their shadows, rendered heavily by Greenwood, have almost as much substance as the living figures. On the evidence of this picture, racial Whiteness is defined by movement and individuality, even if that movement involves falling over or throwing up, even if that individuality was exposed as carelessness, self-neglect or even self-abuse. The White men sleep complacently 'manspreading', while the Black figures sleep in a dark corner. If the contrast is stark, starker than when Black figures appear in many pictures produced around the same time in Europe, it was perhaps necessarily so in a colonial context as a justification for the brute inequities of slave societies, and to deflect attention from the ambiguous moral character of those Whites whose ambivalent 'creole' status between European and colonial worlds might otherwise be more seriously unsettling of their social identities.

Sea Captains flags with lively immediacy the global currency of Hogarth's imagery in the eighteenth century. *A Midnight Modern Conversation*, in particular, appeared in multiple versions in print form across Europe, as well as on earthenware, ceramics and Chinese export porcelain (pp.104–5, 123). Greenwood's painting also exposes questions of racial identity and global economics which are generally deeply hidden within eighteenth-century European visual culture. The tobacco and sweetened punch consumed in Suriname was the same stuff consumed in the taverns and private backrooms of London or Paris or Amsterdam; the coffee or chocolate drunk in numberless European conversation pieces (as in Greenwood's colonial American pictures), and the sugar that sweetened these drinks, originated in the Americas, as did the cottons worn, and the mahogany used for the chairs, tables and pianos often shown gracing fashionable interiors.[3] The tea, silk and ceramics that appear in these same pictures followed the trade routes that brought Chinese porcelain bowls to Europe. It is noteworthy, too, that Greenwood himself was a highly mobile figure: after his years in Suriname, he moved first to Amsterdam, then to Paris and London, where he settled. There he exhibited as an artist and published prints but became most notable as an auctioneer. Strikingly, it was he who managed the sale, in 1790, of Hogarth's studio contents after the death of the English painter's widow, Jane.

Meanwhile, the *Sea Captains* remained in the collection of a family in Rhode Island until the twentieth century.[4] During this time, family tradition identified ten of the White sitters as well-known Rhode Islanders. Merchants from Rhode Island dominated the North American share of the African slave trade, continuing to do so even during the Seven Years' War (1756–63) when, despite being a British colony, Rhode Island maintained a lucrative but illegal trade with the French colonies and those of other nations in the Caribbean.[5] If this is a picture of Rhode Islanders, then, it reveals the conflicting interests within the British colonies and the profound degree to which mercantile and public life intersected in North America.

Greenwood's *Sea Captains* and the migrations of Hogarth's *Midnight Modern Conversation* provide the most striking depictions of cultural mobility in this book. However, across the selection there are pictures and artists who may have travelled less far geographically but nonetheless cross national and cultural boundaries in complex ways.

This is true of the Hervey conversation piece, depicting the family group posed within a classical building, looking out upon a seascape prominently

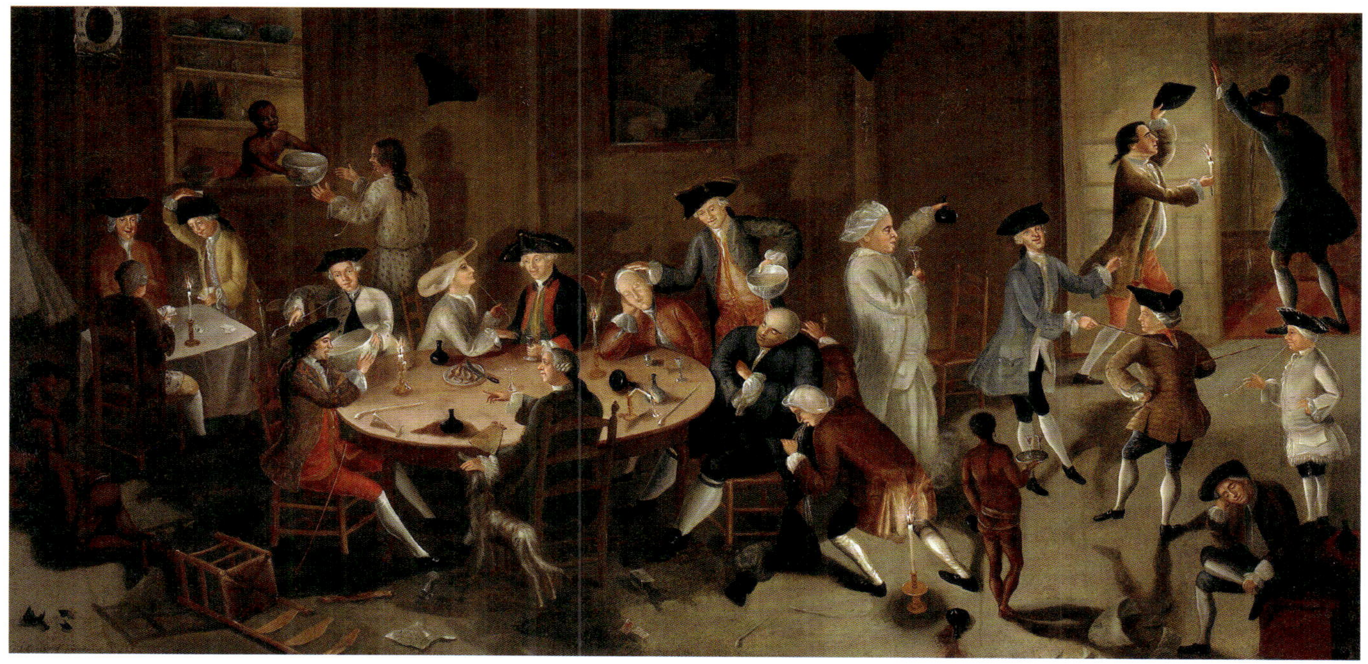

JOHN GREENWOOD   *Sea Captains Carousing in Surinam*   c.1752–8

featuring a Royal Navy ship (p.16). It is now identified as a joint effort by the French draughtsman and printmaker Hubert François Gravelot, the Swiss portraitist Jean-Étienne Liotard and the English painter Francis Hayman. The sitters are accepted as including Mary Lepel, Lady Hervey, seated on the right, with her son, Captain the Hon. Augustus Hervey, in uniform, greeting his two sisters and their husbands.[6] The story of the picture's production is understood to begin between 3 October and 9 November 1750, when the sisters were in Paris together and commissioned a family piece to be composed by Gravelot, but with the faces painted by Liotard. The progress of the painting was delayed when Augustus left Paris; Lady Hervey found the incomplete painting unsatisfactory, refusing to pay Gravelot, and the picture was probably only completed in London, by Hayman, in 1752 (though it has also been suggested that Liotard worked on the picture again when he was in England in 1775). The various contributions of the three artists currently named as the picture's co-producers remain open to interpretation. This history only became clearer with research undertaken in the 1930s, but it is noteworthy that in the 1830s the painting was referenced as 'in the style of Hogarth'.[7]

According to current understanding, the family portrait was produced in Paris and London, by artists who were variously Swiss, French and English, who between them worked in Britain, France and Italy, Switzerland, Austria and Turkey. All six sitters enjoyed cosmopolitan social and working lives, spending time between Britain and Ireland, France and Italy. Augustus Hervey's naval career had already taken in extensive action around the Mediterranean, and was latterly to include notable actions in the Caribbean (the ship in the painting has been identified as HMS *Dragon*, the Royal Navy vessel that Hervey commanded in the Leeward Islands); his sex life was also famously international and adventurous, earning him the title of 'the English Casanova'.

Both Greenwood's *Sea Captains* and the Hervey family picture involve literally physical forms of cultural mobility, with artists and pictures crossing national boundaries. In this, they also vividly highlight the disparate mobilities at play in the eighteenth century, notably the cosmopolitan travel of artists and aristocrats in contrast to the forced migration of the enslaved Africans serving the drunken captains pictured by Greenwood. But there are less tangible trespasses across borders to be found in the selection of works as well.

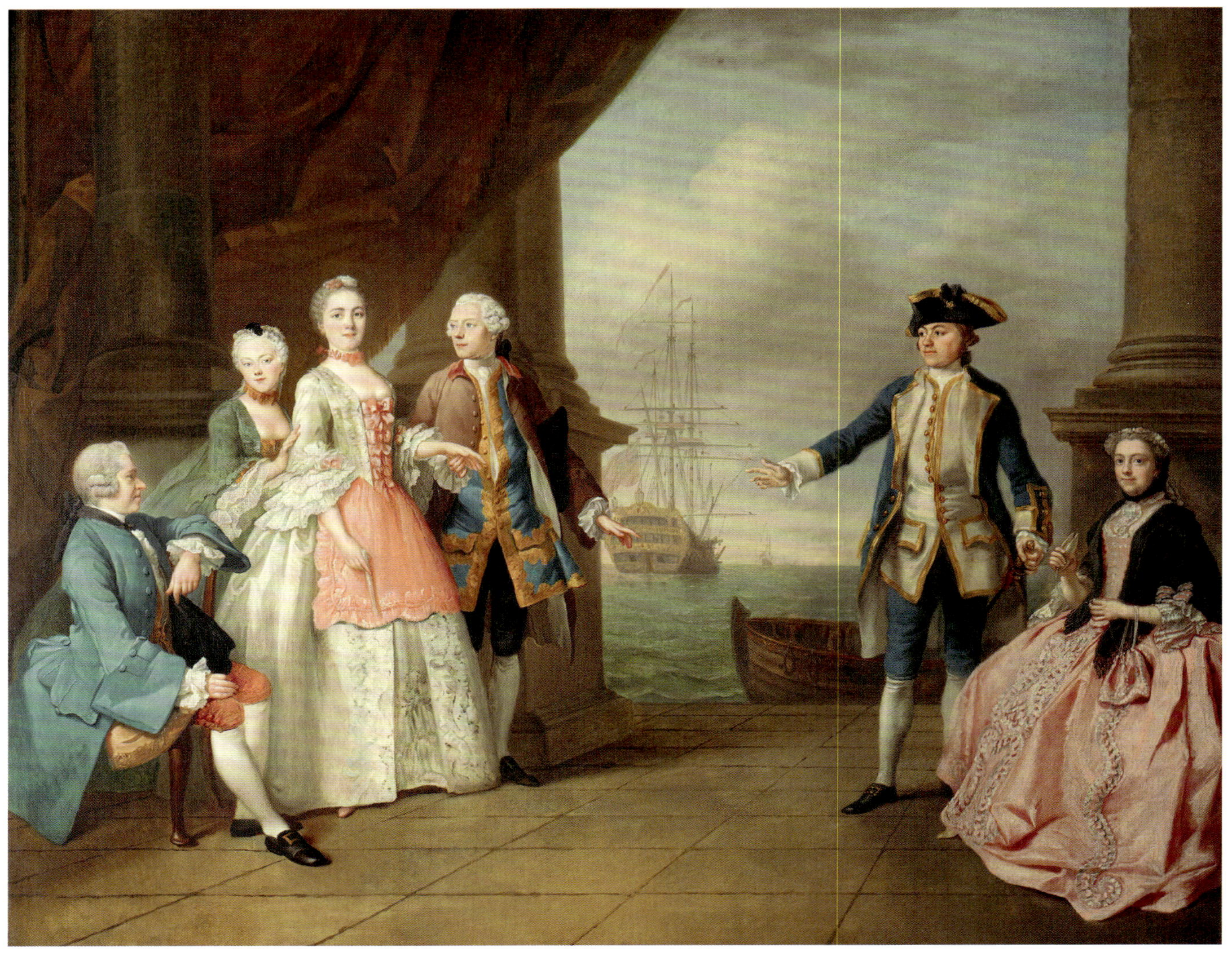

HUBERT FRANÇOIS GRAVELOT WITH JEAN-ÉTIENNE LIOTARD AND POSSIBLY FRANCIS HAYMAN
The Hon. Mrs Constantine Phipps (1722–1780) being led to greet her Brother,
Captain the Hon. Augustus Hervey, later 3rd Earl of Bristol (1724–1779) 1750

A portrait now identified as of Françoise de Castellane, by the French painter Jacques-André-Joseph Aved in Manchester Art Gallery (p.185), was originally acquired in 1904 as a portrait of the English writer and artist Mary Delany by the Scottish portraitist Allan Ramsay.[8] Aved's name was suggested in the 1930s, but other names are recorded in correspondence kept on file by the Gallery, while good authorities doubted on occasion that it was even French.[9] But even now that modern research has confirmed this as securely a 'French' picture, we can note that Aved grew up and trained in Amsterdam, worked in Brussels and The Hague as well as Paris,

and that his painted work was noted as distinctly Dutch in style. Furthermore, in this context we should also note that he is the French portraitist most closely aligned in style with Hogarth, and the two would have met in Paris in 1743 when Aved was embarking on a series of family portraits to mark the marriage of the sitter's son, Victor de Riqueti, Marquis de Mirabeau.[10]

As well as commemorating the marriage, the portrait highlights the reach of familial networks in cosmopolitan Europe. Françoise herself came from Provence aristocracy; her husband's family could apparently trace its ancestry back to thirteenth-century

Florentine nobility.[11] Of her sons, Victor gained fame as a political economist, while Jean-Antoine entered the Navy, journeying to North America, North Africa, Corsica and the Azores before becoming Governor of Guadeloupe in 1752. The brothers' regular correspondence informed their concerns about the political and economic structures of the French empire, particularly the institution of slave labour, and shaped ideas which entered into wider circulation through Victor's celebrated book *L'Ami des hommes*.[12]

This litany of the achievements of her male relations testifies to the often fragmentary records of women of the period – but we might also highlight the signifiers of Françoise's appearance, which convey her dignity and social standing.[13] The Marquise is resplendent in a *robe à la française* – the name speaks to the centrality of fashion and textiles to French cultural identity – lavishly adorned with bobbin lace worked in gold thread, with ribbon bows of woven silk and gold thread, and delicate ruffles of French needle lace at her sleeves and neck. Such opulent fabrics were vital to the French economy and, as foreign export markets opened up, became synonymous with French superiority in matters of taste.[14]

In just three pictures, not otherwise obviously linked by subject matter or artist, we have travelled between European nations, around the Mediterranean, across the Atlantic several times, and connected to globe-spanning routes of trade, communication and empire. Similar stories could be told of most of the pictures included here, providing evidence of the accelerated cultural mobility which characterised mid-eighteenth-century Europe. If the full force of technologically driven transport and communications 'revolutions' lay some way in the future, individuals, ideas and images circulated more extensively, more frequently and more rapidly than in previous eras.

Moreover, the idea emerged at precisely this point that such circulations might be historically significant, by providing a material foundation for progressive new forms of philosophy, political and social thought. Yet the ethos of cosmopolitanism, universalism, equality and free dialogue encompassed by the ideals of 'Enlightenment' sat alongside, and

was arguably underpinned by, forms of exchange and circulation which were far from progressive. The moment at which ever more people in major European capitals felt increasingly liberated, affluent and culturally engaged was also the moment at which urban poverty and deprivation became exacerbated, when hundreds of thousands of impoverished Europeans were compelled into unpaid labour abroad, when millions of African people were enslaved and transported to the Americas, when the reach of European colonialism extended further and bit more deeply around the world, when the commercial and political incursions into the Indian subcontinent and China were proliferating – interpreted then as the civilising progression of global trade, but now more critically seen as seeding modern imperialism. This inequality emerges further still, when following the wealth of Hogarth's patrons: George Arnold (p.191) invested in the Bow Porcelain Manufactory at a time when it used 'uneka', a fine white clay from the indigenous Cherokee people in America, to replicate fashionable Chinese-export porcelain; both his painted series, *A Harlot's Progress* and *A Rake's Progress* (pp.108–11) were bought at auction by William Beckford, whose family were powerful plantation owners in Jamaica. Beckford's own extensive estates amounted to 22,021 acres of land and at his death in 1774 he owned 1,356 enslaved people.[15]

The historical realities involved here were scarcely registered in the visual arts, other than in highly mediated, muted and playful forms – as fancy dress (particularly in the blackface that was a shockingly prominent feature of Dutch art and performance) or in subordinate figures condemned to the margins, in 'exotic' design motifs or in the new visibility accorded to the material artefacts of global trade. These included ceramics, as Lars Tharp explores in his essay in this volume, and mahogany, as Sonia Barrett sets out in her contribution, as well as silks and cotton, tobacco, rum and sugar, tea and coffee.

The eighteenth-century Europe that might once have been characterised as a glorious moment of philosophical Enlightenment, or of rococo playfulness and quotidian cultural pleasure, or even, as tends to be emphasised now, as involving rambunctious satire or socially transformative consumerism, needs to be understood in 'global' terms. As set out in the following four chapters, artists in Europe's major cities demonstrably enjoyed new freedoms – but these newfound liberties must be considered in relation to the kinds of unfreedom or constriction which equally came into play: those concerning the artists themselves (the economic precarity and loss of social status which became themes within the innovative storytelling artworks of the period, see pp.66–9), those concerning the patrons and consumers of art, and those concerning the larger metropolitan, national and international contexts in which art and artists operated, including the divisions of gender, race and class which cut across these. If there are images in this book which seem to speak of new freedoms associated with urban modernity, especially with regard to individual creativity and freedom of comment, the question remains: *at what cost*?

The allure of much of the art presented here lies, of course, in the pleasures it can yield for present-day viewers. This is a version of eighteenth-century urban life amusingly overrun by harlots and rakes, wicked hags, misbehaving clergymen, money-grabbing merchants, cynical quacks and satanical aristocrats. The images showcased here provide much entertainment in this vein. Hogarth has had his name applied to an entire era, giving rise to the familiar periodisation of 'The Age of Hogarth'. Within his lifetime, there was a definite sense that Hogarth was forging a new kind of art that engaged in storytelling in fresh ways, as Henry Fielding set out in his famous commentary: 'It hath been thought a vast commendation of a painter to say his figures seem to breathe; but surely it is a much greater and nobler applause, that they appear to think.'[16] It was not coincidental that this corresponded with the rise of the European novel: literature of the time (including the satires of Fielding himself) explored the variety and specificity of individuality as it developed and changed through time and experience – expressing western ideas around, and emphasis upon, personhood and empirical knowledge.[17]

That Hogarth designated his narrative paintings 'modern' suggests a self-consciousness about modernity. European society and culture was tangibly changing, breaking with past norms as it moved towards a more commercial and less courtly culture, as the growing population became increasingly urban, as traditional social hierarchies were disrupted and blurred by growing wealth, and as the intellectual climate suggested new ways of thinking.[18] Crucially, too, the perception of this as 'modern' relied on defining its opposite, which gave rise to increasingly sharply defined views of nation, personal identity and race. In Britain, these shifts appeared particularly rapid, and were as much a source of anxiety as of pleasure: luxury was both a sign of economic prosperity and a potentially corrupting influence; refinement and sophistication were distinguished from virtue, and associated with spectacle and superficiality.[19] The arts embodied and expressed these tensions, finding new ways of representing and defining the modern experience.

Centring upon the works of the English painter, it is perhaps inevitable that we will, to some extent, reinforce a sense of the uniqueness of Hogarth's achievement. But his pictures are shown here with the work of mainly French, German, Italian and Netherlandish artists, who both inspired and were influenced by Hogarth. The Italian artist Giuseppe Crespi plays a pivotal role in the development of narrative painting, although his series of pictures on the rise and fall of an opera singer survives only in fragments and versions, while the Dutch artist Cornelis Troost evidently took direct inspiration from Hogarth's images, which he presumably encountered in prints, as noted in the essays by Paul Knolle and Josephina de Fouw below. In other cases, there are connections which cannot be readily explained. The parallels between the painting manners of Chardin and Hogarth as they developed in the 1730s are tangible – yet there is no evidence that either painter saw the other's painted work in the flesh before Hogarth's visit to Paris in 1743.[20]

The first section of the book presents portraits and self-portraits of artists to suggest the varying notions of the artist that emerged in the eighteenth century, encompassing the sometimes uncertain and self-mocking as well as the aggrandising, while also highlighting cross-national connections, debts and parallels. Instead of the rigid hierarchies of status

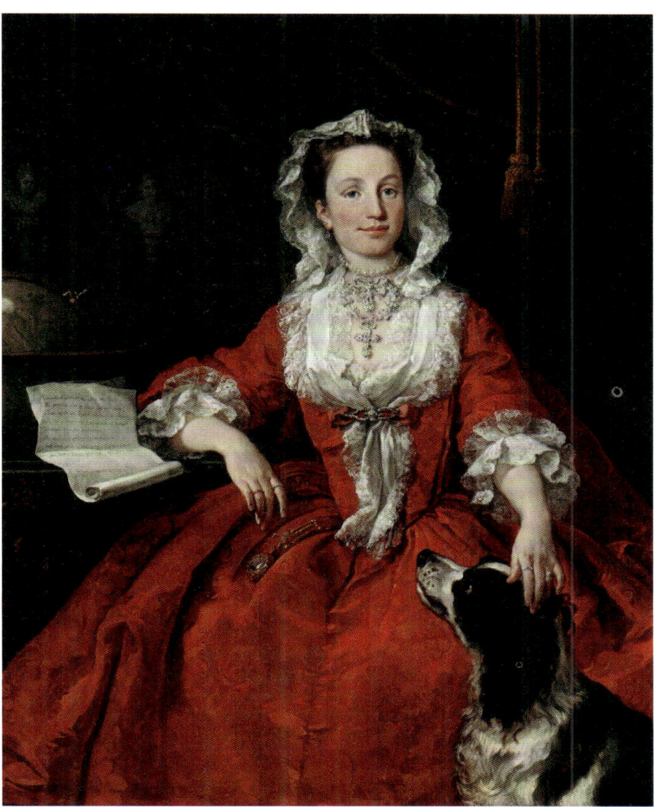

WILLIAM HOGARTH   *Miss Mary Edwards*   1742

and the stiff poses of earlier portraiture, there was fresh emphasis on informality and ease, hinting at the way that the artist was to become the exemplar of a new idea of individuality (a development consolidated in the Romantic era, with profound influences through to our own day). While the question of 'at what cost' remains crucial, it cannot be denied that real freedoms were sometimes secured, if only temporarily: even the most resolute barriers to personal autonomy, class, gender and racial division were sometimes challenged. Responding to the exclusions and possibilities inherent in these works, the contributions here by Temi Odumosu and Cora Gilroy-Ware, Meredith Gamer, Lubaina Himid and Sonia Barrett articulate a more expansive understanding of subjectivity and desire, identity and social critique than are customarily found in art-historical literature on Hogarth and the eighteenth century. In their introductory essays, Stacey Sloboda, Hannah Williams, Paul Knolle and Jonny Yarker examine the highly specific geographical and cultural settings in which most of the

pictures included here were produced – the cities of London, Paris, Amsterdam, and Venice and the Grand Tour. All these commentaries, set alongside the narrative scenes, urban genre and theatrical subjects which occupy the central sections of the book, sharpen and extend our understanding of the costs and opportunities of the developing European modernity these pictures encapsulate, the range of experiences and identities animated by this imagery.

But though the presence of empire and forms of sexual, class and racial violence within the work of Hogarth and his peers is apparent here, and confronted directly at different points, and while there is allusion made to the global networks and the passage of people, ideas and resources, we should stress that we are not laying claim to a comprehensively 'global' or 'decolonised' position (as set out more fully in the preface). The artists represented here are all male, and the moments when we can point to the contributions of women cultural producers and patrons are scarce; likewise, there are few opportunities to represent the agencies of those subject to colonial violence.

The possibility of recovering subjectivities beyond the White, male perspective usually centred by the most familiar idea of the 'Hogarthian' comes into particular focus in the final section. This considers the new images of men and women that emerged in the mid-eighteenth century, and the more informal, direct styles of portraiture that arose around Europe. Hogarth's own sisters, Mary and Anne, independent businesswomen, are rendered by him as individuals, as are his servants (pp.196–7, 199). His portrait of Mary Edwards presents a richly suggestive image of intellectual independence, subtly acknowledging the subject's contravention of gendered norms by surrounding her with attributes more readily found in male portraiture (pp.19, 184): a celestial globe, portrait busts of Alfred the Great and Elizabeth I (both symbolic figures of British liberty), a large hunting dog, and papers at her elbow which include a proclamation of individual rights adapted from Joseph Addison's *Cato*.[21] These assert her political and personal belief in English freedoms and, more subtly, her contravention of gendered norms of the time, as seems appropriate for a woman who chose to describe herself as a spinster rather than acknowledge her husband, Lord Anne Hamilton, in order to retain and protect her estates and fortune, even at the expense of her son's legitimacy. Some of Edwards's implacability may also be detected in *Taste in High Life*, which expresses her scathing attitude towards contemporary fashions and, in her view, the detrimental effects of foreign – notably, French – influence (p.168).[22] Yet it cannot be ignored that her portrait is a consummate example of Hogarth at his most 'French' (nor, indeed, that she wears a fashionable *robe à la française*);[23] its display here provides an opportunity to explore the contradictions and porousness of this relationship in the flesh.[24]

The engraving of Jacobus Capitein (p.188) also presents a singular figure, solemn, learned and spiritual, presented with a directness that is distinctly 'Hogarthian'.[25] Born in Ghana, Capitein had been enslaved but gained freedom by default when his owner, Jacob van Goch, took him to the Netherlands. He went on to study theology at the University of Leiden, becoming the first African to defend his doctorate at a European university and, shortly after, one of the first Africans to be ordained as a minister of the Dutch Reformed church. His thesis, published in 1742, argued that slavery was compatible with Christianity and proved highly popular, less for the novelty of its argument but because of his own origins.[26] Again, the question of 'at what cost' recurs, for Capitein remained dependent upon White benefactors for his education and career; as a missionary and pastor in Elmina in the employment of the West India Company, he became alienated from the European community but also distanced from the local people.[27] His request to be relieved of his position was denied, and he died in 1747, aged only thirty. Capitein was one of the thousands of people with African heritage living and working in Europe in the eighteenth century, not least in Amsterdam where slavery had been made illegal in 1644, or London where it is estimated that the Black community amounted to between one and three per cent of the overall population.

Thinking about Hogarth as a European figure takes us back to the very beginnings of modern Hogarth scholarship, with the émigré art historians Francis Klingender and Frederick Antal. In the context of the profound global upheavals of the 1930s and 1940s, they saved Hogarth from the rather quaint and anecdotal treatment which had prevailed in the literature on the artist and insisted upon a broader, European intellectual and cultural context.[28] In very recent years there has been a new flourishing of scholarly literature on Hogarth in languages other than English, and scholars have renewed efforts to dig deeply into the European cultural contexts and connections of his art.[29] But Hogarth's art was always European: it had an impact and resonance within European contexts, and it emerged and took shape in connection with the social, economic and cultural forces developing across the Continent.

If there is common ground among Hogarth and the other artists represented here, it lies in the outlook that was then beginning to prevail of a bourgeois Europe of merchants and traders, professional men and urban gentry, well-off artisans, artists and creative workers achieving new levels of independence and public visibility. This society was ready to moralise but tolerant of moral contradictions relating to class, race and gender; able to conform but much attracted to nonconformity; rooted in cities and nascent nation-states, but dependent on vast, global networks of exchange, extraction and exploitation that were scarcely made visible then, and have still to be properly excavated now.

Indeed, these contradictions and fault lines are further exposed here, in the very structure and content of this publication. While we might now wish to emphasise the global networks and connections that underpinned the cultural growth and change of eighteenth-century European cities, the authors of the essays on London, Paris, Amsterdam and Venice were asked to establish the concrete, localised urban circumstances in which artists were living and working. As the cultural historian Stephen Greenblatt has noted: 'Cultures are almost always apprehended not as mobile or global or even mixed, but as local. Even self-conscious experiments in cultural mobility … turn out to produce results that are strikingly enmeshed in particular times and places and local cultures'.[30] Yet as our discussion of the several paintings at the start of this essay indicate, such local, European histories can be unsettled and expanded in a variety of ways, and the sense of 'Europeanness' – centralised through historical narratives and aesthetic forms – proves to be far from fixed or coherent. We see some of this unfold in the essays that punctuate the main sections of this book, where the authors were given freedom to explore their own responses to works in the show. Still, the reality of social and ethnic diversity within Europe's cities, each (and London above all) shaped by global commerce and colonialism, is barely surfaced: female autonomy is generally only subtly expressed, if at all; the poor and marginalised of society are ciphers or lampooned; and figures of colour are routinely kept in the margins. More progressive forms of cultural consciousness may have been nascent but, even where they took on as robustly Hogarthian form as did the acute social observations of the famed London writer and abolitionist, Ignatius Sancho (once mooted as the child model for the servant in *Taste in High Life*, see p.168), they remain on the horizon.

We hope that what is offered here is not a single new story about Hogarth and his European contexts or a blunt presentation of the morally compromised nature of eighteenth-century culture, but rather a new set of suggestions about how understandings and engagements with this artist can be further renewed with an appreciation of the shifting contexts for his art – whether local, national, European or global.

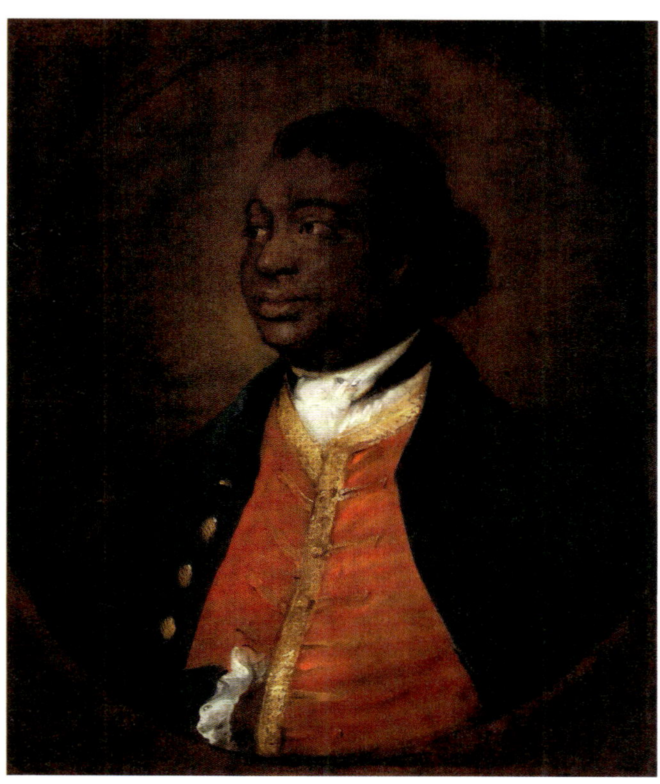

THOMAS GAINSBOROUGH *Ignatius Sancho* 1768

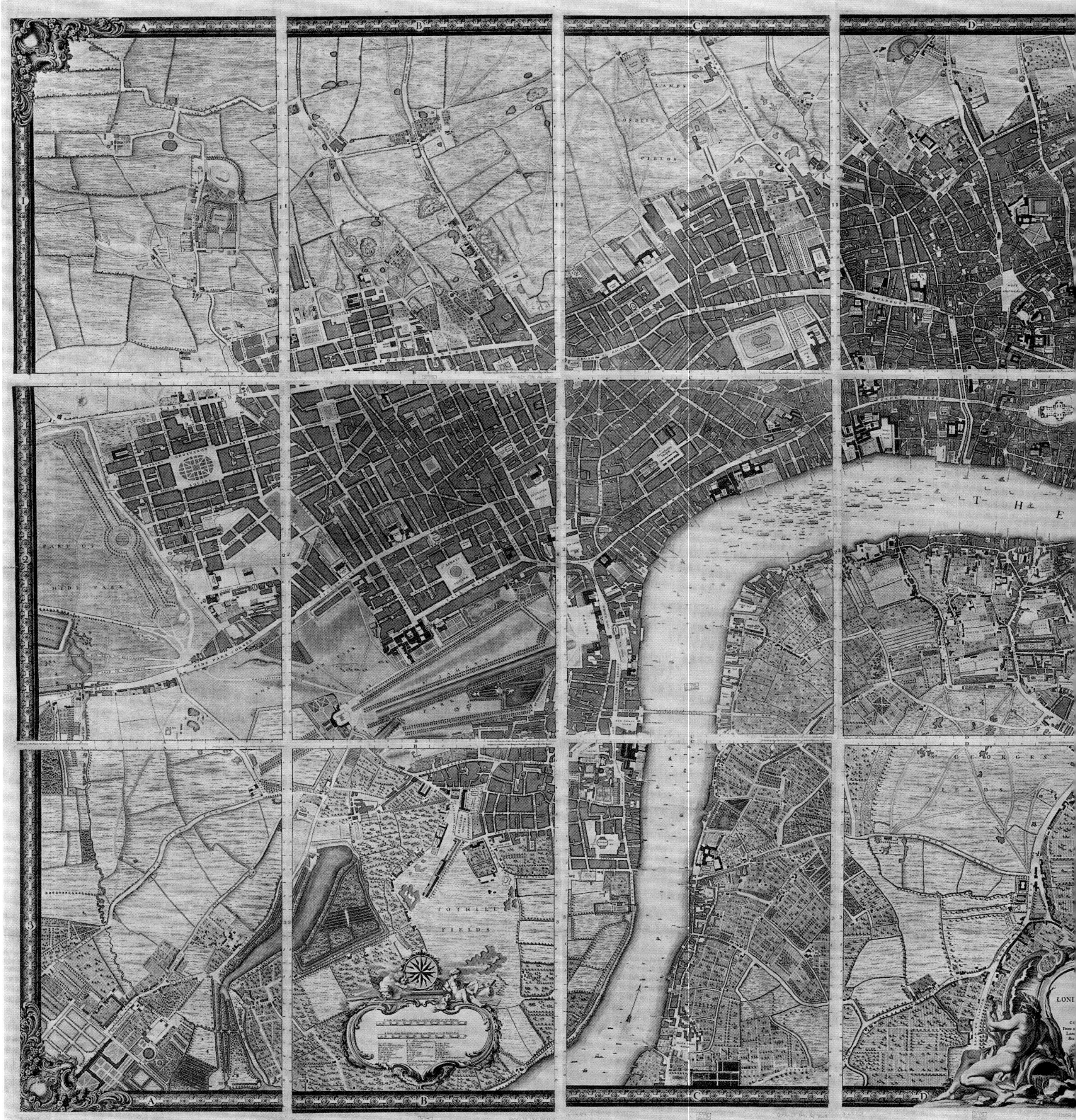

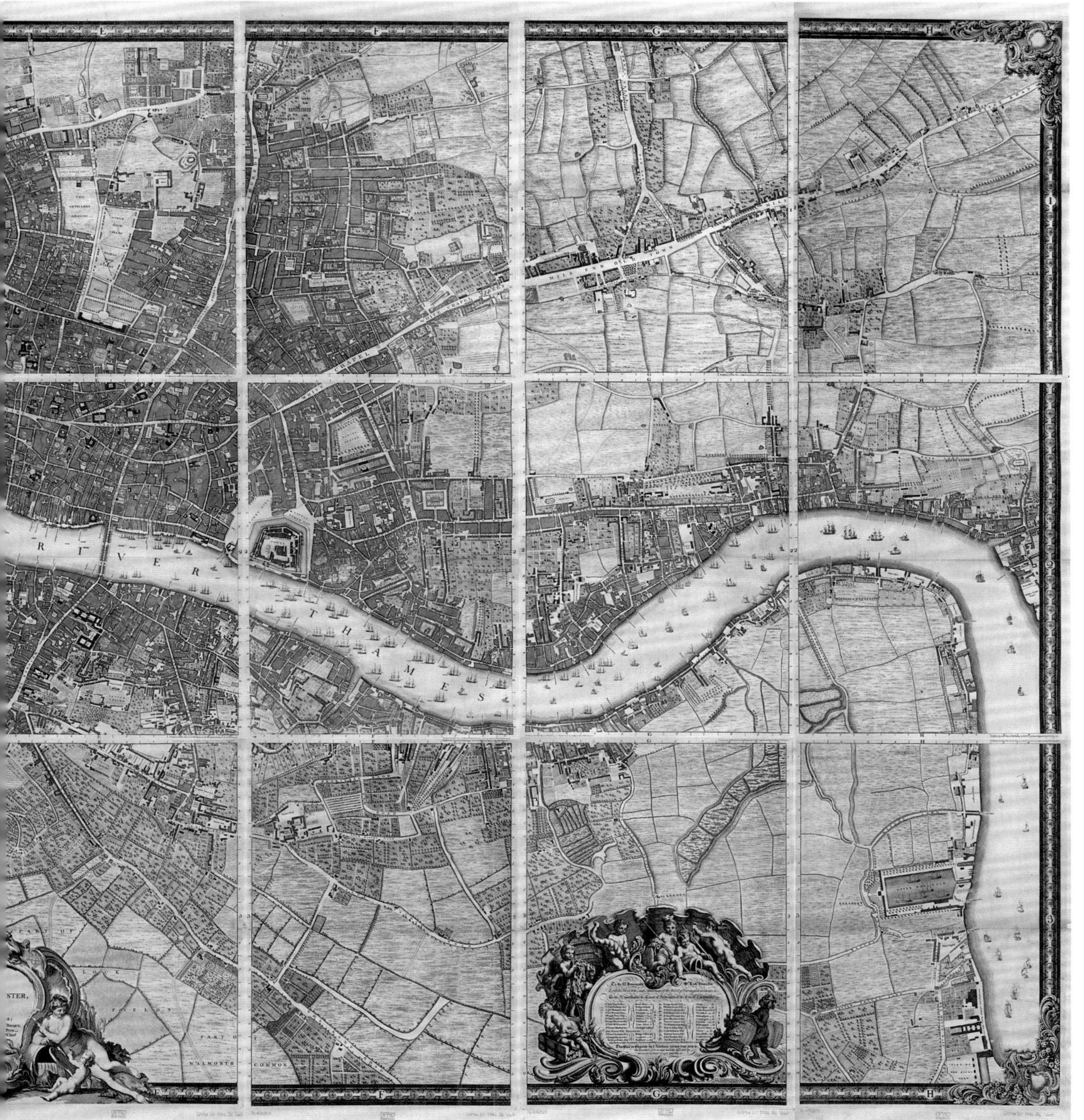

JEAN ROCQUE AND JOHN PINE
*A Plan of the Cities of London and Westminster,
and Borough of Southwark; with the contiguous buildings*   1746

23

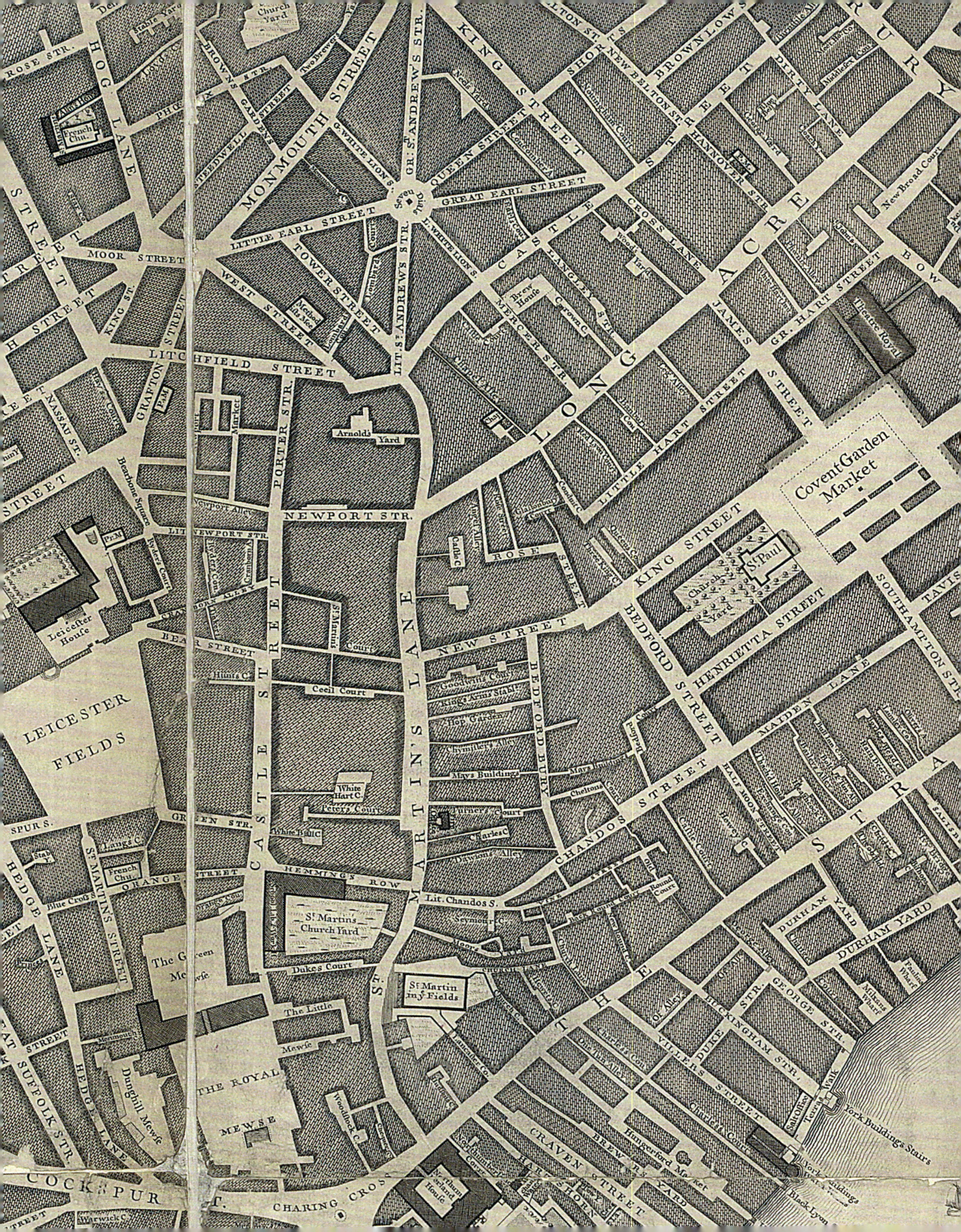

ROSE STR.
HOG LANE
Church Yard
French Ch.
STREET
MONMOUTH STREET
MOOR STREET
KING ST.
BROWNLOW
DIRT LANE
New Broad Court
LITTLE EARL STREET
GREAT EARL STREET
QUEEN STREET
KING STREET
NEW BELTON STR.
HANNOVER STR.
Theatre Royal
WEST STREET
TOWER STREET
ST. ANDREW'S STR.
LIT. ST. ANDREW'S STR.
CROSS LANE
CASTLE
GR. HART STREET
BOW
NASSAU ST.
GRAFTON STREET
LITCHFIELD STREET
Market
PORTER STR.
Arnolds Yard
LONG ACRE
LITTLE HART STREET
Covent Garden Market
STREET
Beaumont Square
LIT. NEWPORT STR.
NEWPORT STR.
ROSE STREET
KING STREET
St. Paul
Church Yard
HENRIETTA STREET
SOUTHAMPTON STR.
Leicester House
BEAR STREET
Hunts C.
Cecil Court
NEWSTREET
BEDFORD BURY
BEDFORD STREET
MAIDEN LANE
TAVIS
LEICESTER FIELDS
ST. MARTIN'S LANE
Goodwin's C.
May's B.
Chelsea
CHANDOS STREET
STRA
SPUR S.
Lane C.
French Ch.
Blue Cross S.
ORANGE STREET
GREEN STR.
CASTLE STREET
White Hart C.
Peter's Court
White Hall C.
HEMMING'S ROW
Lit. Chandos S.
DURHAM YARD
DURHAM YARD
HEDGE LANE
ST. MARTIN'S STREET
St. Martins Church Yard
Dukes Court
St. Martin in y Fields
GEORGE STR.
GREAT SUFFOLK STREET
The Green Mews
The Little Mews
BUCKINGHAM STR.
DUKE STREET
Dunghill Mews
THE ROYAL MEWSE
York Buildings Stairs
CRAVEN STREET
Hungerford Market
BREW STREET
YARD
COCKSPUR ST.
CHARING CROSS
Warwick
Black Lyon

LONDON

STACEY SLOBODA

On 3 March 1738 the engraver and art historian George Vertue discussed plans for a new survey map of London.[1] Though William Morgan's 1682 map *London, &c Actually Surveyed* had been updated as recently as 1732, it did not come close to capturing the rush of property development then transforming London. As a result of large-scale migration from the country and immigration mostly from the Continent, London was the most populous city in eighteenth-century Europe.[2] The fashionable, and those who catered to them, continued a westward expansion from the City to Westminster and beyond, fundamentally changing the footprint of the metropolis. Work on the new map began almost immediately, but not, perhaps, as Vertue had intended. In 1740, the estate surveyor Jean Rocque published an announcement for subscriptions, with John Pine taking Vertue's place as engraver. The map was published in 1746 as *A Plan of the Cities of London and Westminster, and Borough of Southwark* (pp. 22–3). Printed on twenty-four sheets of large imperial-sized paper, it was over thirteen feet long and six high, and claimed to describe 'all the Squares, Streets, Courts, and Alleys, in their true Proportions'.[3] Though not without omissions and errors, it remains today the most accurate cartographic picture of mid-eighteenth-century London.

Rocque and Pine's map was a product of the creative, collaborative, cosmopolitan and commercial art world of the city that it pictures. Jean Rocque's parents were among the more than 20,000 Huguenots who immigrated to London following Louis xiv's revocation of legal protection for French Protestants in the late seventeenth century. That migration produced a large concentration in London of highly skilled artisans trained in the French luxury trades including gold- and silversmiths, cabinetmakers,

painters and sculptors in all media, clockmakers, and textile weavers who found an eager audience among Britain's comparatively wealthy urban populations.[4] By the mid-eighteenth century, London had surpassed Constantinople as the most populous city in Europe: a centre of mercantile trade, retail, banking and government. While London lacked an institutional centre for the visual arts until the establishment of the Royal Academy for Painting and Sculpture in 1768, there was nevertheless a strong commercial demand for all forms of art, which made the capital an important destination for ambitious European artists, designers and craftsmen.[5]

During the span of Hogarth's career from the 1720s until the 1760s, the London art world congregated in distinct, yet overlapping, artistic communities in Lincoln's Inn Fields, Covent Garden, Leicester Fields, Soho and Golden Squares and Spitalfields. The centre of the London art world at the time was undoubtedly St Martin's Lane, a serpentine street between Covent Garden and Leicester Fields that connected Charing Cross to the Seven Dials. It was in this neighbourhood that Hogarth and his circle of British and second-generation Huguenot artists espoused the contemporary rococo style in art and design.

As a young man, Hogarth took drawing lessons at the St Martin's Lane Academy, the artist-run drawing school that flourished briefly in the early 1720s (Hogarth would reopen the Academy in 1735 with the portrait painter and tapestry manufacturer John Ellys as his partner). The Academy was a loosely knit centre of artistic training and community for two generations of British painters, sculptors and architects; after Hogarth, its principal instructors included the painter Francis Hayman, the sculptor Louis François Roubiliac, the illustrator Hubert

François Gravelot and the gold chaser George Michael Moser. At the same time, St Martin's Lane and its adjacent streets were replete with the shops of cabinetmakers, carvers, goldsmiths, print engravers and sellers. By mid-century the best-known cabinetmakers and wood carvers of the period all had workshops in or directly around St Martin's Lane,[6] while Hayman, Hogarth, Joshua Reynolds, Roubiliac and the architect James Paine also had studios in St Martin's Lane or very nearby. The Academy was the focal point of the neighbourhood, and it fostered a range of collaborative artistic projects in various media that shaped the contemporary London art world.[7]

Thomas Sandby's rare picture of the street includes a view of the house of John Pine's son Robert, who had established himself as a painter in St Martin's Lane by 1750.[8] The open windows of his studio are visible, as is the shop sign of the Noble brothers, who operated a bookshop and circulating library in St Martin's Court. The availability of a wide range of English and French books at the Nobles' and other bookshops in the neighbourhood was complemented by a large concentration of printsellers and engravers, many of them trained on the Continent, around Newport Street, Long Acre and the Strand. Printsellers such as James and Céleste Regnier sold contemporary English prints,

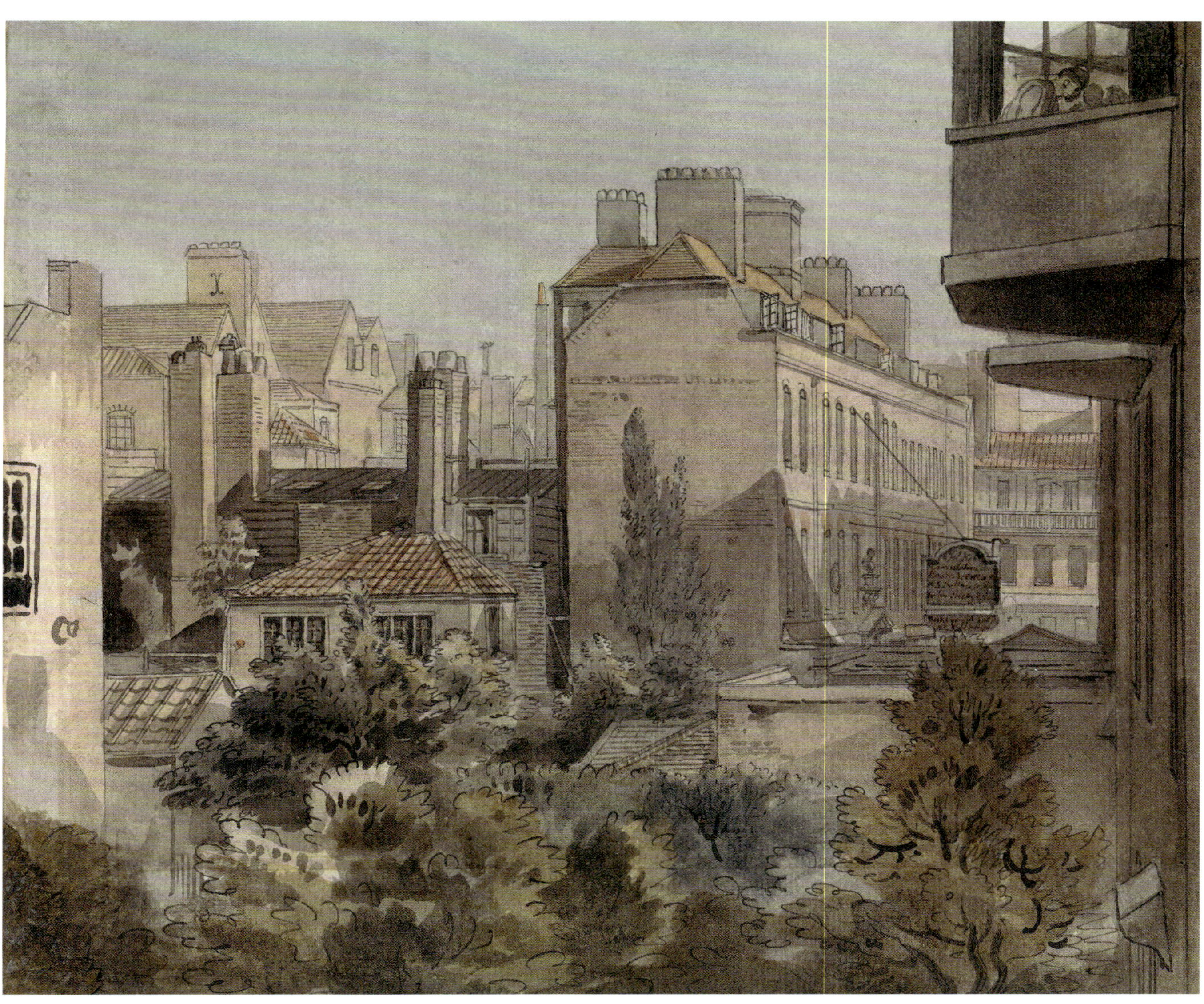

   THOMAS SANDBY *A View of St. Martin's Court* c.1765

including authorised editions by Hogarth as well as French and Italian old master prints, from their shop in Newport Street, as did their neighbours Francis and Susan Vivares, who specialised also in ornament prints from the Continent. Matthias and Mary Darly sold their prints from multiple addresses around the neighbourhood. George Bickham the Younger kept his own press in the basement of his shop in St Martin's Lane, though when arrested in 1745 for the presence of over 150 'obscene' (although possibly just politically incendiary) prints in his shop, he claimed innocence, averring that the business of the shop was exclusively carried out by his wife, Elizabeth.[9]

The artists living and working in and around St Martin's Lane were supported by a concentration of suppliers, dealers and skilled artisans that made their work possible. Many painters supplemented their income with sign painting, coach painting, book illustration, and scene painting for the theatre. The theatres of Covent Garden and Drury Lane gave artists such as Hayman their start, and were the lifeblood of artists such as George Lambert and Samuel Scott. Retail shops, coffeehouses, pubs, bathhouses and offices – all yet without street numbers and in need of identifying signage – provided steady, if not illustrious, employment for painters. The coachbuilding industry that flourished along Long Acre utilised decorative painters as well as wood carvers, gilders, and upholsterers. Likewise, painters' constant need for framemakers and the large workshops of cabinetmakers made the area around St Martin's Lane and Long Acre particularly attractive to wood carvers and gilders, who resided there in large numbers.

The auction rooms of Christopher Cock and Abraham Langford in Covent Garden and Richard Ford in the Haymarket dominated the sale of Continental prints and paintings, as well as auctions of furniture and other household goods. These auctions made it possible for the public to at least glimpse some of the large amount of art that was imported through private agents and dealers to London from Italy, France and Holland in the mid-eighteenth century. Numerous collectors exhibited their collections in their houses in London and the country.[10] These private museums were accessible to artists and visitors with the knowledge and connections to visit them, but there was no public institution in London with an express purpose to display contemporary art until the Society of Arts began their temporary exhibitions in 1760.

Until then, private, charitable and commercial ventures exploited the potential of contemporary art to provide a genteel thrill for their visitors, while London artists, particularly those based around St Martin's Lane, used those venues to exhibit their work. Under Hogarth and Hayman's leadership, fifty paintings to decorate the supper boxes at the Vauxhall Pleasure Gardens were collaboratively produced by colleagues and students at the Academy, including Gravelot and Thomas Gainsborough. Roubiliac had already contributed the life-size sculpture of Vauxhall's musical director, George Frideric Handel, in 1738 and St Martin's Lane Academy instructor George Michael Moser designed the interior decoration of the Rotunda.[11] Beginning around the same time, Roubiliac, John Michael Rysbrack, Henry Cheere and Joseph Wilton also began to turn Westminster Abbey into a de facto art gallery, after a spree of privately funded monument building provided a public venue there for exhibiting contemporary sculpture.[12]

The use of the visual arts to uplift and entertain a polite audience was implemented even more strategically at the newly established Foundling Hospital in Lamb's Conduit Field by Hogarth and his St Martin's Lane collaborators. In 1746, the Court Room (p.28) was opened to the public, with paintings donated by Hogarth, Hayman, Lambert, Gainsborough, Reynolds, Scott, Samuel Wale, Joseph Highmore, James Wills and Richard Wilson, grand sculptural frames donated by the St Martin's Lane cabinetmaking firms of William Hallett and William and John Linnell, and ornate stucco decoration by William Wilton, creating a permanent gallery of English contemporary art in the capital.[13]

New, collaborative print publications gave contemporary London artists and designers another venue to exhibit their work to the public. The strategy of issuing a series of prints by subscription was already well-established by the time

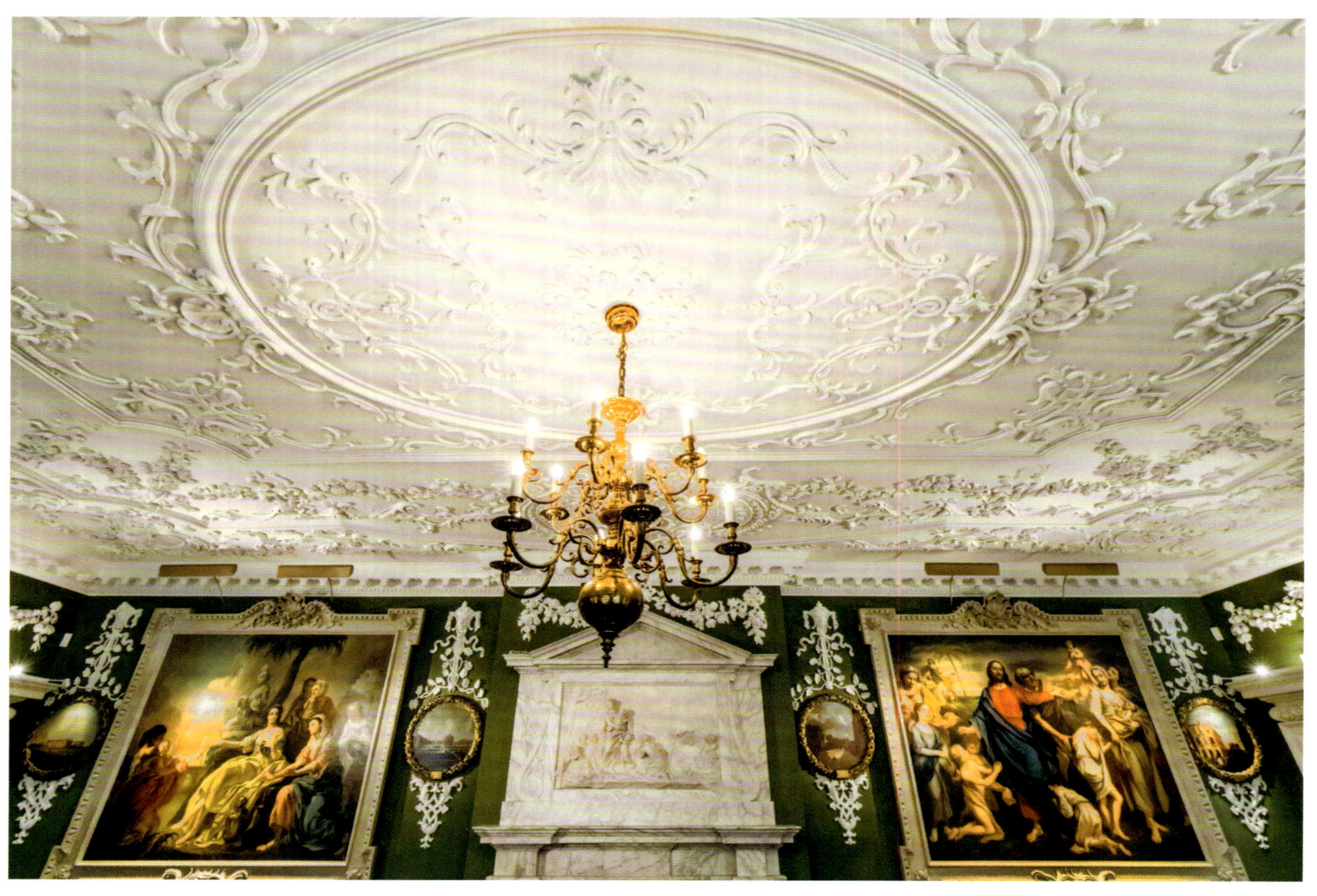

The Court Room of the Foundling Hospital

Hogarth took up the practice in the early 1730s. Large-scale publications such as George Bickham's *The Musical Entertainer* 1737 and *The Universal Penman* 1743 compiled serially issued prints by a range of artists, engravers, writing masters and designers to create a printed gallery of the contemporary London rococo style. Such publications inspired carvers and cabinetmakers in and around St Martin's Lane to translate their work into published designs.[14] Thomas Chippendale's *The Gentleman and Cabinetmaker's Director* was produced collaboratively with the engraver and designer Matthias Darly and published from Chippendale's new address in St Martin's Lane. By the mid-1750s, London was a centre of the European print trade, with the Overton and Bowles families, as well as Robert Sayer, dominating the trade in illustrated print publications from their shops in Fleet Street and St Paul's Churchyard.[15]

This focus on exhibiting and publishing art and design by living English artists (though many were first- and second-generation immigrants from the Continent) was a direct response to the perceived excellence of the French and Italian art and artists who continued to dominate the London art market.[16] England, with its comparatively wealthy population, was seen as a lucrative destination for European artists. The principal large-scale English painting commissions of the early eighteenth century had been dominated by Italian and French artists, and London continued to attract European artists throughout the eighteenth century. For instance, Hubert François Gravelot came to London in 1732 after studying at the Académie Royale under Jean Restout and François Boucher; though an artist of minor reputation when he left Paris, his Covent Garden studio and drawing school strongly influenced a generation of London artists in French

28

academic principles of drawing and design, and when he returned to France from London in 1745, he reputedly did so with £10,000 in his pocket.[17]

Though Covent Garden was a focal point of the mid-eighteenth-century London art world generally, foreign artists gravitated slightly northwestward around Golden Square. Giovanni Antonio Canal (known as Canaletto) spent spent nine years in England, with a base in London at a cabinetmaker's shop in Silver Street, Golden Square. That street (now called Beak Street) had also been the address of both the Venetian painter Jacopo Amigoni, who encouraged Canaletto to cater to English patrons on their own ground (see pp.52–3), and the Bolognese artist Gaetano Brunetti, in the 1730s. When Canaletto arrived in London in 1746, his fellow Venetian artist Antonio Joli was busy with scene paintings for the Haymarket Theatre. Mid-eighteenth-century Europe's most prolific travelling artist, Jean-Étienne Liotard, resided in and around Golden Square on his two visits to London from 1753 to 1755 and again from 1773 to 1774, and fellow Swiss artist Angelica Kauffmann also set up her studio and exhibition space in Golden Square in the 1780s. Dorothy Mercier's tradecard gives some sense of how artists and amateurs were supplied there, as her shop sold Continental prints as well as all manner of fine European paper, pencils, chalk and watercolour paints.

Great Queen Street and Lincoln's Inn Fields had been another centre of the London art world since the early eighteenth century. Godfrey Kneller carried out his portrait practice from a house in adjacent Great Queen Street and directed the Great Queen Street Academy in the second decade of the century. The French painter Jean-Baptiste van Loo spent five years in London residing in a house in Great Queen Street, which was taken over in the 1740s by the portrait painter Thomas Hudson, who moved there from just down the road in Holborn Row on the north side of Lincoln's Inn Fields. The painter Joseph Highmore and his wife, the poet Susanna Highmore, resided four doors down in Holborn Row, and Arthur Pond sold prints and old master paintings from his house in Great Queen Street. When the painter and St Martin's Lane Academy director John Ellys purchased the Vanderbank family's Soho Tapestry Works, it came with their house in Great Queen Street.

This brief sketch of the mid-eighteenth-century London art world emphasises its collaborative and materially diverse nature. The commercial nature of English art in this period made shops, exhibition spaces and print publications especially significant sites. In this way, neighbourhoods took the place of institutions in the role of fostering contacts between clients, suppliers and artists themselves.

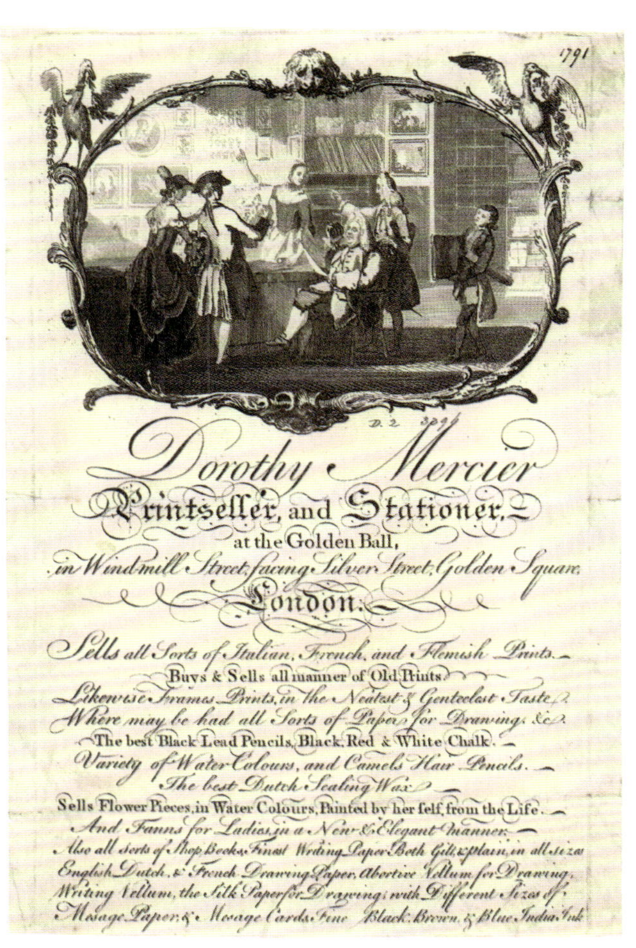

DOROTHY MERCIER *Tradecard* 1791

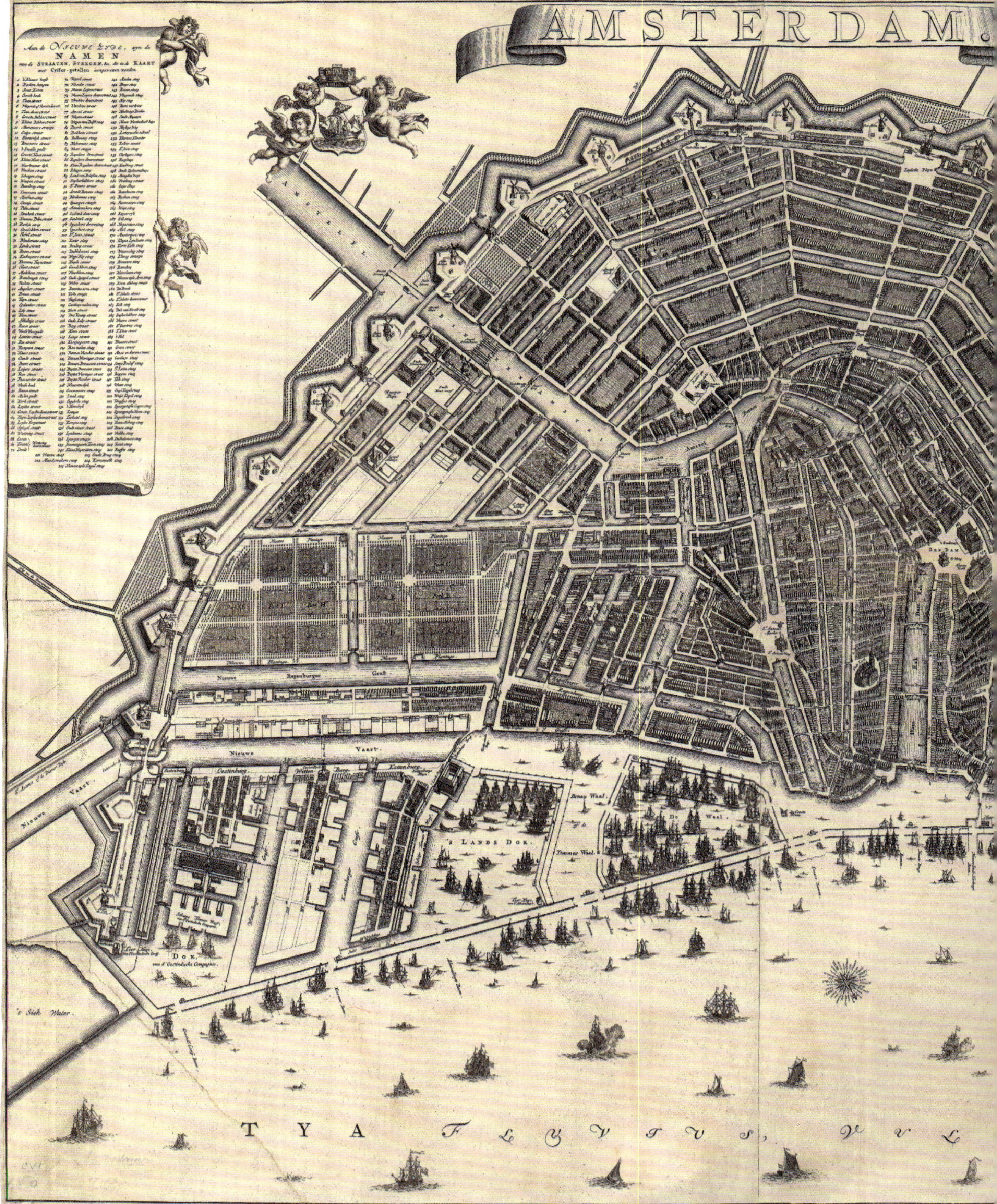
AMSTERDAM.
Aan de Nieuwe Zyde, zyn de
NAMEN
van de Straaten, Stegen, &c. die in de Kaart
met Cyffer-getallen aangewesen worden
's Lands Dok.
Braau Waal.
De Waal.
Timmer Waal.
Oostenburg.
Wittenburg.
Kattenburg.
Nieuwe Vaart.
Dok.
van d'Oostindische Compagnie.
'S Siek Water.
T Y A   F L U V I U S,   v u l

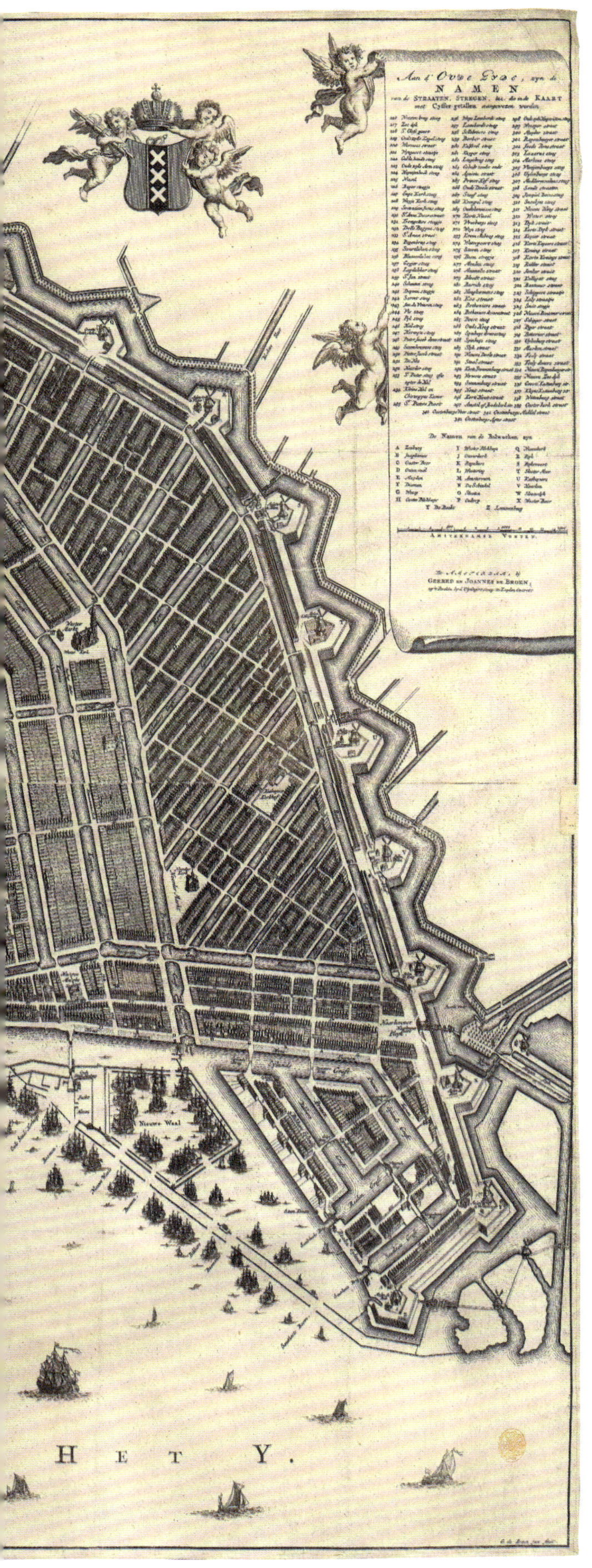

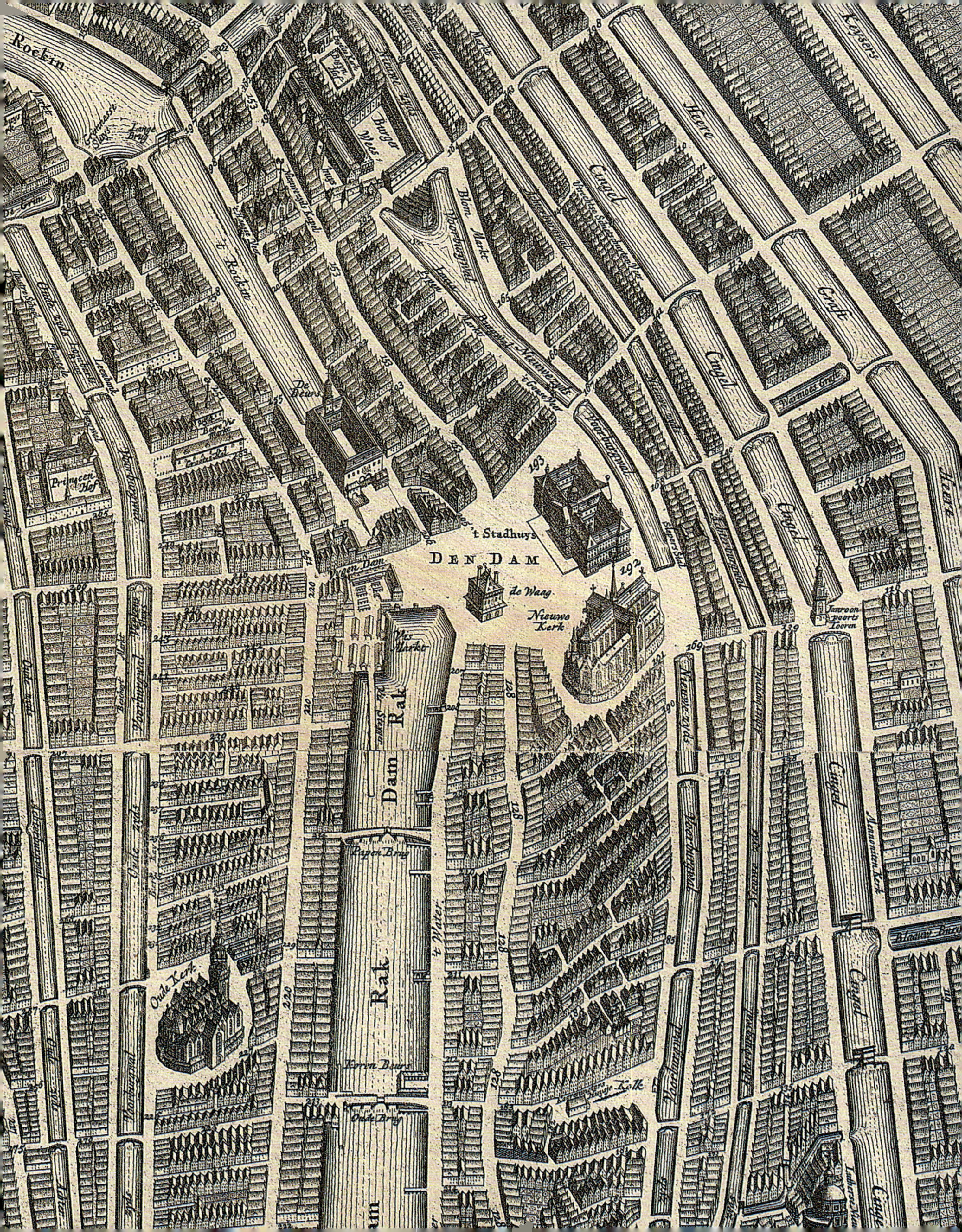

Rockin
Koysors
Heere
Cingel
Cingel
Cingel
Cingel
Cingel
't Rockin
Burger Wees
Blom Mark
't Rockin
De Beurs
Princen Hof
't Stadhuys
Den Dam
de Waag
Nieuwe Kerk
Dam Rak
Vis Markt
Papen Brug
Oude Kerk
Rak
Tooren Brug
Oude Brug
Amstrelkerk
Reael Burg
Cingel
Cingel

AMSTERDAM

PAUL KNOLLE

Amsterdam's historical and contemporary cultural riches have appealed to art lovers for centuries. Besides the freedom to think and act that the city has traditionally offered its own citizens and Dutch and foreign visitors alike, it owes a substantial part of its reputation to its seventeenth-century attractions. The legacy of the Dutch 'Golden Age' is inescapable to anyone who explores central Amsterdam and must-see institutions such as the Rijksmuseum or Rembrandt House.

Other than the fact that art was still held in private collections at that time, rather than museums, the same is true of the period in which Cornelis Troost produced the work that would earn him the nickname 'the Dutch Hogarth'. Street life might have altered dramatically over the centuries, but the backdrop of canals, old houses, churches and public buildings has remained. Then as now, the city was culturally extremely fertile for the arts, including music, theatre and literature.

Contrary to the long-standing perception of the Netherlands as staid, the first half of the eighteenth century was an exciting period for the country. Amsterdam, in Troost's lifetime, was an important trading centre with a large harbour and a population of around 200,000, making it one of Europe's largest cities. Commerce and shipping flourished, as did the arts and sciences. What follows is an impression of the city as if viewed through Troost's eyes.

By the start of the eighteenth century, the centre of Amsterdam had already assumed the street layout that did so much to shape the image of this 'Venice of the North'. Its main canals – the Singel, Herengracht, Keizersgracht and Prinsengracht, lined with opulent residences and warehouses – were dug concentrically during several phases of urban expansion in the seventeenth century and linked by smaller canals running at right angles to them.[1] Construction of the Town Hall on Dam Square, a symbol of Amsterdam's newly acquired power and status, commenced in 1648 after a design by the architect Jacob van Campen and was completed in 1665.

An expansive view of the city can be found in the map published in 1732 by the engraver and bookseller Gerrit de Broen II (pp.30–1) – the first monumental plan of the city to show the 'New Layout' (Nieuwe Uitleg) begun in 1660. By 1780, seven editions of De Broen's map had been published, some adjusted to take account of more recent construction.[2]

There were no crowds of shoppers as yet, though large markets already existed.[3] Stores selling everyday necessities were mostly located on the radial streets, with luxury and durable goods available for purchase in a cluster of centrally located thoroughfares such as Nieuwendijk (home to numerous textile sellers), and Kalverstraat and Rokin (where you could buy books and prints).

People could meet over a snack and a drink in coffee houses and inns, where a wide variety of activities took place, from business meetings and the discussing and signing of commercial deals to placing orders with artists or arranging for paid sex.[4] On Kalverstaat, Café Quincampoix – named after the Parisian street – became famous (or notorious) for its stock trading: it was here that risky speculative trade in 1720 left duped citizens nursing substantial losses.[5] In the wake of this debacle there was a decline in both the number and popularity of such establishments – of the thirty-two operating in Amsterdam in 1700, only seventeen remained by 1750.[6]

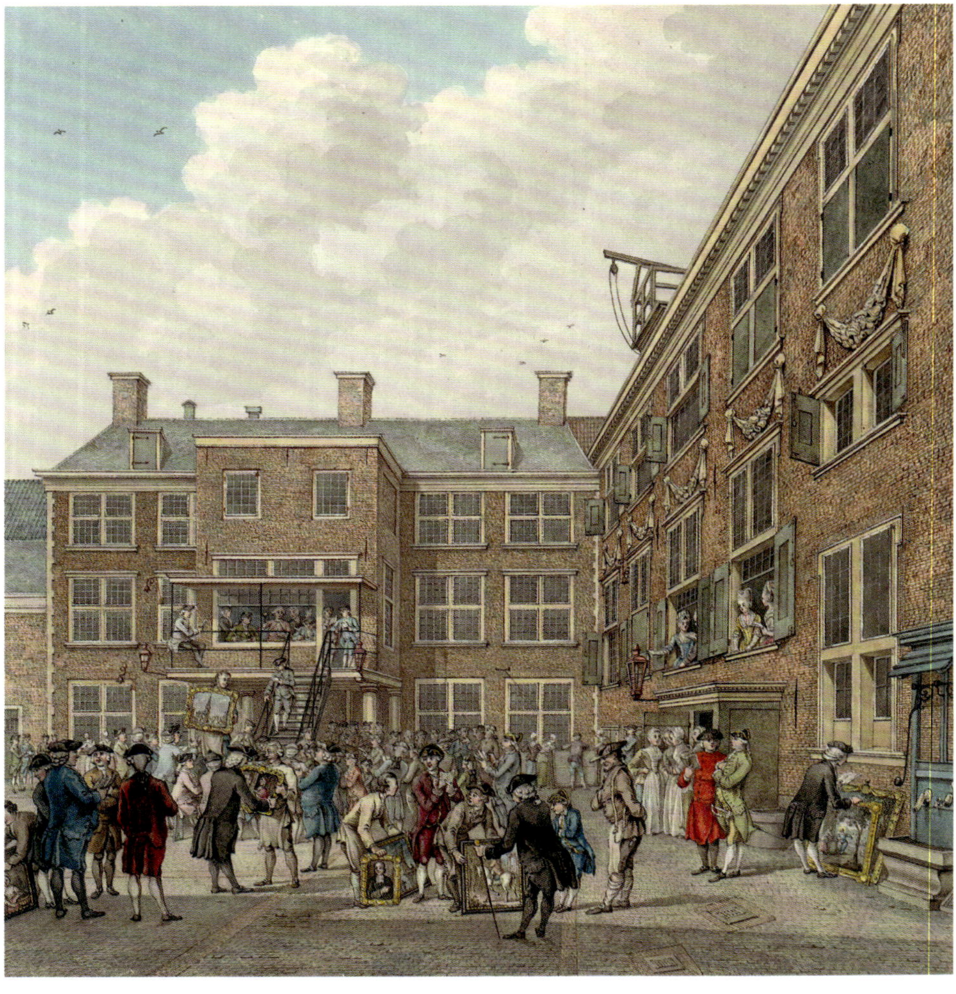

HERMANUS PETRUS SCHOUTEN   *Picture Sale at the Oudezijds Herenlogement*   1771

The administration of the city was the preserve of a close-knit group of regent families who held political power and supplied burgomasters (mayors) for almost the entire eighteenth century.

It goes without saying that Amsterdam's citizens regularly sought entertainment. A stimulating conversation at a coffee house or a visit to a fair might be enough, or else they could attend a concert, play or ballet performance. Farces, comedies and all sorts of spectacular shows were staged, while those who preferred serious drama could opt for a tragedy – mostly a French classical play, with heroes or princes from antiquity.

Amsterdam's most important theatre was built on the Keizersgracht in 1637, designed once again by Jacob van Campen. The building went up in flames in May 1772, when a candle used to light the stage for a performance of the lyrical drama *The Deserter* ('De Deserteur') set fire to the scenery. The conflagration spread rapidly, causing panic in the audience and leaving eighteen people dead. The city council immediately ordered the construction of a new theatre, the Stadsschouwburg, which was opened on the Leidseplein in 1774.

Visual art and drama came together in the theatre. Many of Troost's paintings, drawings and prints from 1733 onwards depict scenes from plays – comedies especially – of which he had personal experience.[7] A professional actor between 1719 and 1724, Troost designed stage sets for the Stadsschouwburg and married the actress Susanna Maria van der Duyn in 1720. Troost was not alone in painting theatrical scenery; the perpetually serious artist Gerard de Lairesse, who had come to Amsterdam

34

from Liège by way of Maastricht in 1665, also did work of this kind.[8]

Music had a prominent place in the cultural life of the Dutch Republic. It was frequently played at home, but there were public concerts as well, given by both amateur and professional musicians. They grouped together in societies or collegia, but could also perform solo.[9] The musical climate evidently had an appeal further afield, too: celebrated composers and musicians who spent varying periods of time in Amsterdam include Antonio Vivaldi (in 1738) and Pietro Antonio Locatelli, who died in the city in 1764. When Mozart visited the Netherlands with his father Leopold and little sister Nannerl in 1765–6, he performed a month-long series of concerts in Amsterdam. Local and visiting companies staged operas in French, German and Dutch at the Stadsschouwburg and other theatres.[10]

The climate was excellent for literature as well: publishers supplied a wide variety of books and many well-heeled citizens owned libraries of their own. Enlightenment ideals meant that reading was increasingly encouraged throughout the bourgeoisie. Besides Dutch and translated prose and poetry, a great many magazines were published in this period. Periodicals inspired by the British literary and society journals *The Tatler* and *The Spectator* were popular, especially after the publication of Justus van Effen's *Hollandsche Spectator* (1731–5).[11]

Artists were naturally also expected to read – as a minimum, the literature relevant to practising their trade. In 1751, for instance, the artists' biographer Johan van Gool declared that Cornelis Troost was a 'wise and well-read man' who was able to judge all aspects of art.[12] Troost clearly read widely: a relationship can be demonstrated between the content of his work and the moral message – the fostering of virtue – found in *Spectator*-style writing.[13]

It will be clear by now that the Dutch art world presented a very rich, varied and appealing picture in the eighteenth century,[14] with no question of 1700 having marked an abrupt break with the previous century's 'Golden Age'. Painters continued to supply a variety of genres of high quality, but the *number* of artists was lower than it had been in the exceptional seventeenth century, in Amsterdam too. Few women artists were active in this period, although Rachel Ruysch – daughter of the renowned anatomist Frederik Ruysch – did achieve international acclaim with her still lifes.

At the same time, tastes were changing among artists and their public. By the early eighteenth century, the subtle, refined style known as 'fine painting' (*fijnschilderkunst*) was preferred to the some-what rougher approach of Frans Hals and the late Rembrandt. Many artists, including Nicolaas Verkolje – the painter with the velvet touch – combined a variety of genres: in addition to interior decorations, Verkolje painted history scenes that were highly regarded by many art theorists, but also portraits, which scored much lower in the artistic hierarchy (history painting being the most highly prized). He had to earn a living, after all, and that he certainly did: he and his family lived on the prestigious Prinsengracht.[15] Although several prominent Dutch artists, among them Rotterdam's Adriaen van der Werff, were recruited as court painters by German princes, many others remained active in Amsterdam. Some – such as Tibout Regters, who seems to have been inspired by British portrait painters (pp.180, 187) – travelled around the country, wherever their commissions took them.[16]

In the meantime, a new market for interior decoration had opened up in the late seventeenth century, with wealthy citizens commissioning artists to decorate the ceilings, walls and chimney breasts of their city mansions or country retreats with fashionable paintings of mythological scenes and Arcadian landscapes. Cornelis Troost's versatility is further demonstrated by the fact that he also painted 'rooms and chambers in the round' (*Zaelen en Kamers in 't ront*). Some of the best-known artists supplying decorations of this kind were Gerard de Lairesse (before he lost his sight around 1690), Jacob de Wit and Isaac de Moucheron. The latter was a sufficiently wealthy artist to live in just such a patrician residence himself.

Troost, too, lived in a grand style with his family – initially on the Binnen-Amstel in Amsterdam, before moving to the Prinsengracht.[17] With an annual income of a thousand guilders, more than three times the average, he could afford it.

Many cultivated Amsterdam people owned a collection of objects from nature ('naturalia') and curiosities, in addition to art.[18] Leading art collectors included Jeronimus Tonneman (whose 1736 portrait by Troost is one of the artist's masterpieces), Gerrit Braamcamp (a successful distiller and timber merchant), Leendert Pieter de Neufville (a merchant and banker trading in silk, linen and grain) and Pieter Testas the Younger (also an art dealer).[19] Works were sourced directly from the artist or, where the maker was deceased, from dealers, intermediaries or at auction, as in the case of the Braamcamp painting collection which was sold at the Oudezijds Herenlogement in 1771.

Many collectors in Amsterdam were interested in a type of image that can be identified as a Dutch speciality of the period, namely topographical art – a genre that flourished in the first half of the eighteenth century. Some buyers focused on a particular city or region and collected topographical and historical scenes, portraits and depictions of morals and customs, especially in the form of drawings and prints. Assembling 'atlases' of this kind was popular in the eighteenth-century Dutch Republic,[20] and numerous artists travelled around to perform commissions for collectors. Individual atlases were sometimes combined in large ones and still exist, like the example in the Amsterdam Municipal Archive.

The well-travelled artist Cornelis Pronk, who nurtured young talents like Jan de Beijer, was one of those behind the explosive growth in the number of Amsterdam city views. Beginning in the 1720s, he made precise drawings of locations in the city such as the Town Hall and the Weighhouse on Dam Square. Draughtsmen like De Beijer, Herman Schouten and Jacob Cats followed his example and a 'Drawing Society' (*Teeken Collegie*) of artists specialising in topographical subjects formed around him in about 1750; in June 1760, Simon Fokke drew the group on a day out aboard the famous passenger barge service (*trekschuit*) between Haarlem and Amsterdam.

Cornelis Pronk's drawing society is unlikely to have been a tightly organised company. Professional associations for artists existed in cities throughout the Netherlands, and in Amsterdam it was the Guild

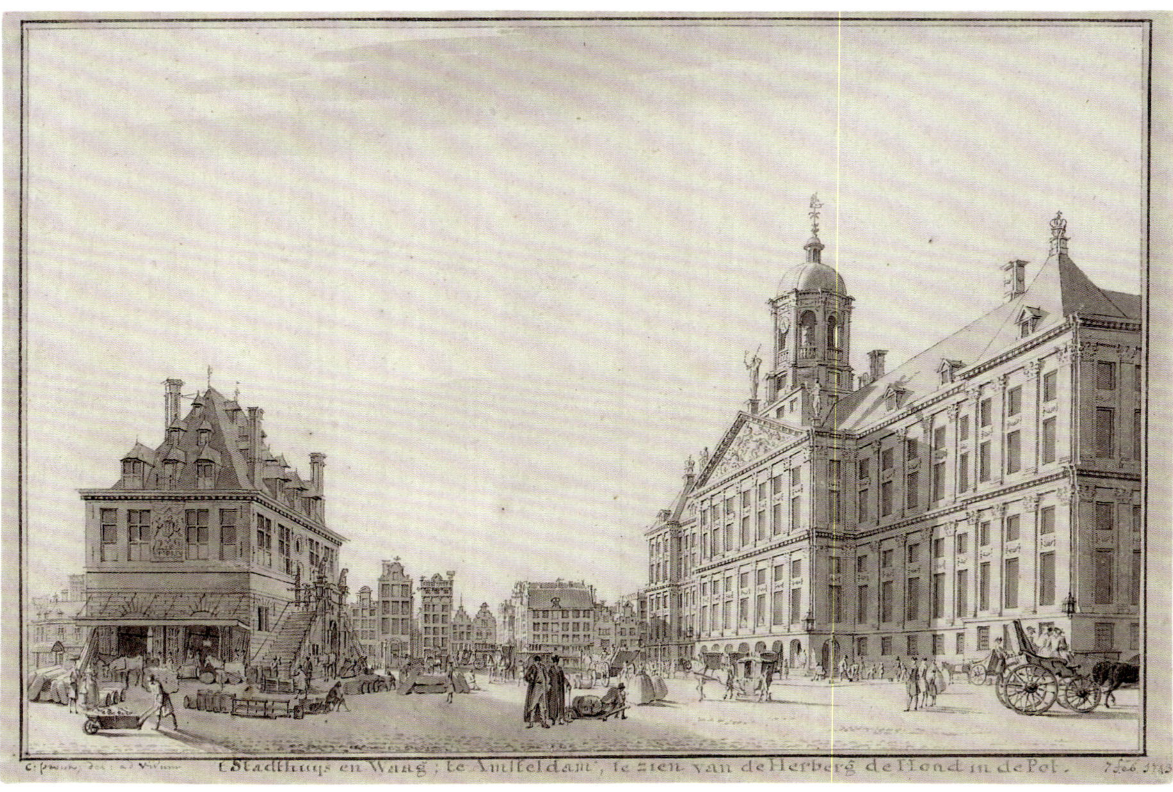

   CORNELIS PRONK   *The Town Hall and Weighhouse on Dam Square*   1743

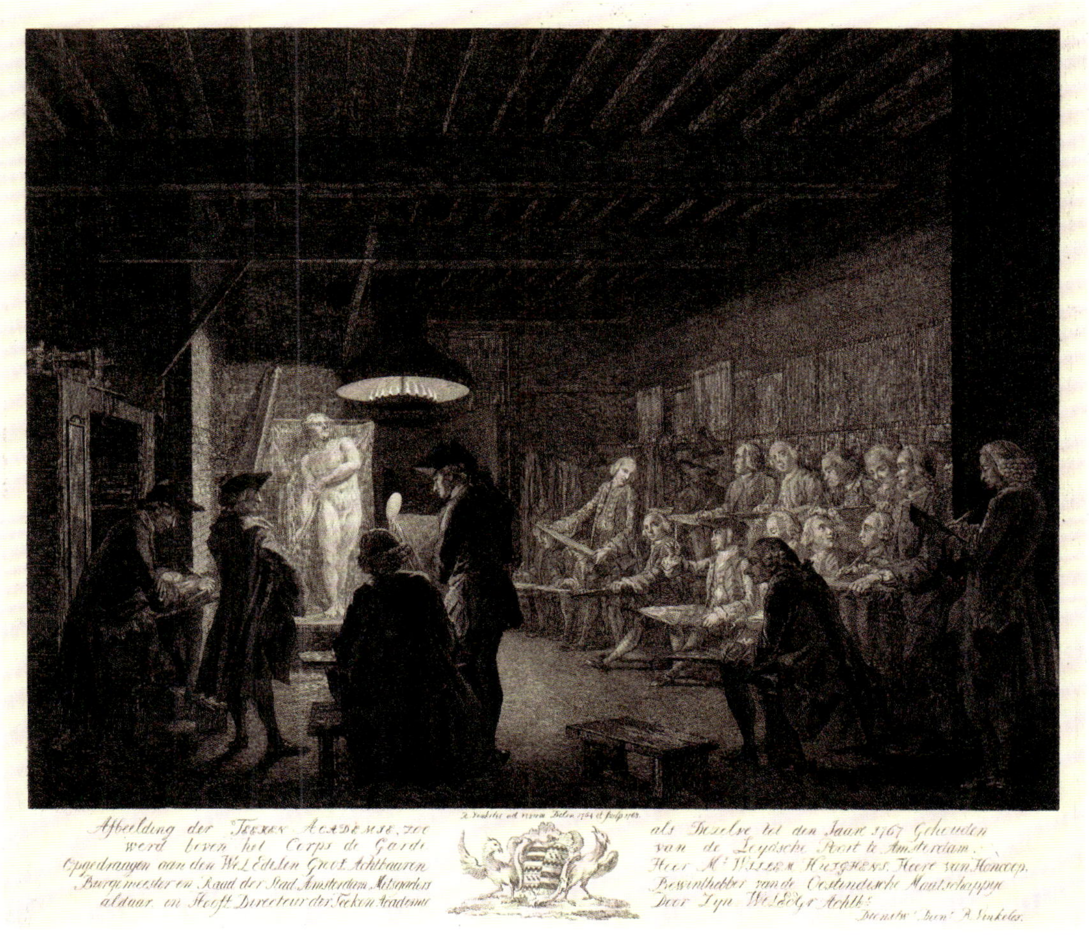

REINIER VINKELES *Drawing after a nude model in the City Drawing Academy in the Leidsepoort* 1764

of St Luke that regulated artistic training and production, including quality control. Alongside this, twelve Amsterdam artists began to meet twice a week in 1718 in the Leidsepoort to study and practise life drawing. Clubs, societies and associations became a well-established feature in Dutch life after 1760, and in 1765 this group transformed into the strictly organised City Drawing Academy (*Stadstekenacademie*), complete with regulations, a director-in-chief (usually one of the burgomasters) and six directors, life-drawing contests and, not least, speeches by connoisseurs and scholars, the content of which could be genuinely innovative.[21] Essentially a drawing association with ambition, the new academy, which later took up residence in the Town Hall, numbered fifty draughtsmen amongst its members in 1768, along with sixty-seven honorary members.

There were other important organisations for artists and amateurs. Members of the drawing section of the large-scale Felix Meritis society, founded by Amsterdam citizens in 1777, were exceptionally active in stimulating their own and other people's skills and Dutch art in general. The goal, firmly in keeping with the spirit of the Enlightenment, was to pursue 'happiness through merit' (hence *'felix meritis'*).

But all this was well after the era of Cornelis Troost – an artist whose own merits gave him every right to feel happy. His appealing work continues to stand up well in the twenty-first century, not just among Dutch artists but also when highlighted in an international context.

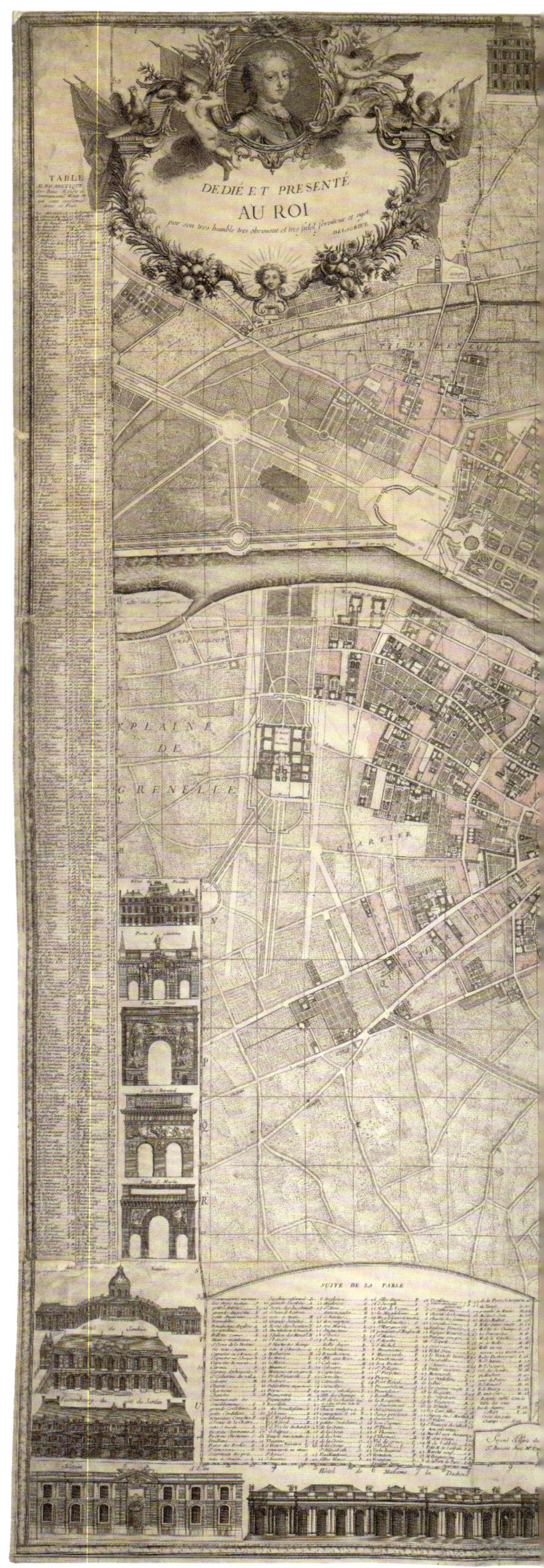

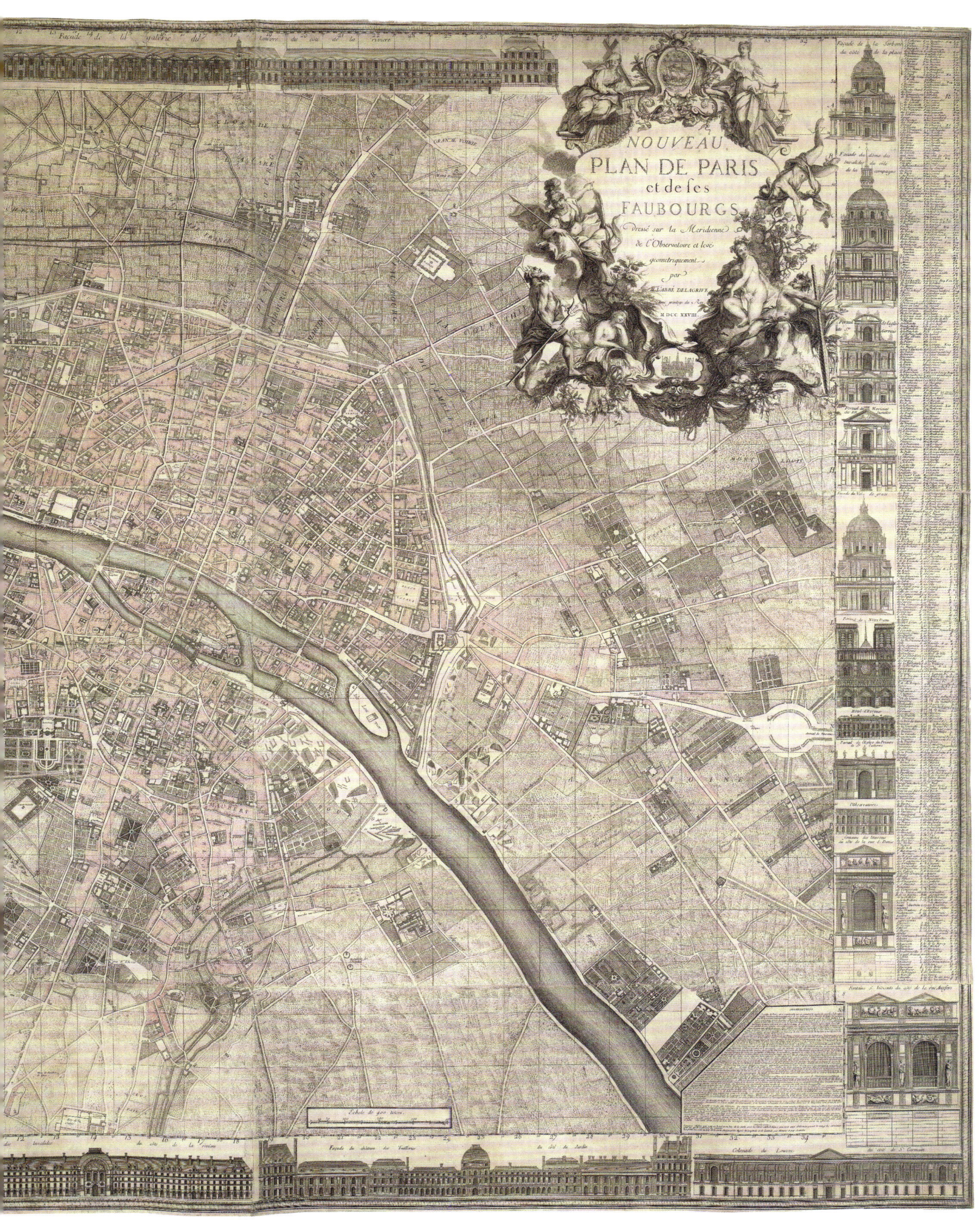

NOUVEAU
PLAN DE PARIS
et de ses
FAUBOURGS
dressé sur la Meridienne
de l'Observatoire et levé
geometriquement
par
M. L'ABBÉ DELAGRIVE
avec privilege du Roy
M DCC XXVIII

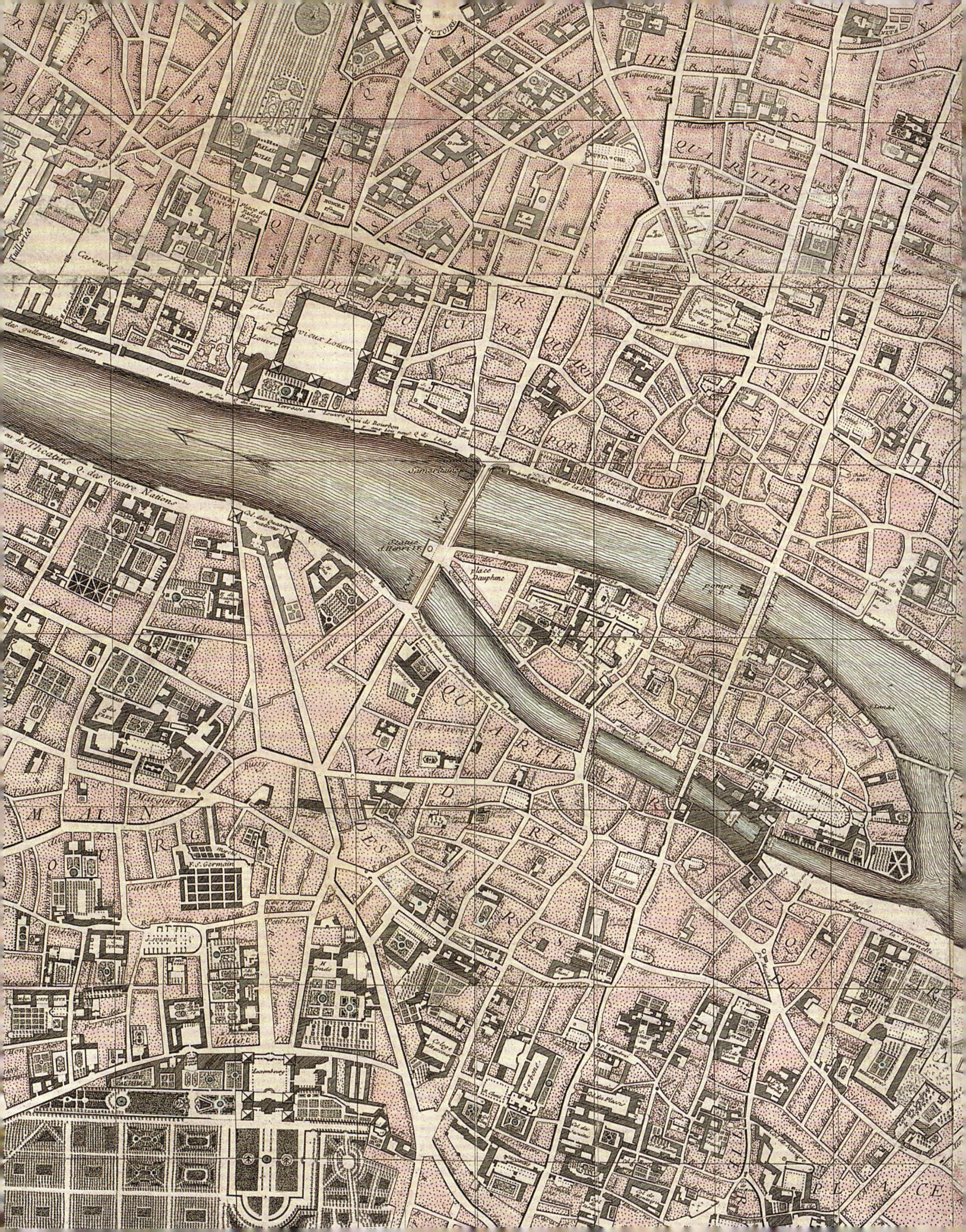

PARIS

HANNAH WILLIAMS

Being an artist in eighteenth-century Paris meant following one of two paths. Restrictions in the commercially controlled and socially hierarchical world of the city's professions meant that, to practice legally, an artist either had to become a member of the king's Royal Academy, or be admitted to the city's medieval guild.[1] The story of art in eighteenth-century Paris is often told as a tale of rivalry between these two institutional worlds, represented in this book by artists such as the Academy's Jean-François de Troy or Jean-Siméon Chardin, and the guild's Jacques Autreau. It is a tale of ideological division, in which the virtuous and learned academicians sought to rescue the arts from the guild's rabble of money-grubbing tradesmen – a narrative which, as that bias might suggest, was constructed by the Academy itself and perpetuated long afterwards through the enduring traditions it established.[2] Whatever the more complicated facts and experiences behind this story, in art history it has given rise to a vision of the Paris art world based in oppositions, which nearly always fall along institutional lines: liberal art vs mechanical trade; art for art's sake vs making money; elite vs common; cosmopolitan vs parochial. For the artists who belonged to these institutions, it has also created an idea of two supposedly distinct social worlds – two artistic communities defined against each other, operating in separate spheres, to achieve divergent endeavours.

Yet as this exhibition suggests, when we turn from institutional histories to social and urban histories, and from art theory to art objects, much more complex and entwined views of Paris's art world emerge. In the city's cultural geography, we find academicians and guild artists living and working in the same streets and neighbourhoods, even while carving out their own professional and commercial spaces in different parts of the city. In artists' social and financial lives, we find a broad socioeconomic spectrum and diverse networks that do not neatly follow institutional lines. And in the artworks they produced, as is evident in the paintings in this exhibition, we find shared interests despite differing markets and institutional contexts.

It is perhaps no coincidence that this alternative view should be granted to us thanks to Hogarth, that inveterate observer who encouraged his audiences always to look at things differently. Far from the conventional art-historical privileging of the Academy's world – its famous artists, elite patrons, and hierarchical elevation of history painting – this exhibition's effort to explore a Hogarthian perspective on Europe's art recovers a more multifarious vision of Paris's artistic communities, traversing social boundaries to retrieve common experiences, and challenging traditional theoretical constraints to find the period's emerging artistic engagement with the city in which all these artists lived.

*

Hogarth visited Paris twice in his life: in 1743 to hire engravers for *Marriage A-la-mode* and then again in 1748, when, on the return journey, he experienced his unfortunate arrest in Calais.[3] One of Europe's largest eighteenth-century cities, Paris's population reached half a million in this period and expanded physically to such an extent that it required a new administrative perimeter (the wall of the Ferme générale) by the 1780s. The Paris art world that Hogarth would have encountered on his Parisian trips was geographically concentrated in certain neighbourhoods, though to explore it in its entirety would have led the traveller all over the city. For the Academy, life was centred on the Louvre, where the institution had been granted apartments in 1692 and where, since 1737, it had held the Salon exhibitions that became a biennial art-world spectacle. Since the reign of Henri IV (1589–1610), small numbers of artists working for the French crown had been granted lodgings in the Louvre, but during the eighteenth century, the palace became a veritable artistic neighbourhood, with more and more of the building given over to artists' homes and studios, first in the long Galerie extending along the banks of the Seine and later in the main palace itself.[4] Priority for these coveted lodgings usually went to the Academy's history painters and sculptors, but some practitioners of the 'lesser' genres were accorded the privilege, such as André Rouquet, the miniaturist who painted Hogarth's enamel portrait (p.64). Rouquet in fact holds the dubious distinction of having been forcibly evicted from his Louvre home, when a mental health episode and drug addiction led to a pattern of escalating antisocial behaviour (like throwing furniture out of windows and nearly setting fire to his lodging) that eventually became too much to bear for his artist neighbours and the palace authorities.[5]

By the end of the eighteenth century, the Louvre had become the epicentre of the Academy's professional sphere. But while more and more of the institution's artists gravitated towards the palace, either to live within the building or in the surrounding neighbourhood, there were always academicians who chose to set up homes and studios (one and the same in this period) elsewhere. Indeed, in the first half of the century, when Hogarth visited Paris, most members of the institution (and most of the academicians represented in this exhibition) were living in other neighbourhoods. De Troy, for instance, lived fairly close by on Rue Neuve des Petits Champs, near the Palais Royal, while Jean-Baptiste Pater lived over near the Marais on Rue Quincampoix.[6] Others, meanwhile, chose the Left Bank of the Seine. Chardin lived for much of his career on Rue Princesse in the Faubourg Saint-Germain, until he was eventually granted a Louvre studio in 1757, while Étienne Jeaurat lived for over twenty-five years on Rue des Fossés-Saint-Victor, out near the Jardin des Plantes, which is where he was living when he painted his *Interior of the Artist's Studio* (p.69). Another crucial art-world neighbourhood on this side of the river was around Rue Saint-Jacques, an area that Hogarth would certainly have visited, because it was home to the city's printing and bookselling district and thus the preferred quarter for Paris's engravers.[7]

The distribution of artists across the city turned the neighbourhoods of Paris into contact zones for the otherwise institutionally divided members of the Academy and the guild, not least because the guild's artists were even more widespread than the academicians. The guild had premises housing its school – the Académie de Saint-Luc – in central Paris on the Île de la Cité near Pont Notre-Dame, the bridge that was home to many of the city's commercial picture dealers and other shops. But unlike academicians, the guild's artists were not granted lodgings onsite; nor did they generally gravitate towards their institutional headquarters. Instead, when it came to choosing a home, guild artists seem to have been more influenced by other trade networks in which their practice might be embedded.[8] Some, for instance, lived out east in the furniture-making district of the Faubourg Saint-Antoine, and one of the most popular neighbourhoods was in the north of the city near the Porte Saint-Martin, another artisanal quarter that was a key commercial and industrial zone for the trade and manufacture of colours for painting and dyeing. Indeed, some guild artists actually pursued far more active careers as colour merchants than as art-makers (an avenue not open to academicians, whose Statutes directly prohibited any kind of commercial activity).

Demographic concentrations in these two different art-world neighbourhoods – the Louvre and Porte Saint-Martin – might seem to confirm the idea of the socioeconomic divide between the 'elite' Academy, in its central fashionable quarter of noble and wealthy bourgeois residents, and the more 'common' guild artists, out with the labourers of the northern faubourgs (suburbs). But whatever cultural capital came with an address in eighteenth-century Paris, it did not always reflect an artist's financial status.

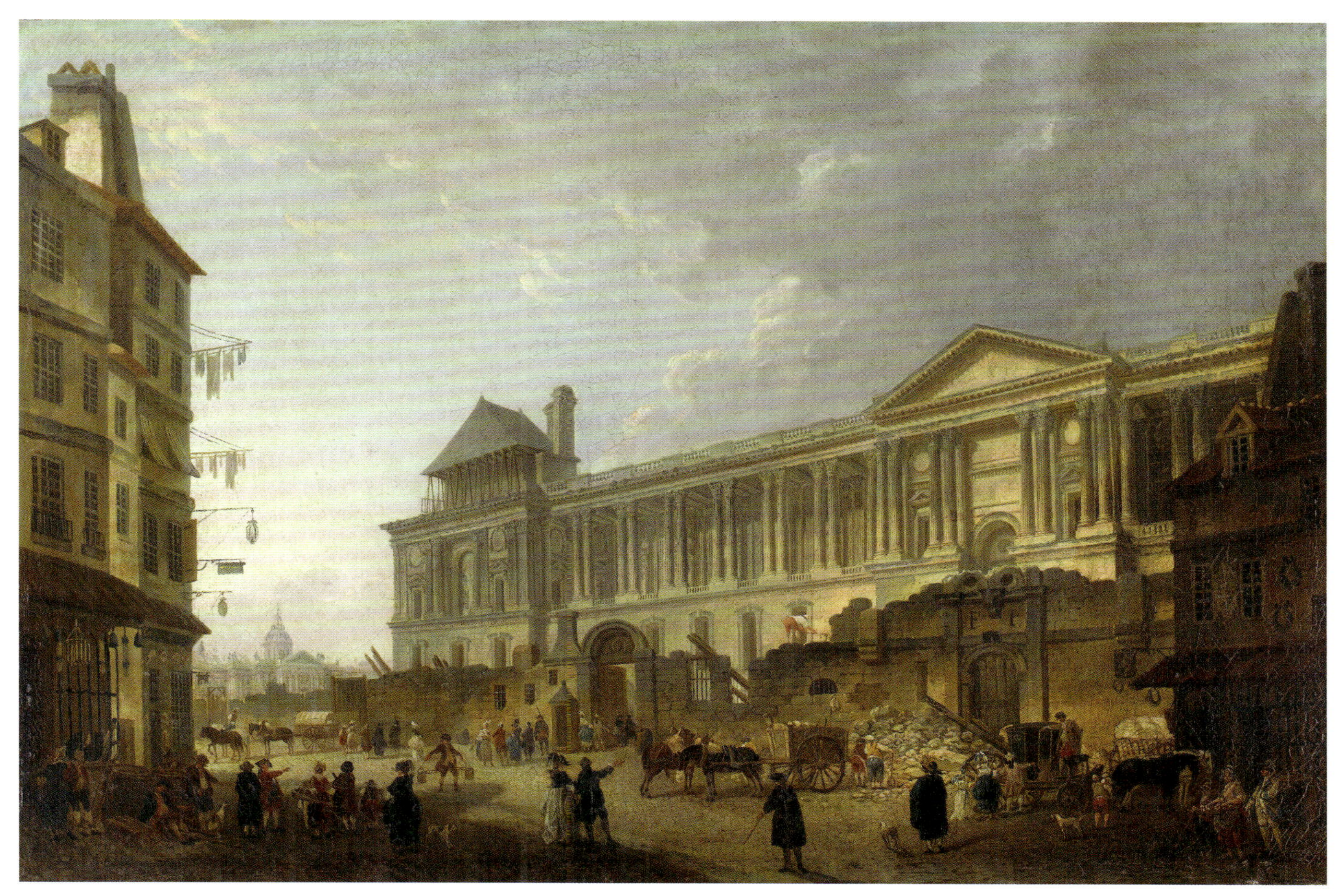

PIERRE-ANTOINE DEMACHY View of the Colonnade of the Louvre 1772

Some of the guild's artists might be leading lucrative careers as colour merchants or art dealers, while some of the academicians in the Louvre could be living in utter poverty, like the sculptor Edmé Dumont, whose home was once described by the director of the Academy as 'a complete rat's nest without any furniture'.[9] Moreover, as we have seen, notwithstanding certain concentrations, artists of both institutions were living all over the city, allowing for intermingling interactions in neighbourhood shops and social spaces like taverns and churches. Some were even neighbours on the same street, like the academicians Gabriel Allegrain and Gilles Allou who in the 1740s both lived on Rue Meslay, one of the most popular addresses for guild artists in the Porte Saint-Martin neighbourhood. Inter-institutional connections could even occur in the same family, like Jacques Autreau, a guild artist whose son Louis became an academician, or Jean-Baptiste Oudry,

an academician whose father, Jacques, was a guild painter.[10] Oudry himself began his career in the guild before being admitted to the Academy, which was not an uncommon trajectory; Alexis Grimou, more unusually, abandoned a career in the Academy to become a member of the guild.

The life of the street that Paris's artists experienced in their neighbourhoods did not often feature in their art in the same way that urban London did for Hogarth. This was not for want of interest, but because subject matter in French painting was far more controlled. In the Academy especially, with its restrictive hierarchy of genres, painters were only supposed to practice in the genre for which they had been admitted (history painting, portraiture, still life, etc.) and thus the only artists for whom 'the street' was really a legitimate subject were landscapists (painting architectural views of the city) and genre painters (in scenes of everyday urban life).

43

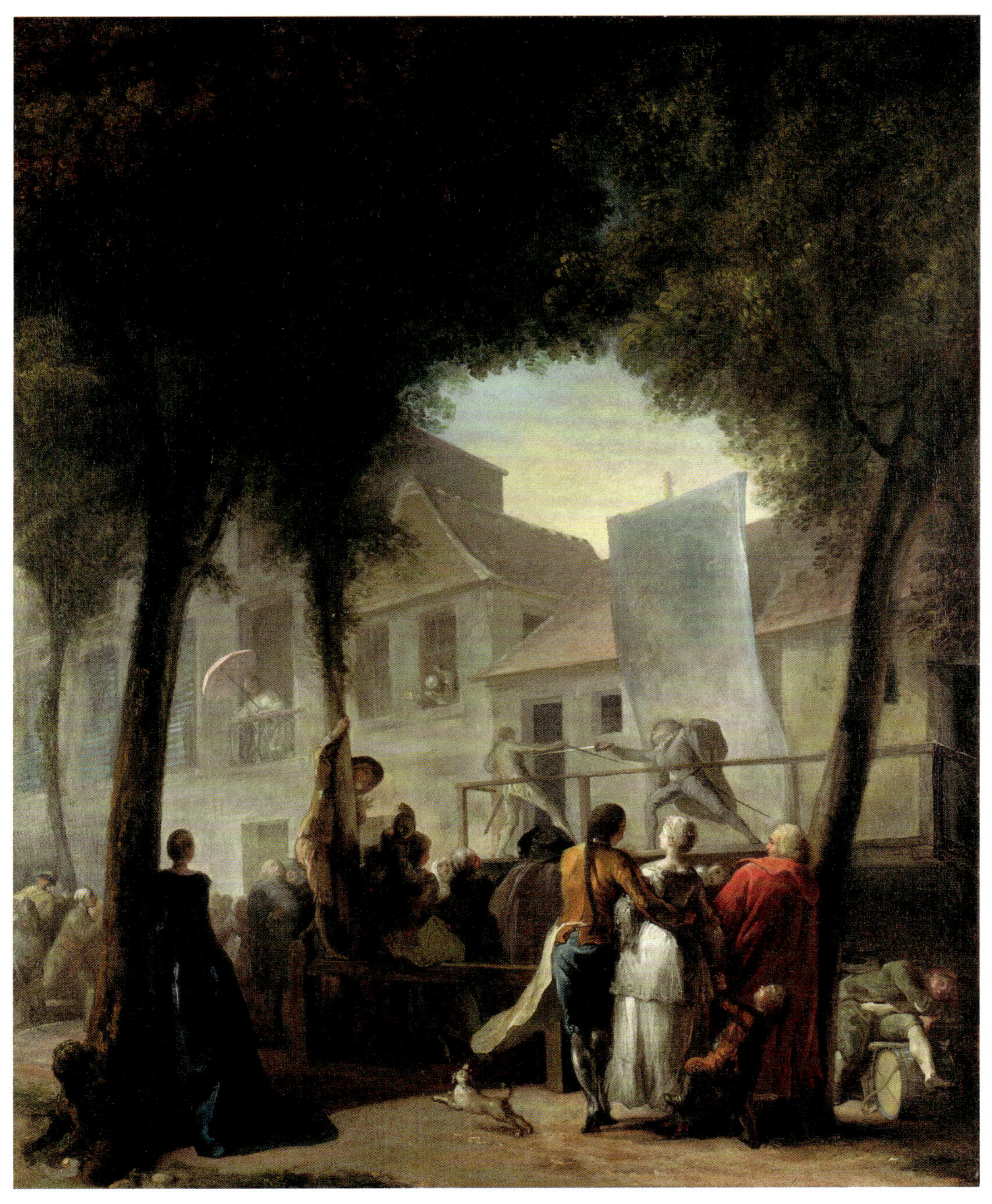

44

Pierre-Antoine Demachy was one of the Academy's landscapists who made Paris a particular focus of study, especially his own neighbourhood around the Louvre, depicting the area's urban transformations in works like *View of the Colonnade of the Louvre* 1772 (p.43), while also capturing a sense of city life in the foreground.[11] One of the most habitual observers of everyday life was the guild artist Gabriel-Jacques de Saint-Aubin, who often worked as a draughtsman, but also produced painted vignettes like *A Street Show in Paris* 1760 (p.44), which includes a performance by commedia dell'arte actors – familiar figures also in Jean-Antoine Watteau's theatrical paintings – acting on a temporary stage rigged up on a city square.

While French art-theoretical restrictions meant that the city never became a dominant subject in eighteenth-century art, artists did push against the hierarchy of genres to find ways of engaging with urban life, many examples of which are included in this book. The sculptor Edmé Bouchardon, for instance, made a series of drawings creating an artistic taxonomy of Paris's hawkers and street-sellers (p.86).[12] The history painter Jeaurat executed several lively street encounters, such as his depiction of *Sex workers being taken to Salpêtrière near the Porte Saint-Bernard* 1757, a scene set very near his Left Bank studio. Watteau, meanwhile, invented an entirely new genre with his *fêtes galantes* (p.140), which turned parks and gardens into evanescent fantasy spaces for theatrical and aristocratic escapades.

Such creative efforts suggest the depth of engagement with urban life (and its escape) during this period of significant expansion and urbanisation, which witnessed the very beginnings of 'Paris' as a subject in its own right in French art. In art history, this is a story that has become far more familiar from the nineteenth century, when, following the dismantling of the ancien régime's art-world institutions and the rapid expansion of the city, Paris established itself categorically as the driving focus of avant-garde painting. Yet, as the collection of works in this exhibition reveals, it was in the everyday experiences and artistic interests of eighteenth-century Parisians that the modern city first emerged as urban muse.

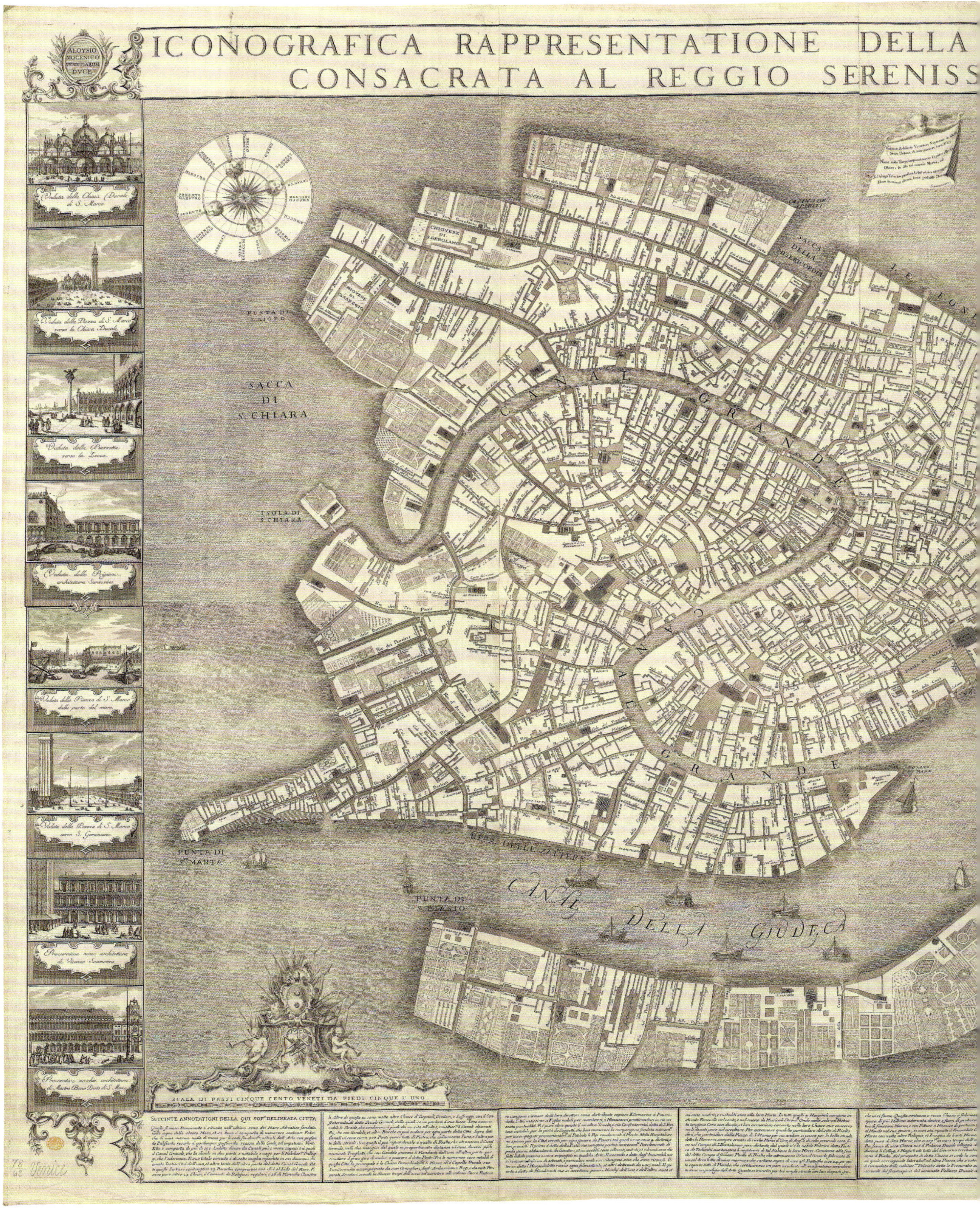

ICONOGRAFICA RAPPRESENTATIONE DELLA ... CONSACRATA AL REGGIO SERENISS...

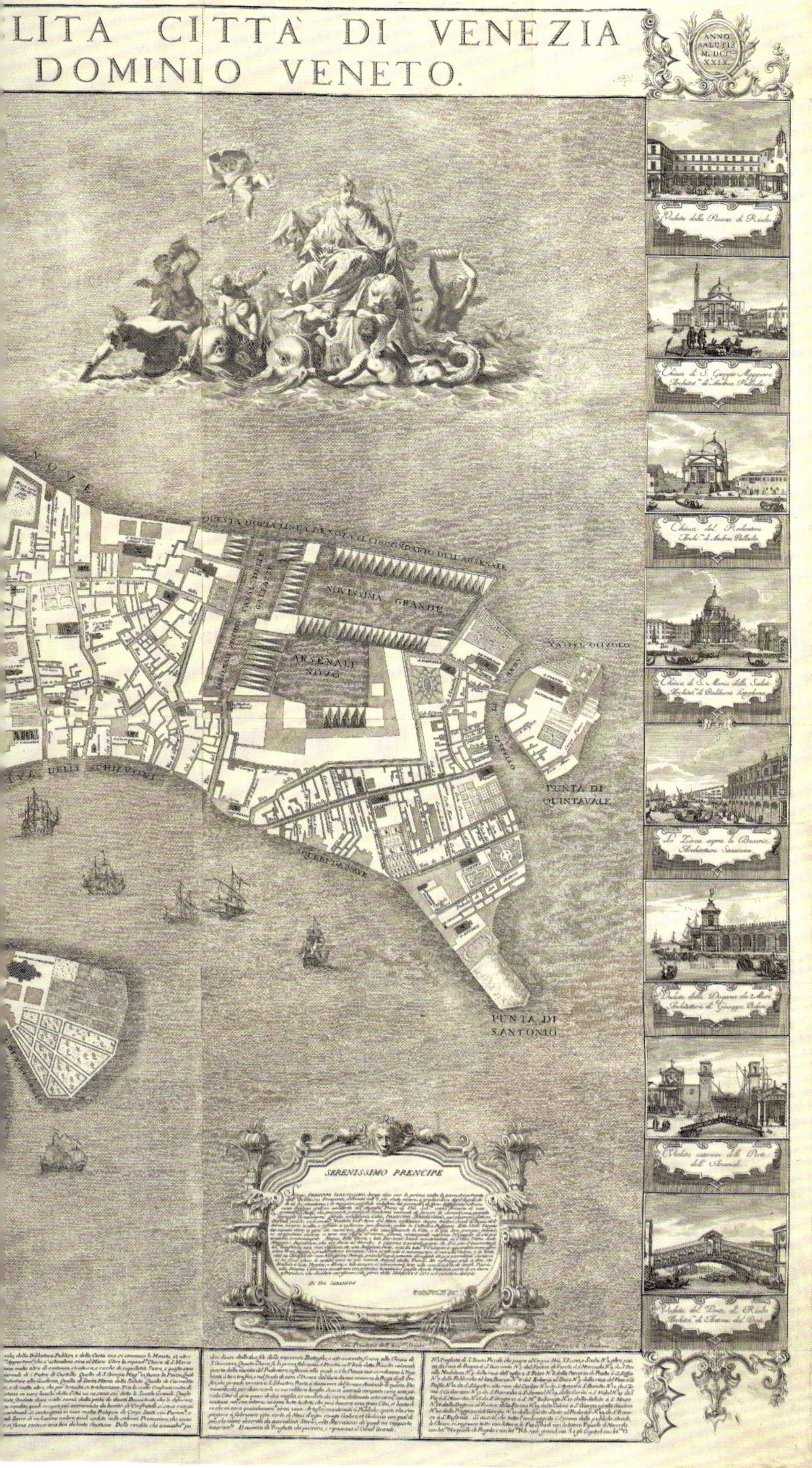

LODOVICO UGHI
*Iconographic Representation
of the City of Venice*   1729

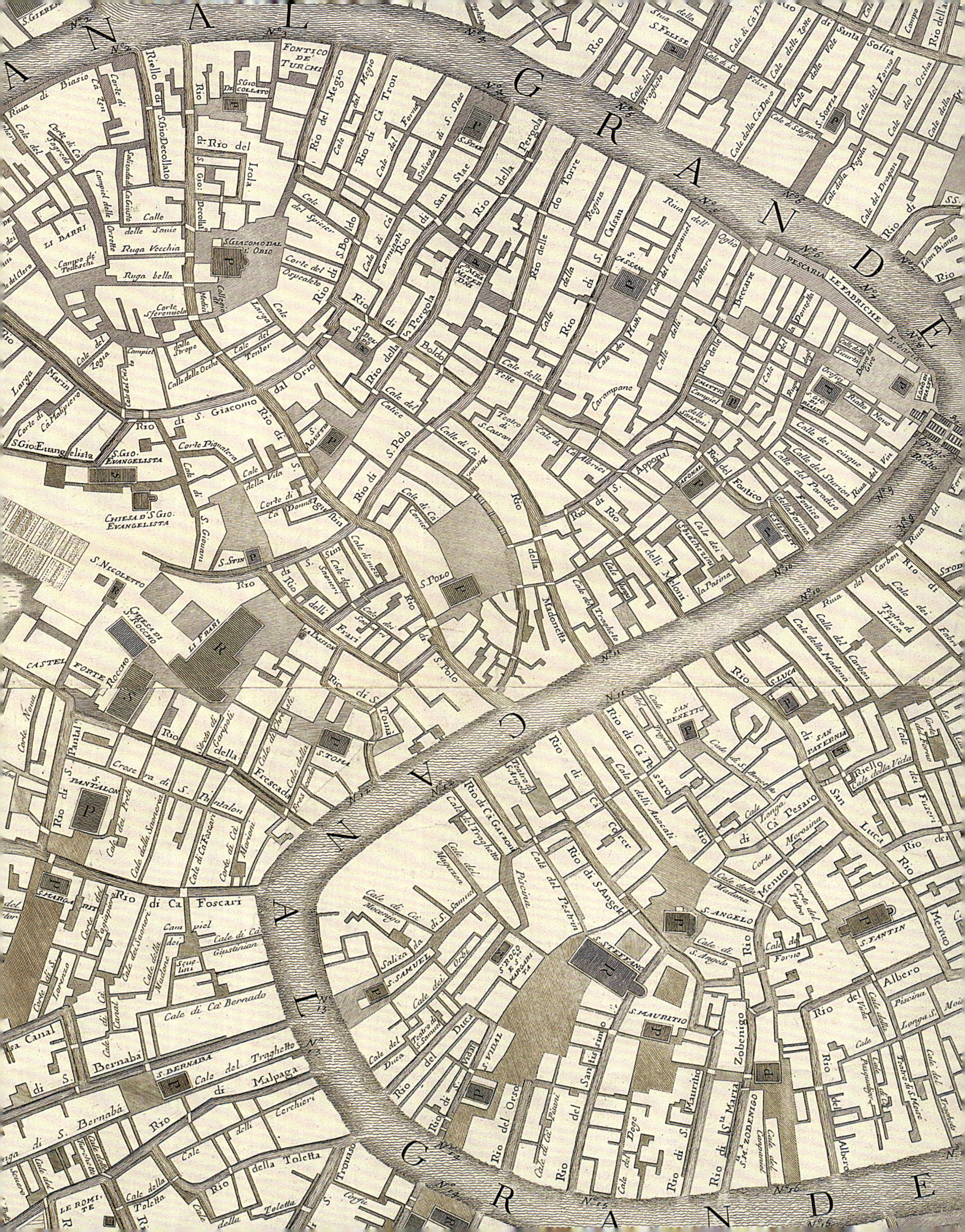

CANAL GRANDE
FONTICO DE TURCHI
Riva di Biasio
S.Gio.Decollato
S.Gio.Decollato
Rio del Isola
Campiel delle Oreste
Ruga Vecchia
Ruga bella
LI BARRI
Campo de Todischi
S.GIACOMO DAL ORIO
Corte del Oyesdade
S.Boldo
Carmini
Rio del Mago
Rio di Cà Tron
Rio della
Pergola
PESCARIA LE FABRICHE
Rialto Novo
Rio di S.Cassan
Calle del Campanil
Beccarie
La Donzella
Carampane
S.Gio.Evangelista
S.GIO. EVANGELISTA
CHIESA D'S.GIO. EVANGELISTA
S.Giacomo dal Orio
Corte Piguntera
Corte della Vila
S.Spirito
S.POLO
Teatro di S.Casson
Calle di Cà
Rio di S.Polo
S.Polo
Madonetta
Calle del Traghetto
S.NICOLETTO
S.Gio.
L'FRARI
CASTEL FORTE
Rocca
Rio di S.Tomà
S.TOMÀ
Frescada
Calle della Madona
SAN BENETTO
SAN PATERNIA
Rio di Cà Pesaro
S.Luca
S.PANTALON
Rio di S.Pantalon
Croxe
Rio di Cà Foscari
Cà Bernado
Cale di Cà Bernado
BERNABA
S.BERNABA
Cale del Traghetto
Malpaga
SAN ANGELO
S.ANGELO
S.STEFFANO
S.FANTIN
S.MAURITIO
S.SAMUEL
S.VIDAL
S.MARIA ZOBENIGO
Rio del Orso
Rio di S.Maurizio
Piscina
ALBERO
Rio della Toletta
LE ROMITE
Toletta
CANAL GRANDE

VENICE

JONNY YARKER

Pietro Longhi's *The Painter in His Studio* c.1741–4 (p.68) shows an artist at work on the portrait of an aristocratic woman, fashionably dressed and clutching a lapdog. Her *cicisbeo* – young escort – is shown hovering behind her chair dressed in the distinctive *bautta*, or masked costume, typically adopted during the Venetian carnival; apparently bored, he looks eager to return to the festivities. The quiet interior is typical of Longhi's work: the limited number of figures, the curious, shallow room, the carefully observed costume, the suggestion of narrative and trace of satire. It is perhaps not surprising that scholars have long sought to link Longhi with William Hogarth.

At first glance there are some intriguing parallels between the two painters. Longhi often hangs his interiors with old master paintings, designed to amplify the narrative message; there is evidence he conceived works sequentially, and his recently published correspondence with Giuseppe Wagner proves that, like Hogarth, he was assiduous in monitoring the production of prints after his own paintings.[1] But it is perhaps in the response of contemporaries to their respective work that we find the greatest analogies. Longhi's paintings were praised by a group of Venetian writers who were invested in artistic reform. The playwright Carlo Goldoni, who had rejected classical tragedy, the commedia dell'arte and all their hybrid combinations in opera for a greater naturalism, specifically compared his work to the naturalism of Longhi's paintings: in a famous sonnet, written in 1750, Goldoni starts with the lines: 'Longhi, tu che la mia musa sorella del tuo pennel che cerca il vero' (Longhi, you summon my sibling muse; your pen like mine is seeking truth).[2] Longhi received praise in the reforming press: writing in 1760 in *Gazzetta veneta*, a journal modelled on *The Spectator*, Goldoni's follower Gasparo Gozzi celebrated Longhi's faithful interiors over the baroque grandeur of Giovanni Battista Tiepolo. But here the parallels end. Longhi's work is completely devoid of the biting satire or moral imperative of Hogarth's. Whilst Longhi might have seen Hogarth's prints, it is highly unlikely Hogarth would have known work by Longhi, whose patrons were almost universally Venetian aristocrats.

The desire to see formal links between the two artists does, however, raise the intriguing question of what Hogarth knew of Venice and its artists.

*

During the eighteenth century the Italian peninsula was composed of autonomous states (it would not become a single country until 1861). Despite declining fortunes, the Venetian Republic – which comprised fourteen provinces in northern Italy and the eastern Mediterranean – remained a major artistic force centred on its principal city, Venice. The Republic's contracting trade and enfeebled aristocratic government meant there was a diminishing indigenous patronage base for artists, but the city remained a centre of the Grand Tour. Travel as a component of elite education rapidly increased following the conclusion of the War of Spanish Succession, and by 1730 a steady stream of aristocratic British men were travelling to Italy, frequently in the company of a tutor, to experience the Continent, learn new languages, visit notable monuments and tentatively enter society. Whilst Rome and her ruins were the principal goal, Venice formed a fashionable diversion, often visited during the carnival, which ran from Boxing Day until Shrove Tuesday every year.[3]

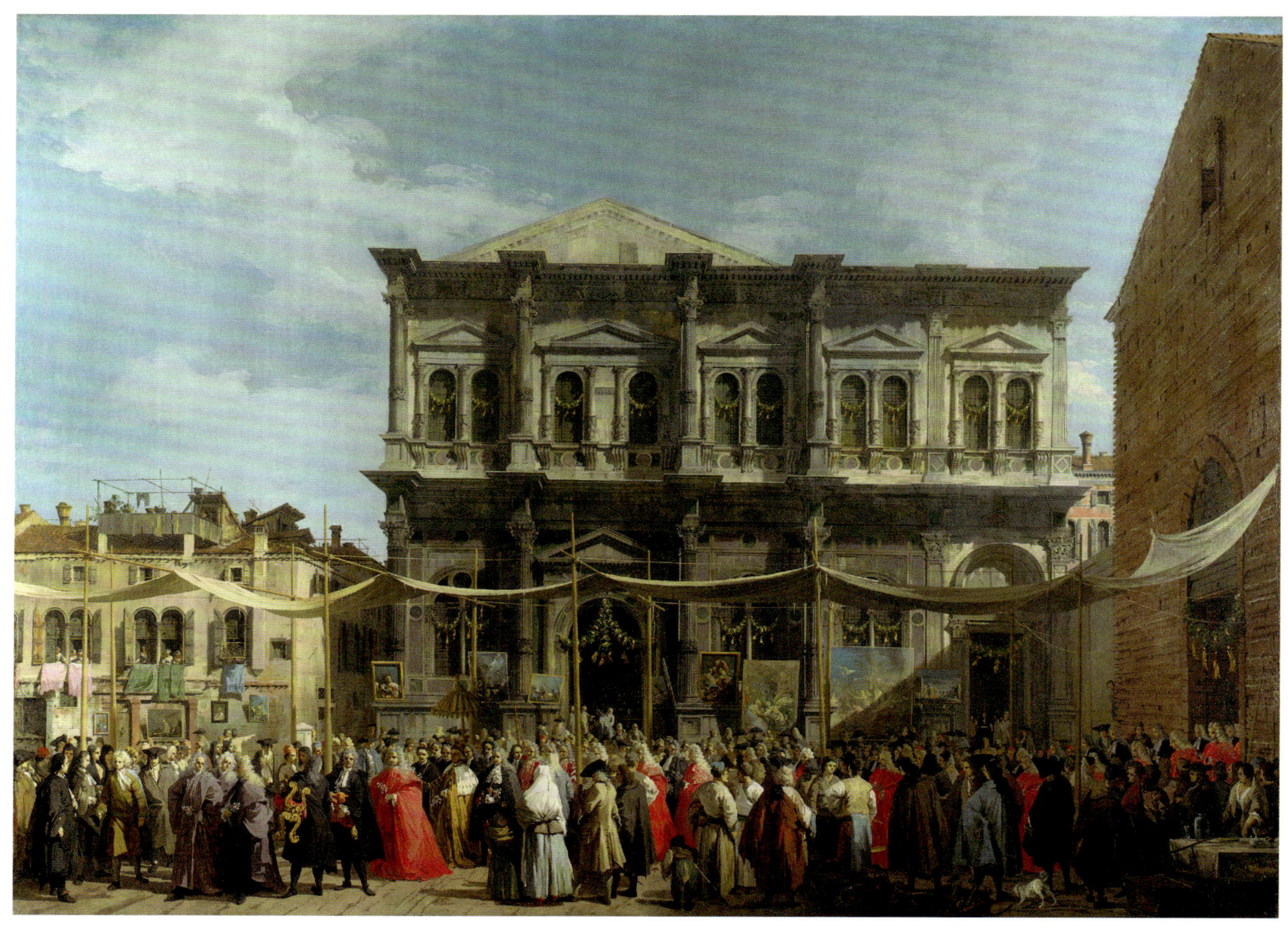

CANALETTO *The Feast Day of Saint Roch* 1735

We can visit the city in the company of one of Hogarth's sitters, Martin Folkes, who arrived in Venice in June 1733. Folkes was not the average Grand Tourist: at 43, he was already an eminent scientist and was travelling with his wife, daughters, 'dog, cat, parrot and monkey'. As he recorded in his journal, despite purchasing an up-to-date plan to help him get around, Folkes found the city difficult and confusing to navigate: the absence of a regular street plan meant the visitor was confronted by a labyrinthine network of canals and *calle* crisscrossing haphazardly from parish to parish. As a celebrated disciple of Isaac Newton, he was called upon to make various optical demonstrations and made accurate measurements of the Campanile and Rialto Bridge. He also followed other tourists in visiting the most celebrated artist in the city, Rosalba Carriera. Folkes recorded in his journal:

I went to Signa Rosalbas whos pictures in crayons have been with justice esteemd the most excellent pieces of art of that sort. She is now better than 50, and was formerly as deservdly famous for her works in water colours; I was there extreamly well entertaind with a great number of fine portraits some of my acquaintance very like.[4]

Carriera was almost sixty when Folkes visited her studio on the Grand Canal and since early in the century her pastel portraits and allegorical heads had been highly esteemed across Europe. Amazingly, much of Carriera's correspondence survives and it demonstrates how well connected she in fact was.[5] Through the peripatetic French painter Nicolas Vleughels, she had begun corresponding with the principal cultural figures in Paris, exchanging letters with the collectors Pierre-Jean Mariette, Pierre Crozat and Jean de Jullienne. As a result she

50

visited Paris in 1719 where she was introduced to, amongst others, Jean-Antoine Watteau and she was, unusually for a woman, elected a member of the French *Académie*.

Venice had no formal art academy at this date; painters belonged to a guild (the *Collegio dei pittori*) which itself had only seceded in 1679 from a guild including housepainters and whitewashers. An annual open-air exhibition was held in the Campo S. Rocco on 16 August (p.50), timed to coincide with the annual visit of the Doge, Venice's elected ruler. It offered, in a modest way, a forum bringing artists and their public together. Without an academy, painting was learnt in the studio of an established artist. This had the result of making painting a family affair: sons followed fathers in the profession, and apprentices often married their master's daughters, as Hogarth himself had done.

On his visit to Rosalba Carriera, Folkes also met her sister Angela, noting she was the 'wife of Sigr Pelegrini and was with him in england, for which she expresses a great regard'. This was the painter Giovanni Antonio Pellegrini, who had visited London in 1708 at the invitation of Charles Montagu, Earl (later Duke) of Manchester. Together with the landscape painter Marco Ricci, Pellegrini worked on a constellation of fashionable interiors in Britain, covering the walls of Kimbolton Castle and Castle Howard with richly coloured late-baroque murals. The pair also worked on scenery for the newly fashionable Italian opera at the Haymarket theatre. Ricci brought the popular Italian art of *caricatura* to bear on the creative world he encountered in London, producing a series of satirical interiors filled with musical celebrities: *Rehearsal of an Opera* c.1709 (p.79) lampoons the portly castrato Niccolini, who is accompanied by Handel's collaborator, Nicola Francesco Haym.

Within Venice's tight-knit art world, caricature flourished. Ricci shared his rapidly drawn pen and ink portraits of operatic performers, artists and visiting tourists with the great Venetian patron, promoter and critic, Anton Maria Zanetti. Zanetti in turn, made copies, drew his own cartoons and shared them with a network of European connoisseurs (p.52). Diminishing domestic demand meant that Venetian artists increasingly sought patronage abroad, and Pellegrini and Ricci were the first in a succession of Venetian artists who travelled to London. Ricci returned for a second trip with his uncle, Sebastiano Ricci, whose works, inspired by Veronese, were lionised by those Whig patrons busily reviving the architecture of Palladio. The draw of London can be partly explained by this taste for sixteenth-century Venetian architecture, partly by the professional – and familial – ties among this group of painters and partly by the presence in Venice of dynamic British agents.

One upshot of the increase in tourists travelling to Italy was the emergence of an ecosystem of resident agents to support them. Carriera's correspondence shows that it was Montagu's secretary, Christian Cole, who taught her English and first promoted her to visiting British travellers. Owen McSwiny, an operatic impresario who washed up in Venice following commercial failure in London, introduced travellers to Carriera and other artists, negotiating commissions, payment and the return shipment to Britain; once the traveller was home, McSwiny could help them continue buying by correspondence.[6] In this capacity he conceived a remarkable project: a sequence of large-scale paintings of the fictive tombs of celebrated British public figures associated with the reign of William III. The project, by multiple hands, was apparently conceived without a patron, but after meeting Charles Lennox, Earl of March (later 2nd Duke of Richmond) in Venice, McSwiny convinced him to underwrite the enterprise. In seeking artists for his tombs, McSwiny commissioned some architectural elements from a young painter, Canaletto, and became his first agent, responsible for selling sets of Venetian views to patrons in London.

McSwiny lodged at Palazzo Balbi on the Grand Canal, the premises of the British merchants Williams & Smith, who dealt in the import of meat, dried cod and other foodstuffs from Amsterdam and London. The 'Smith' was Joseph Smith, who would form the greatest collection of contemporary Venetian painting in the city. He supplanted the chaotic McSwiny as Canaletto's principal agent, acquiring no fewer than fifty of his works and brokering commissions with a series of British clients; as a result, for the next decade, almost all Canaletto's sun-drenched views of Venice were dispatched on Smith's ships to Britain.

At Palazzo Balbi, Canaletto and other young artists were exposed to new ideas from across Europe. Smith, with his partner Giambattista Pasquali, ran a publishing house, printing the works of Newton and an Italian edition of Ephraim Chambers's *Cyclopaedia*. They promoted reformist texts on architecture, espousing a more scientific approach to the work of Andrea Palladio, this in turn prompting Smith to commission from Canaletto and others a sequence of depictions of Palladio's buildings (both built and unbuilt) and celebrated neo-Palladian structures in Britain. Like Carlo Goldoni and Gasparo Gozzi, Smith preferred Longhi to Tiepolo, acquiring a pair of Longhi's finest interiors which, along with Smith's exceptional collection and library, were purchased in 1762 by George III.

Travel and trade dwindled thanks to the European war in the 1740s, prompting Canaletto to try his luck in London. He may have been encouraged by the return of the ambidextrous Jacopo Amigoni from a decade in Britain. Amigoni had followed commissions across Europe, working for the court at Dusseldorf, on decoration at Nymphenburg Palace, and at the Benedictine abbey at Ottobeuren before arriving in London in 1729 with his assistant Giuseppe Wagner and in the company of the great castrato, Farinelli. Amigoni's pastel-coloured, putti-filled histories appealed to the new queen, Caroline of Ansbach, and, as Vertue

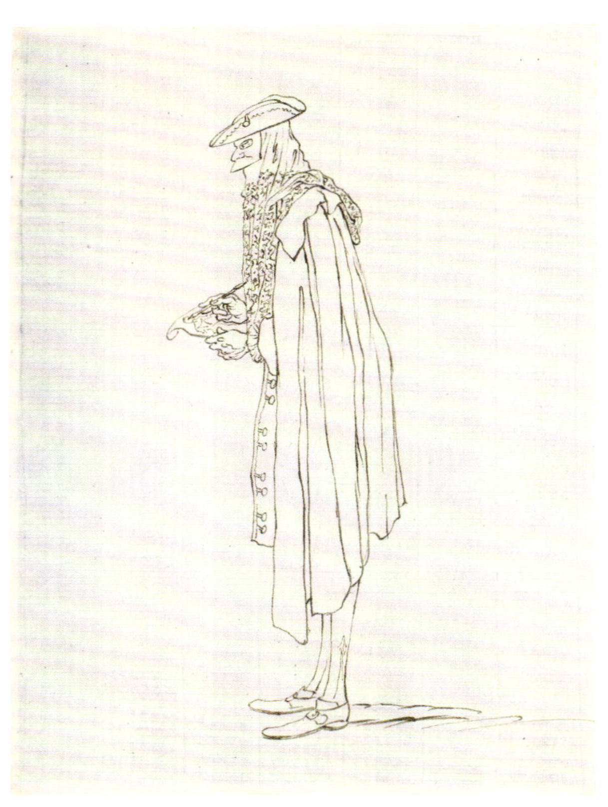

ANTON MARIA ZANNETTI THE ELDER
A Self-portrait in carnival costume, sketching c.1740

noted: 'courtiers and quality presd him, to imploy him in portraits'. Amigoni transposed the putti and saccharine palette to his portraits and 'got 4 or 5 thousands pounds' which he 'carryd away with him to Venice'.[7] Canaletto found patrons just as receptive to his British views; he produced a definitive depiction of eighteenth-century London and a remarkable sequence of views of – and from – country houses.

The question remains: what would Hogarth have known of all this? He would certainly have been aware of the works of Sebastiano Ricci and Pellegrini in Britain, conscious of their competition with his father-in-law, James Thornhill.

Whilst Hogarth was outspoken in his criticism of Continental training for British artists, he mixed in a decidedly European milieu and many of his most sympathetic patrons had spent time in Venice. Sir Edward Walpole – dedicatee of his print *The Polling* – had been in Venice with Gustavus Hamilton, 2nd Viscount Boyne, where both sat for Carriera, Boyne for the flashiest of her portraits, shown wearing a *bautta* (p.53). Boyne in turn commissioned Hogarth's satirical portrait of another friend from Venice, Sir Francis Dashwood, a painting that revels in the homosocial humour of a shared Grand Tour. Hogarth peppered his works with savage depictions of the fashionable castrati, possibly indebted to Venetian caricatures such as Ricci's.

But it was the success of Amigoni in London which reveals Hogarth's feelings about Venetian painting. In 1734 rumours started swirling that

Amigoni had received the commission to decorate the stairs of the newly built St Bartholomew's Hospital. Hogarth countered by offering to paint the stairs for free. What followed was a dirty campaign against Amigoni: he was ridiculed by Hogarth's supporter James Ralph in his *Weekly Register*, and two of Amigoni's prints, from a set of the *Cries of London*, were pirated (with the addition of lewd inscriptions).[8] Hogarth had effectively mobilised his supporters to squeeze out the Venetian and, in the process, make a concerted statement about the future of British history painting. One final footnote: all Amigoni's prints had been made by his assistant, Giuseppe Wagner, and sold from his printshop in Great Marlborough Street. It was Wagner, on his return to Venice, who went on to become Pietro Longhi's engraver – offering a hitherto unknown link between Longhi and Hogarth, between the raucous interiors of *Marriage A-la-Mode* and the quiet *palazzi* of *settecento* Venice.

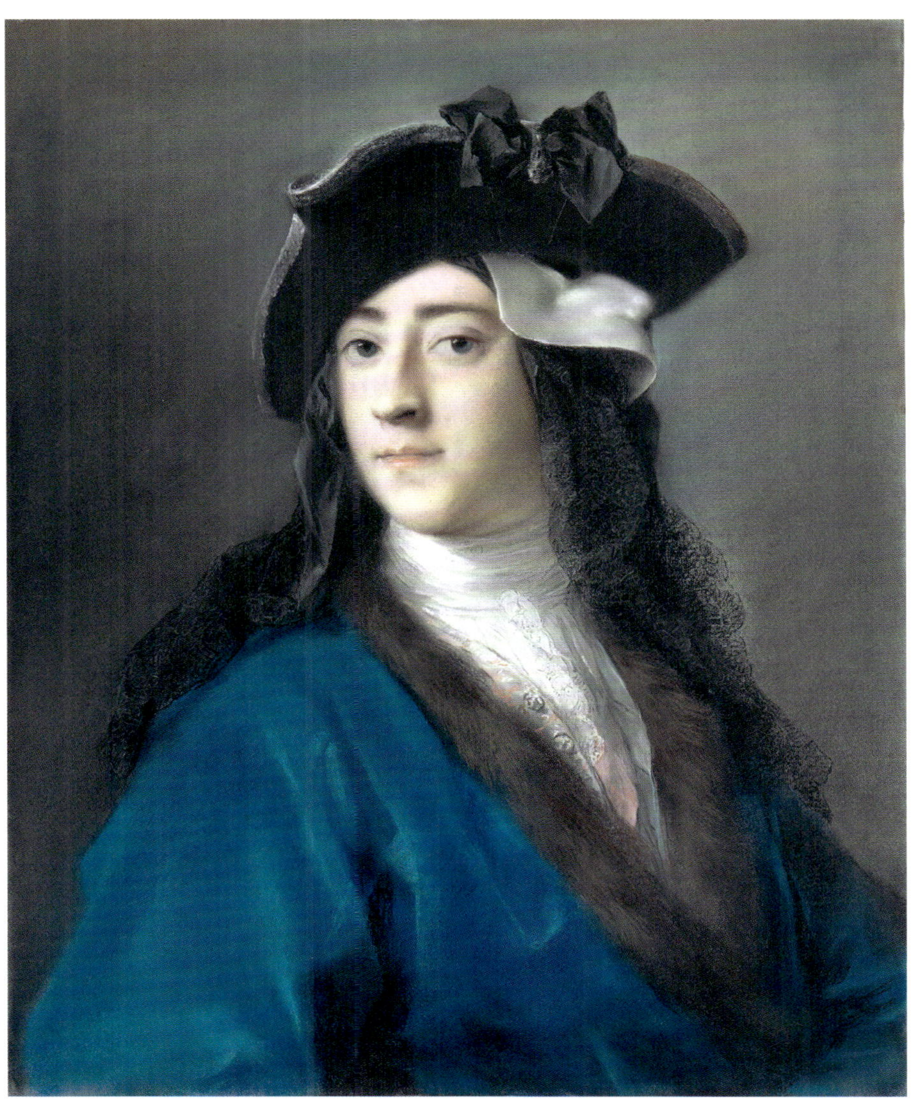

Gustavus Hamilton, 2nd Viscount Boyne in Masquerade Costume   1730–1

MODERN PAINTERS

The social changes of the mid-eighteenth century created new opportunities for artists, to different degrees and in different ways around Europe. Particularly in the commercial nations of Britain and the Netherlands, but also in the cosmopolitan tourist centre of Venice and in the increasingly unstable ancien régime of France, artists became less reliant upon the patronage of the state, church or court. Many became what we would today classify as 'freelancers' or 'independent' creatives: instead of having long-term employment or the protection of a princely patron, they worked opportunistically, responding to, and sometimes actively creating, market opportunities. The guilds and civic bodies that had once claimed authority over the production of art, limiting who could produce art and where it could be sold, continued to weaken in their practical influence.

As cities grew and as newspapers and printed materials proliferated, there emerged new possibilities for addressing potential clients directly. Visual artists became entrepreneurial, developing a new sense of professional independence even as their economic situation became more vulnerable. Where many painters and sculptors had been locked into a tradition of workshop practice, some now became prominent figures in metropolitan cultural scenes alongside musicians, actors and writers. This route was more available to men than to women, but the commercialisation of culture did offer some prospects for women to engage in cultural production, especially through patronage, publishing and writing.

Hogarth was acutely aware of these changes. His father aspired to be a man of letters but ended up imprisoned for debt after the failure of a business venture involving a coffee shop where the customers would speak Latin. Hogarth was initially apprenticed to a silver-plate engraver but soon broke from his master to set up as an independent copperplate engraver producing book illustrations, tickets and tradecards. His career as a portrait painter and self-published artist mapped out new routes to public prominence and creative independence. The reflections on the art world included in his autobiographical notes, and his determined efforts to ensure creative artists' copyright (successfully made law in 1735), demonstrate a sharp sense of how creative workers were exposed to commercial exploitation and risk.

The images gathered here reflect on these various shifts, and the different national contexts in which they were played out. Images by Hogarth in England, Chardin in France and Longhi in Italy reflect the humour and masculine self-parody that accompanied the sometimes uncomfortable shift in artistic identities over the middle decades of the eighteenth century. These artists were no longer the suave, educated courtiers who served kings and princes and could claim a certain aristocratic identity themselves. While there were still such 'court painters', they were now often viewed with suspicion, as lacking independence and creative integrity. Nor were they the stolid artisans who served as painters for churches and civic bodies, and whose skills were imagined to be dependably passed on from generation to generation, but who were now increasingly viewed as lacking imagination and freedom, supposedly bound and limited by the guilds that controlled their activities. Yet nor, still, were these artists the Romantic figures which came into focus in a later age: creative individuals, driven by inner passions, who rejected the hierarchies and expectations of mainstream society. These artists' relationship with the societies they inhabited was more complicated and compromised. Chardin, for instance, enjoyed a state pension later in life; Hogarth aspired to the role of Serjeant Painter to the king and, towards the end of his career, lent his satirical skills to supporting the government. Nonetheless, they might all be considered 'modern painters', not just because of the subjects that they chose, nor even because of the directness and immediacy of the ways they painted, the jokes and social criticism played out in their imagery, but because of their uneasy, emerging place in a burgeoning urban world.

JEAN-SIMÉON CHARDIN   *Still-life: The Kitchen Table*   c.1733–4

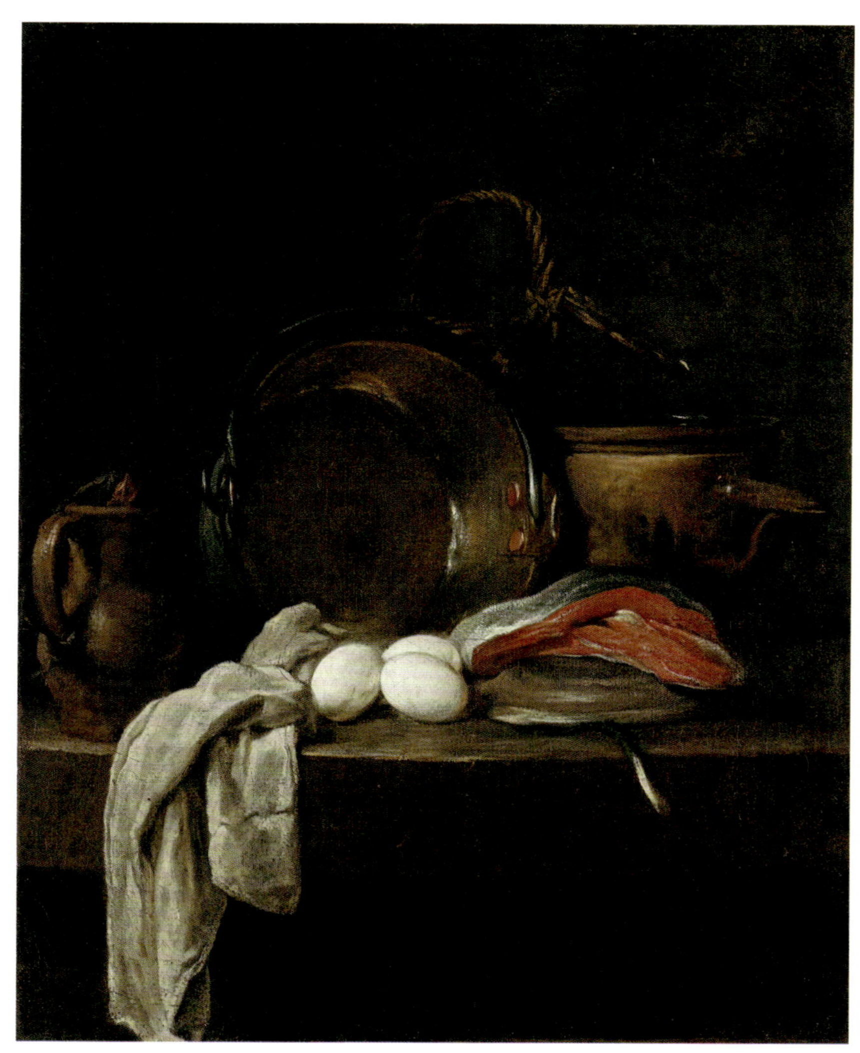

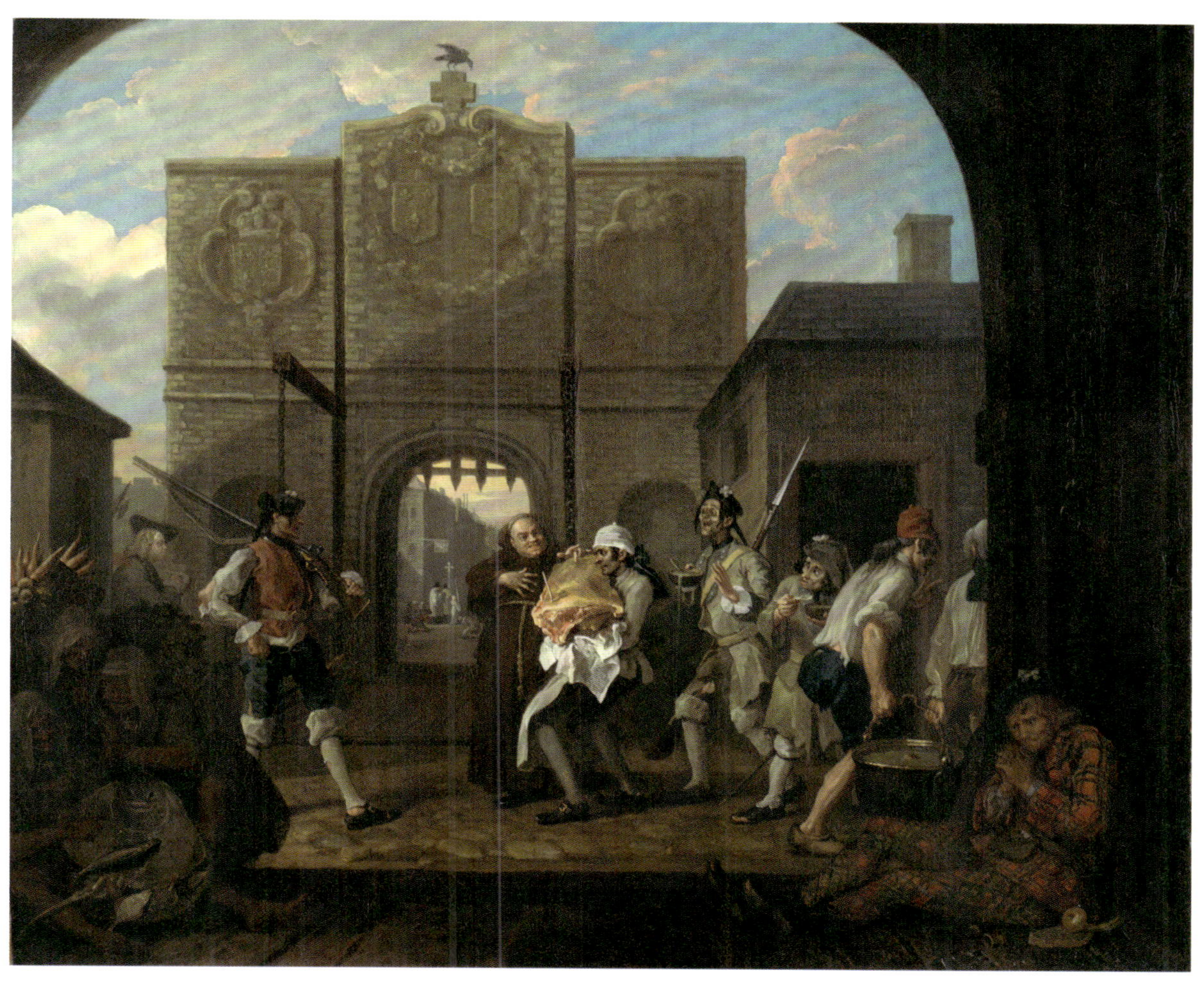

WILLIAM HOGARTH   *O the Roast Beef of Old England ('The Gate of Calais')*   1748

Although based on a documented incident, when
Hogarth was arrested as a suspected spy in Calais
in summer 1748, this picture serves as an allegory
of English nationalism. To the left, Hogarth casts
himself as a sharp-eyed social critic sketching his surroundings. The rest of the picture, though, provides
a compendium of xenophobic stereotypes, including
exploited French soldiers and superstitious women.
But the sumptuous still-life details echo the paintings
of the French artist Chardin, whom Hogarth had met
in Paris.

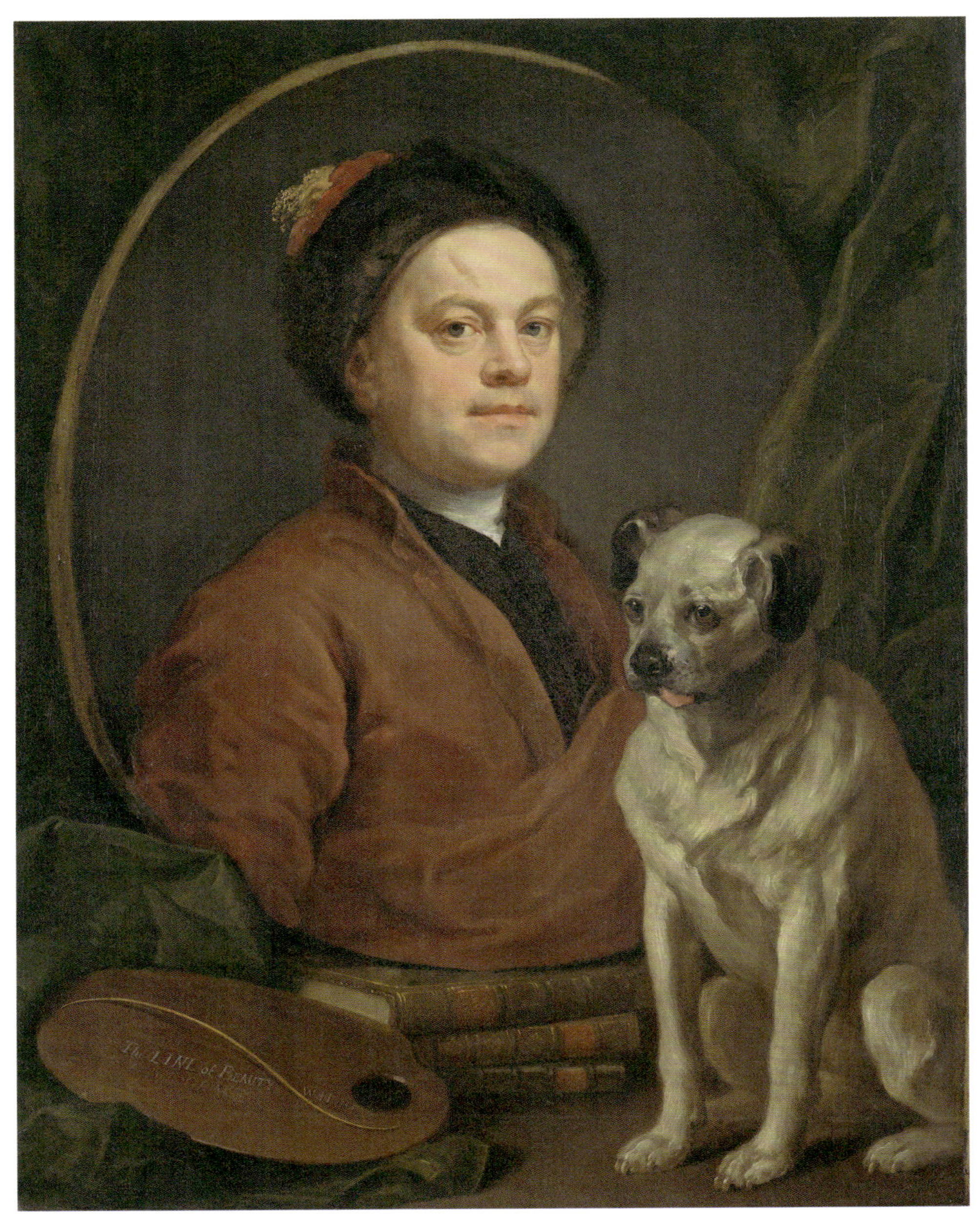

WILLIAM HOGARTH *The Painter and his Pug* 1745

58

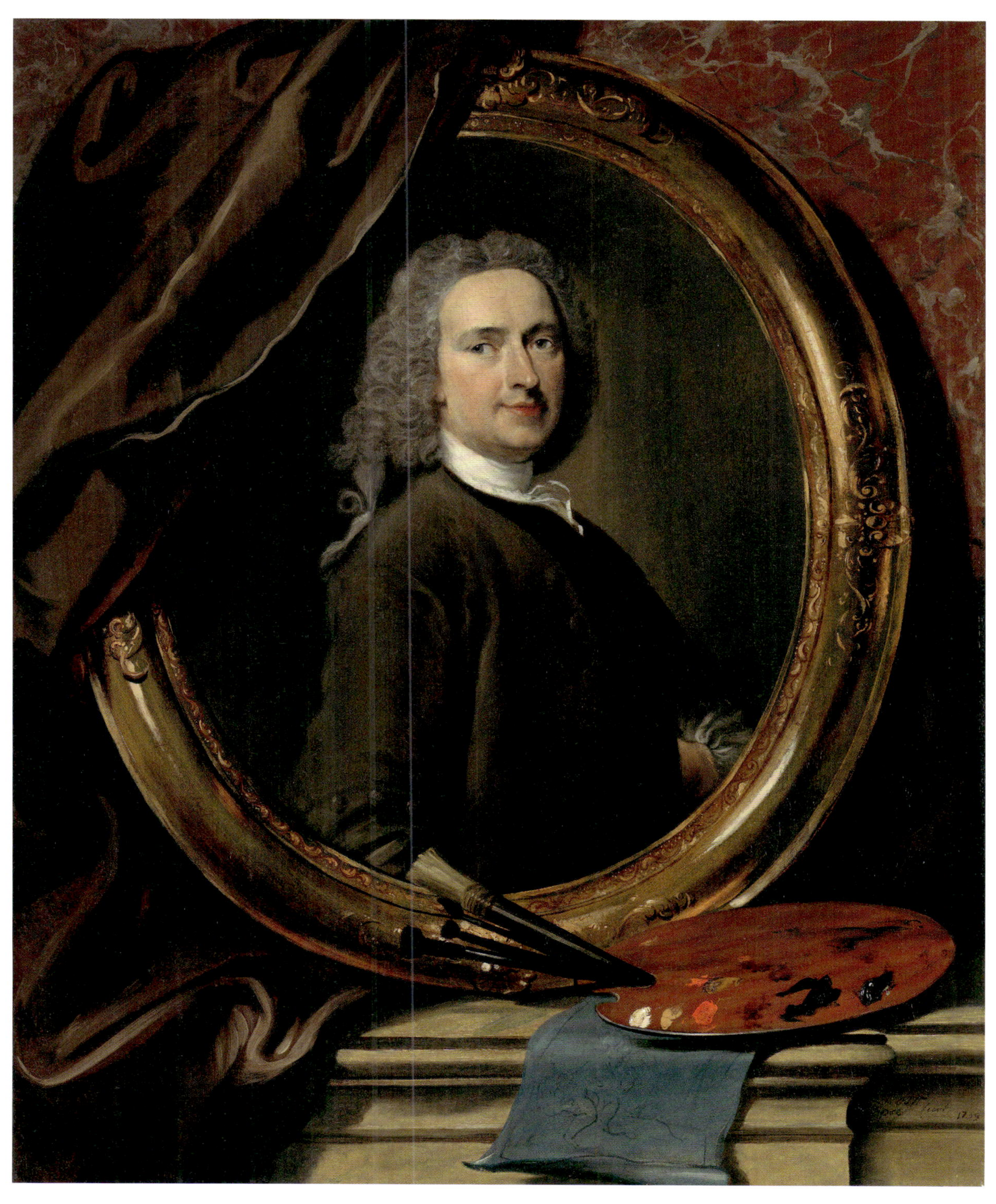

CORNELIS TROOST *Self-portrait* 1739

'THE DUTCH HOGARTH': CORNELIS TROOST

JOSEPHINA DE FOUW

When Cornelis Troost painted his self-portrait in 1739 (p.59), he was one of the most popular artists in the Dutch Republic. Six years later, William Hogarth finished his self-portrait (p.58), the same year he published his renowned print set *Marriage A-la-Mode*. The similarity in the form they chose is striking: both are portraits within a picture, and both are oval. The curtain pushed aside presents each portrait as if on a stage, a trick that emphasises the deceptive nature of painting and showcases the artist's skill. They were doubtless familiar with this pictorial device from Dutch paintings of the second half of the seventeenth century.[1]

Despite these similarities of form, there are fundamental differences too. The paintings are likenesses of the two and, at the same time, reflections of their position as artists and their views about art. Hogarth's self-portrait can be seen as a manifesto of his artistic ambitions: the self-portrait in the painting is propped up on books by the writers who most inspired him – William Shakespeare, Jonathan Swift and John Milton. The palette on the left bears the words 'The Line of Beauty and Grace' and the line itself – the serpentine line that Hogarth asserted was the key to all beauty. It was a principle that he later enlarged upon in his controversial book *The Analysis of Beauty* (1753). On the right, as a counterweight to this art theory, is a lifelike rendition of one of Hogarth's favourite pugs, indifferent to his master and oblivious to his lofty ideals.[2]

Troost's self-portrait is less assertive and programmatic than Hogarth's. In his portrait, Troost presents himself, deliberately and with pride, as an artist. The palette and brushes and the drawing on blue paper allude to the art forms he practised. The work also shows the painter's technical skill: the methodical construction of the composition and the strong chiaroscuro suggest considerable depth in the setting, reinforcing the illusion of a framed portrait on a plinth. Troost actually took it a step further than Hogarth in deceiving the eye: the colours are not painted on the palette, but put on in thick blobs, blurring the distinction between illusion and reality.

There is also a noticeable difference in the way the two artists present themselves. Troost is fashionably dressed in a grey coat, a black waistcoat and a white neckcloth. He has tucked his left hand into his waistcoat in a confident gesture. In a sketchy self-portrait that Hogarth made a little earlier, now in the Mellon Collection, the artist presented himself similarly formally attired, in wig, cravat and reddish-brown coat. Possibly this sketch was a preparatory study for the manifesto portrait of 1745.[3] The portrait had begun life as a more conventional representation of the artist, much closer to Troost's: x-rays have revealed that initially it showed the artist in a formal coat with gold buttons and a wig. Around 1745, possibly following his trip to Paris, Hogarth radically changed his approach, picturing himself unequivocally as an artist in his informal jacket and cap.[4] He made no attempt to disguise the scar on his forehead – rather, he emphasised it. While Troost's portrait is a gentlemanly representation of the artist, Hogarth presents a more straightforwardly artistic image of himself. Appropriately, Troost's self-portrait in its gilded rococo frame stands on a marble balustrade, and Hogarth's, unframed, balances on a stack of books.

The portraits were also made for different reasons. Although Troost's was later produced as a print by others, it was most probably commissioned by an admirer of his work.[5] Hogarth, by contrast, was looking to disseminate his likeness as widely as he could. He made his own engraving of the portrait, which he used in 1749 as the frontispiece for bound volumes of his prints.[6]

The comparison between the self-portraits can be extended to a degree to the artists' oeuvres. Troost was already being compared with Hogarth in the eighteenth century, earning him the nickname 'the Dutch Hogarth'.[7] There is certainly some artistic kinship. Both began their careers – Troost after a spell as an actor (see p.34) – as portrait painters, and played a key role in the development of the conversation piece or informal family portrait in their respective countries. They both made genre works in which they mocked the morals of the upper classes. Both loved the theatre and illustrated stage scenes; this was the genre that brought Troost unprecedented popularity in his own country.[8]

One of the finest examples is *Johanna and the Jewish Merchants*, a scene from the popular comedy *De Spilpenning of de verkwistende vrouw* (1693) by Thomas Asselijn (p.146). Troost presents the moment when the spendthrift Johanna sells the clothes that had been made for her at great expense not two months earlier to two Polish Jewish rag-and-bone men. In fact, they are her father and husband, who have disguised themselves to trap the profligate Johanna. The stereotyping in Asselijn's play shows the chasm that existed at that time between the wealthy middle classes and Jewish retailers. The scene is set not in a theatre, but in an opulent room with red wall coverings, a painted ceiling and a variety of objets d'art, including statues and Chinese porcelain. A ring-tailed lemur sits on a chair on the left as a symbol of wastefulness and destruction.[9]

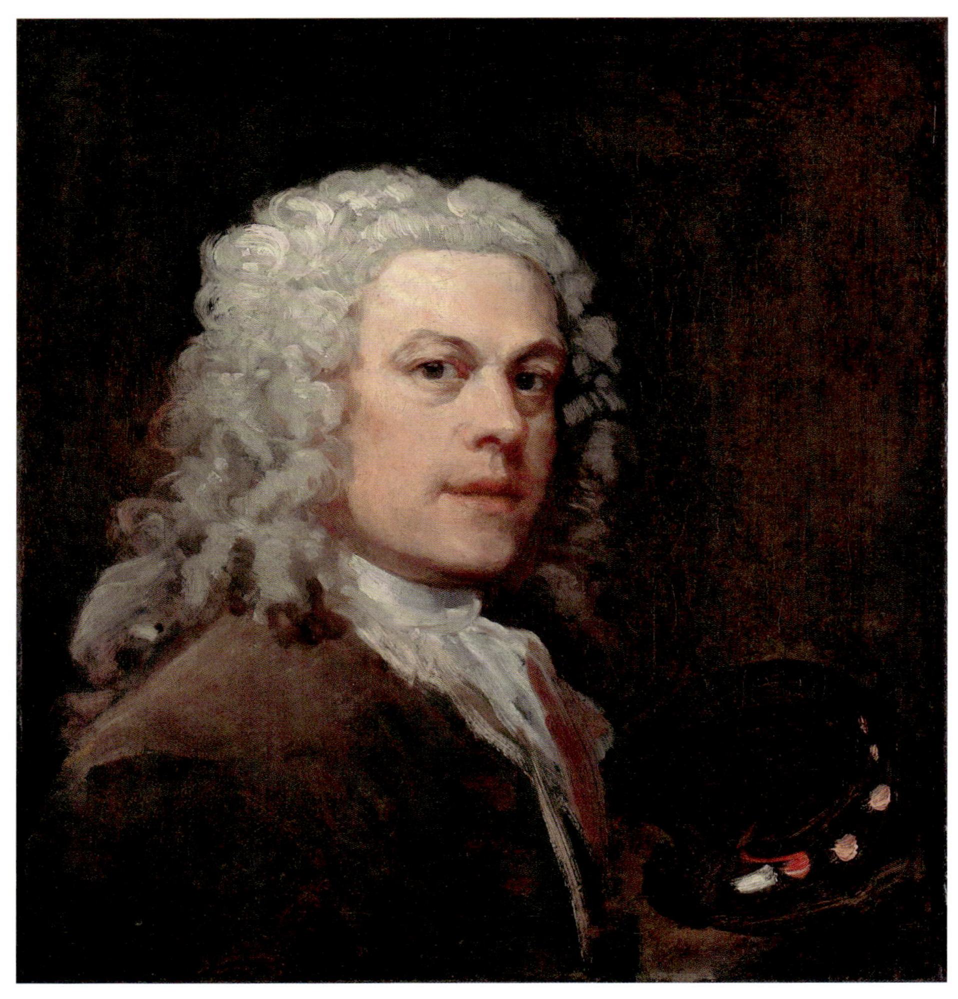

WILLIAM HOGARTH *Self-Portrait* c.1735

Although Troost was a dyed-in-the-wool Amsterdammer and his work was virtually unknown outside the Republic,[10] he was well aware of the trends in art in other countries. Motifs in some of his stage scenes and genre works were derived from Hogarth, and he also took inspiration from prints after the work of Nicolas Lancret and François Boucher.[11] As was customary at that time, he did not follow them slavishly, rather borrowing motifs to improve his own art – as he did with seventeenth-century Dutch masters. There is one series of pastels, however, in which Troost probably took Hogarth's example more literally. There can be almost no doubt that Troost had Hogarth's famous series *A Rake's Progress* (pp.108–11) in mind when he drew his 'Five Scenes in the Life of a Rake, or the Consequences of Frivolity'.[12] Sadly, the set has vanished without trace, so we can only guess at Troost's interpretation, but it is likely that Troost treated the libertine's downfall more light-heartedly. Although Hogarth and Troost had much in common, their personalities were very different. Hogarth was more engaged, sought publicity and savagely lampooned the morals of his time. His vicious moralisations are light-years away from Troost's gentle mockery.[13] This difference in approach is evident in the way they presented themselves in their self-portraits. Troost the gentleman, as elegant as his patrons, in a gilded rococo frame. Hogarth the social critic, straightforward, as frank as the messages he conveyed.

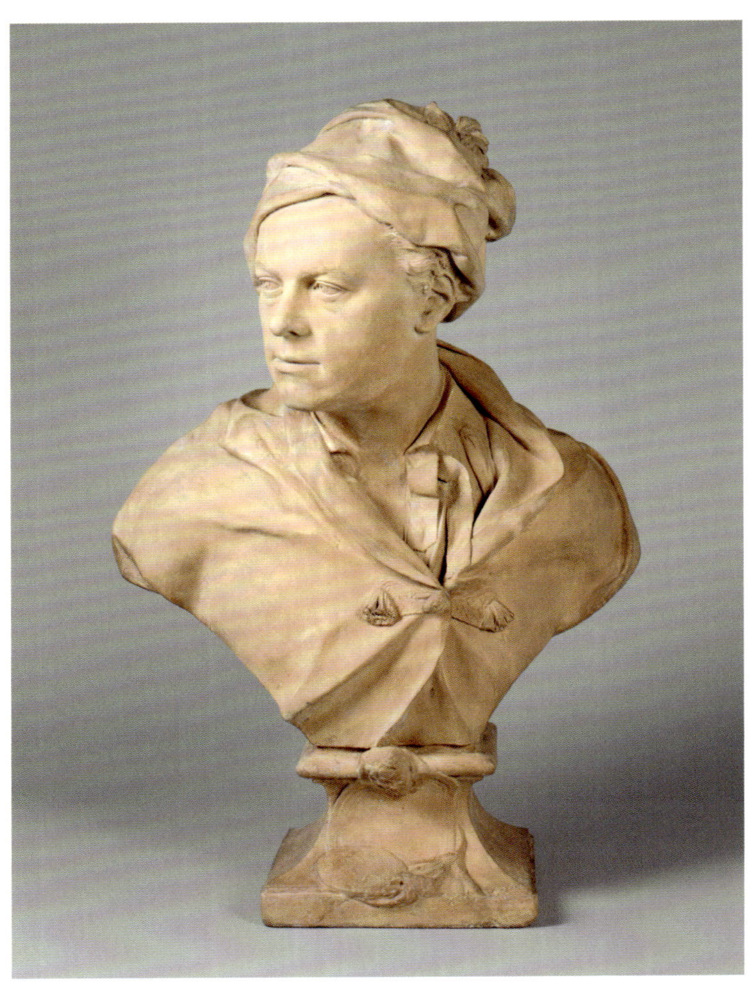

LOUIS FRANÇOIS ROUBILIAC   *William Hogarth*   c.1741

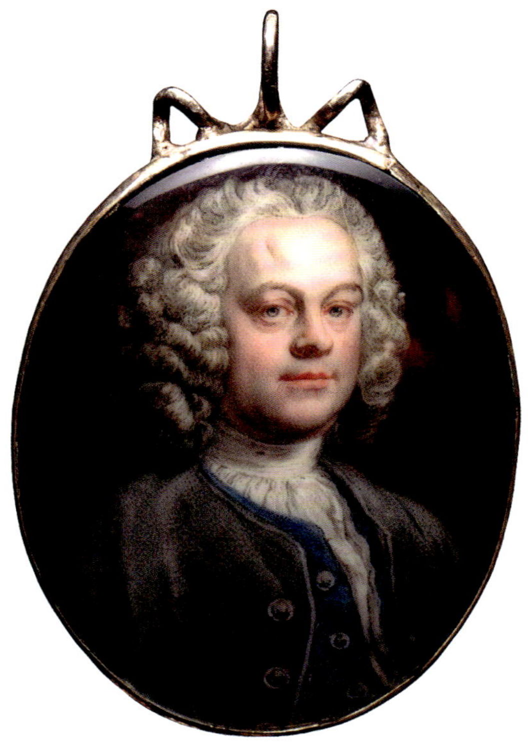

ANDRÉ ROUQUET   *William Hogarth*   c.1740–5

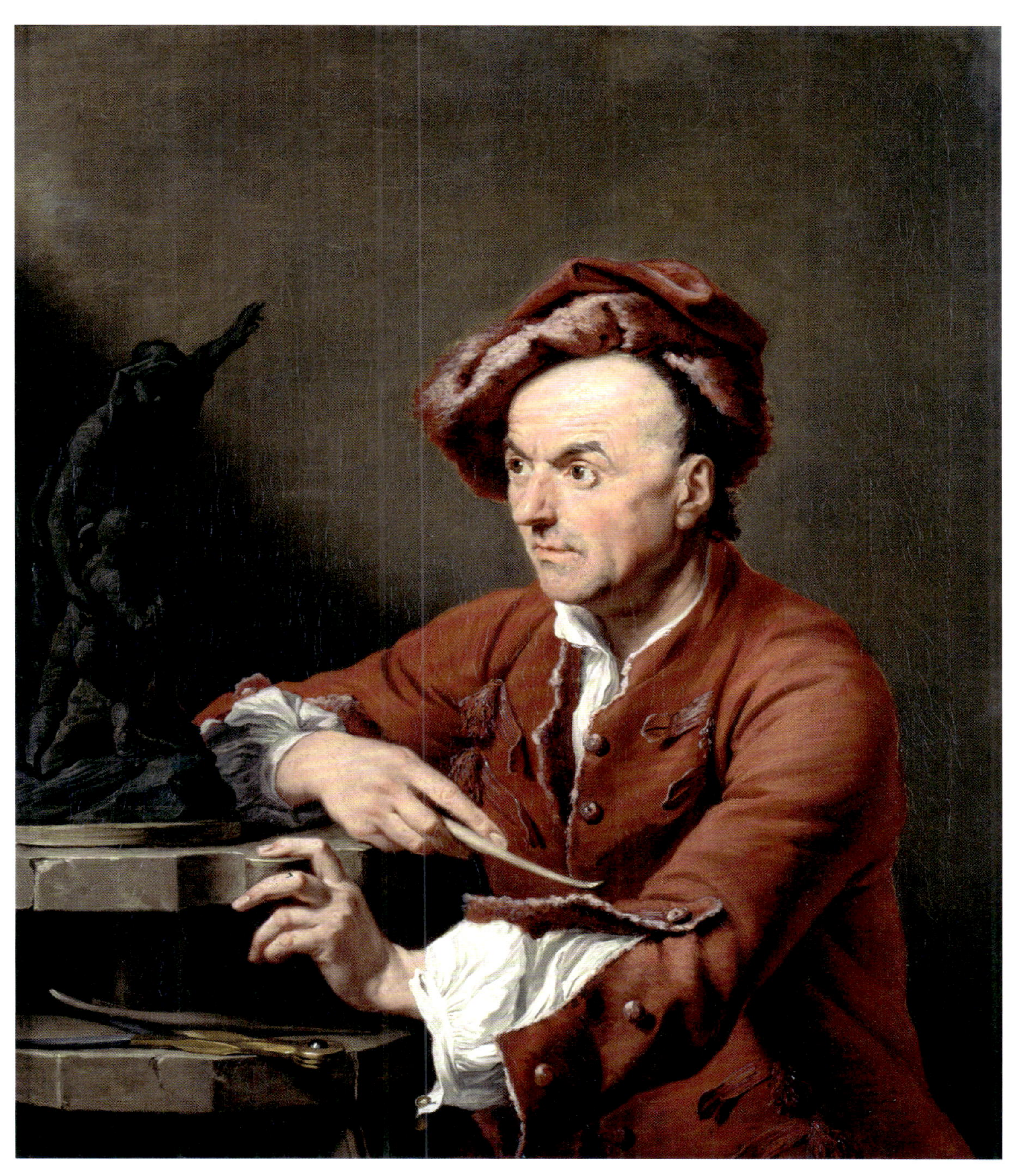

ANDREA SOLDI *Louis François Roubiliac* 1751

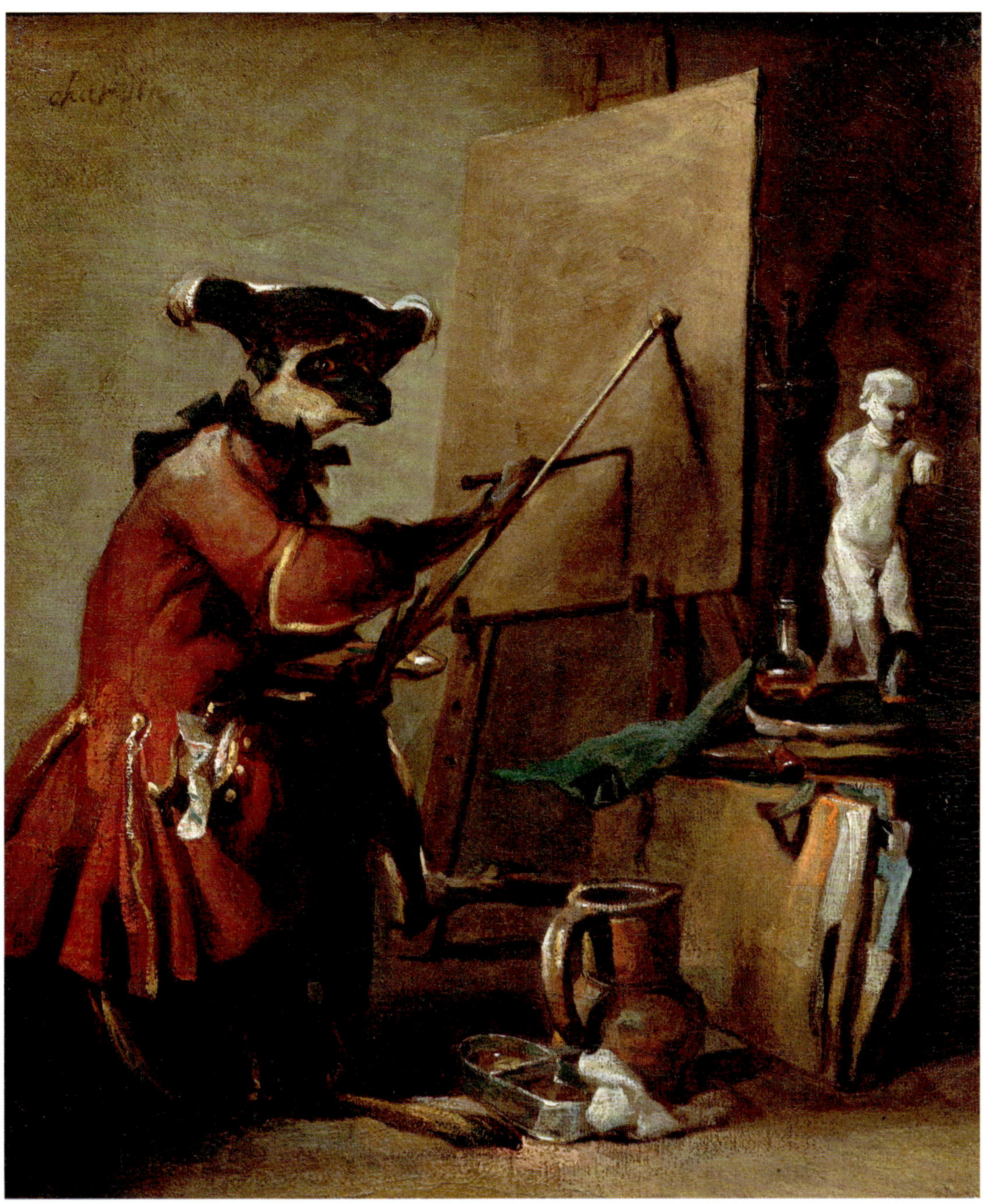

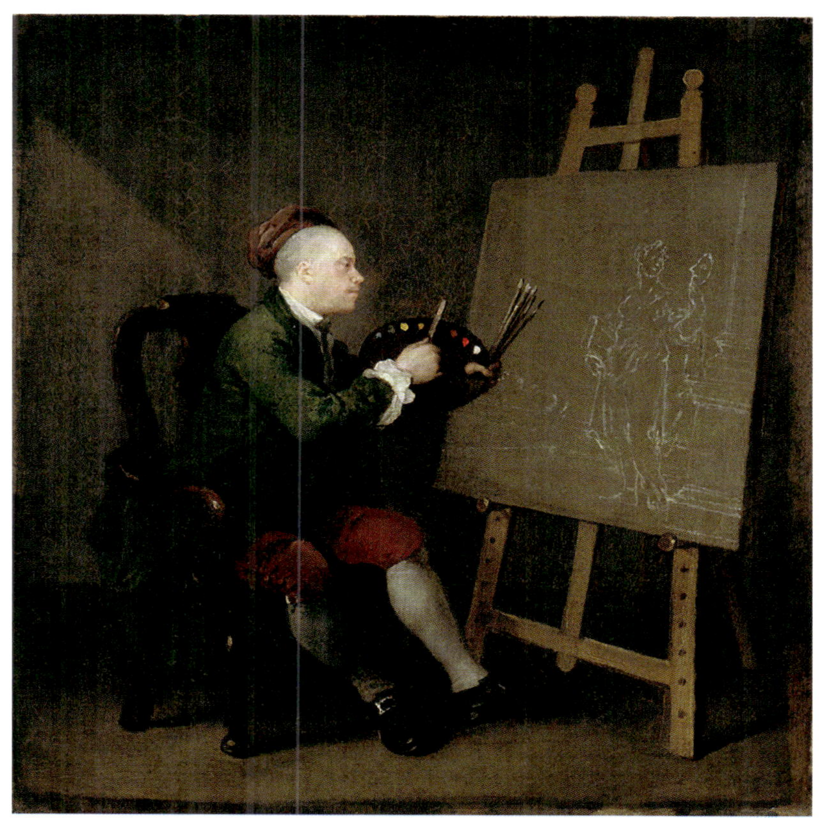

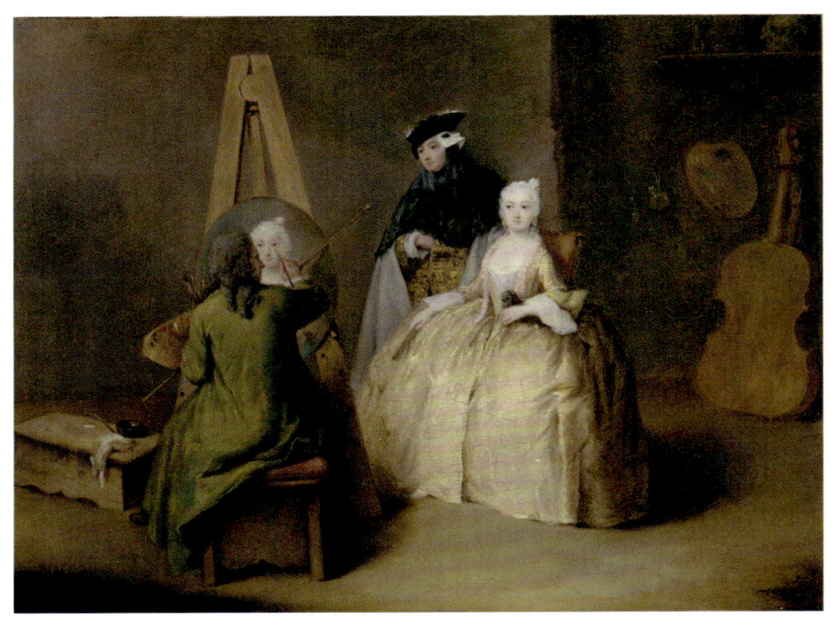

PIETRO LONGHI   *The Painter in His Studio*   c.1741–4

WILLIAM HOGARTH   *The Distressed Poet*   1733–5

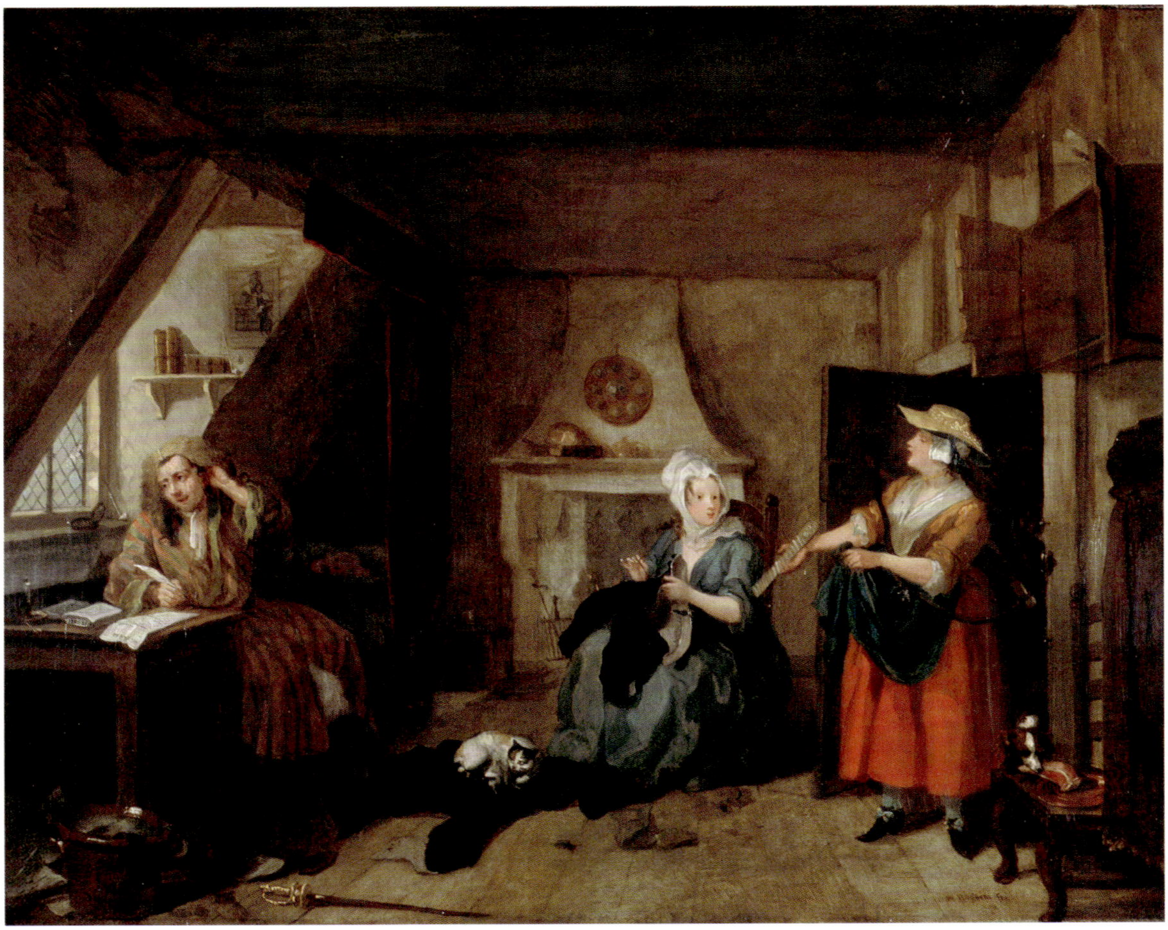

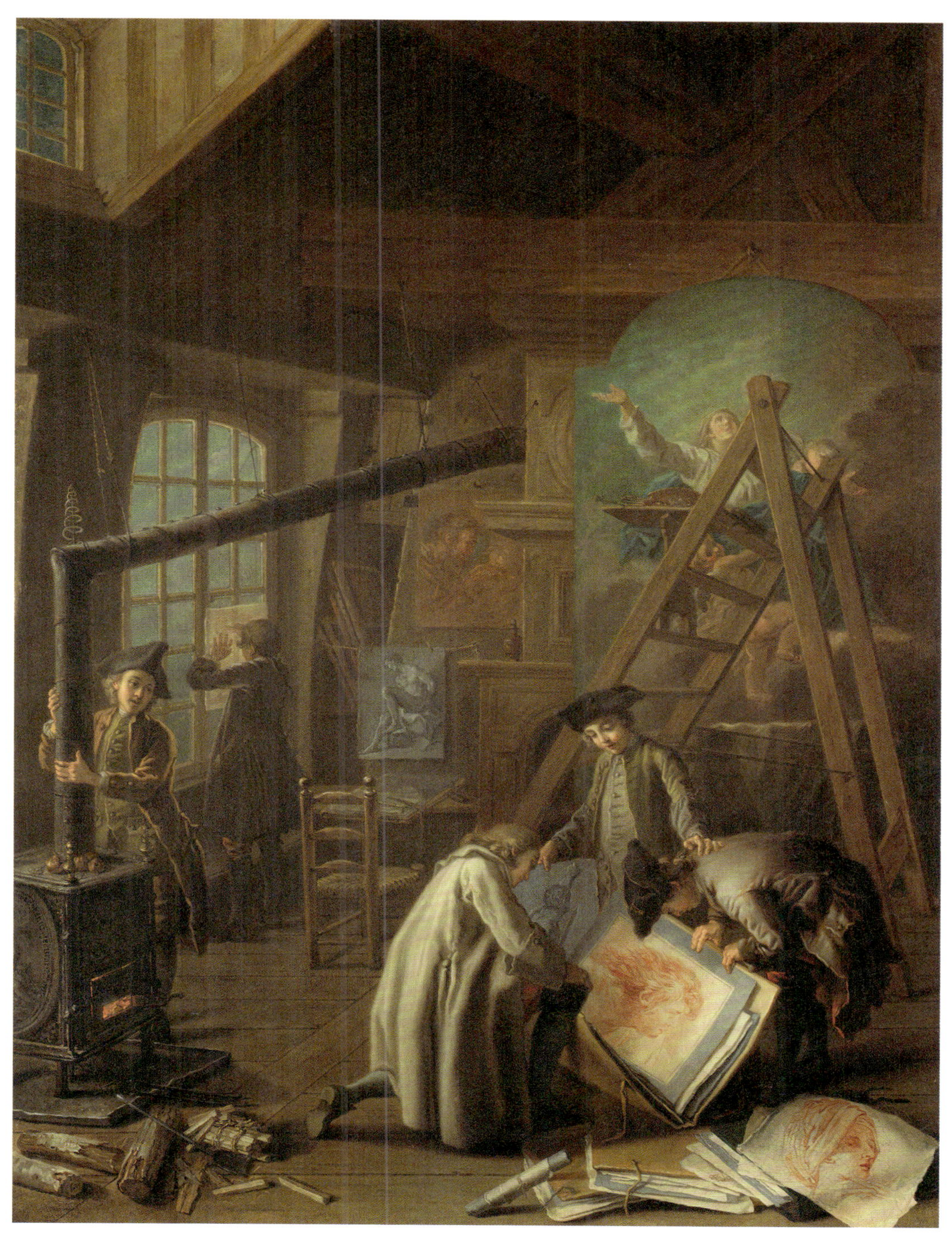

ÉTIENNE JEAURAT   *Interior of the Artist's Studio*   1755

ARTISTS AND CITIES

The first half of the eighteenth century saw new efforts to record and map the major cities of Europe as they grew in size and influence, notably London, Paris, Venice and Amsterdam (pp. 22–3, 30–1, 38–9, 46–7). The sheer size of these maps evokes the scale and complexity of these cities, revealing them in unprecedented detail. We can see the multitude of individual streets, squares and yards, the graphic blocks signalling churches and public buildings, sometimes even the lineaments of individual domestic homes. The city emerges in these elaborate images as not just a political entity, the possession of a king or an expression of state authority, but a teeming mass of sites – of houses jostling against one another, streets meeting and crossing, and increasingly of open spaces, parks and squares where people could meet, interact or engage in commerce.

Assembled from multiple printed sheets, these maps also demonstrate the flourishing art of engraving and the proliferation of prints as highly mobile commodities. Sometimes, too, they include allegorical devices that allude to the wider world, and the networks of exchange and empire that crossed the globe. While physical travel remained time-consuming and even dangerous, the commerce in printed materials meant that the world beyond most peoples immediate experience could appear more readily accessible: other cities, other countries and the further reaches of the known world – including the territories in Asia, Africa, the Caribbean and the Americas being colonised, terrorised and exploited to support this urban growth.

Most of the artists included in this book were based in one or other of these cities. Many visited or lived in several such urban centres over the course of their careers, travelling to find work and seek out new opportunities. The city became a prevalent subject in visual art for the first time, with street scenes and views showing urban growth and social encounters that might be thrilling, funny – or threatening.

The city was the dominant setting and subject matter of Hogarth's art, the place where various human comedies and tragedies were played out. His paintings and prints depict real places that his viewers could be expected to know at first hand, but project narratives which people the urban space with exemplars from across a spectrum: the crowded market or fair becomes the site of multifarious human vices, colliding with calamitous effect. His *Southwark Fair*, *Gin Lane* and *Beer Street* are actual places that many of his viewers would recognise, but they are also symbolic in making visible themes of disorder and order, prosperity and decline. As his characters are moved or displaced across different places in the city, their fortunes are transformed, providing lessons and warnings like myths or fables. But Hogarth was not alone in this approach; Cornelis Troost's projection of theatrical subjects into the streets and taverns of contemporary Amsterdam give a vivid immediacy to city experience, while Étienne Jeaurat's evocations of the streets of Paris expose the sometimes harsh realities of everyday life, rendering these as urban entertainments. Further afield still, artists such as Zoffany in Lucknow in the 1780s, or Charles D'Oyly later in Calcutta, brought a 'Hogarthian' lens to their satirical representations of the burgeoning colonial cities.

The reality of the high-risk commercial ventures, the complicity of the state, the exploitation of labour and the colonial expansion on which these burgeoning European centres relied was, however, only sometimes acknowledged explicitly. But the signs are there in the depiction of the material cultures fostered by empire and trade (tea and coffee, sugar, mahogany, silks and china), in the figures of African and Asian heritage who can be detected sometimes in crowds, or even in the racialised caricatures and allegorical figures which were stock features of visual iconography. Underpinning all of this was the prevailing idea in western thought that however depraved or corrupt European society might be, it remained a great 'civilising' force.

Hogarth's picture of the annual fair at Southwark is so filled with individual incidents and different characters that it becomes a kind of allegory, open to multiple interpretations. The over-riding theme is the risk of ruination or collapse, signalled most clearly by the performers falling from the toppled stage to the right. In the centre a Black boy playing a trumpet accompanies the female drummer. Just behind him a dog walking upright is dressed as a gentleman, mocking social class but also risking an obviously racist juxtaposition with the trumpeter. Throughout, theatre and reality, classical allusion and bawdy humour abound, but above all the chaos a Union Jack flies.

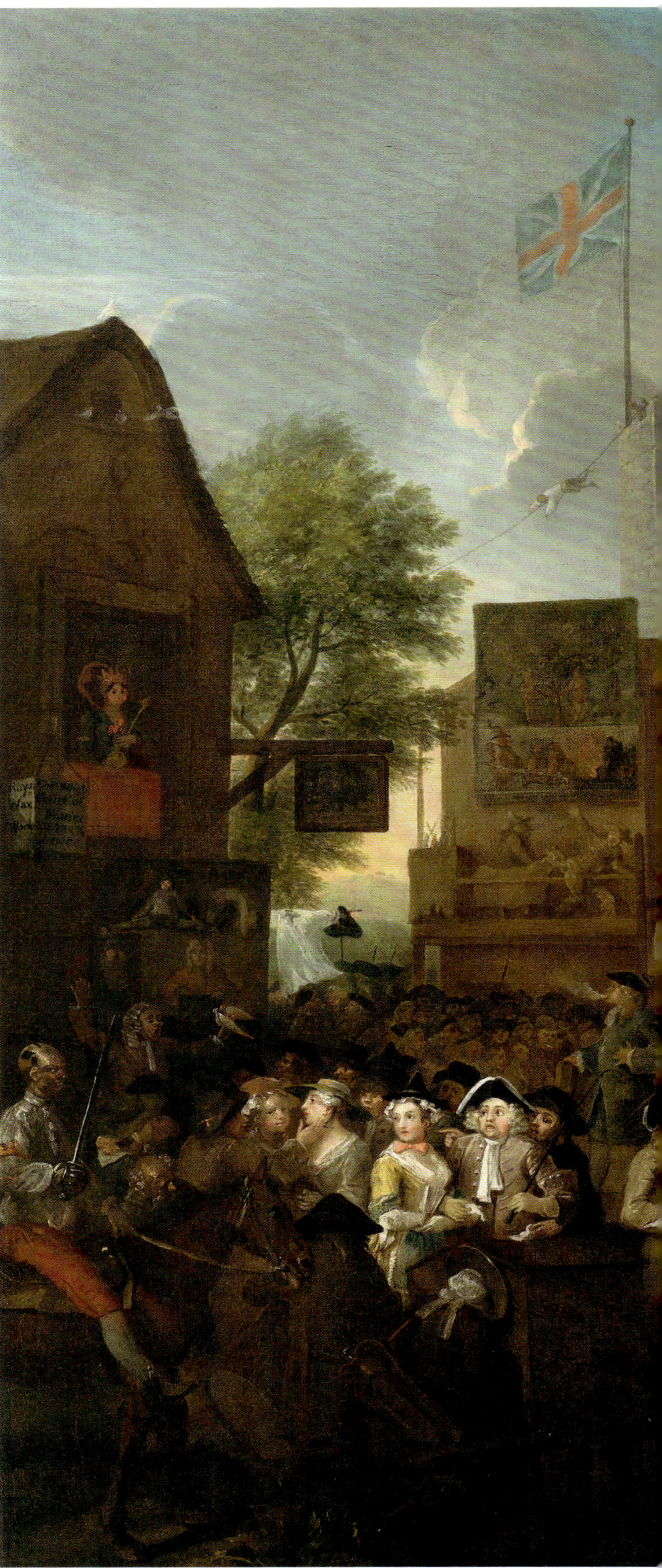

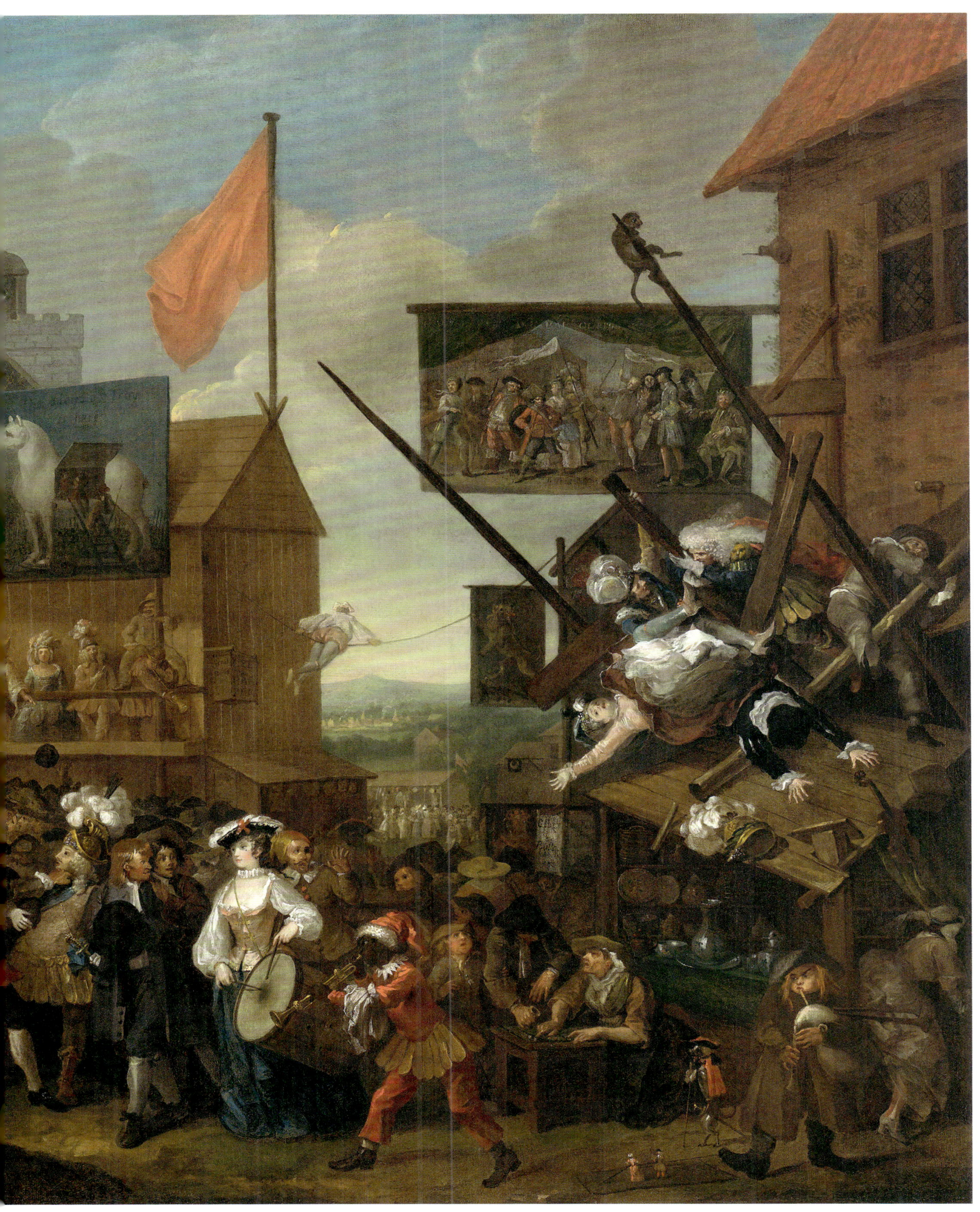

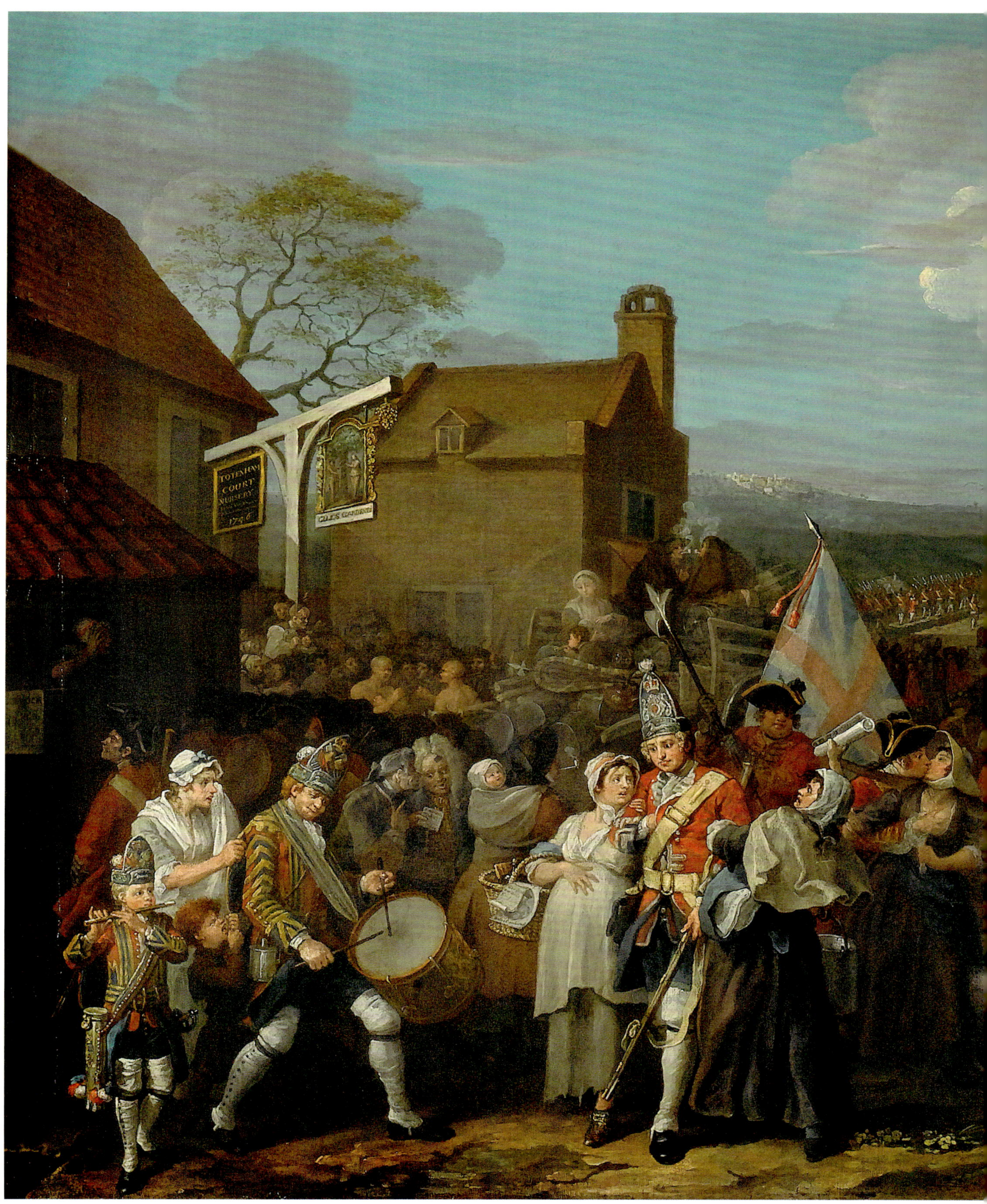
TOTENHAM
COURT
NURSERY
1746
GILES GARDINER

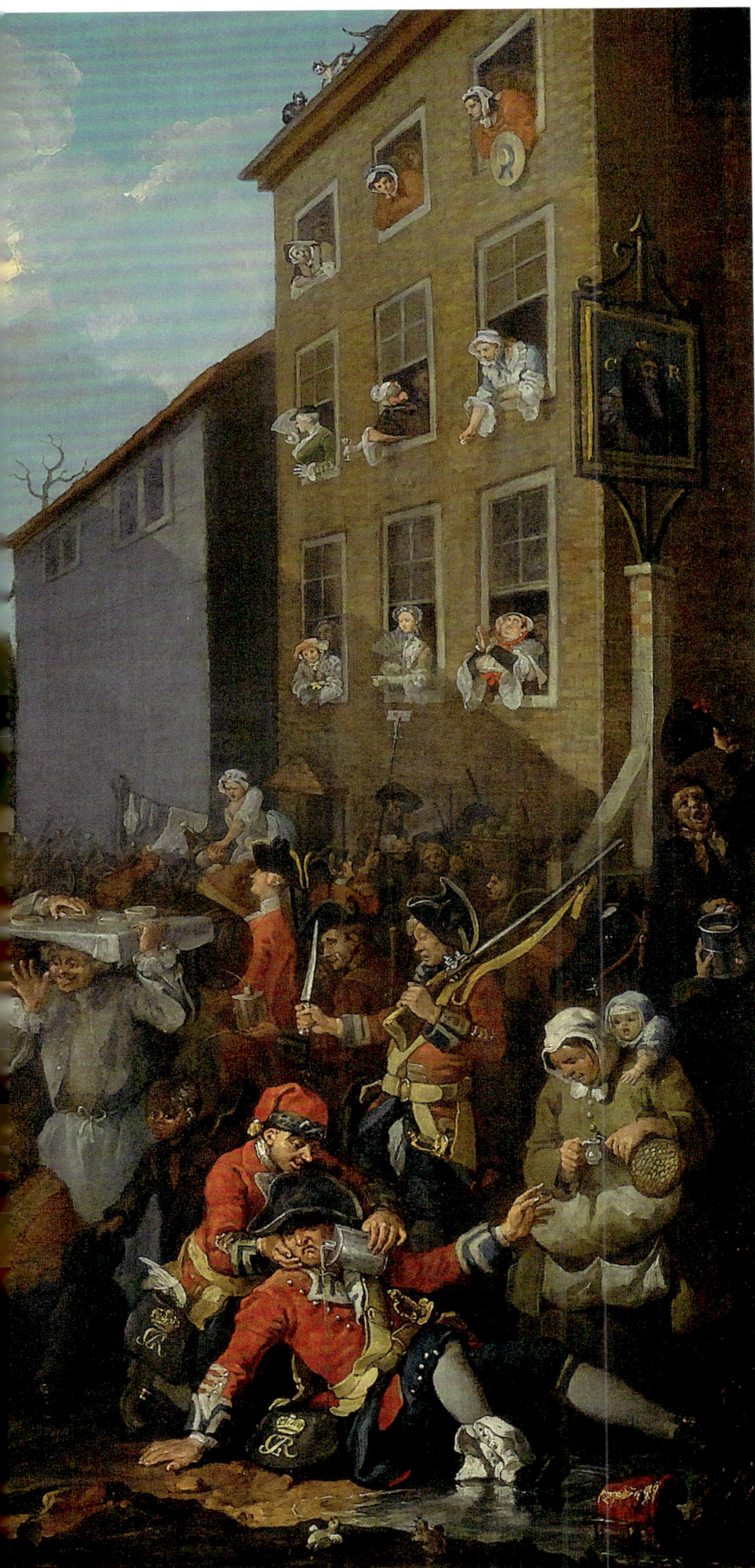

This imaginary scene alludes to the many soldiers that assembled at Tottenham Court turnpike in late 1745, preparing to defend London from the threat of the Jacobites (supporters of the exiled Catholic Prince Charles Edward Stuart). The soldiers in the foreground seem like an unruly mob – badly hung-over or still drunk, reckless bruisers or lustful molesters. But the guardsman illuminated in the centre shows dignity in parting from his pregnant wife, while the neat lines of soldiers in the distance suggest what all these men might become.

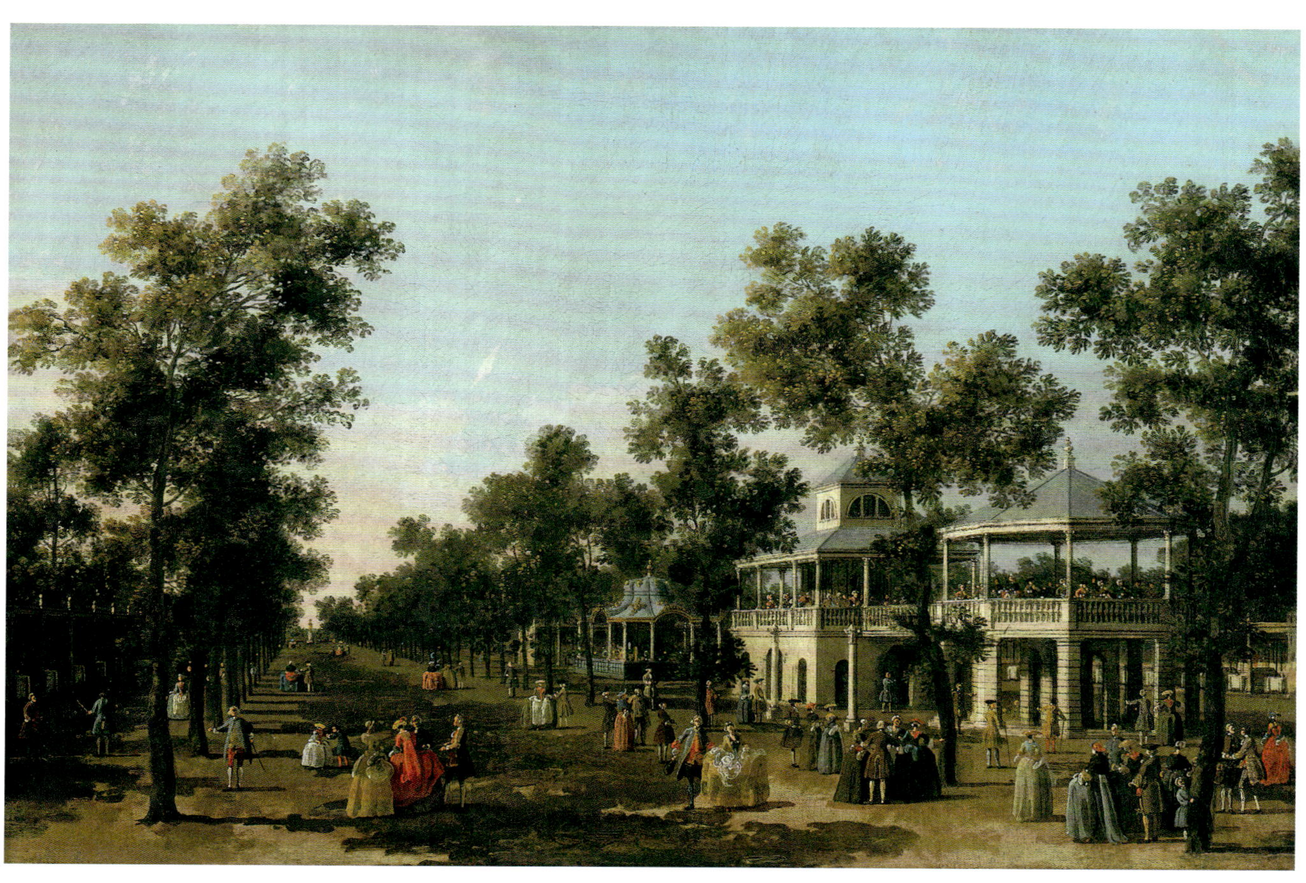

     CANALETTO   *The Grand Walk, Vauxhall Gardens*   c.1751

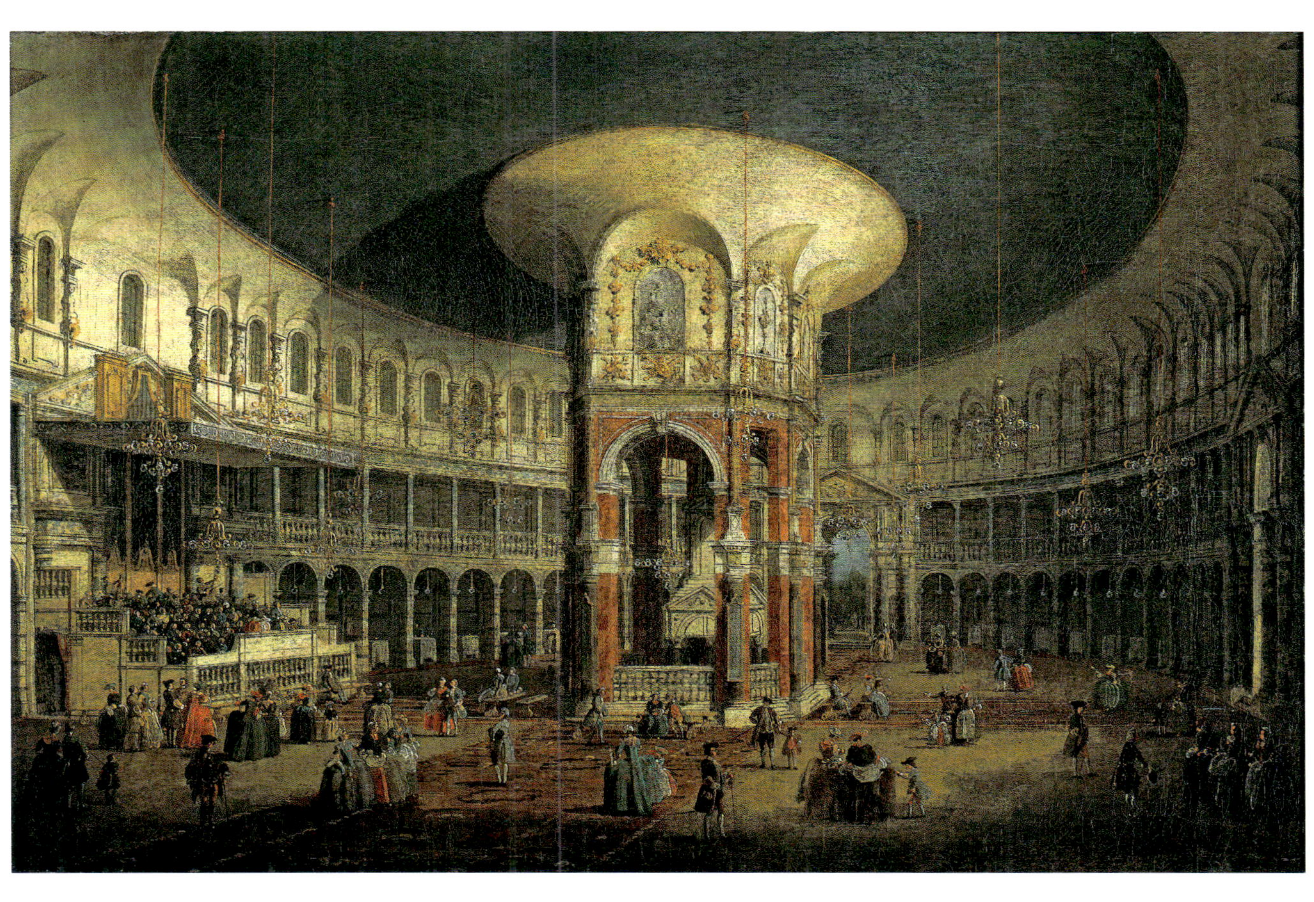

CANALETTO   *The Interior of the Rotunda, Ranelagh*   c.1751   77

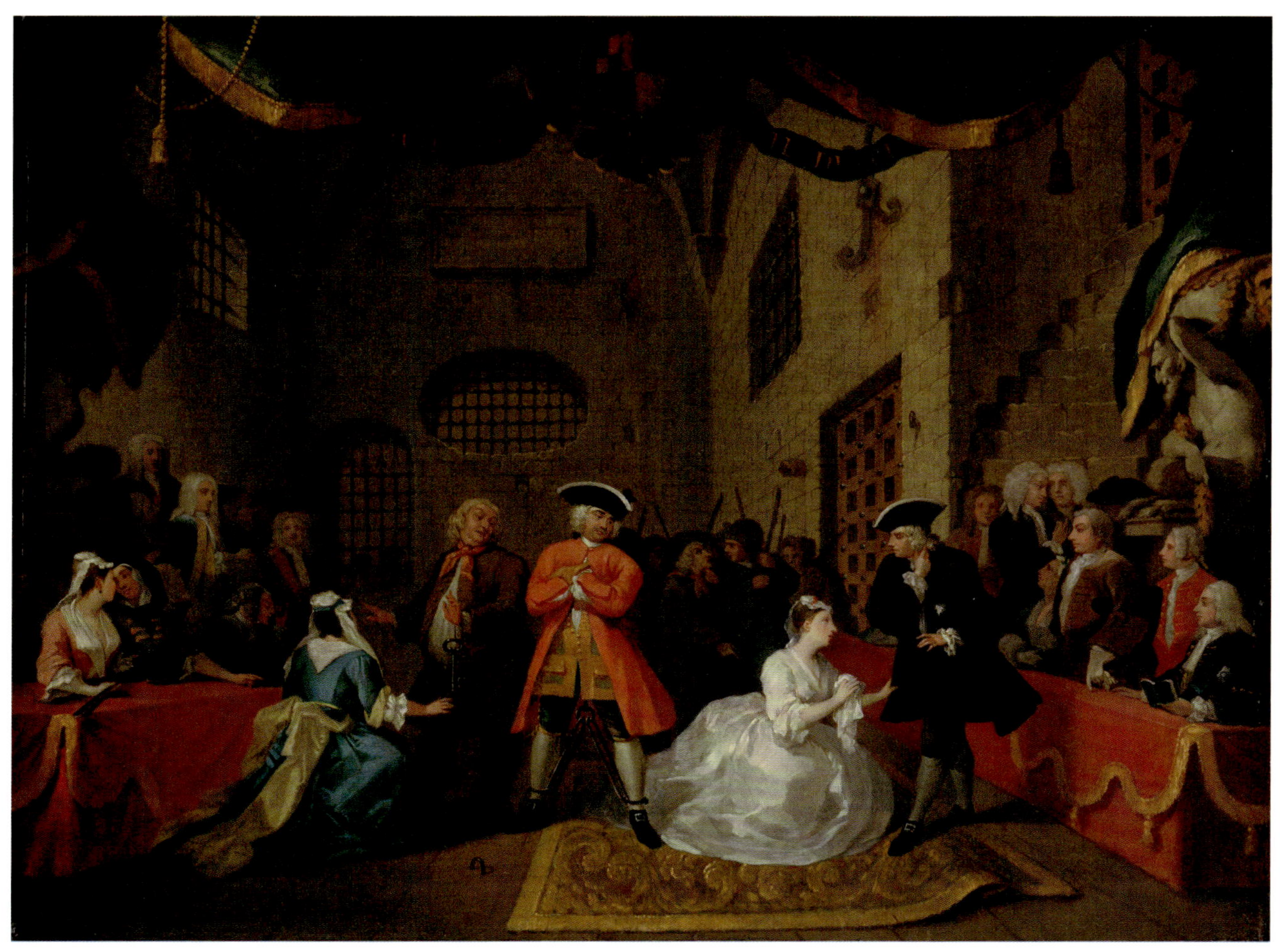

Hogarth's theatrical scene depicts the climax of John Gay's *The Beggar's Opera* (1728). The imprisoned highwayman, Macheath, stands at the centre, while two women who both believe themselves his wife plead for his release. The actor in white, Lavinia Fenton, later had her portrait painted by Hogarth too (p.192).

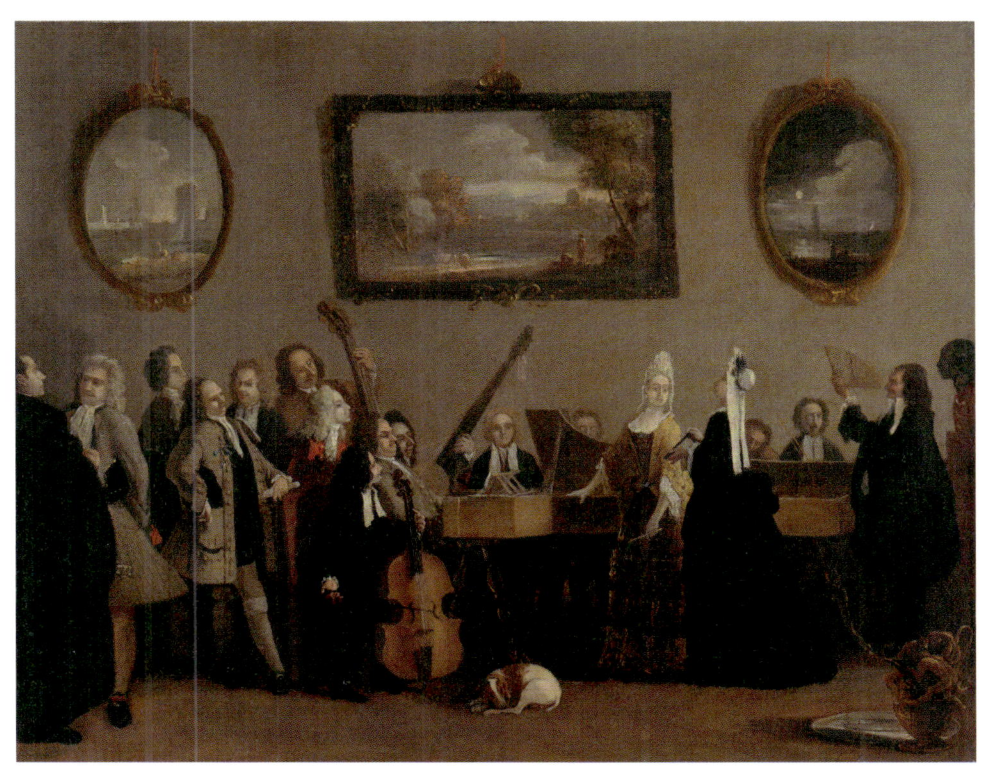

MARCO RICCI   *Rehearsal of an opera*   c.1709

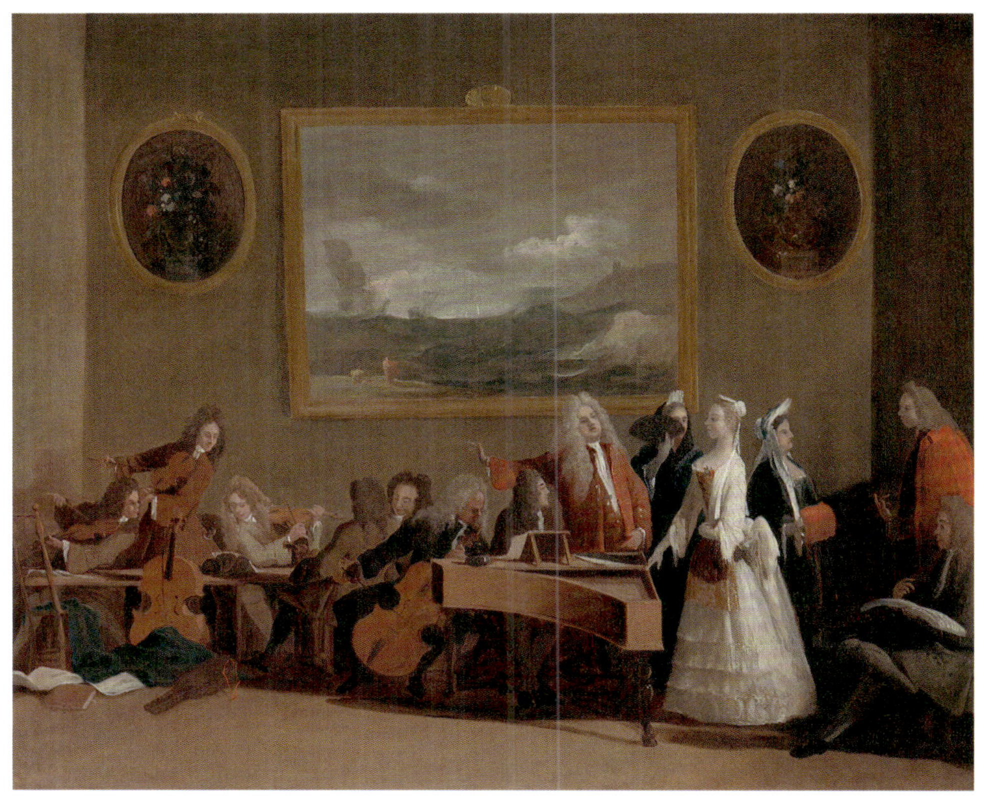

MARCO RICCI   *Rehearsal of an opera*   c.1709

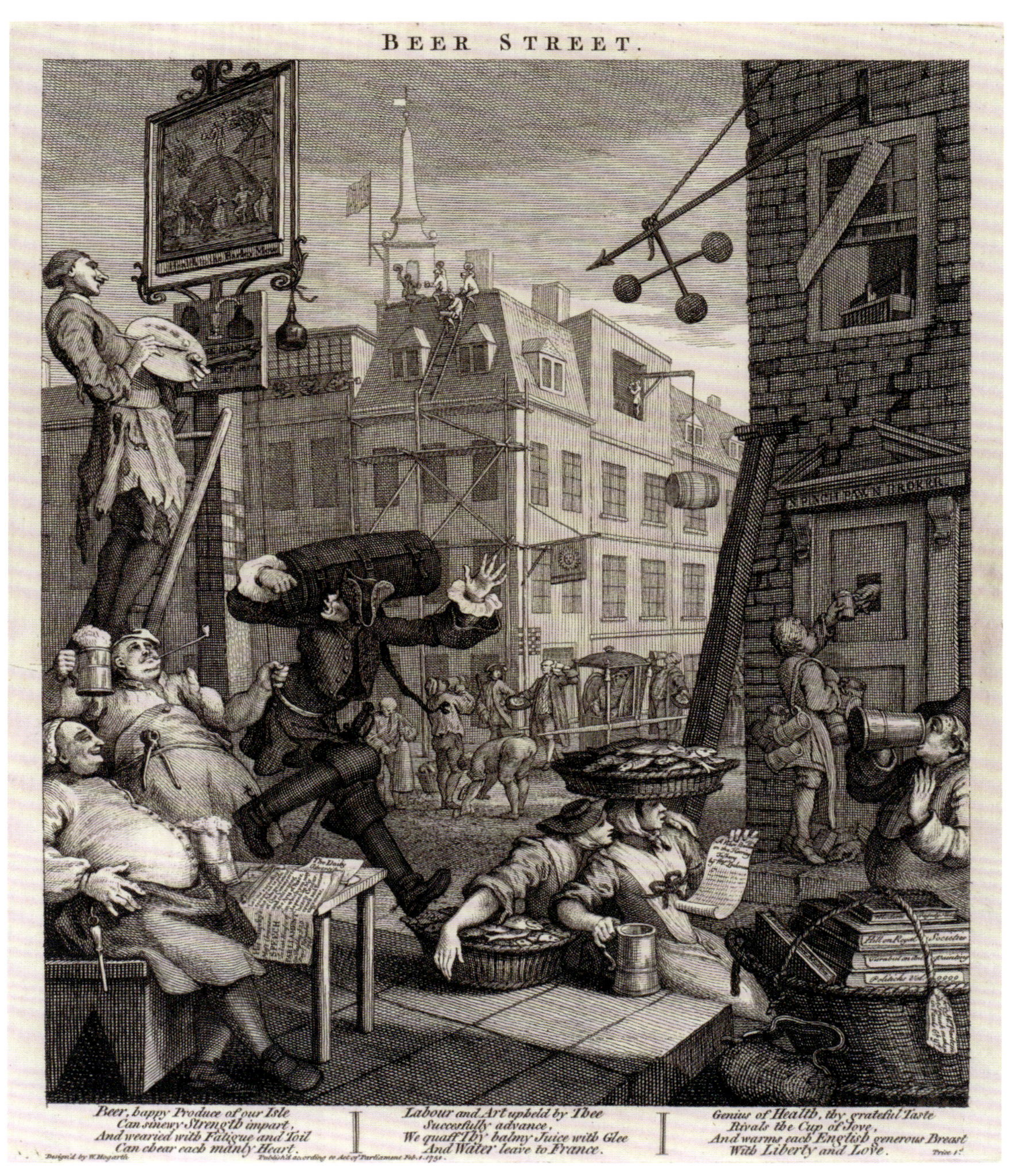

BEER STREET.

Beer, happy Produce of our Isle
Can sinewy Strength impart,
And wearied with Fatigue and Toil
Can chear each manly Heart.

Labour and Art upheld by Thee
Succesfully advance,
We quaff Thy balmy Juice with Glee
And Water leave to France.

Genius of Health, thy grateful Taste
Rivals the Cup of Jove,
And warms each English generous Breast
With Liberty and Love.

Design'd by W. Hogarth   Publish'd according to Act of Parliament Feb. 1. 1751.   Price 1.ˢ

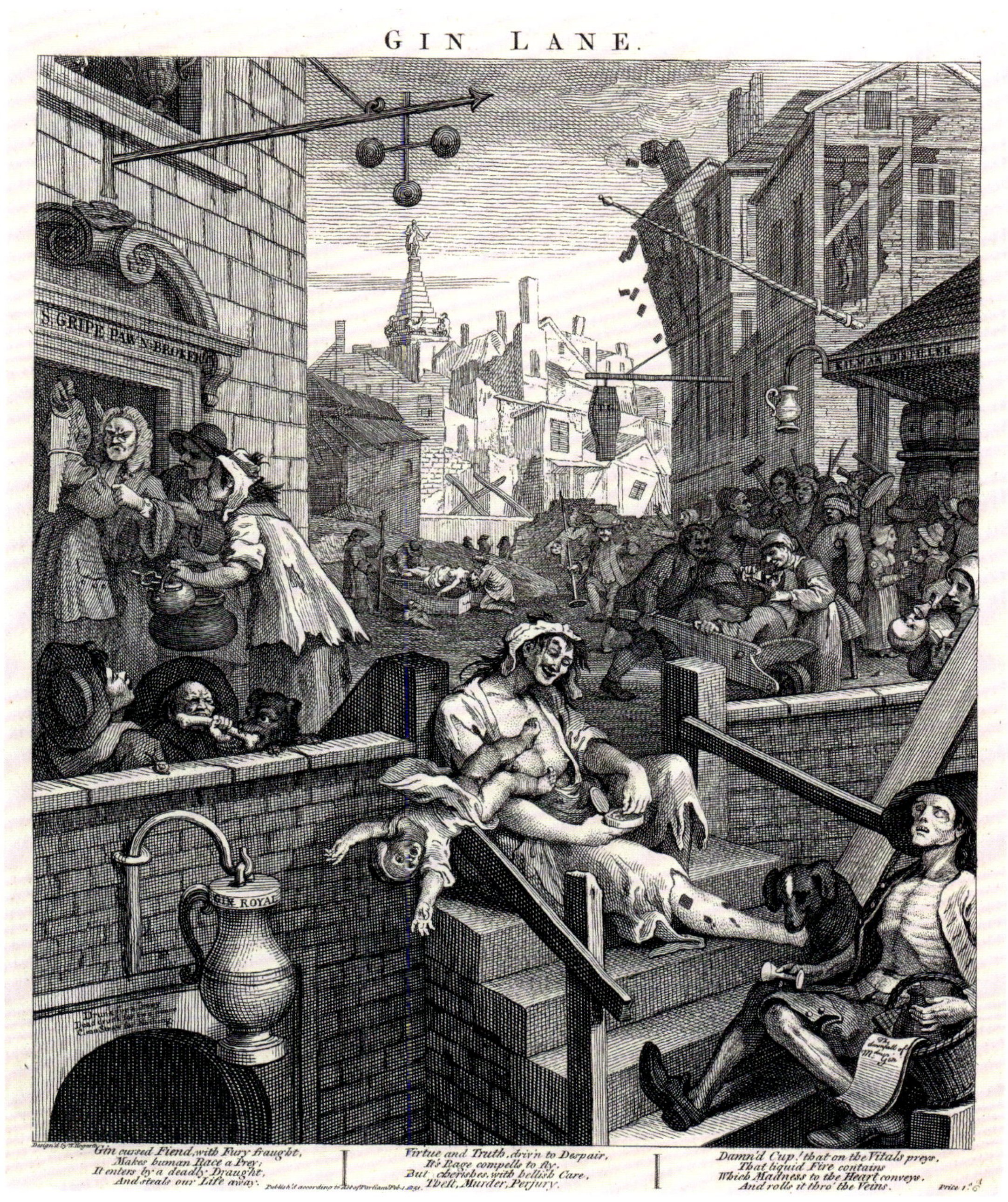

WILLIAM HOGARTH *Gin Lane* 1751

Hogarth's pair of prints were intended as propaganda, supporting the Gin Act of 1751. The act was meant to curtail the spirits consumption which was widely associated with rising crime and depravity among the urban poor. Hogarth contrasts the ill effects of gin to the life-enhancing effects of beer-drinking.

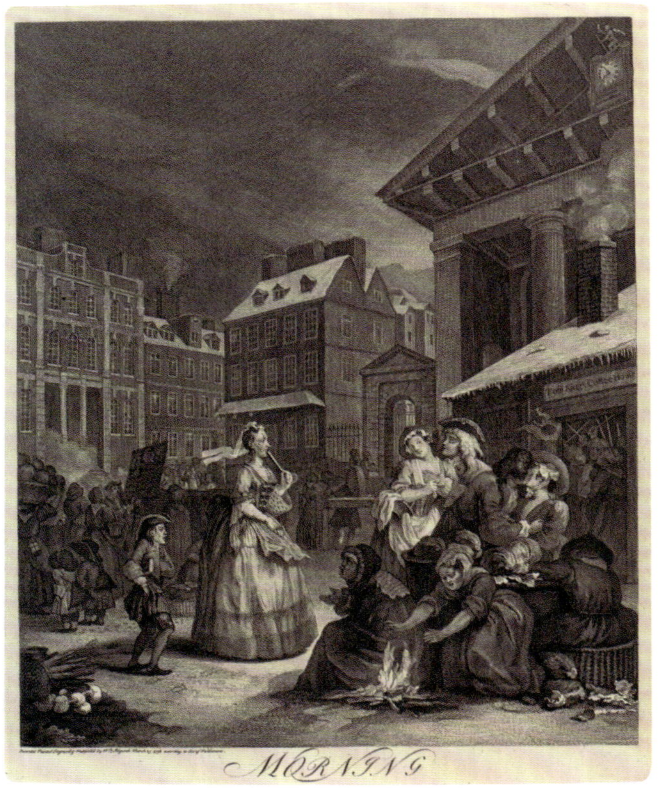

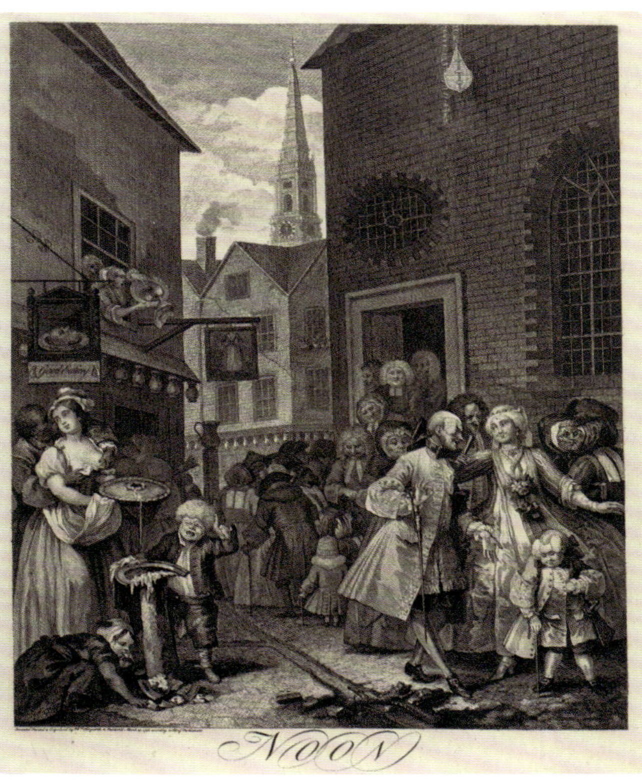

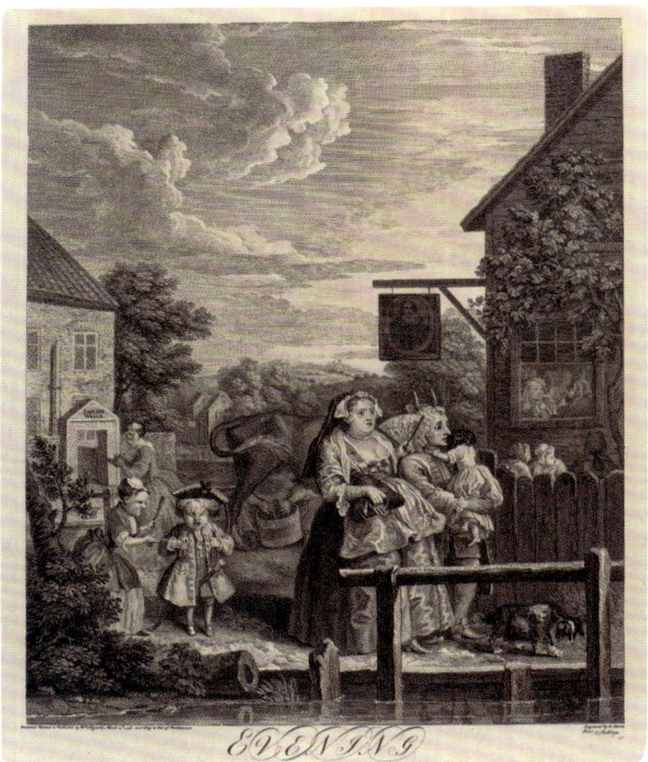

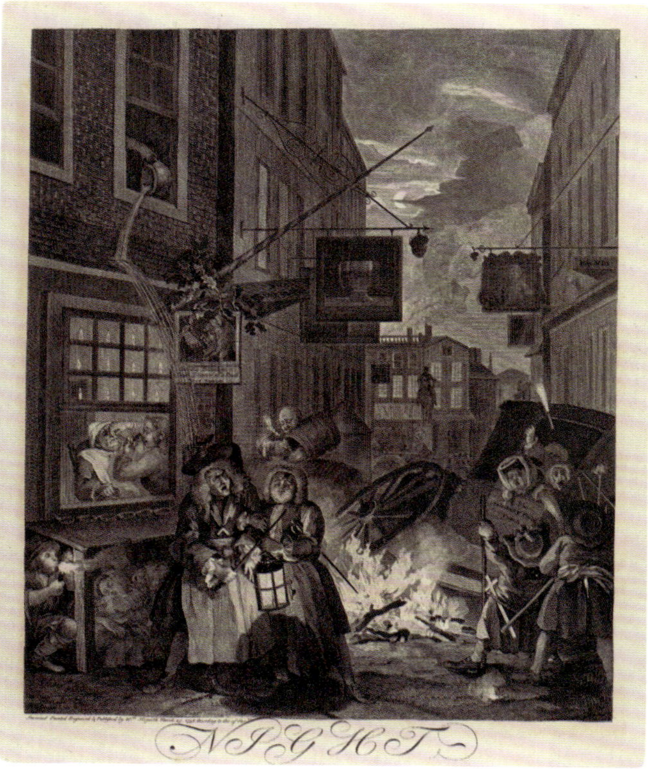

WILLIAM HOGARTH *The Times of Day* 1738

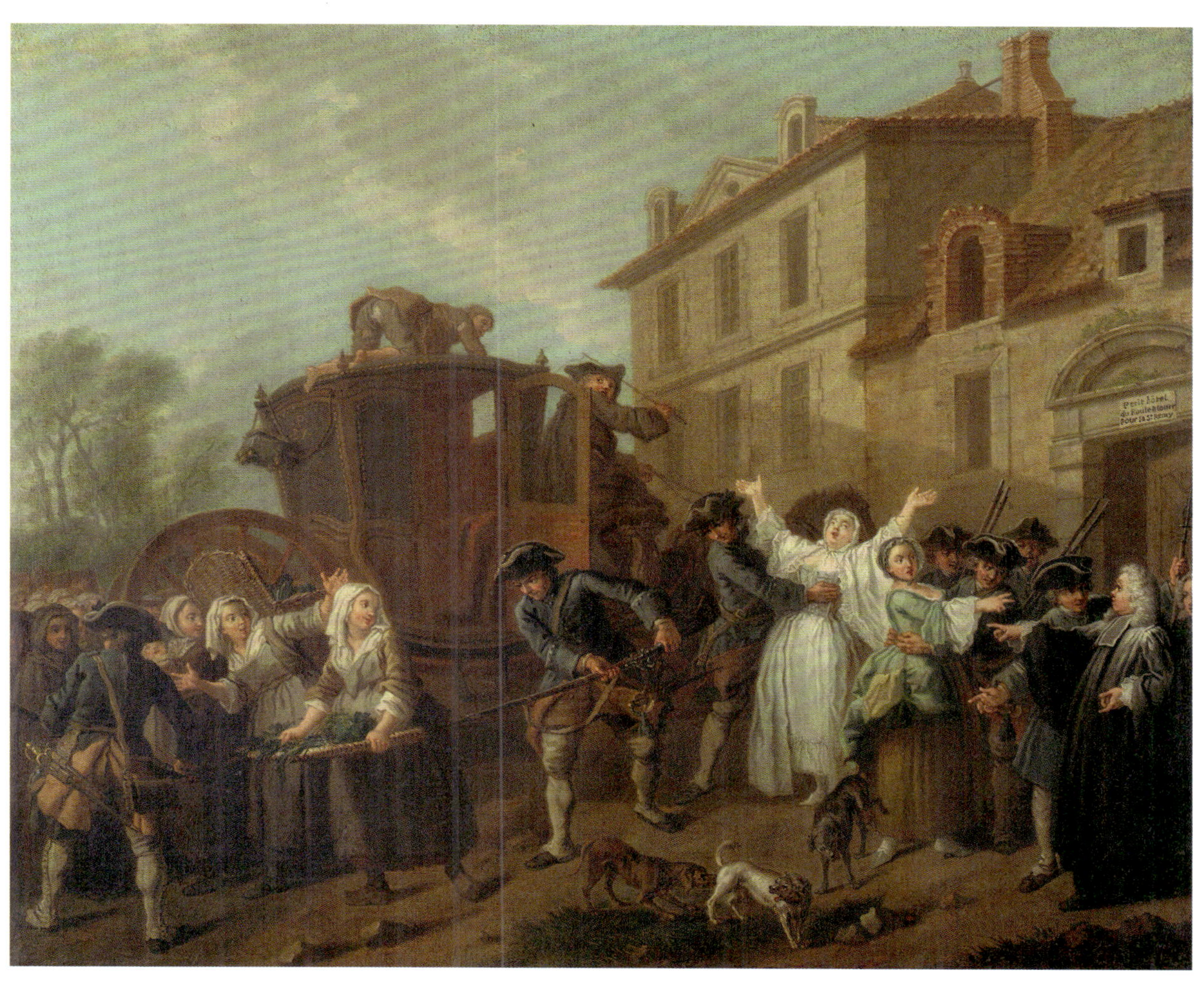

ÉTIENNE JEAURAT   *Arrest by the Watch*   1743

← Over four identifiable London scenes, at four
different times of day, Hogarth charts the social
life of the city. This sort of sequential format was
lifted from European prototypes, apparent in sets
of landscape paintings, or in the domestic scenes
of Lancret's *Four Times of Day* (pp.152–3).

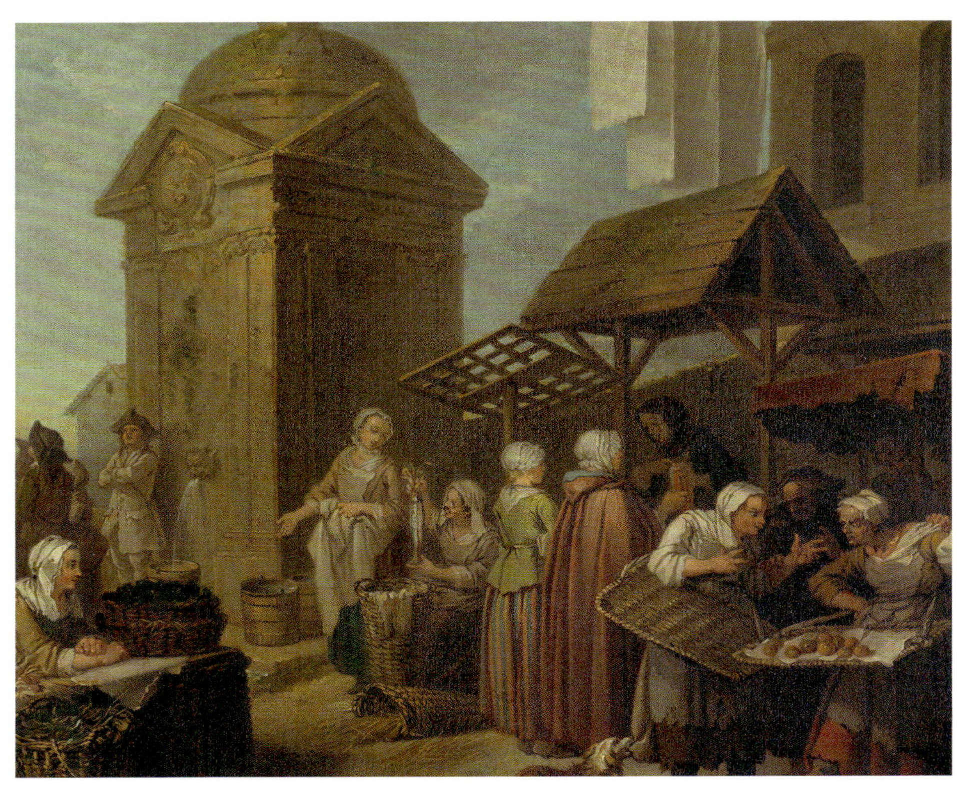

ÉTIENNE JEAURAT   *The Place Maubert, Paris*   1743

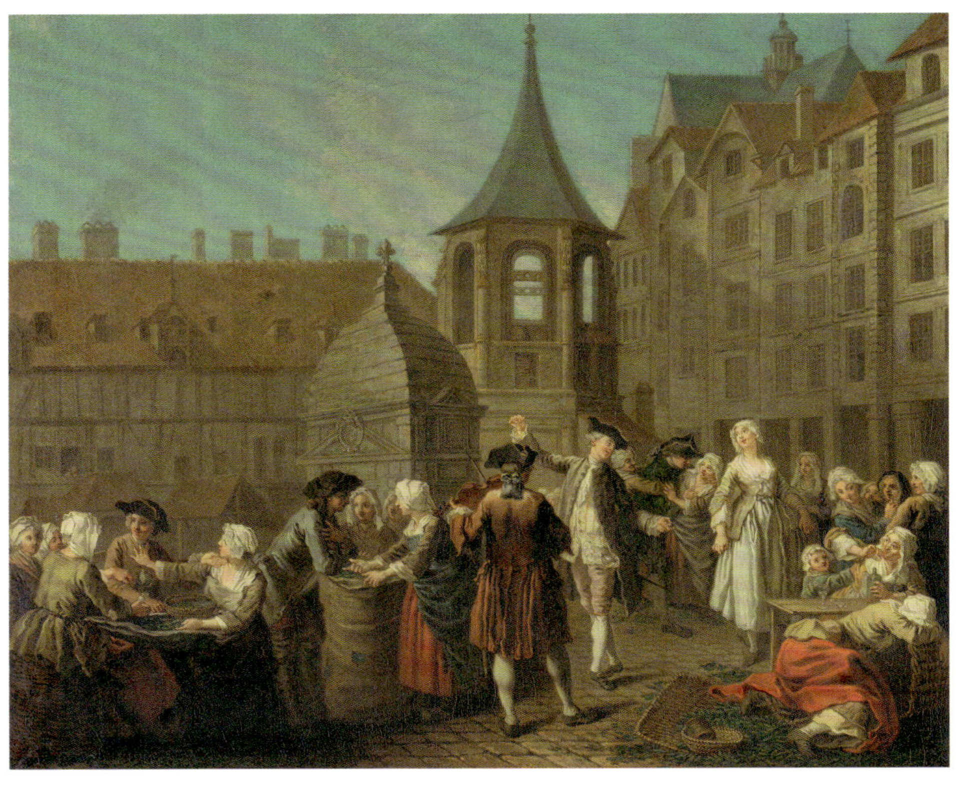

    ÉTIENNE JEAURAT   *The Market 'Des Innocents', Paris*   1743

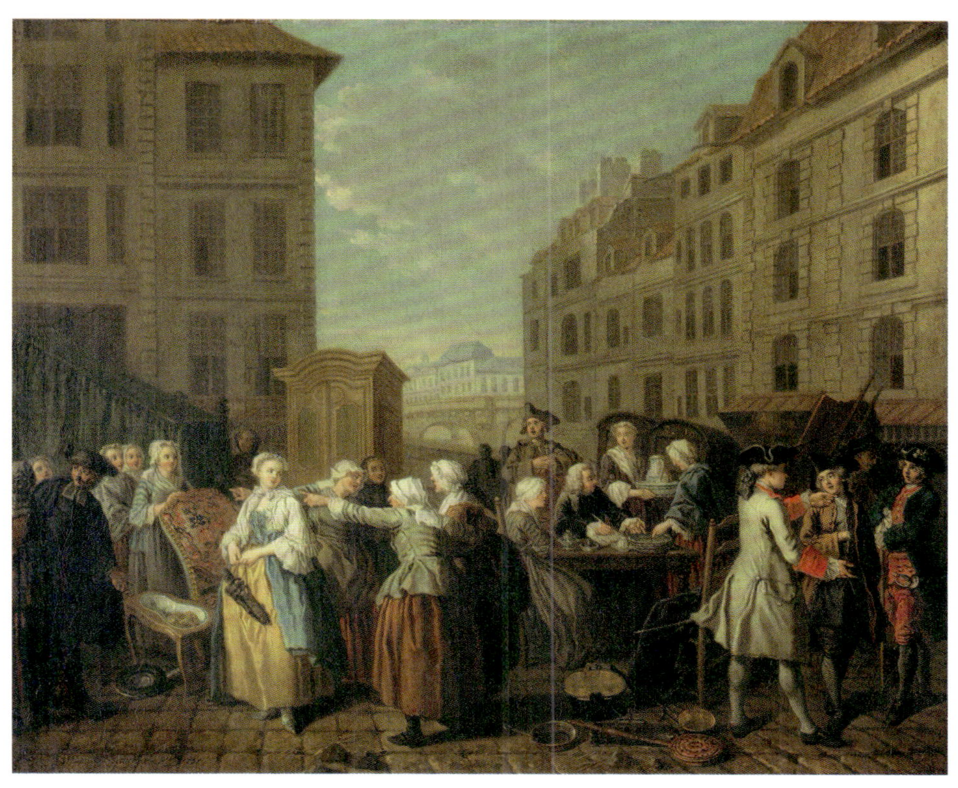

ÉTIENNE JEAURAT   *Scene in the Streets of Paris*   1743

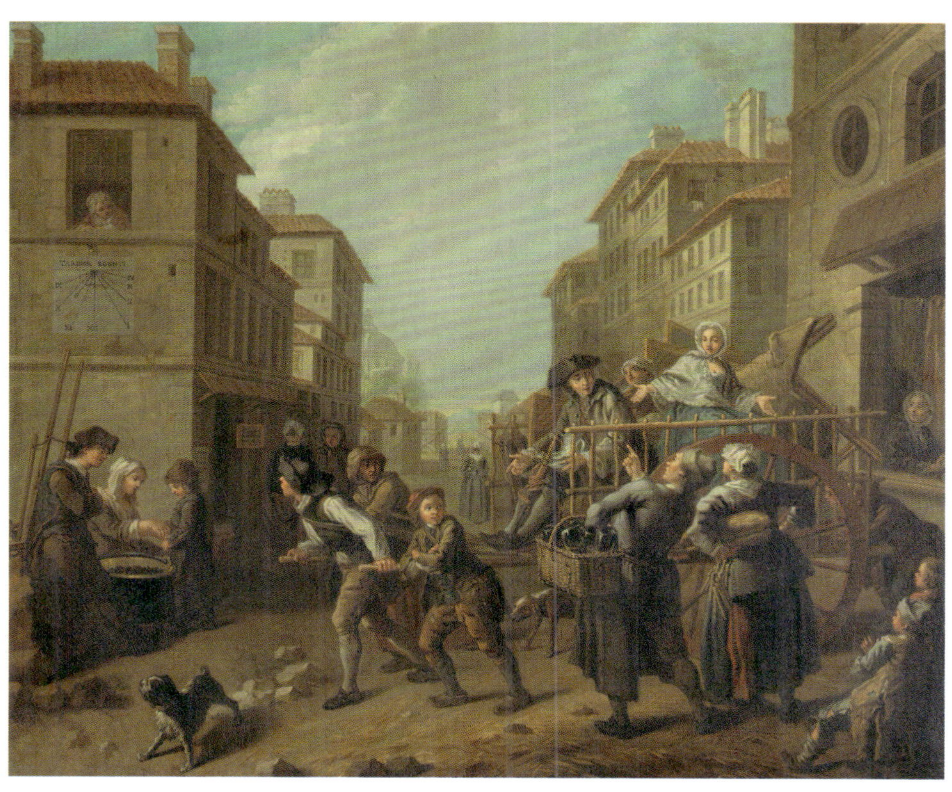

ÉTIENNE JEAURAT   *Removal of the Effects of a Painter*   1743

PAUL SANDBY
London Cries: Last Dying Speech and Confession
c.1759

PAUL SANDBY
London Cries: A Girl with a Basket of Oranges
c.1759

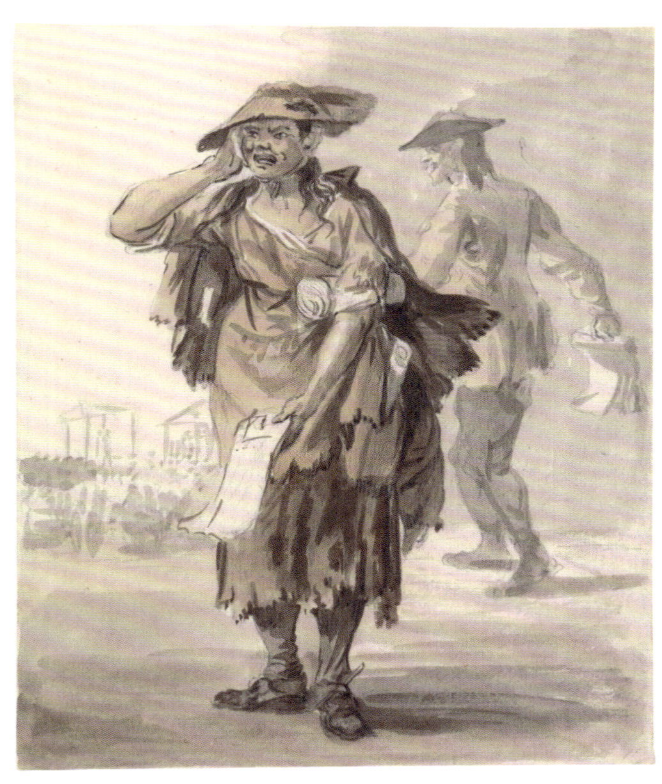

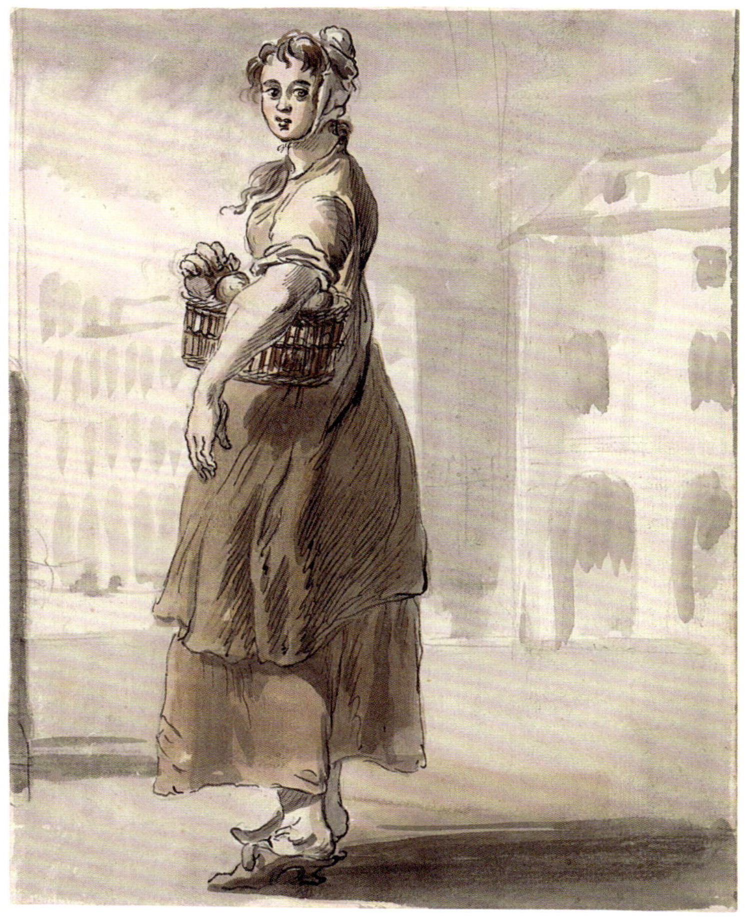

86

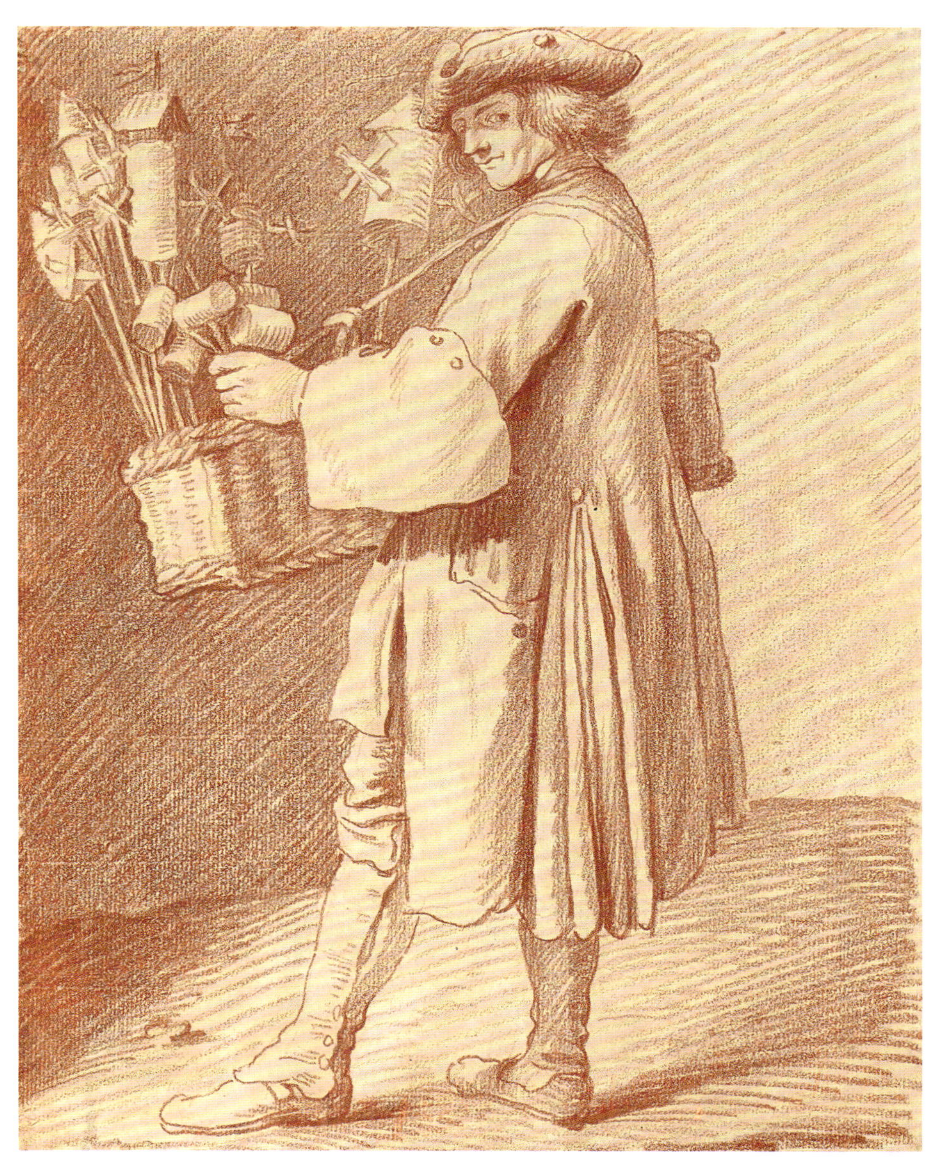

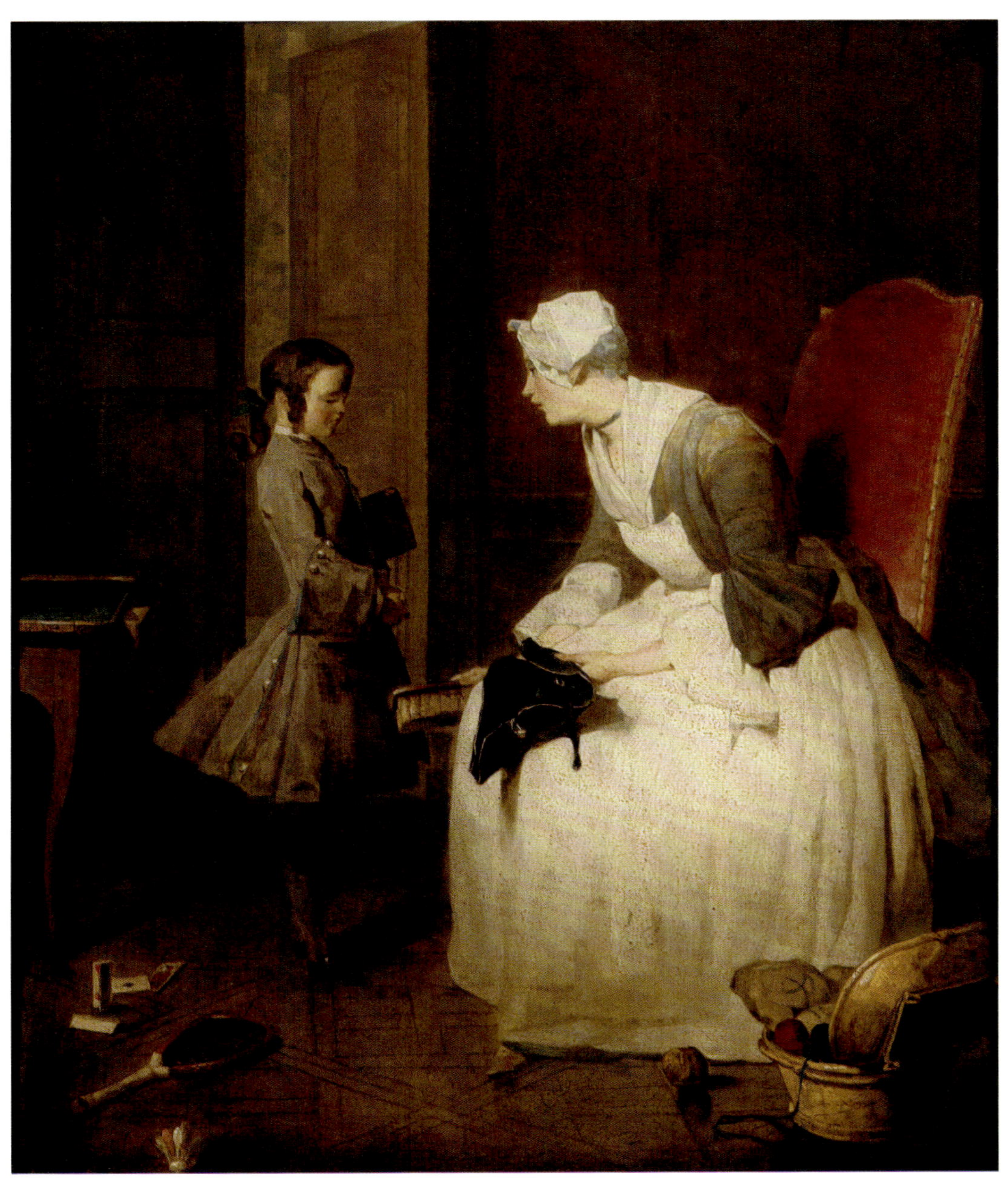

Jean-Siméon Chardin *The Governess* c.1738

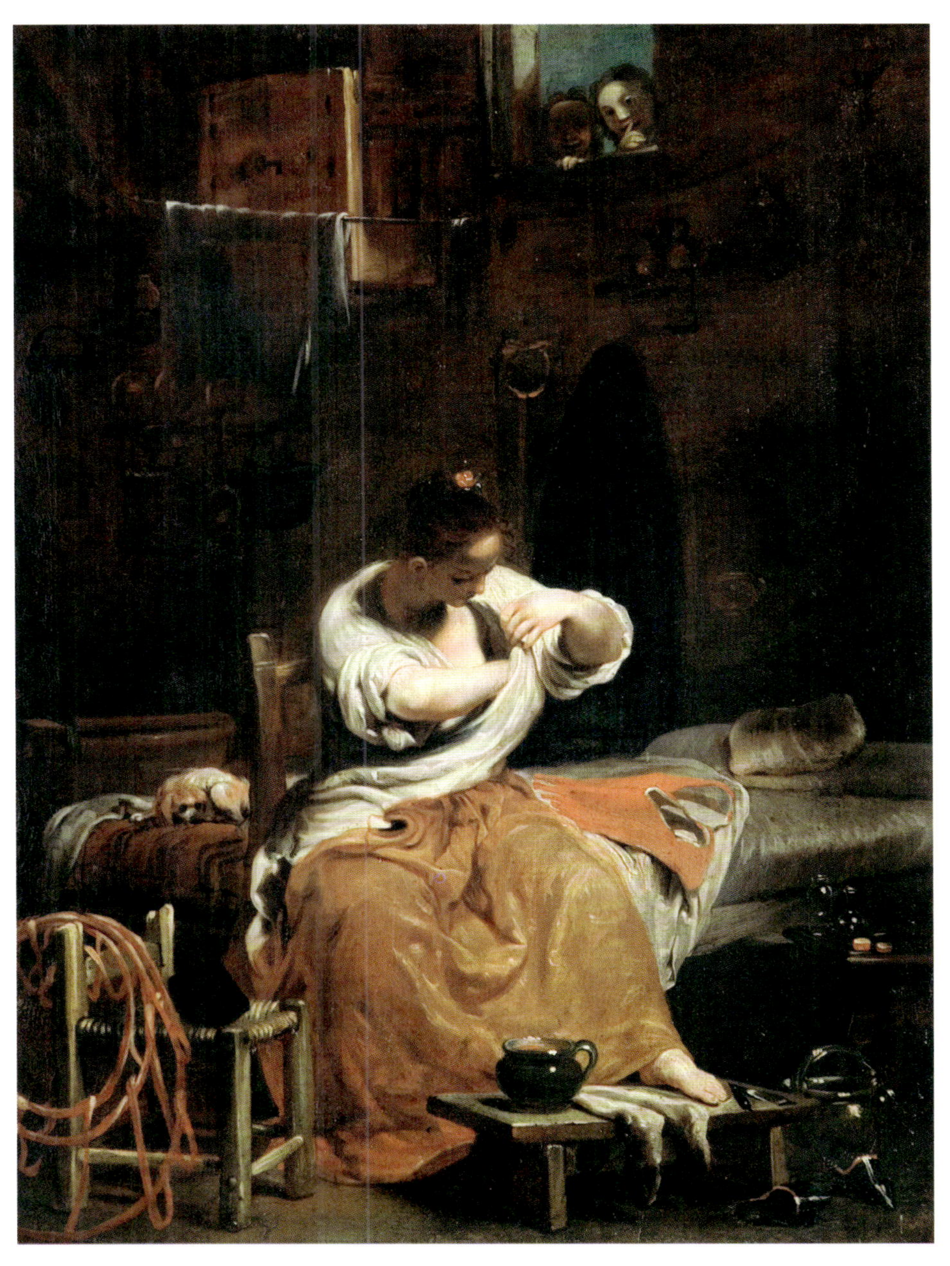

GIUSEPPE MARIA CRESPI   *A Woman Looking for Fleas*   c.1715–20

Troost gained particular popularity for his pictures of stage performances. In *Misled* a sober-looking Protestant couple dressed in black sit in front of a tavern, oblivious to the exposed buttocks in the window above, painted to resemble a face and heralded by trumpeters who appear to be in 'blackface', an obviously racist but prevalent feature of eighteenth-century Dutch theatrical and popular culture.

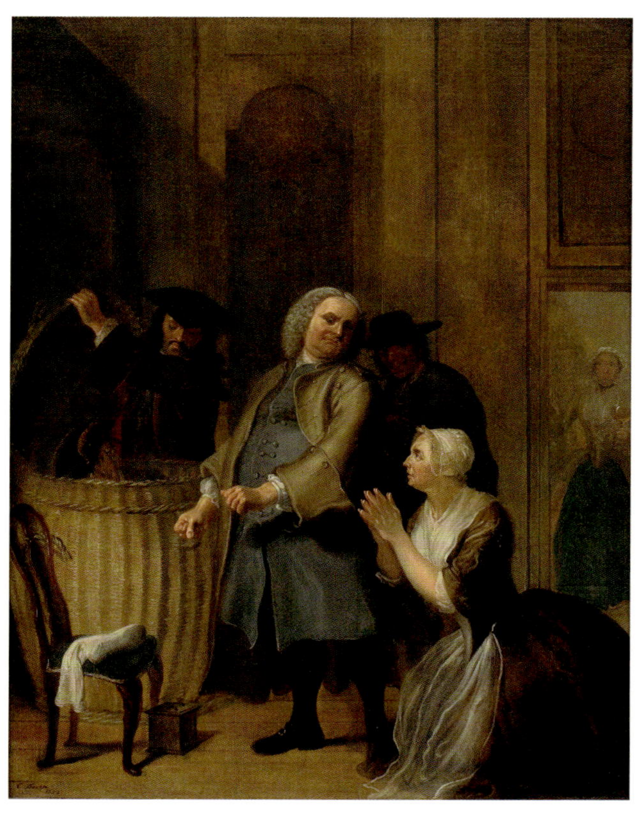

CORNELIS TROOST *False Virtue Discovered:
the discovery of Volkert in the basket* 1735

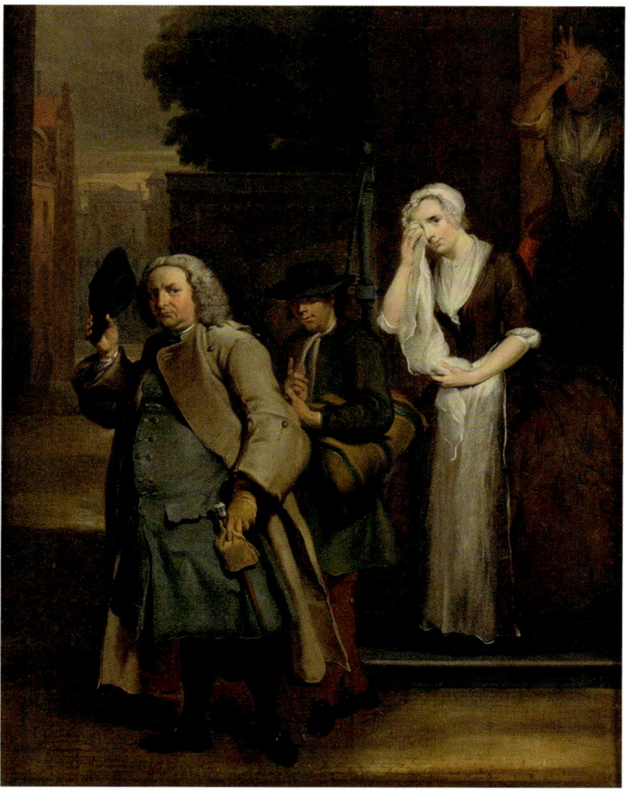

CORNELIS TROOST *False Virtue Discovered:
the feigned sadness of Geertruy* 1745

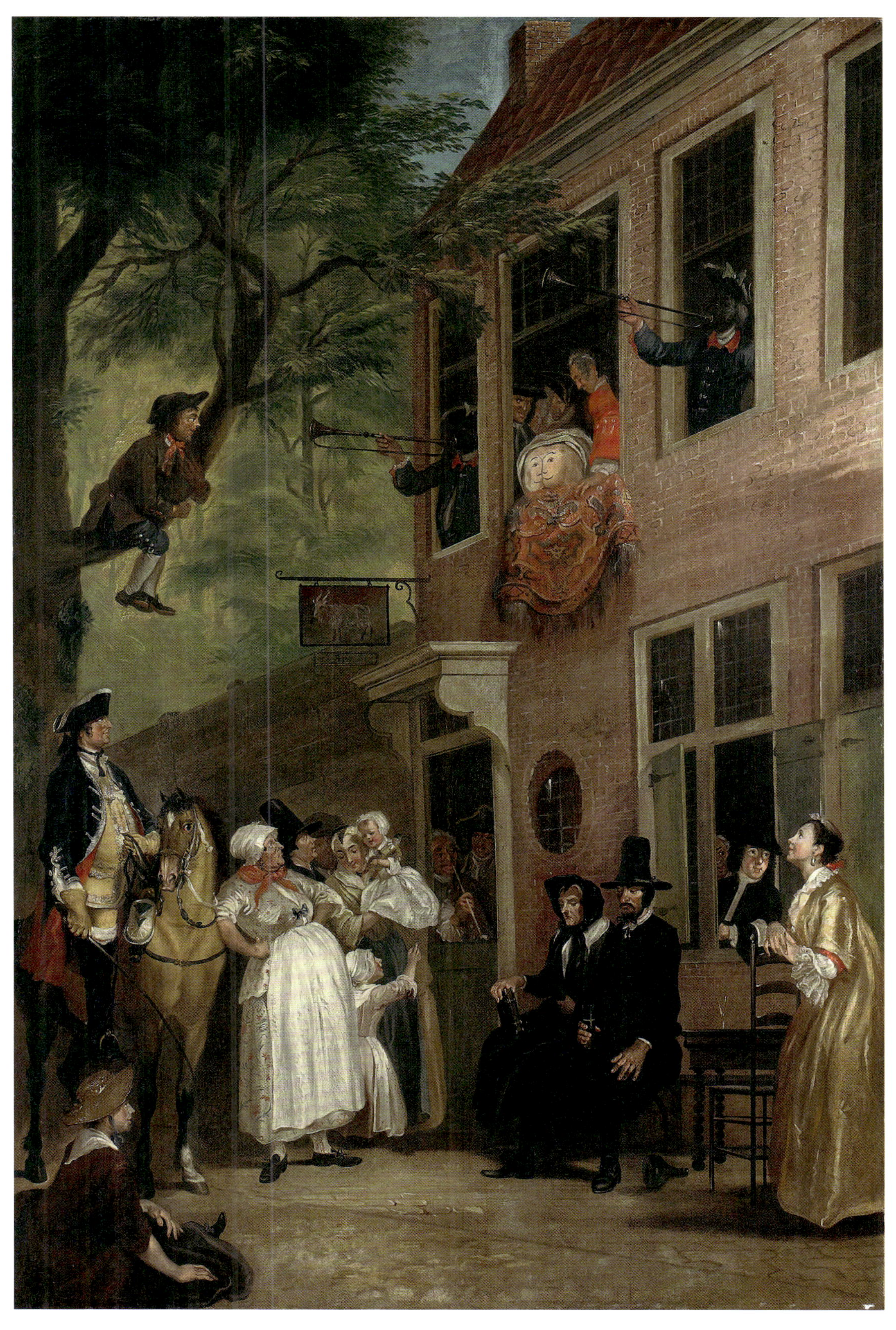

CORNELIS TROOST   *Misled: The Ambassador of the Rascals Exposes himself
from the Window of 't Bokki Tavern in the Harlemmerhout*   c.1739–50

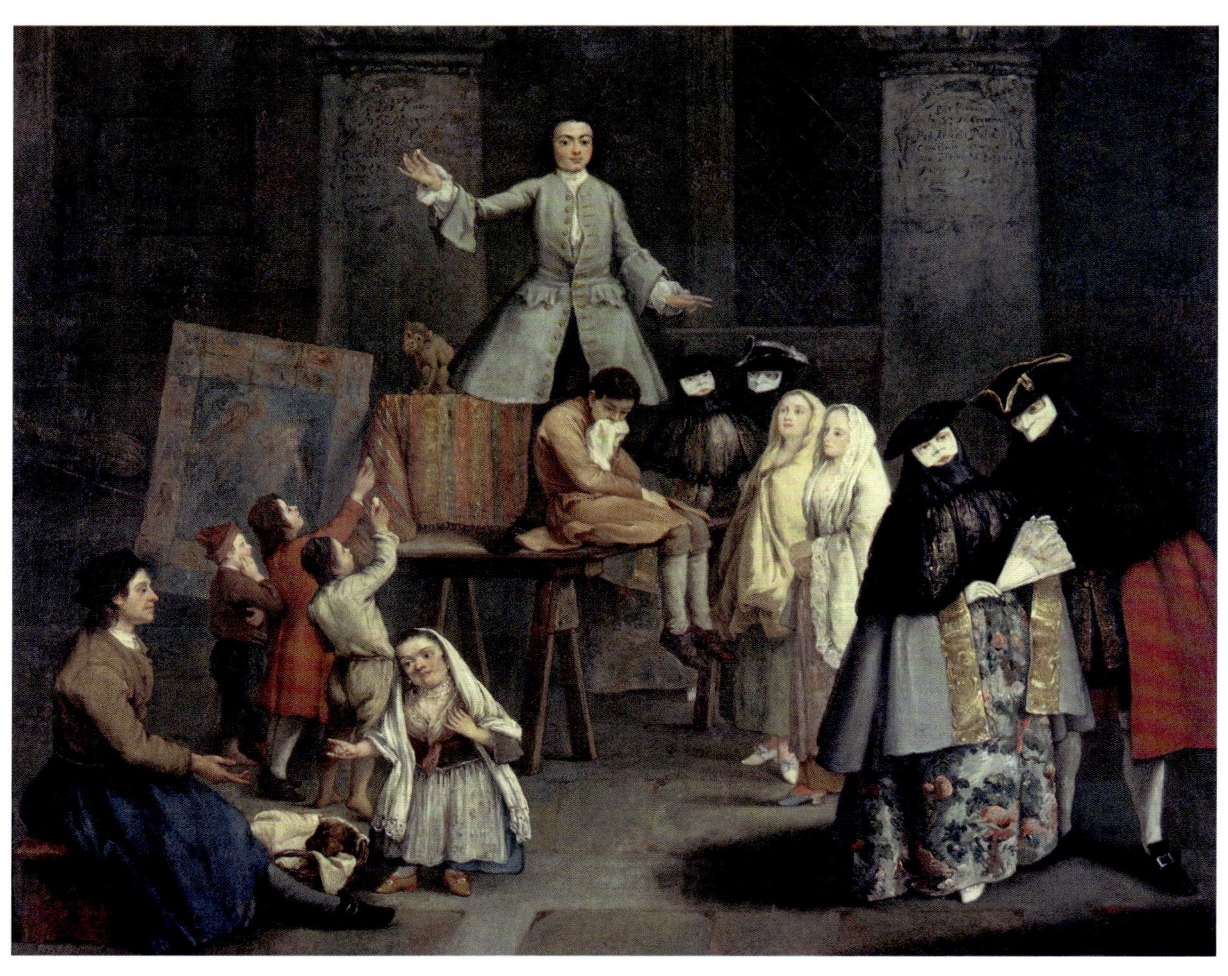

PIETRO LONGHI   *The Tooth Puller*   1746–52

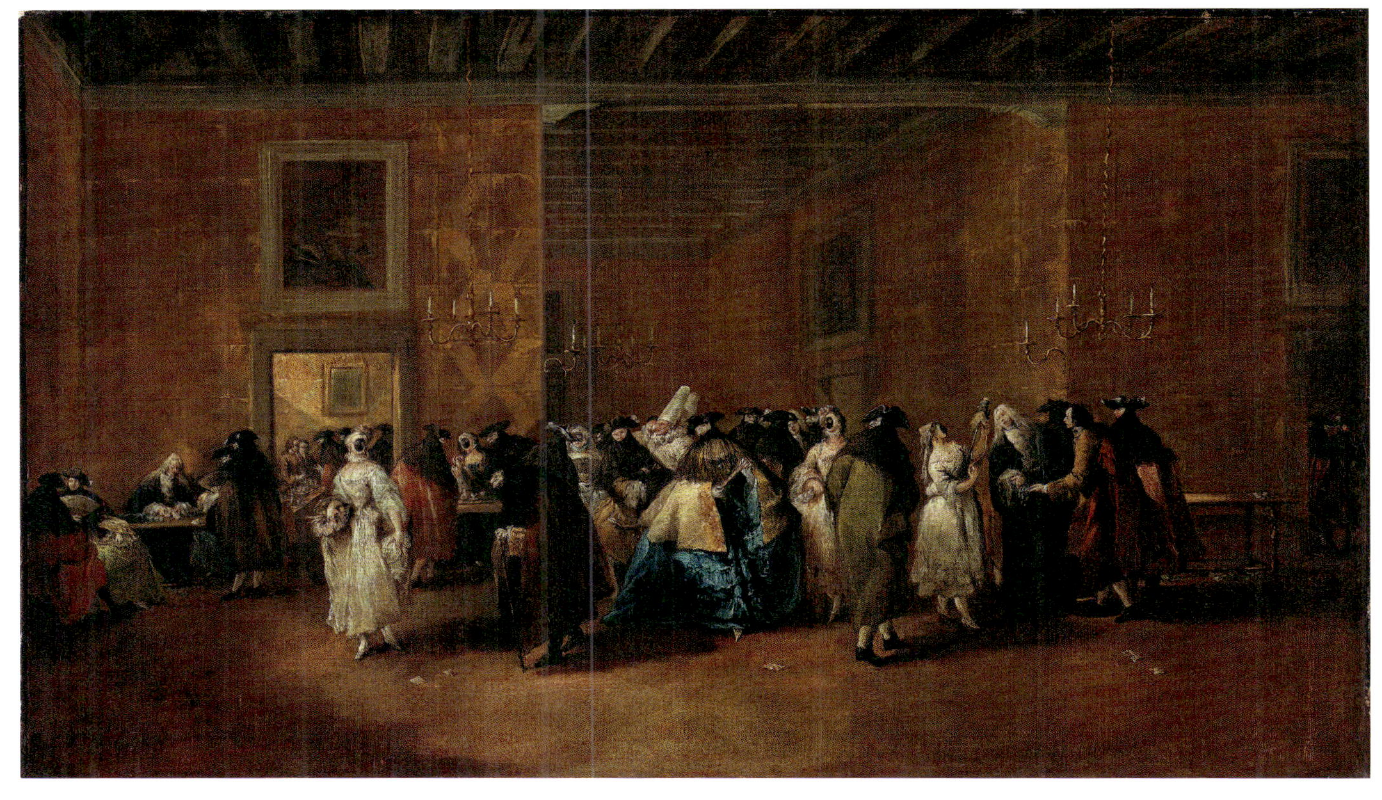

ANTONIO GUARDI   *The Sala Grande of the Ridotto, Palazzo Dandolo, San Moise*   1755–60   93

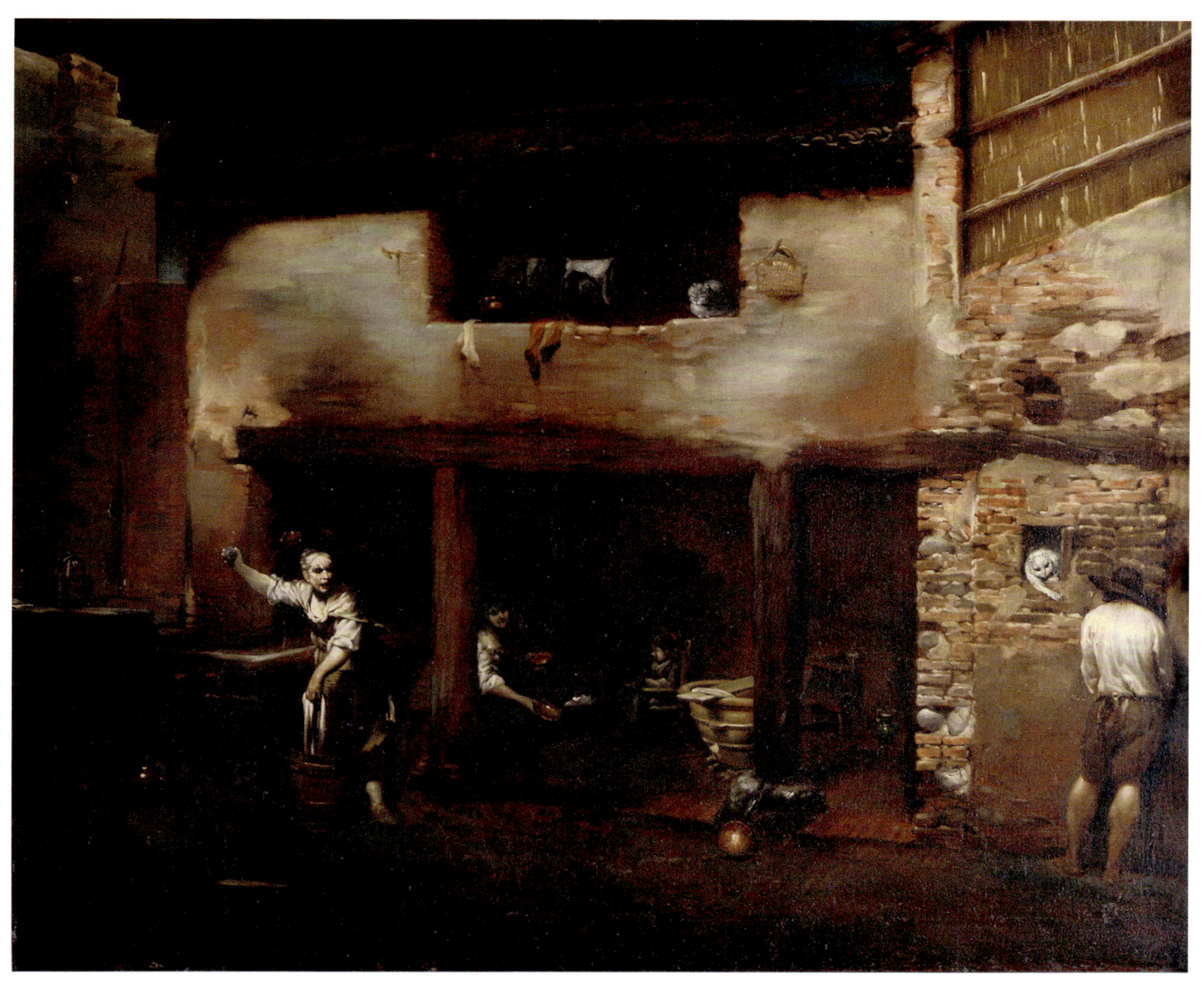

   GIUSEPPE MARIA CRESPI   *Courtyard Scene*   C.1710–15

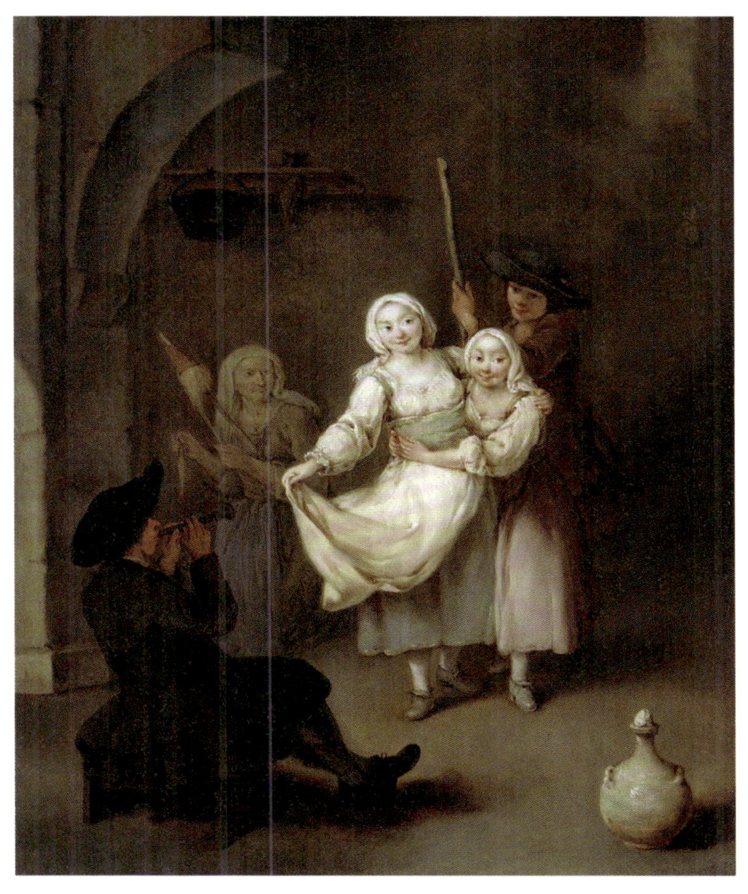

PIETRO LONGHI *The Dance* c.1750

MODERN MORAL NARRATIVES

The early 1700s saw the emergence of a new kind of narrative painting. While this drew upon seventeenth-century Dutch and Italian paintings of everyday life, it was novel in its reflection on modern experience. Artists tackled urban themes with a sometimes surprising frankness, following the adventures or misadventures of individual characters over a series of images. These stories were intended to engage and entertain a growing metropolitan audience for art.

While portrait painting had in the past included elements of humour and informality, there were now brazen images showing drunkenness and depravity. Especially important was the innovation of narrative pictures dealing with modern life, sometimes as a sequence or series of images. The Italian Giuseppe Crespi was a pioneer, creating single images of low life and an influential series setting out the ups and downs of an opera singer. In England, Hogarth's 'modern moral subjects' presented stories and characters of his own invention but which spoke to contemporary types and preoccupations.

The first of these, *A Harlot's Progress*, follows the fateful tale of a young woman from the countryside, who takes up a new life as a mistress and sex worker in the city, able for a short time to exploit her client for her own ends. Ultimately, though, her fortunes decline and she succumbs to venereal disease. Caught up in the commercial machinery of the modern city, in which her body is a product which she can exploit for profit, she experiences highs and lows – although with a definitely moralising fate assigned to her by the artist. The second, *A Rake's Progress*, develops a narrative involving class and new wealth, self-delusion and selfishness, exposing the unsteady mechanics of social change. The pictures include a multitude of details which position the actors in precise social and physical contexts, starting with the house of the protagonist's father, a merchant grown rich, whose wealth has enabled him to build a fancy house, but cannot compensate for the lack of 'taste' to execute the project well. The story of the son, the 'Rake', driven by his passions to a terrible fate in the asylum and an early death, reveals for the viewer's entertainment all the temptations of the modern city but also operates as a moral lesson about the disruption of the old social order. In this regard, Hogarth's narratives served to uphold the social status quo and to define the boundaries of acceptable, or polite, behaviour for the emerging bourgeosie.

Reproduced in engravings, these innovative works became internationally famous and enormously influential. These series represent Hogarth as an exemplary artist-entrepreneur, the creator of urban narratives intended to directly address a contemporary public. As such, they have elicited sustained interest over the generations, being reworked and repeatedly re-imagined by artists, as well as being remediated in literary and musical forms.

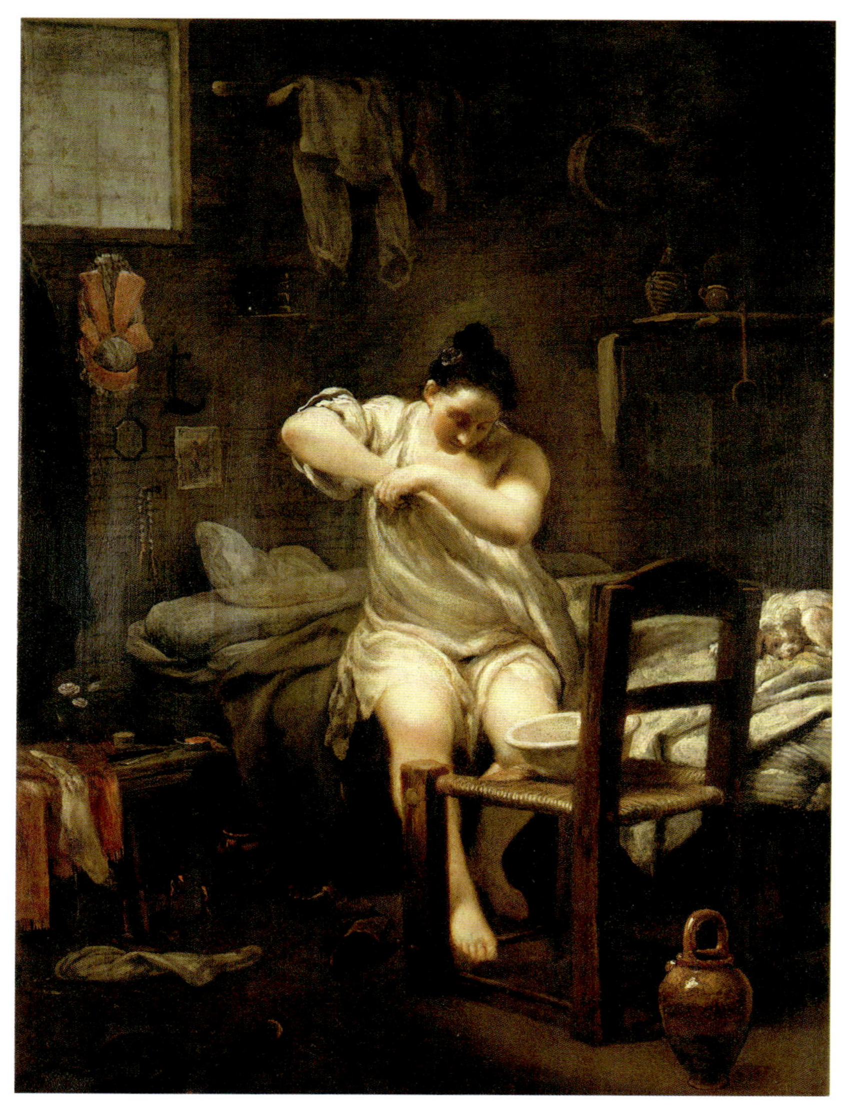

GIUSEPPE MARIA CRESPI *The Flea* 1707–9

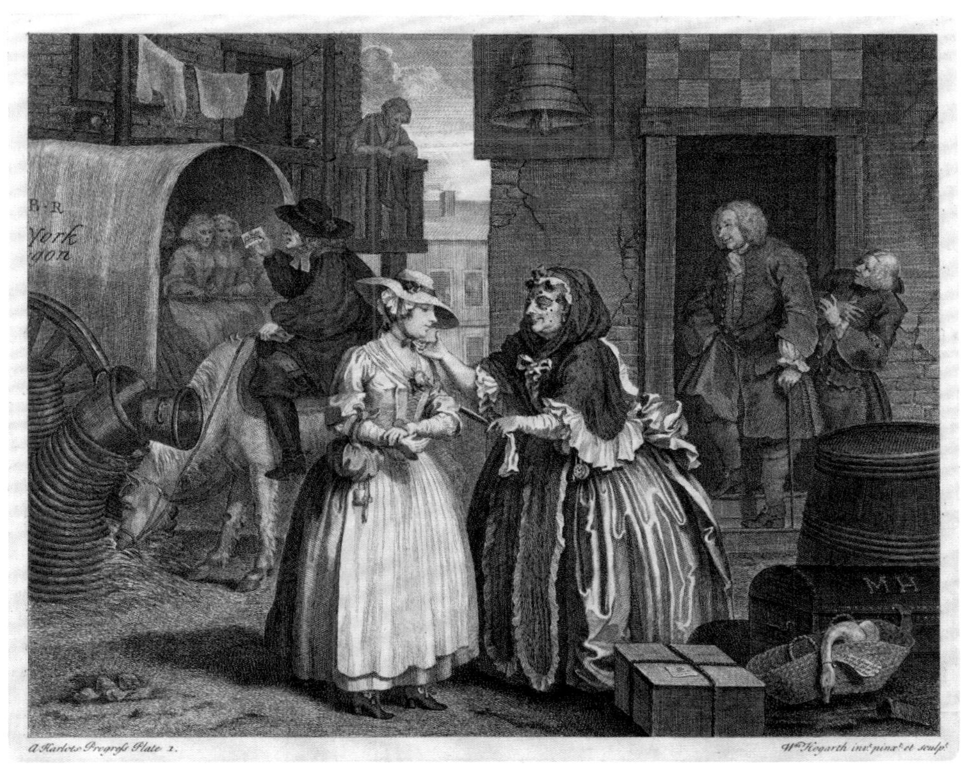

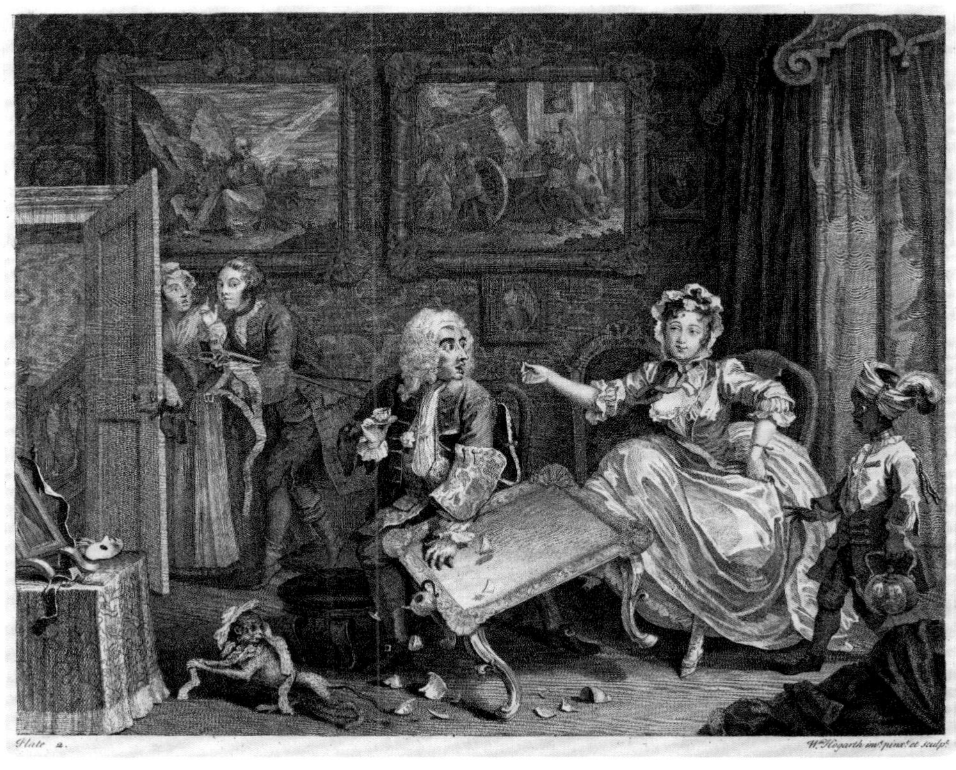

WILLIAM HOGARTH   *A Harlot's Progress*   1732   Plates 1–6 (and overleaf)

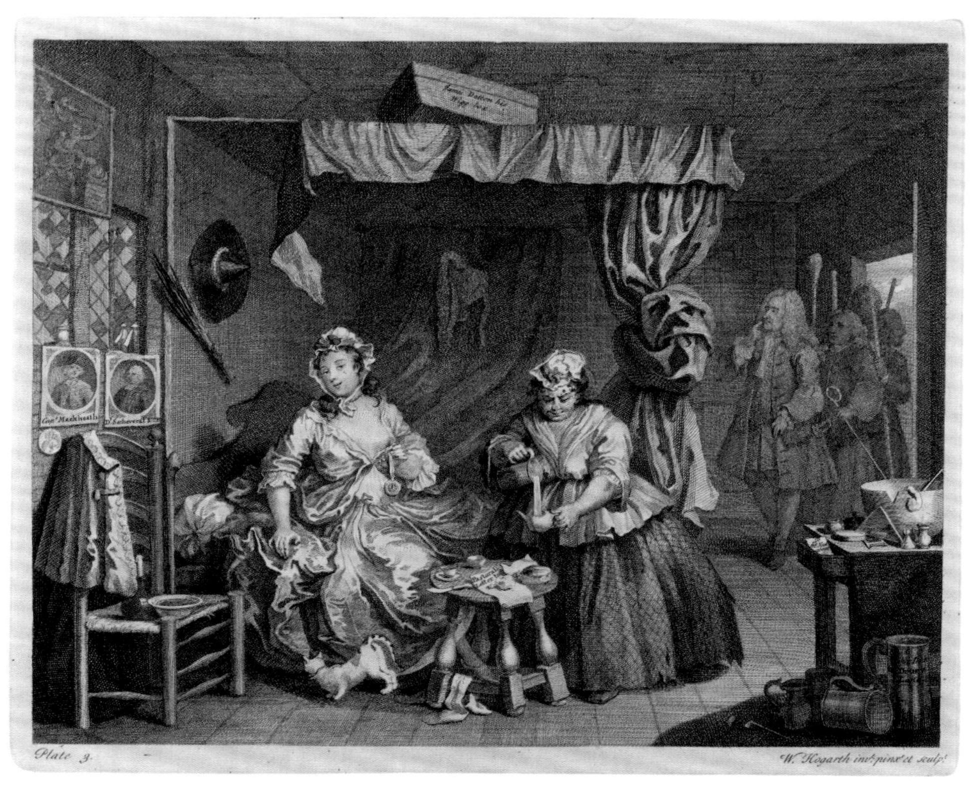

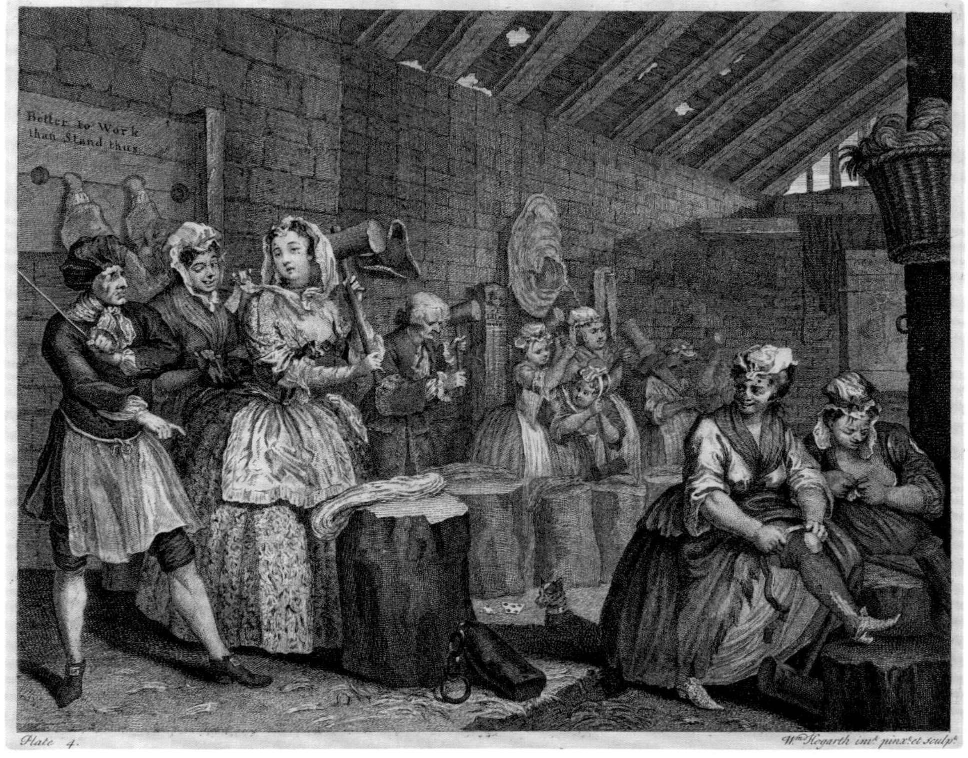
Better to Work
than Stand thus.

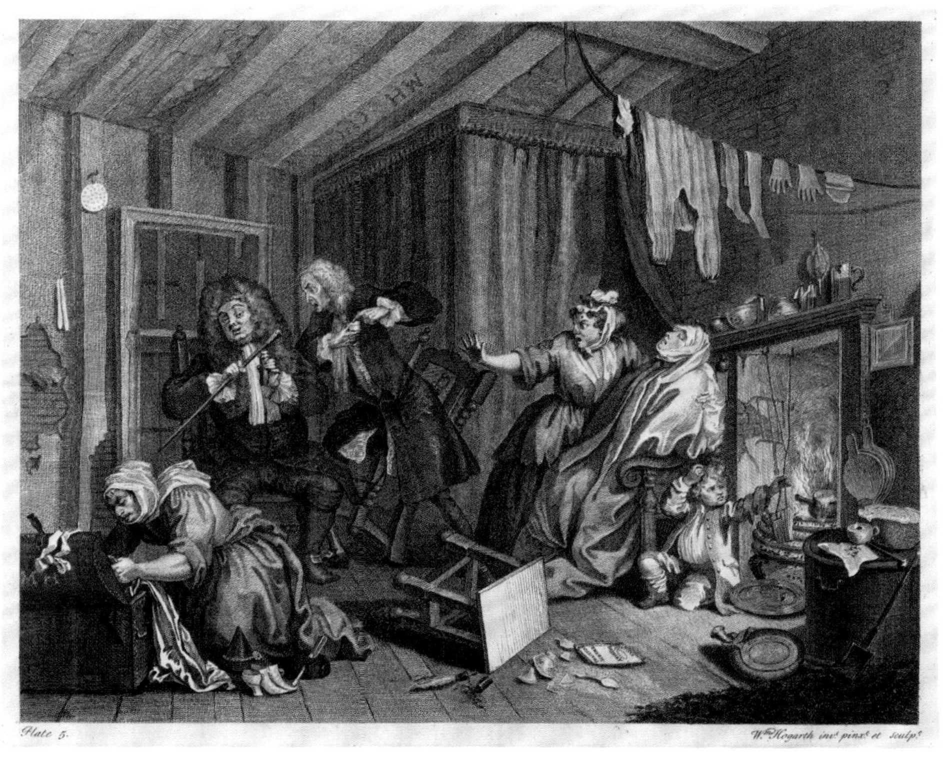

Plate 5.
W. Hogarth inv. pinx. et sculp.

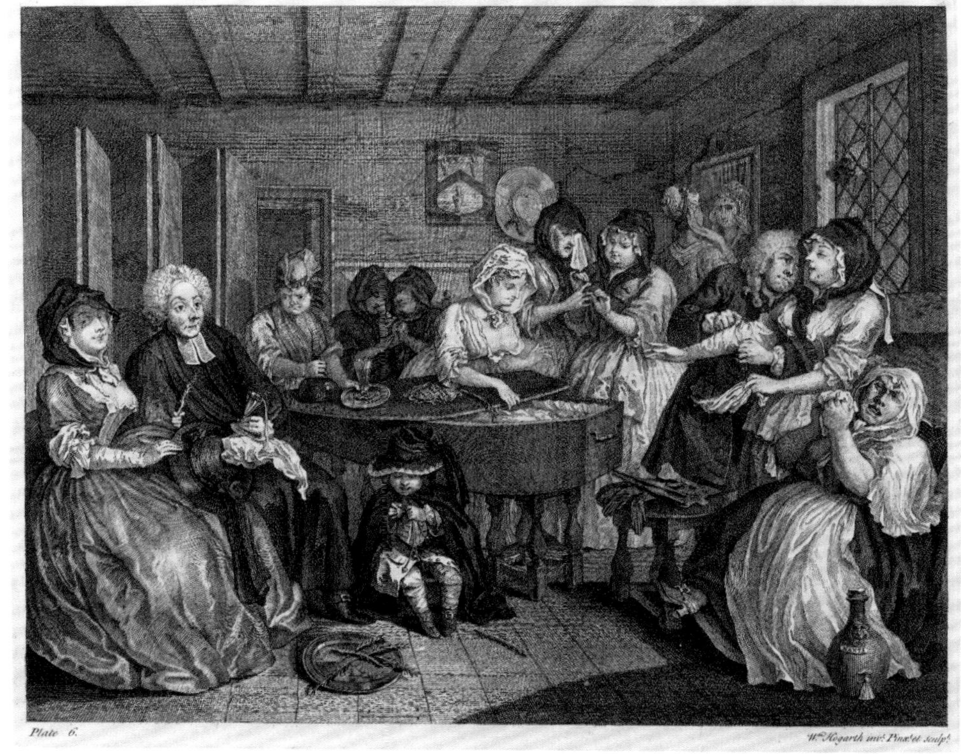

Plate 6.
W. Hogarth inv. Pinx. et sculp.

POTS IN HOGARTH

LARS THARP

My picture is my stage, and men and women my players,
exhibited in a 'dumb' show.[1]

As Hogarth candidly admits, he is a Man of the Theatre. Throughout all his 'dumb shows' – from his *Beggar's Opera* of the late 1720s through all his conversation pieces, whether public or intimate, to his fictional *Progresses*, right through to his four great *Election* canvases twenty-five years later – he constantly takes us to the theatre of Life. He strews his stage with props, trappings of his material world. Prominent among these are his Ceramics, things made of clay: dishes, vases, birds' nesting bottles, flagons, priapic apothecary jars, fantastic Chinese idols, sparkling porcelain services, foaming jugs, lurching punchbowls and flying bricks. A cacophony of clay and crockery. 'Dumb' these props are not.

Many of Hogarth's ceramics are real, attributable to the three basic traditions of earthenware, stoneware and porcelain. However, sometimes the artist cannot resist stretching reality into caricature. For example, in *The Tête à Tête*, Scene 2 of *Marriage A-la-Mode* c.1743 (p.161), Hogarth truly lives up to Henry Fielding's flattering observation: that his characters do not merely breathe, but *they appear to think*. The

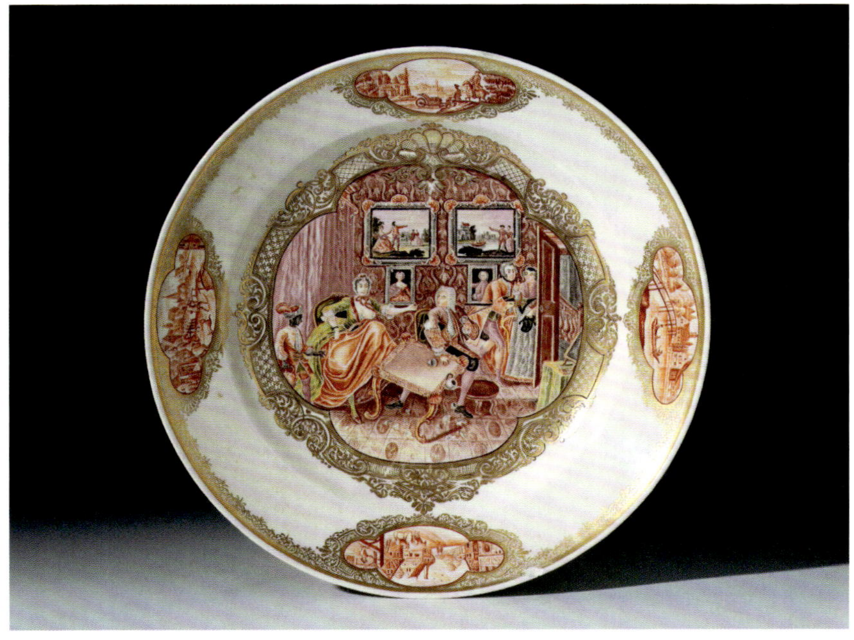

MEISSEN PORCELAIN FACTORY
Plate featuring scene 11 of Hogarth's 'A Harlot's Progress'   c.1740

psychological realism of the bored marquis opposite his flushed, libidinous wife is real and ominous. The teapot on the table between the couple is also real, instantly identifiable as a piece of Chinese export ware.[2] The perspective of connected rooms is real, too, but as our eyes rise to the mantelpiece, reality is trounced: we enter a forest of white vessels bookended by two booby-headed figures, their massive hands splayed wide. While outwardly *suggesting* porcelain, these figures have no real equivalents in the ceramic world, they are pure fabrication.[3] Some of their ceramic neighbours, though, have a basis in fact: the Buddhas, the snuff bottles, the vases and even the frogs. With this mantelpiece Hogarth declares war on 'stuff' and on the epidemic of Luxury.

*

Hogarth was barely ten years old when, in 1707, the East India Company was re-licensed for trade to Asia. The catastrophes of the seventeenth century – plague, civil and foreign wars, dynastic ructions – had given the Dutch Republic carte blanche in maritime trade from Europe to Asia. With relative calm and trade restored, London began rising from the ashes to become a northern Rome, and the English East Asia trade soon grew to outflank that of Holland.

Of all the many exotic consumables imported into England from the 1660s, Chinese tea proved the most influential on several levels. Tea arrived alongside all its associated ceramic accessories, its redwares and (above all) its translucent porcelain. European attempts to discover the manufacturing secrets of Chinese porcelain had hitherto foundered. But with the accession of Mary and her Dutch husband, William, the London court was injected with a European mania for all things Chinese and Japanese. Hard-pressed European potters, lacquerers, silversmiths and weavers were forced to join the chinoiserie craze.

Throughout his life Hogarth was tangled in the aesthetic and ethical debates swirling around the pursuit of Luxury – with its economic potential to undercut 'native' industry and to deplete the nation of silver bullion, and its moral potential for decadence. On several counts, Chinese porcelain inevitably came into his sights.

Initially Hogarth kept his satirical tongue firmly in his cheek: in the milling 'assembly' scenes of his two early conversation pieces, *The Wanstead Abbey Assembly* c.1728–31 and *William Wollaston and his Family* 1730, an amused decorum emanates from the serving of tea – in both cases, supervised from a tea table garnished with Chinese porcelain and silverware. To us such compositions may appear a little stilted, yet with his love of theatre and his interest in humans, Hogarth playfully injects life and humour into the known dynastic connections between his sitters. The resulting 'conversations', flaunting the taste and wealth of the sitters, are proudly displayed for all to see.

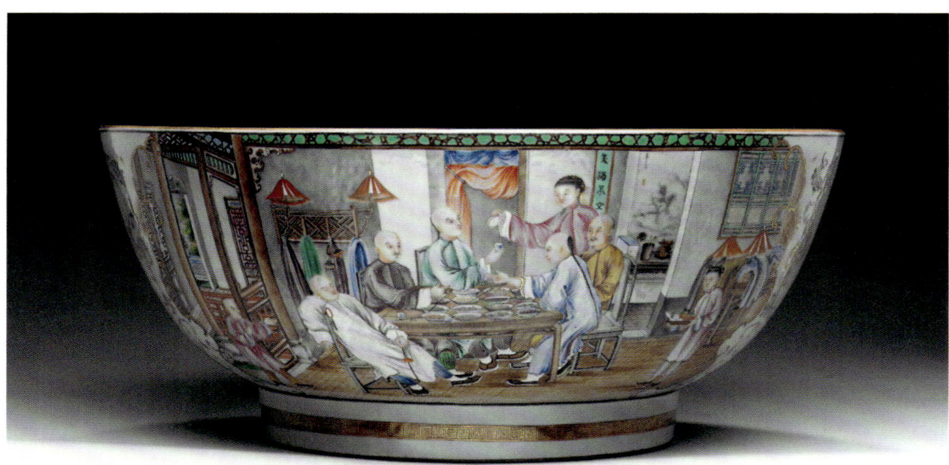

Meanwhile, Hogarth's satirical impulses were astir. Painting in parallel with the literary works of Jonathan Swift and Alexander Pope, Hogarth created a story entirely his own, *A Harlot's Progress* 1732 (pp.99–101). Moll Hackabout, an innocent country lass recently arrived from Yorkshire, untutored in taste or vice, is intercepted by a procuress and installed as mistress to a wealthy London merchant. In scene two they sit beside a silvered tea table, laden with a fashionable, expensive Chinese porcelain *equipage*; allowing her younger lover to quit her patron's bedroom undetected, Moll diverts attention and topples the precious table. Hogarth catches the moment mid-flight, mid-gasp, as porcelain sails through the air, the teapot still pouring, falling to its destruction on the ground. Hogarth here recalls the pretension of the real-life 'players' in his earlier Wanstead and Wollaston tea gatherings.[4] In another work, *Children at Play*, painted around this time, it's a dramatic device he uses to emphasise the fragility of childhood. Many of his ceramics are on the edge, or actually falling.

In Hogarth's lifetime the quantity of Chinese tea shipped into London multiplied fifty-fold. Despite the initially high taxation rates, the increasingly wealthy classes were hooked, and orders for porcelain wares for tea as well as coffee and chocolate followed. An estimated one to two million pieces of Chinese porcelain arrived in London *each year* in the 1700s. This influx of a magical, translucent, heat-resistant material challenged the native pottery traditions of Britain and Europe. It was only in the mid-1740s that Britain saw the emergence of an indigenous porcelain industry.

*

Although the English tea ceremony encouraged the social mixing of the sexes, gentlemen still sought the unbuttoned company of other

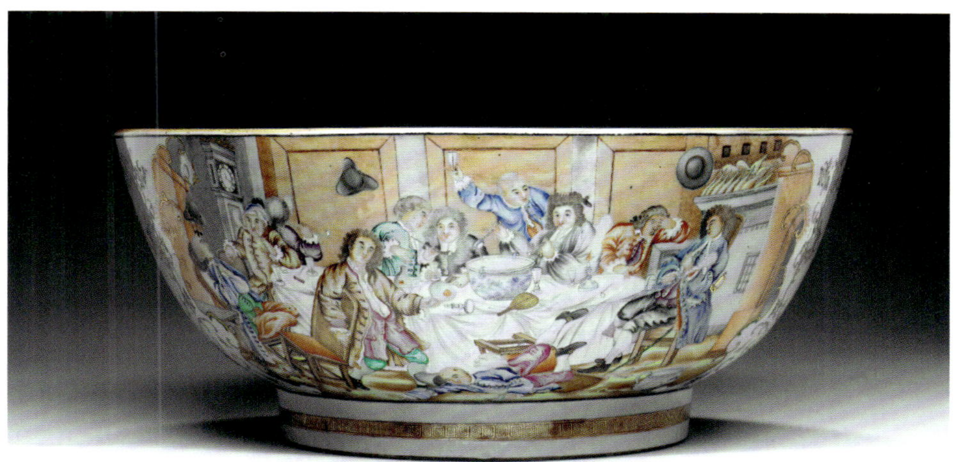

gentlemen, gathered around the convivial bowl of toddy, negus, shrub – or punch.

Punch – its name possibly derived from the Hindi word *pāñć* meaning 'five' (the supposed number of ingredients) – first came to England in the 1660s or 1670s. It was enjoyed even on board ship (see p.115, *Captain Lord George Graham, 1715–47, in his Cabin* – in the corner a sturdy 'famille-rose' enamelled Chinese exportware punchbowl) as on-board beers tended to spoil in the warmer latitudes on the East India routes. The mixture typically comprised arrack (any distilled spirit), sugar, lime or other fruit juice, water and spices. One description from sailors in Canton states the punch was taken hot – heated with hot cannonballs – and consumed after dinner.

The popularity of punch spread to Europe through all the East India companies; just as tea required bespoke porcelain, so punch gave rise to the typical wide, deep punchbowl form. To anyone involved in the East India trade, whether on board ship or through the Company's London headquarters in Leadenhall Street, punchbowls became a standard order along with tea sets and bespoke dinner services – to be decorated with a coat of arms or with a favourite European subject.

Steep-sided wide punchbowls lent themselves to being decorated with landscape-format images. A popular subject for those associated with the East India Company was the Canton waterfront filled with its various European warehouses, each identified by its national flag. Once the desired image had been chosen for reproduction on porcelain, the detailed order plus a printed image would be relayed via the HEIC office into the supercargo's portmanteau. Once safely arrived in Canton, all orders were entrusted to a Chinese intermediary through whom they were conveyed up-country to the city of Jingdezhen in Jiangxi Province. There they were distributed among suitable manufacturing and decorating workshops. Once completed, maybe after several months, the goods were carefully packed and transported, by river and human porterage, down to Canton for eventual stowing for the return journey to Europe. Little wonder that, once safely delivered after epic human efforts by land and sea, Chinese porcelain was highly valued. Even after the eventual emergence of the first European porcelain factories, Chinese potters continued to enjoy their already thousand-year advantage of potting technology over Europeans.

Before and after Hogarth's death in 1764, prints of his images were in widespread circulation throughout Europe. His *Midnight Modern Conversation* was particularly popular. The whereabouts of his original painting are unknown, but the prints of the *Conversation* abound (p.122). To a ceramics historian, a particular focus sits at the centre of the table: the punchbowl. In the print we see on its steep sides the silhouette of a long figure coiffed with a chignon and holding an umbrella or parasol. It is impossible to say whether Hogarth has copied this figure from a Chinese porcelain original, or from a European Delftware chinoiserie. The latter seems probable. Nonetheless *Chinese* porcelain vessels copying *European* chinoiseries – i.e. Chinese painters copying European copies of original Chinese images – do exist. As a matter of interest, Hogarth's own English Delftware blue and white punchbowl, probably potted and painted in Lambeth, copies the Chinese 'dragon' pattern.[5]

So popular did punch become that English potters in the earthenware and stoneware traditions copied Hogarth's 1733 print, sometimes including title, onto mugs, jugs and, of course, punchbowls. Likewise in mainland Europe the *Conversation* appears frequently in several ceramic media: on a very steep-sided Dutch blue and white Delftware bowl in the Rijksmuseum; on Meissen, Ansbach and later Berlin porcelain examples (with lids, for hot punch). In many of the porcelain examples the entire *Conversation* is 'lifted' from an interior setting and 'pasted' into a garden – the long-case clock incongruously transported out-of-doors. But how does the decorator fill the three remaining surfaces of bowl and lid? With a whole supply of Hogarth's images to be found throughout Europe, other Hogarthian elements were likewise edited and 'lifted' into available spaces on the bowl or cover; e.g. from *The Enraged Musician* 1741; and from *Industry and Idleness* 1747. Thus Hogarth's images continued to appeal, and to be available to the ceramic manufacturers of Continental Europe well into the nineteenth century.

The intercontinental 'reach' of Hogarth's images can be seen in two superb examples of his *Midnight Modern Conversation*, painted in China in the 1770s and 1780s and exported to Europe at the time. The *Conversation* fills one full side of each bowl but thereafter the bowls differ. On one (pp.104–5) the second side is filled with a scene of

Chinese gentlemen enjoying a civilised meal, accompanied by a modest quantity of wine. A notice on the door of the establishment reads *mei jiu bu kong* ('beautiful wine not empty'). Whoever commissioned this bowl clearly intended to contrast the dissolute London scene with the altogether different behaviour of Chinese literati. It is an eloquent encapsulation of the view then held in Europe that China was the very epitome of civilisation, superior to the coarser culture of Europe. (This Voltairian view was to be overturned within a few decades.)

The second *Conversation* bowl, in the possession of KODE Art Museums in Bergen, Norway, has an entirely different second scene: a finely detailed 'portrait' of a Danish East Indiaman, flying the split flag of the Danish Asia Company ('DAC') whose gold cypher centres the flag (p.123). The ship's stern carries the name *Mars* and above the ship is an arc of five gilt monograms, four of which, ending in 'M', testify to the association of the bowl with the Danish-Norwegian family Mørch. No Mørch has, as yet, been found in the DAC register but, as prominent timber merchants and shipwrights based in Kristiansand, the direct connection is clear, the bowl having been acquired from the Mørch family via a dealer in the 1890s. From Company records we know the Danish East Indiaman *Mars* sailed three times from Copenhagen to Canton (Guangzhou) and back (1781–3; 1784–6; and 1787–9). And it was on such ships that treasure from the East arrived into Europe. One can only speculate about the commissioning of these two bowls. As Guangzhou was a melting pot of all the European merchants trading with China, one of these bowls may already have been on a decorator's shelf (by the 1780s in Canton, not Jingdezhen) when another merchant demanded a repeat, though one with a different 'side B'.

European designs sent to China for copying onto porcelain were often misunderstood by the painter. On the 'American' example the bowl on the table centre has blue handles, but Hogarth's image actually depicts lemon rinds – yellow, not blue. Also, Hogarth's 'parasol stroller' has been replaced by a beautiful miniature Chinese landscape – a painter's revenge?

*

Ceramics abound in Hogarth's images. Falling or static, humble crockery and swanky porcelain all presage disaster, morals in peril. And porcelain in particular interrogates the contemporary obsession with Stuff and Luxury. It is a pleasing irony that many of Hogarth's images are to be found sealed into the surface of the very material he lampoons.

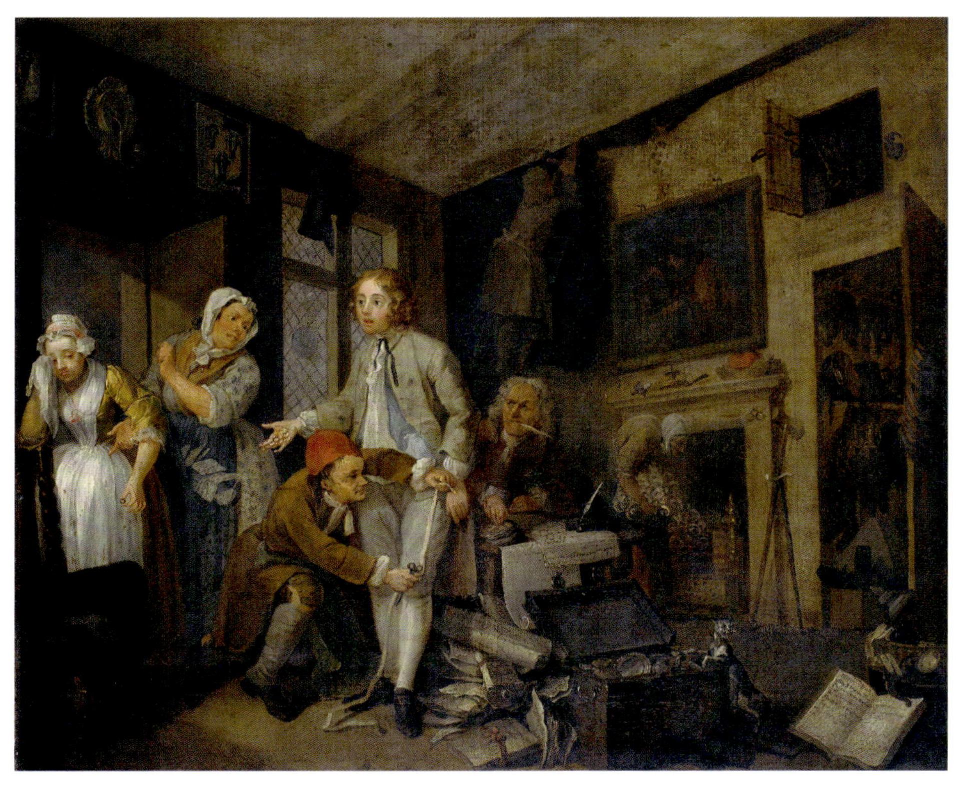

WILLIAM HOGARTH   *A Rake's Progress I: The Heir*   1734

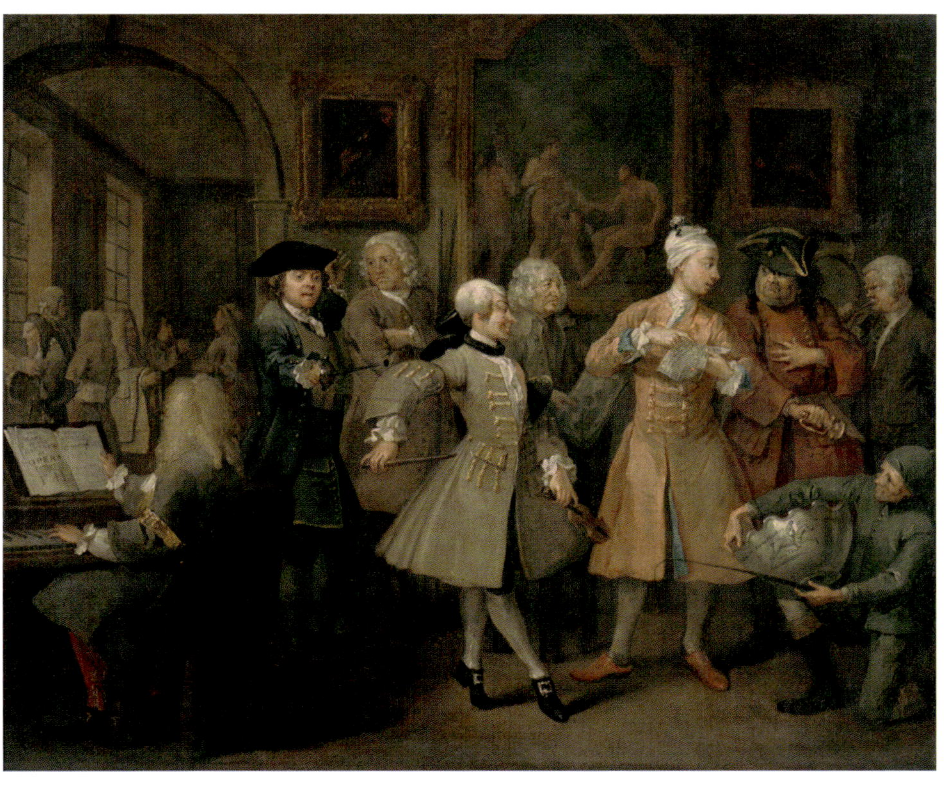

    WILLIAM HOGARTH   *A Rake's Progress II: The Levée*   1734

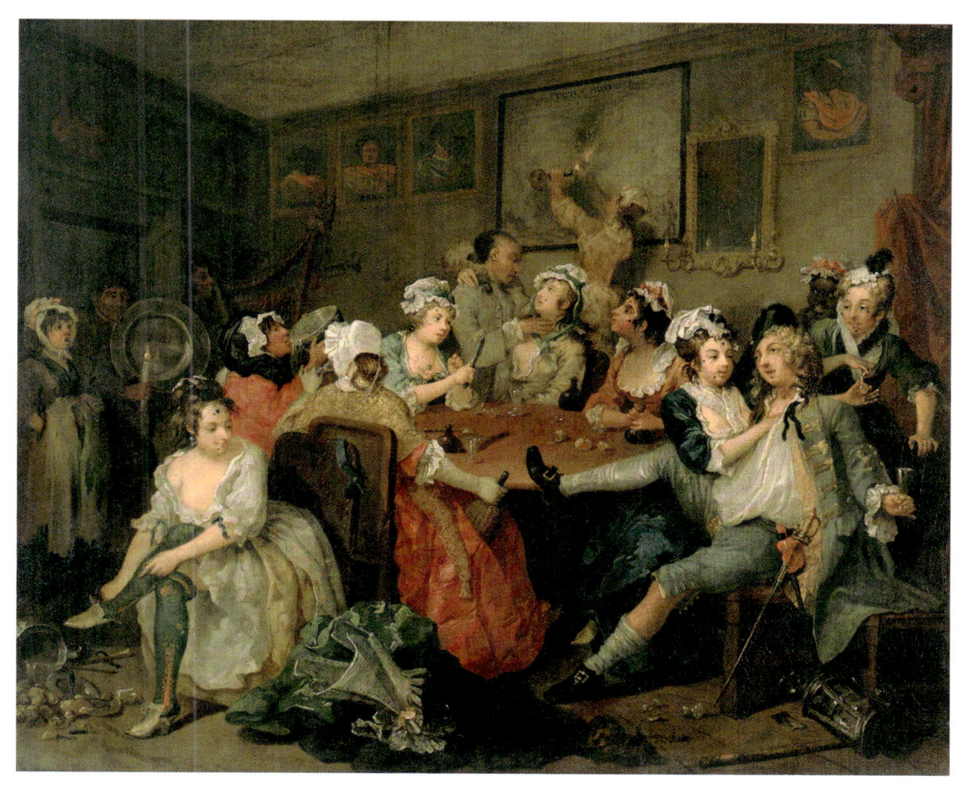

WILLIAM HOGARTH   A Rake's Progress III: The Orgy   1734

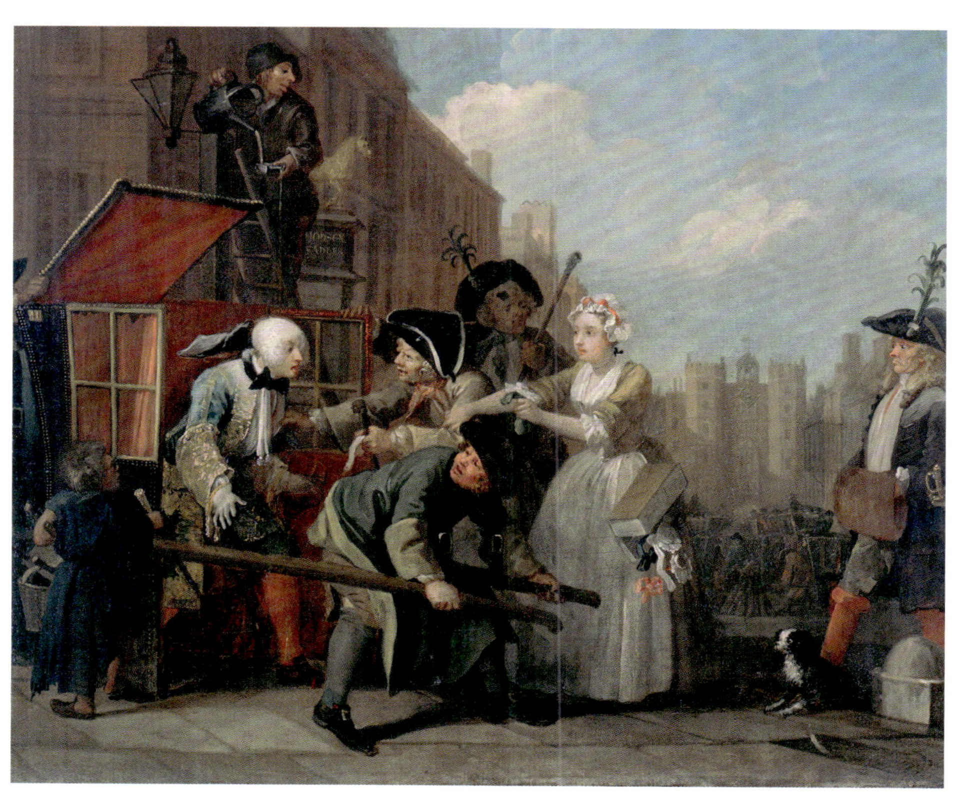

WILLIAM HOGARTH   A Rake's Progress IV: The Arrest   1734

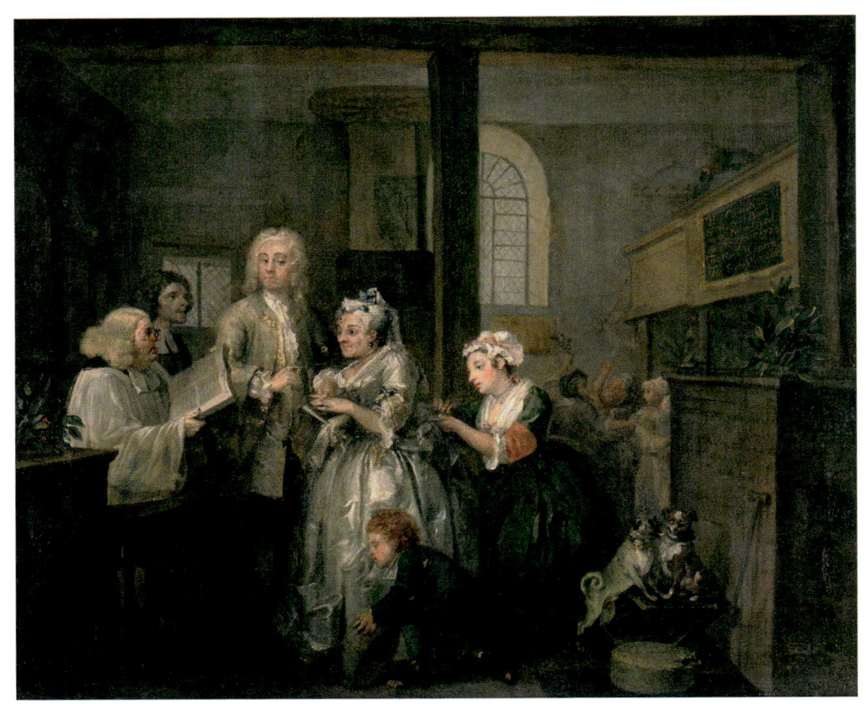

WILLIAM HOGARTH   *A Rake's Progress V: The Marriage*   1734

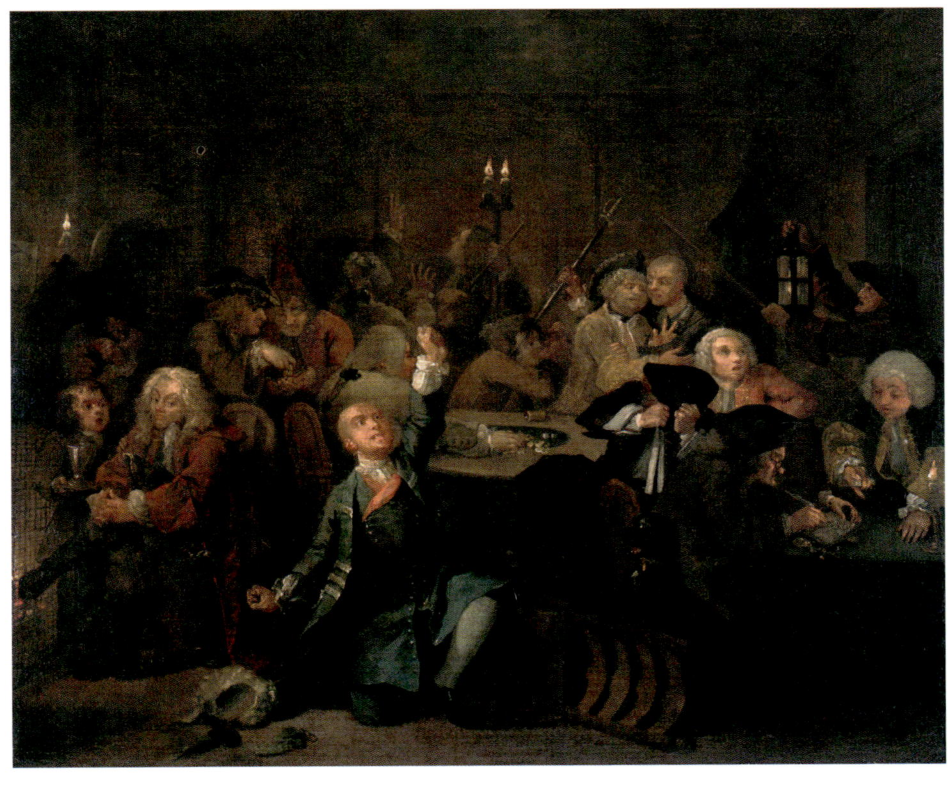

    WILLIAM HOGARTH   *A Rake's Progress VI: The Gaming House*   1734

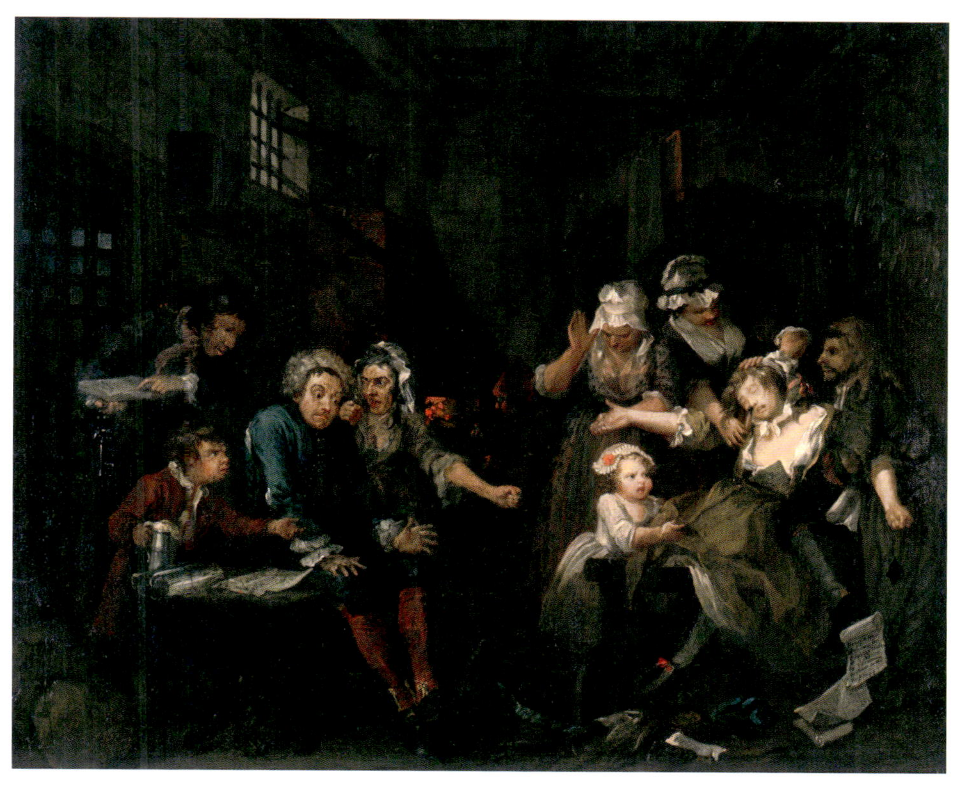

WILLIAM HOGARTH   *A Rake's Progress VII: The Prison*   1734

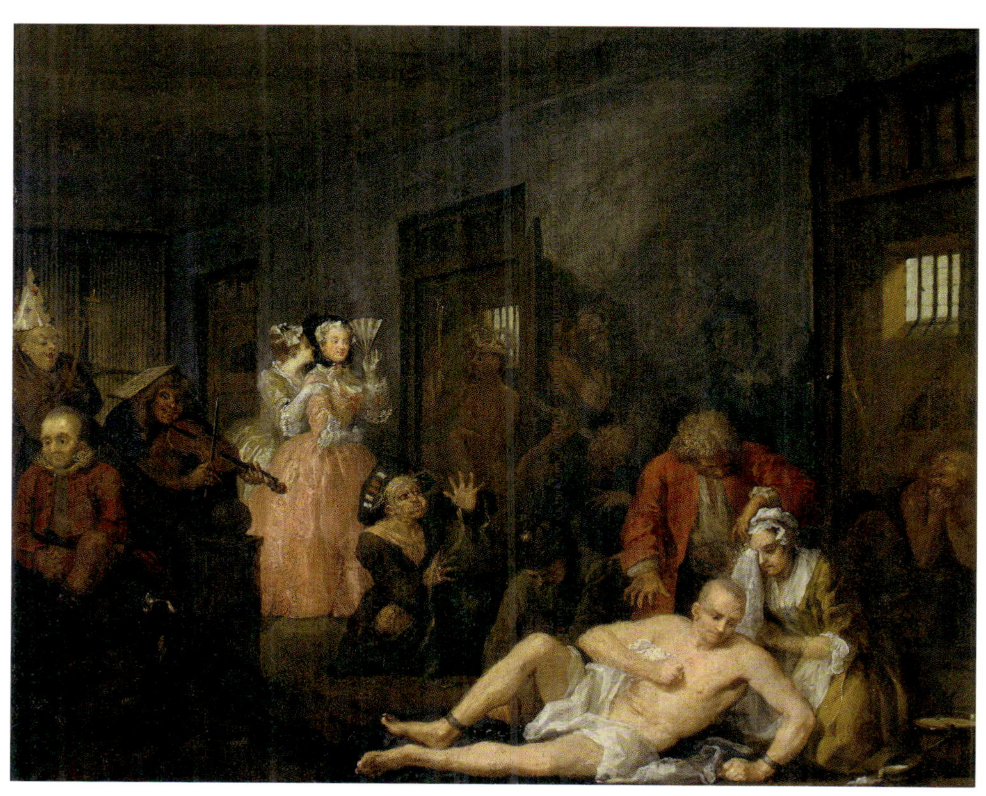

WILLIAM HOGARTH   *A Rake's Progress VIII: The Madhouse*   1734

IN THE COMPANY OF MEN

The raucous humour, visual excitement and apparent anti-establishment tone of Hogarth's narrative pictures have attracted huge admiration over the centuries. His pictures have often been located at the beginning of a modern tradition of social criticism, feeding into the political satire and caricature which achieved radical force in later eras. 'Hogarthian' was a term in use even during the artist's lifetime, suggesting an entire worldview: satirical, independent, insightful.

This flattering interpretation of the Hogarthian perspective helped attract clients for his portrait practice, perhaps surprisingly so. His likenesses can be disarmingly frank, including elements of unconventional behaviour or appearance which would not previously have featured in portraiture. Sometimes this involves relatively gentle humour: the emphatic treatment of a portly frame or spindly legs; the direct treatment of the signs of aging beneath a fancy headdress and behind fine silks. Among male subjects, this tendency towards unconventionality could sometimes become outrageous, even blasphemous. Occasionally the intention appears to have been satirical, but far more often the sitters were in on the joke. The irony is that for men to tolerate such rough treatment – being cast as odd, eccentric or disreputable – they needed to enjoy a degree of status and stability. The Hogarthian image flattered property-owning men who looked at themselves as possessing independence, robust good humour, conviviality and unconventionality.

The satirical and oppositional elements involved in the Hogarthian have often appealed to people holding far more strongly oppositional or radical political and social views than the artist himself appears to have done. But Hogarth's images include elements which we perhaps should find disturbing. The Hogarthian relish in themes of sexual violence, violation and exploitation, his use of anti-Semitic and racist tropes, and his moralising approach to social change are all far from straightforward. While many of his images of boudoirs, brothels and drinking holes have entered mainstream culture as entertaining insights into a past world, there are also overlooked or under-explored aspects of his work.

The print of *The Discovery*, rarely acknowledged as part of Hogarth's canon, is explicitly racist. His lost painting of *A Midnight Modern Conversation* has achieved genuinely iconic status as an image of comically outrageous male conviviality, copied, reproduced and emulated multiple times in a range of media. Shown here with a version produced in a Dutch colonial context by the American painter John Greenwood, the elements of exploitation and subjection immanent in the image may be more readily seen. The sugary drinks and foods guzzled by men in the taverns and brothels of Europe, the mahogany of their furniture, the tobacco they smoked, the silks and cottons they wore – all were the products of colonial violence and unfree labour. With its colonial setting, Greenwood's image is exceptional in expressing visually, in the bowed and collapsed bodies of the enslaved Black figures, the structures of exploitation this involved. These are, surely, hard to swallow as merely humorous props, and the image of male conviviality they support is disturbed. This might be disregarded as merely an offensive colonial variation on an authentic and far more appealing Hogarthian type. But perhaps, too, our placid acceptance of the Hogarthian point of view should also be questioned?

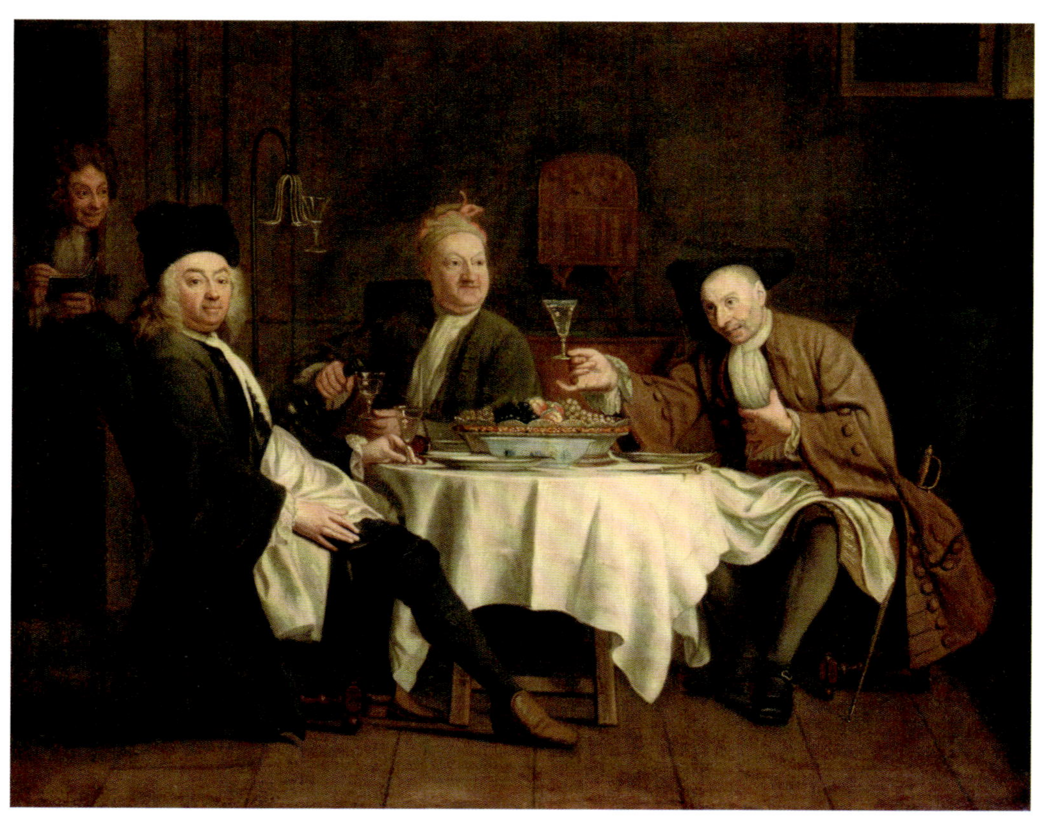

JACQUES AUTREAU   *The Wine Drinkers, or The poet Piron (1689–1773)*
at table with his friends Vadé and Collé   1747

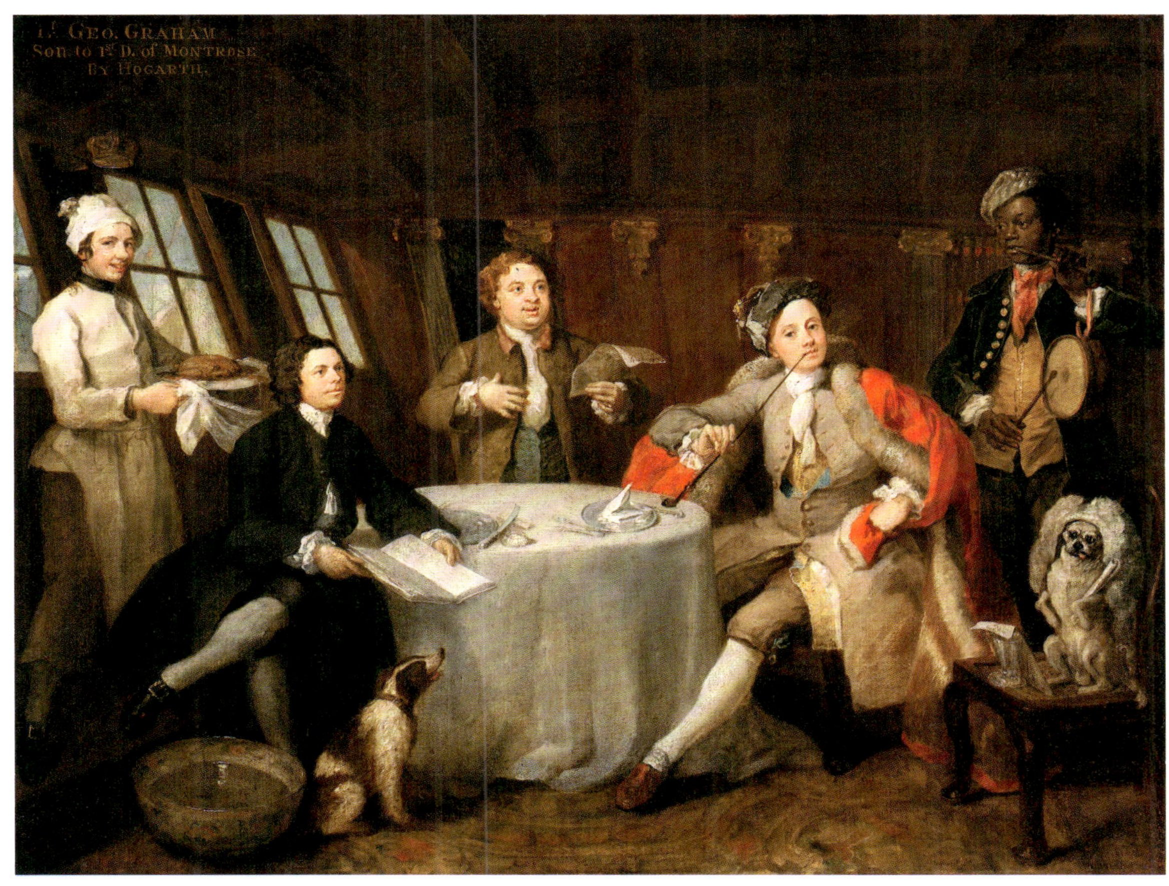

WILLIAM HOGARTH   *Captain Lord George Graham, 1715–47, in his Cabin*   1742–4

Unusually the punchbowl in this scene of male socia-
bility is filled with water, not alcohol, reflecting Lord
George Graham's recuperation from a breakdown.
But the trappings of masculine conviviality remain:
Graham is dressed in a turban, suggesting the informality of the gathering, and his wig rests comically
on the pug (perhaps a stand-in for Hogarth). Food is
being brought to the table, while they are entertained
with singing and music played by a Black servant
boy, positioned in the margins of the picture frame.

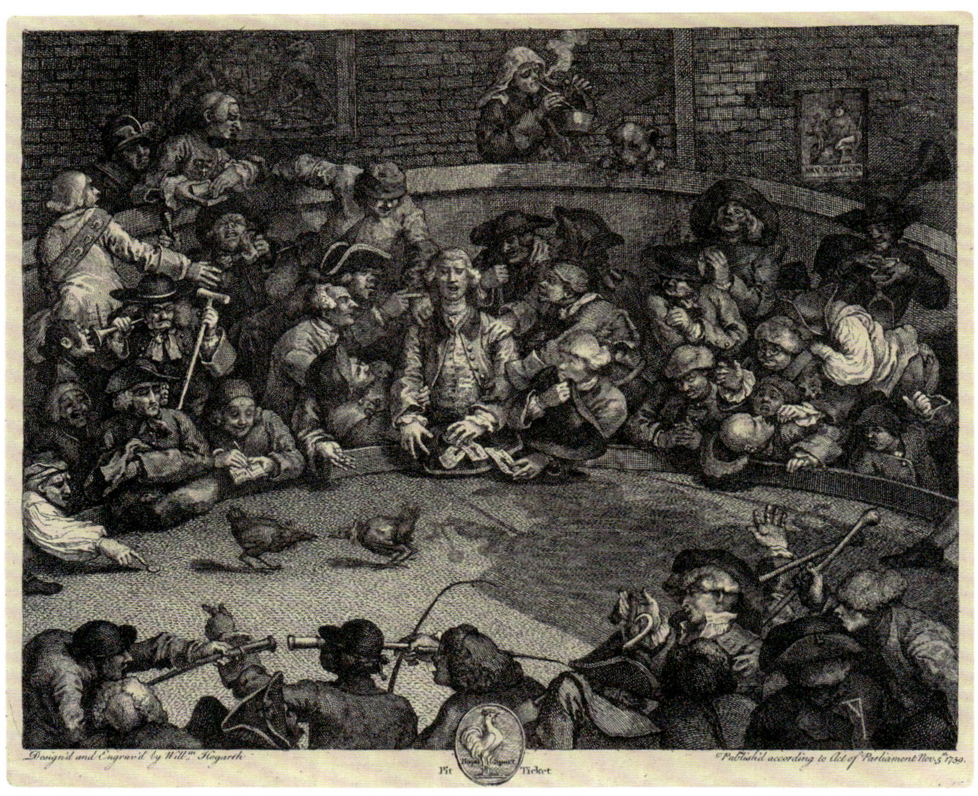

WILLIAM HOGARTH   *The Cockpit (or Pit Ticket)*   1759

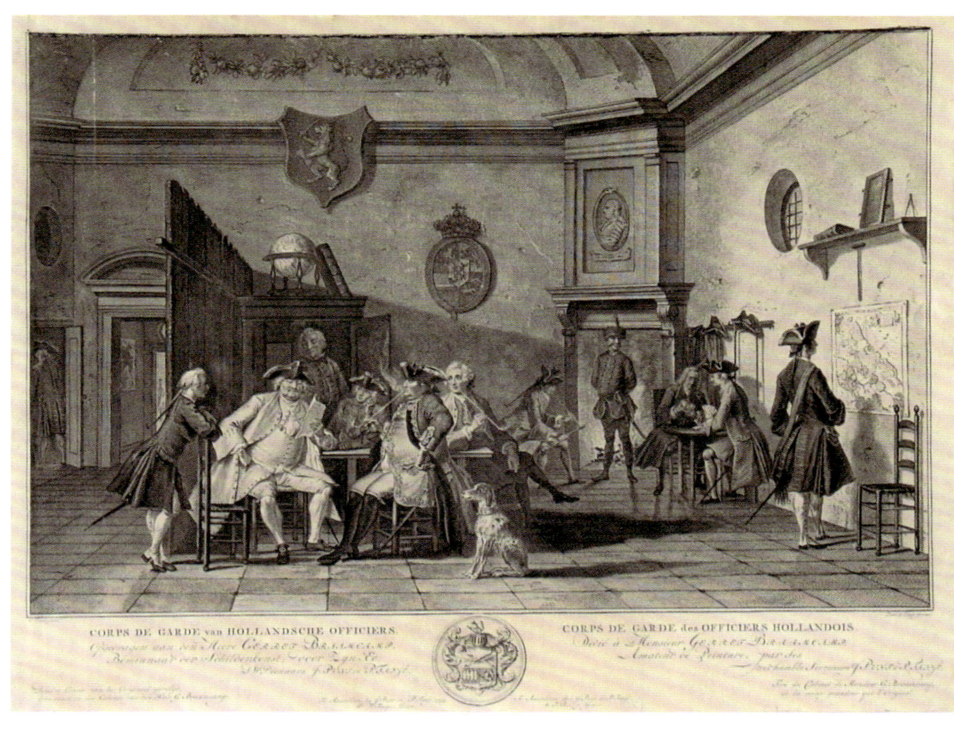

JAN PUNT AND PIETER TANJÉ AFTER CORNELIS TROOST
Guardhouse of Dutch Officers   1754

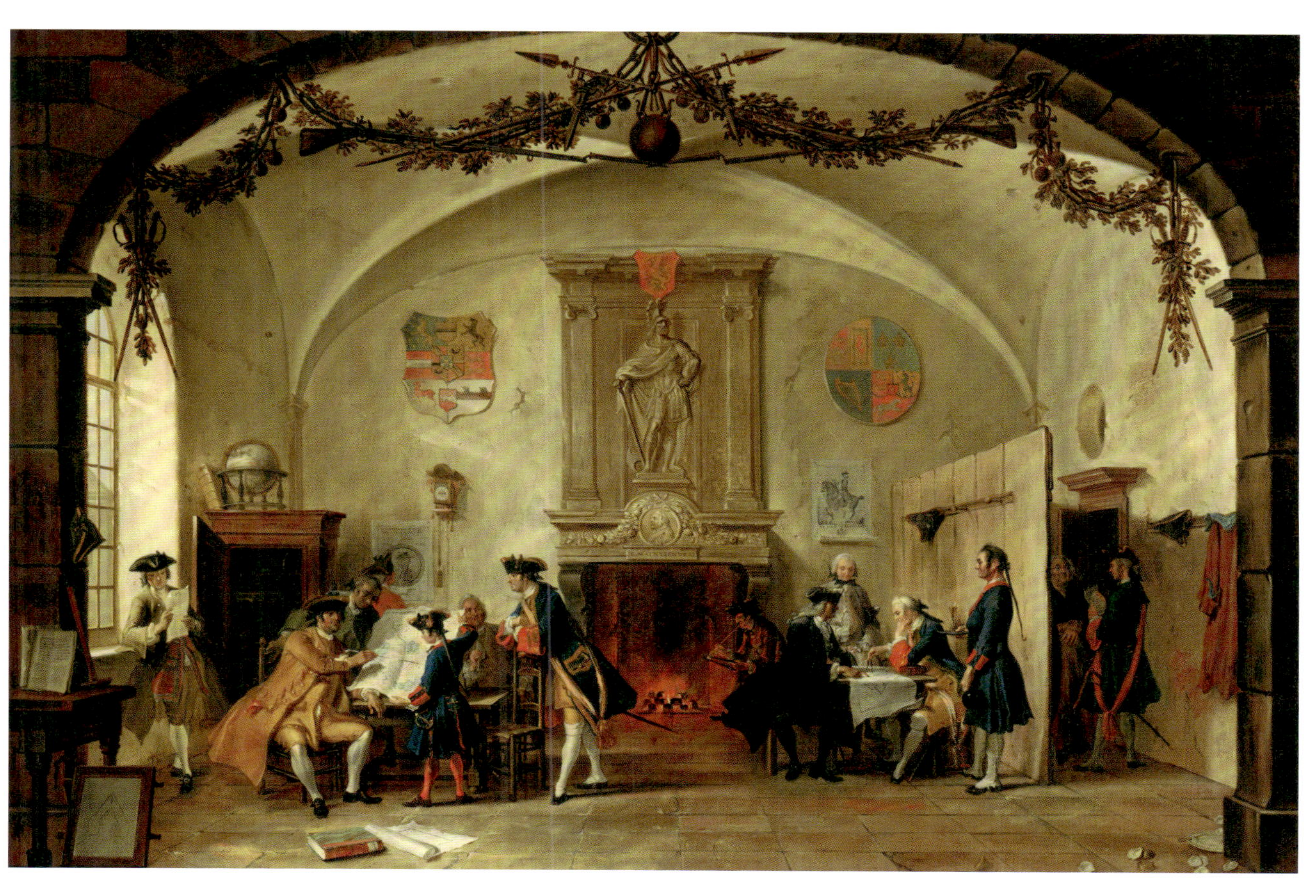

CORNELIS TROOST *Guardroom Scene* 1747

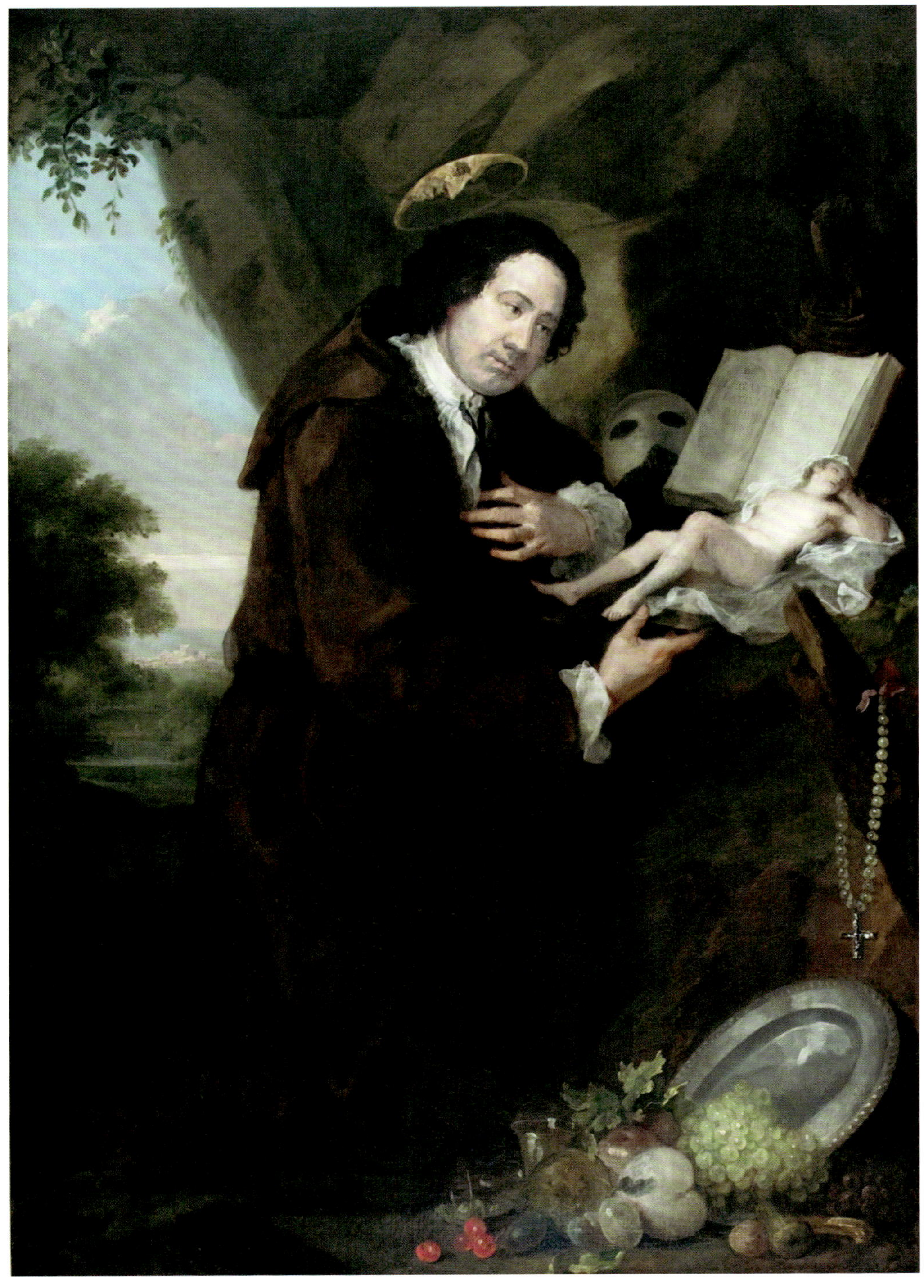

WILLIAM HOGARTH   *Sir Francis Dashwood at his Devotions*   c.1733–9

118

This portrait plays upon Dashwood's reputation as a notorious libertine. He is blasphemously shown dressed as a monk and worshipping a nude woman in the place of a crucifix.

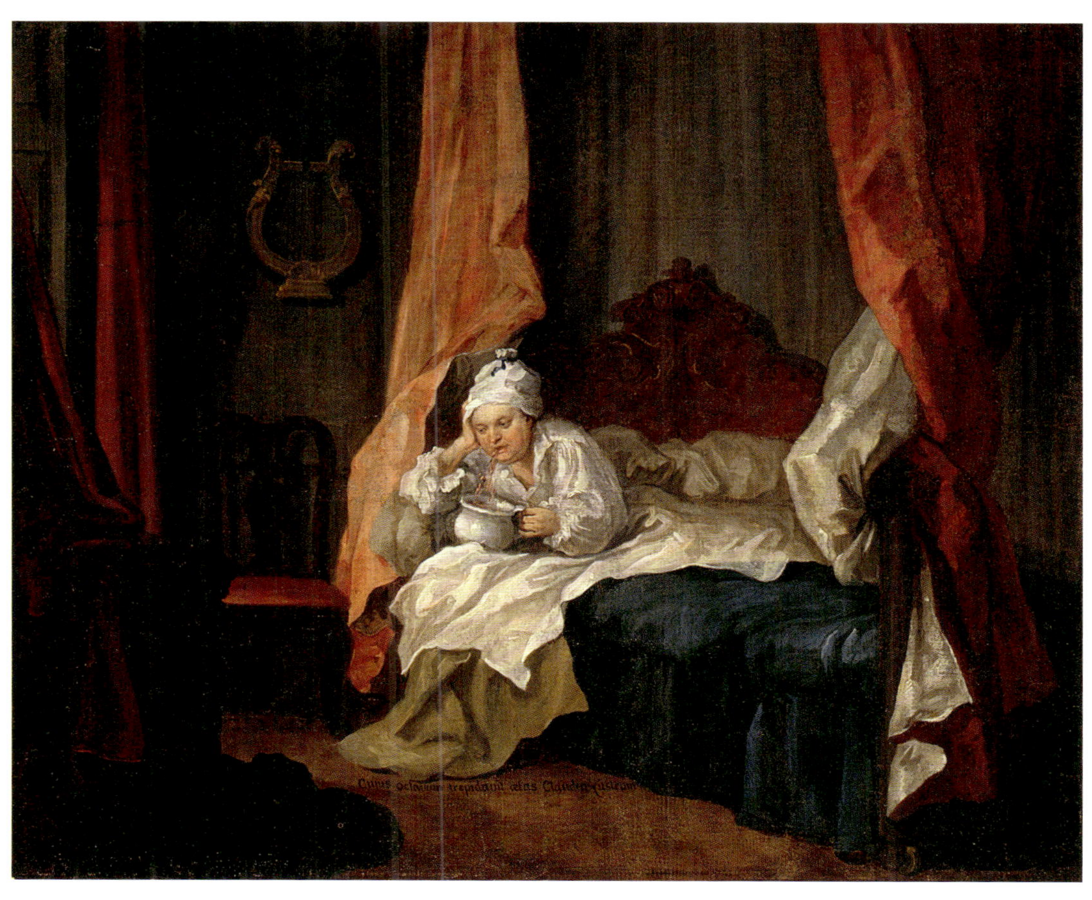

WILLIAM HOGARTH   *Francis Matthew Schutz in Bed*   c.1755–60

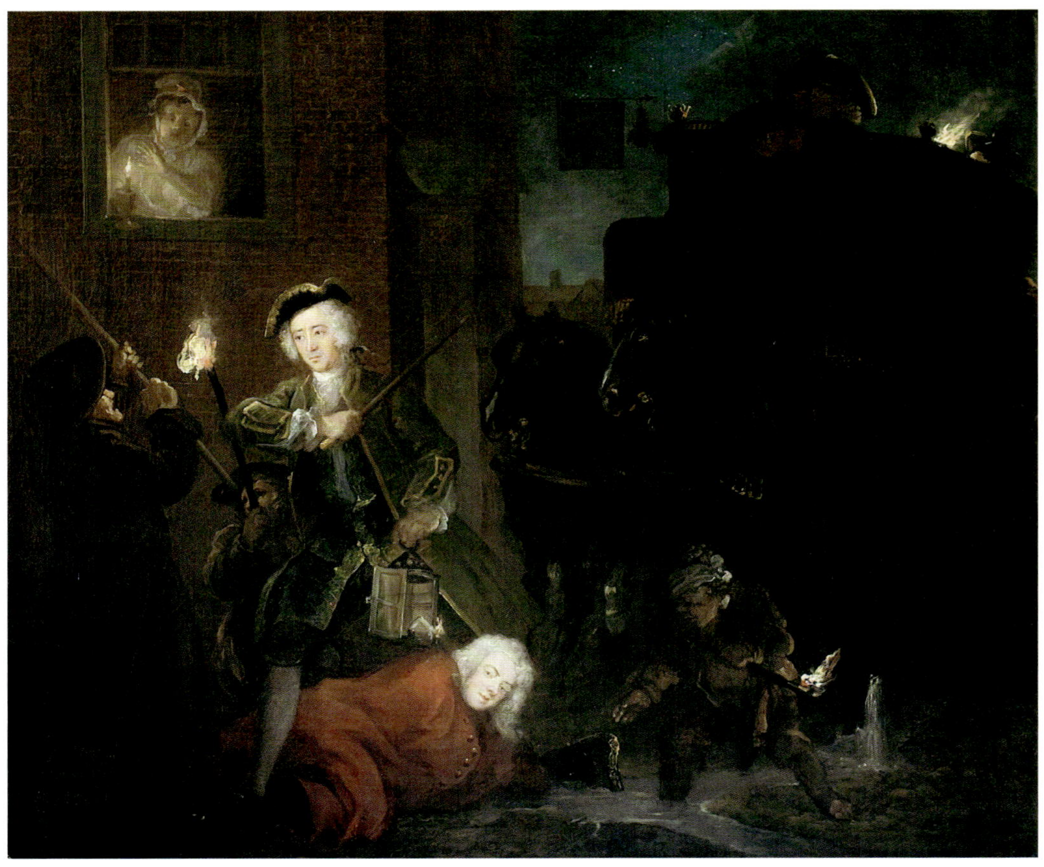

WILLIAM HOGARTH   *A Night Encounter*   c.1738–9

GEORGE VERTUE AND WILLIAM HOGARTH
The Reverend Mr Benjamin Hoadly BD   1704–16

A conventional engraved portrait of the bishop
'customised' by the addition of devilish horns,
asses ears and wings. The print's early history and
a personal testimony suggest the additions were
made by Hogarth. A handwritten inscription in Latin
satirically states, 'Painted from life by his wife'.

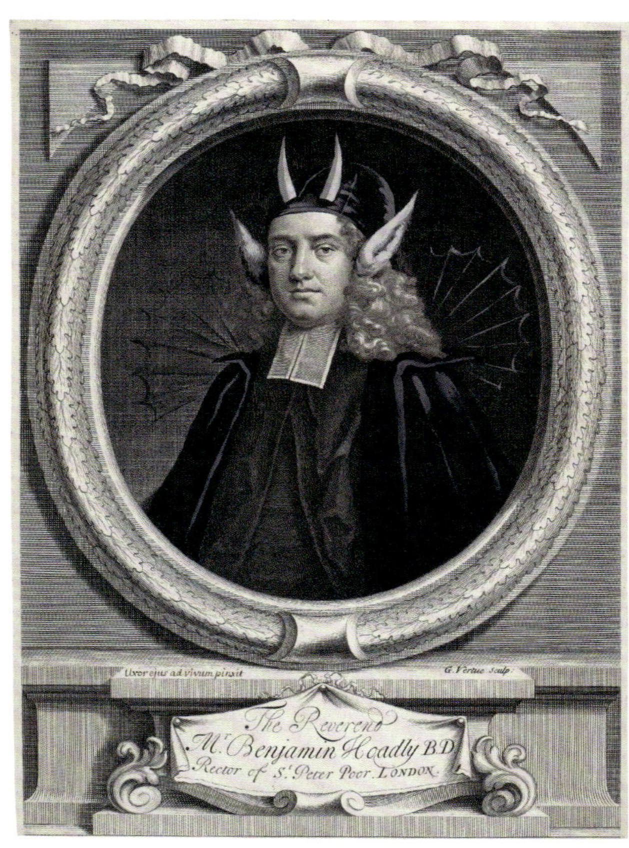

120

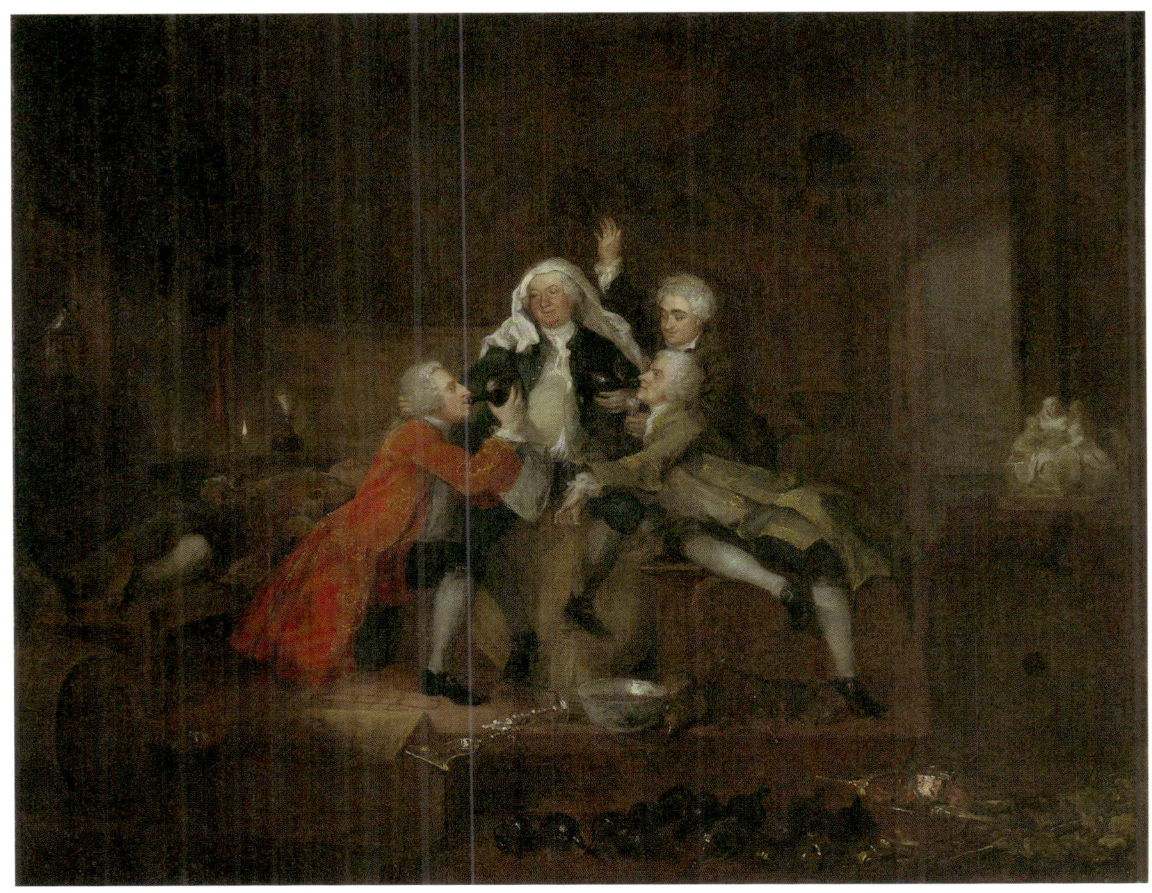

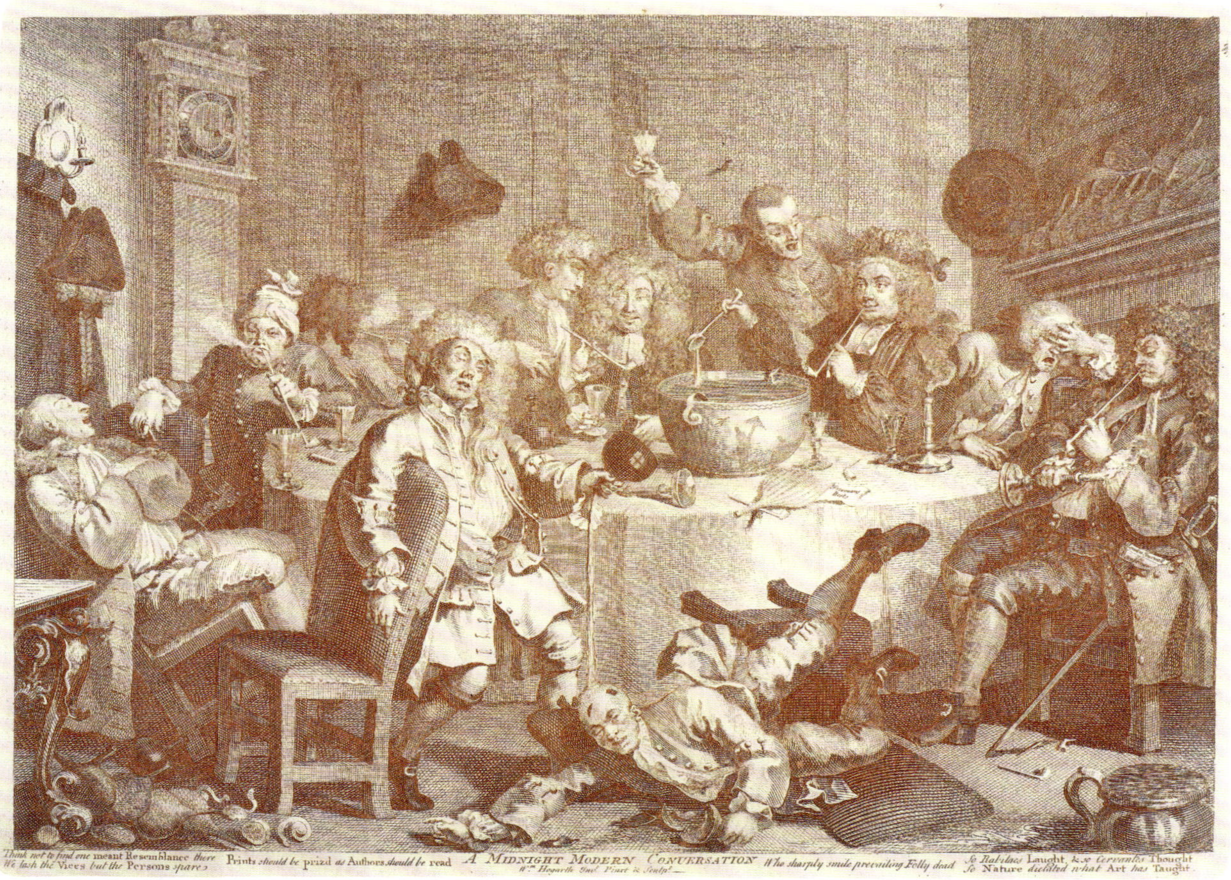

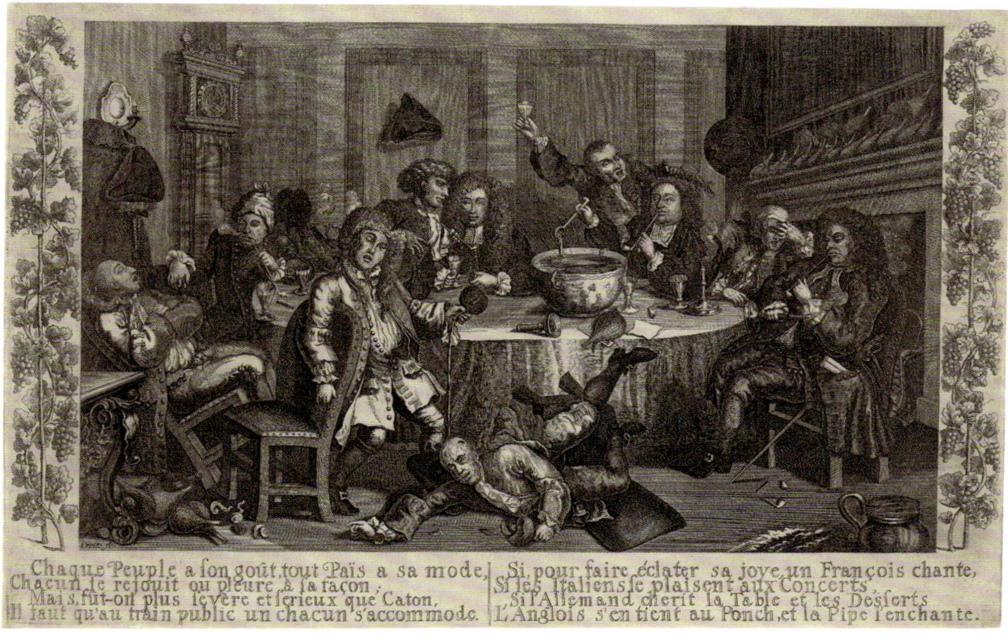

WILLIAM HOGARTH   *A Midnight Modern Conversation*   1733

ERNST LUDWIG CREITE AFTER WILLIAM HOGARTH
A Midnight Modern Conversation   1733–50

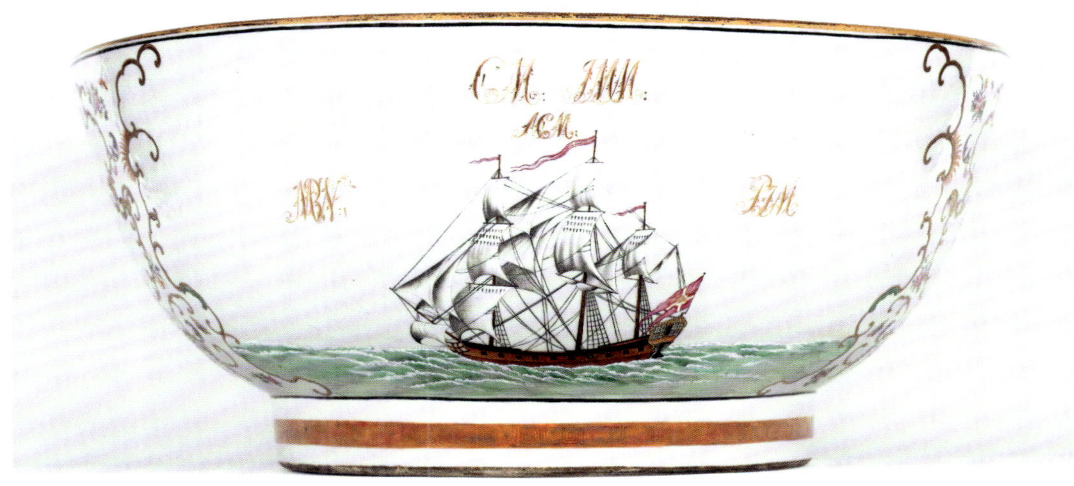

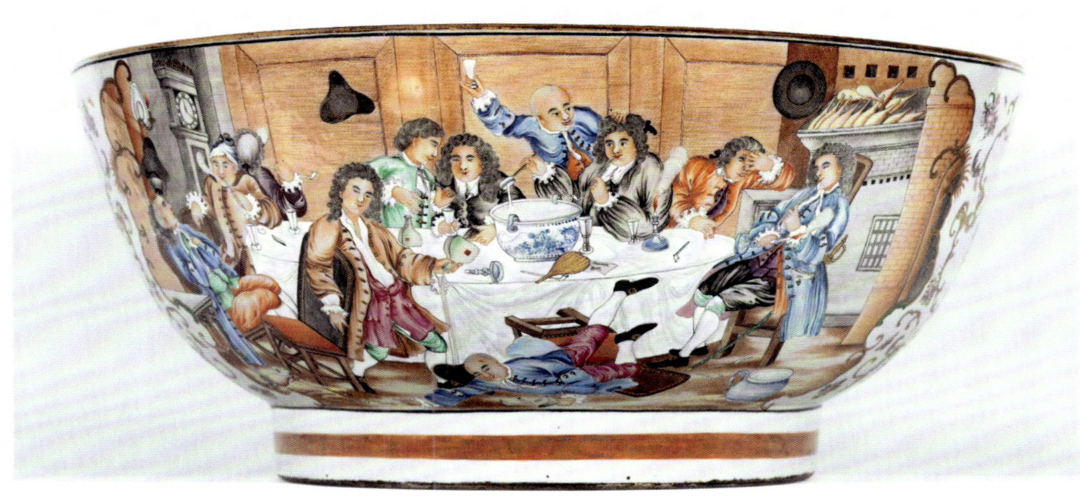

UNKNOWN ARTIST AFTER WILLIAM HOGARTH
Punchbowl featuring Hogarth's 'A Midnight Modern Conversation'   1780s

← Hogarth's *A Midnight Modern Conversation* was widely reproduced and circulated. The German-Dutch artist Ernst Creite made this engraving and included a French inscription to appeal to the larger European market.

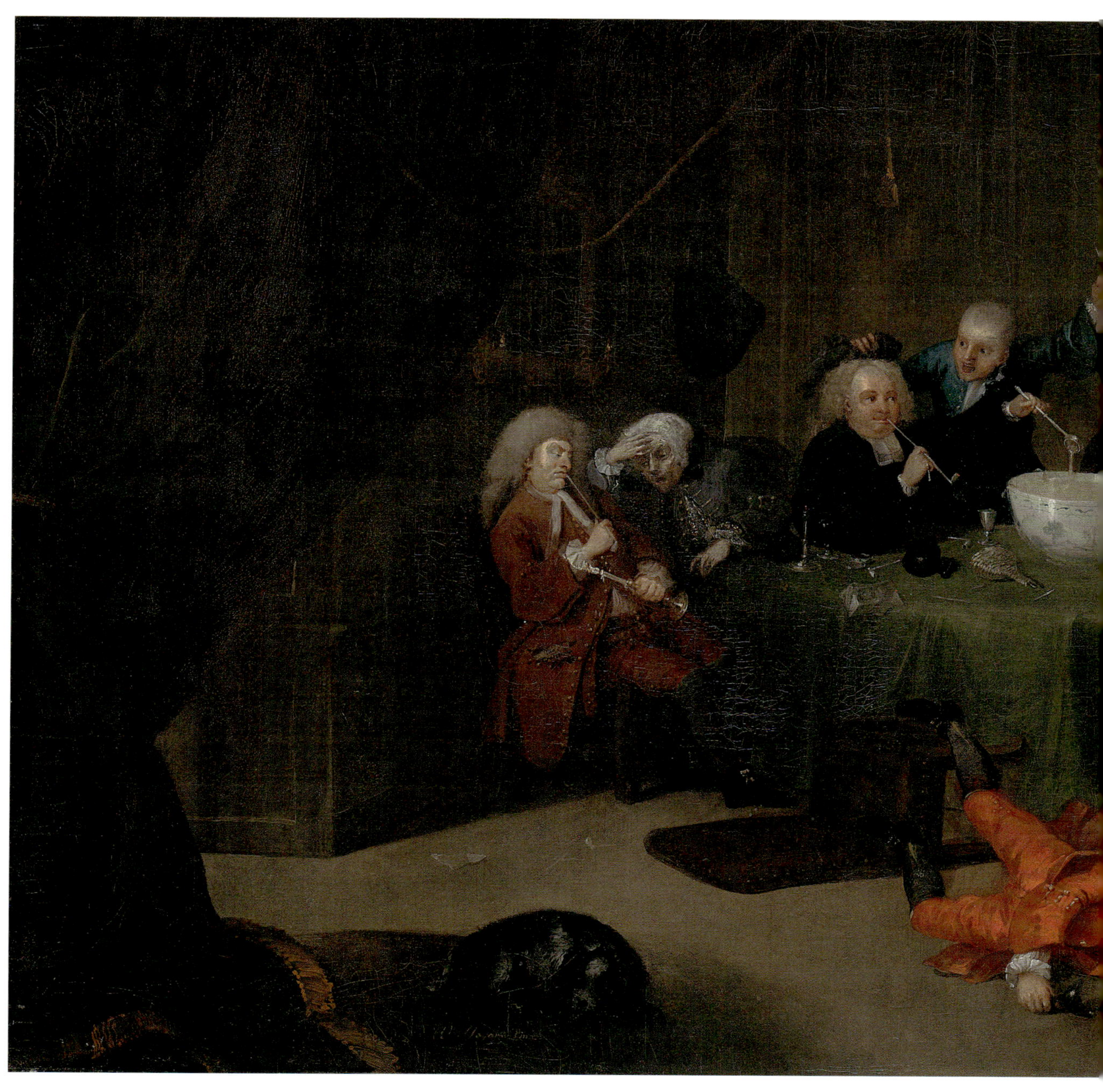

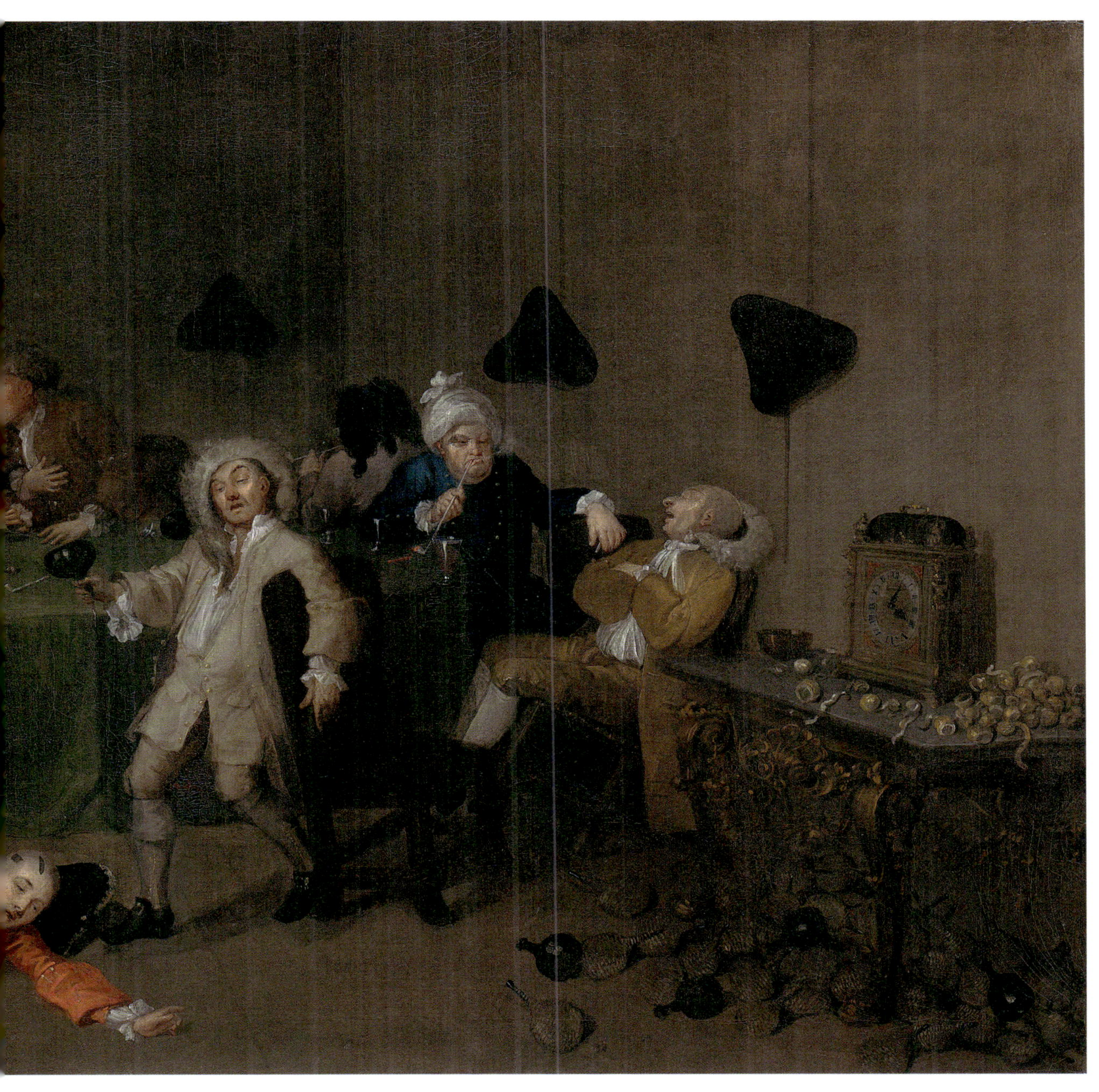

UNKNOWN ARTIST AFTER WILLIAM HOGARTH
A Midnight Modern Conversation   c.1732

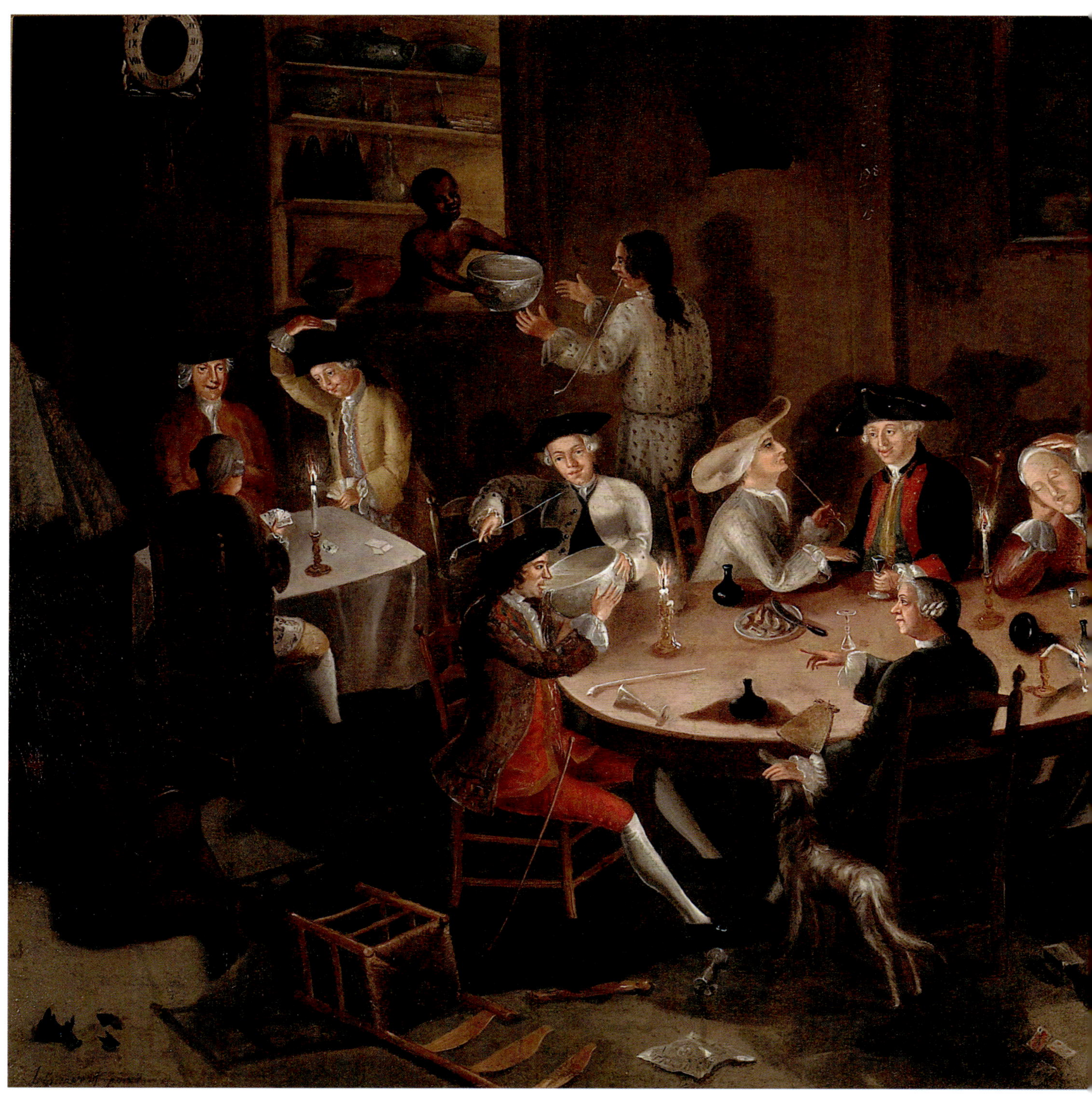

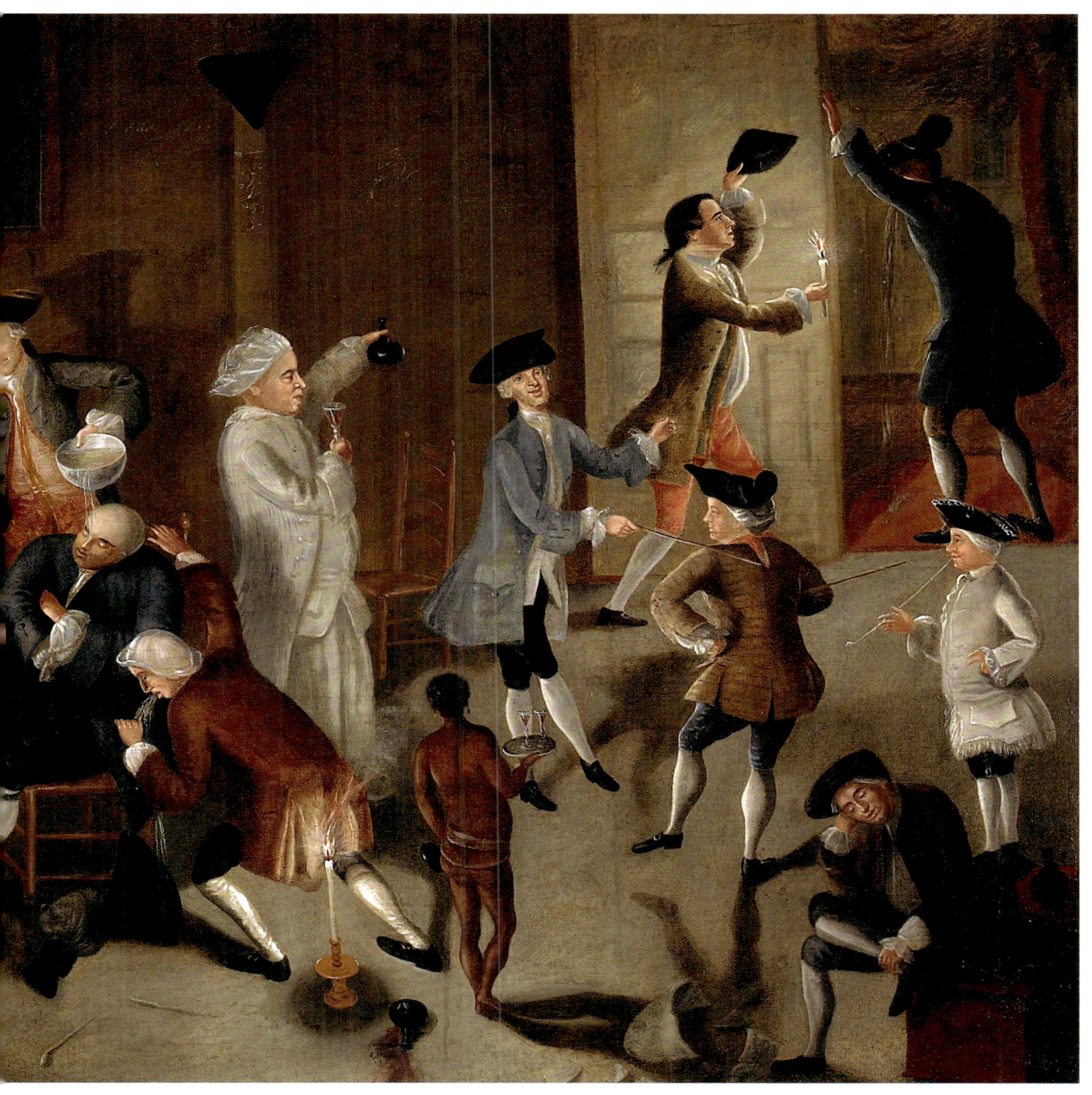

JOHN GREENWOOD   *Sea Captains Carousing in Surinam*   c.1752–8

AN AMERICAN PARTY
IN A DUTCH COLONY

GERHARD DE KOK

From the diary that the painter John Greenwood kept during his stay in Suriname (1752–8), one gets the impression that the inhabitants of this Dutch colony loved strong drinks. The men started the day with a good liquor and switched to wine in the afternoon. 'They hold it very healthy,' wrote a disapproving Greenwood.[1]

One of the best-known paintings by Greenwood depicts a group of men in Suriname overindulging in alcoholic beverages. *Sea Captains Carousing in Surinam* c.1752–8 (pp.126–7) shows a chaotic tavern scene, clearly inspired by William Hogarth's *A Midnight Modern Conversation* (pp.122, 124–5). Inebriated men fill the picture, although a bowl filled with punch is still going around. But the captains depicted in the painting were not inhabitants of Suriname, nor were they Dutch. Instead, the painting shows a group of Americans hailing from New England ports, and Greenwood himself was also an American. Born in Boston, the young painter left his hometown for Suriname in 1752, arriving there aboard the *Rebecca* in December of that year. But what was he doing in a Dutch colony on the South American mainland, and why did he find so many of his countrymen in its capital Paramaribo?

Suriname was first settled by English colonists from Barbados in 1650. It quickly grew into a sugar-producing plantation colony, where enslaved Africans, transported from various parts of Western Africa, toiled the plantations for White colonists. For the planters, the fertile ground of Suriname promised great riches. Nature had been 'luxuriant in filling this part of the world', Greenwood noted in his diary a century later, and the soil supported 'every thing that is planted into it'.[2] The burgeoning colony attracted international attention and, during the Anglo-Dutch war of 1665–7, a Dutch fleet appeared in front of Paramaribo. Within a day, Suriname became a Dutch colony and the hostile takeover was made official in the Anglo-Dutch Treaty of Breda (1667).

One of the main attractions of Suriname for the Dutch were the sugar plantations. Hidden in the upper left corner of the Greenwood painting, behind the bartender, are two sugarloaves. These cone-shaped lumps of sugar belonged in the bar because the sugar was used to sweeten the punch. But the loaves also signify a prime reason why the Dutch were so keen to acquire Suriname in the 1660s. In their minds, the sugar-producing colony could replace Dutch Brazil, which they had conquered from the Portuguese in 1630 and which was reconquered by the Portuguese in 1654. Raw sugar, harvested from sugar cane by enslaved Africans, was a valuable commodity. It was also an indispensable input for the Dutch sugar refineries, which constituted an important part of the Dutch economy.

These high expectations were not immediately met. The first decade under Dutch rule brought about an exodus of English planters, who took many hundreds of enslaved Africans with them. To make matters worse for the colonists, the indigenous peoples of Suriname started an all-out war to try and expel the Europeans once and for all. This did not succeed and in 1682 the Dutch States-General laid down a new charter for the colony. It was the start of a remarkable growth in the plantation economy of Suriname. This growth was to benefit the Dutch Republic, which is why the charter stipulated that all trade and shipping with Suriname was only allowed to Dutch citizens sailing from Dutch ports. According to this original charter, the American captains in Greenwood's painting had no right to be in Paramaribo at all.

At the turn of the eighteenth century, there were about a hundred plantations in Suriname. This number grew to about 300 plantations by around 1750.[3] Many of them produced sugar, but another commodity was on the rise: coffee. After the successful introduction of coffee planting in the 1710s, the number of plantations producing this valuable commodity quickly rose. By the time Greenwood arrived in Suriname, the number of sugar plantations was in a steady decline as coffee became increasingly important. When Greenwood stepped off the *Rebecca* in 1752, Suriname numbered about 40,000 inhabitants.[4] An astounding ninety-five per cent (38,000) belonged to the Black enslaved population, who had either been born in the colony or brought on one of the many slave ships that arrived every year. The European community was small and diverse, consisting not only of people of Dutch descent, but also immigrants from France, the German lands, Scandinavia and England.

The slave society of Suriname was widely seen as one of the harshest in the region. Voltaire seemingly alluded to this in his *Candide* (1759), when his protagonist meets a beaten-up, enslaved Black man in 'Surinam, belonging to the Dutch'. 'This is the price at which you eat sugar in Europe', Voltaire lets the Black man proclaim.[5] The most famous images of Suriname slavery accompanied John Gabriel Stedman's book *The Narrative of a Five Years Expedition against the Revolted Negroes of Surinam* (1796) and these depict gruesome forms of punishments against enslaved Africans.[6] Such punishments must have made an unforgettable impression on all who witnessed them, including Greenwood. During his time in Suriname, the painter attended some executions of Black people and made notes about it in his diary.[7]

The Black men he painted in his tavern scene were likely enslaved persons from the owner of the place and from visitors, having to serve and entertain the guests or wait for their owners to finish drinking.

Early modern Suriname was an isolated place. The colony was surrounded by dense forests and the ocean to the north was its most important link with the outside world. The main international (trading) connections of Suriname connected the colony to the Dutch Republic, either through bilateral shipping or via the triangular (slave ship) route. The Dutch States-General would have liked these connections to be the only connections of the colony, but the strict rules of the mercantilist charter turned out to be highly impractical. The colonists imported a large part of their foodstuffs from overseas and Dutch ships were unable to meet the demand. Especially damaging to the economic viability of the colony was the shortage of draft animals: horses were used on plantations to power sugar mills, but the European horses seldom survived the long transatlantic crossing. Suriname needed another lifeline, a lifeline connecting it to the North American mainland.

Since the last decades of the seventeenth century, American vessels had regularly brought horses and food to Suriname. While the legality of this trade was disputed by the Dutch directors of the Suriname Society – the Amsterdam-based institution that was responsible for governing the colony – it was clear to the colonists that this American connection was indispensable. For this reason, it was finally legalised in 1704, although it remained heavily regulated. American captains were only allowed (and even required) to import horses and a small selection of necessities, including soap and tobacco. As exports, the American vessels could only carry molasses, rum and wood. Lucrative products such as raw sugar, coffee, cocoa and cotton were reserved for the Dutch market.

Despite the restrictions, Suriname attracted many American vessels, especially from New England. From the American perspective, the trade was also important. Many of the northern colonies had a negative balance of trade with Europe, and the Suriname connection helped Americans to pay for European imports on their home market. The North America to Suriname route was heavily traversed by ships: in the first half of the eighteenth century, more than 1,550 American vessels anchored near Paramaribo. For the whole period between 1667 and 1795 (when the Suriname Society was dissolved), the number is about 4,000. In the 1740s, the Americans brought more than 600 horses per year to the colony.[8]

This brings us back to the American captains painted by an American painter in a Dutch colony. Many of them have been identified as prominent traders, some of whom went on to play important roles in American politics, including signing the American Declaration of Independence in 1776. Their presence in the plantation colony Suriname was by no means a coincidence, for they followed well-trodden trade routes. Paramaribo was very different from their hometowns: a small, tropical city surrounded by slave plantations. The city offered few opportunities for leisure, while the captains and the crews often had to wait quite a long time until all their trade deals were concluded. Taverns like the one depicted by Greenwood would have been welcome places to pass the time and meet fellow countrymen.

Greenwood also painted himself into the picture: he is in the upper right, holding a candle and about to leave the scene. Greenwood wanted to leave Boston to visit Europe and see the works of the European masters. Why he chose to visit Suriname first is unclear, but it must have been easy for him to arrange a passage to the Dutch colony. In fact, he shared his vessel with at least two horses, because that is the number of horses that made it to Paramaribo alive on the *Rebecca*.[9] Greenwood stayed in Suriname for several years and it acted as a lucrative stepping stone to Europe. The young painter was commissioned for no fewer than 113 portraits during his years in the colony. Unfortunately, they have all been lost.[10] Greenwood finally left Paramaribo for Amsterdam as a passenger aboard the Dutch ship *Coffijboom* (coffee tree) on 15 April 1758.[11] While he continued making art in Europe, Greenwood was even more successful as an art dealer. After a period in the Dutch Republic, the artist settled in London. Coincidentally, one of Greenwood's assignments there was to sell the works William Hogarth had left behind in his studio when he died.[12]

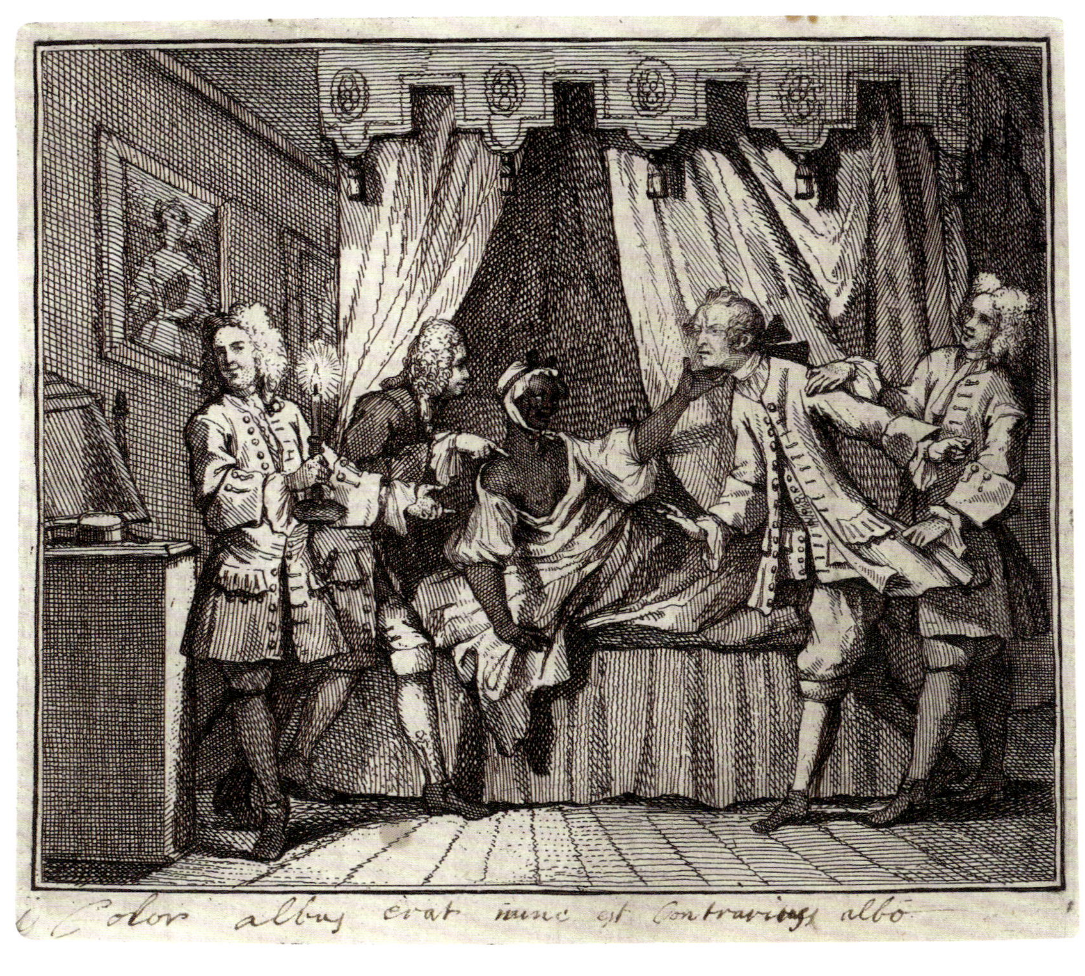

WILLIAM HOGARTH

Qui color albus erat, nunc est contrarius albo. 'The Discovery'   1743

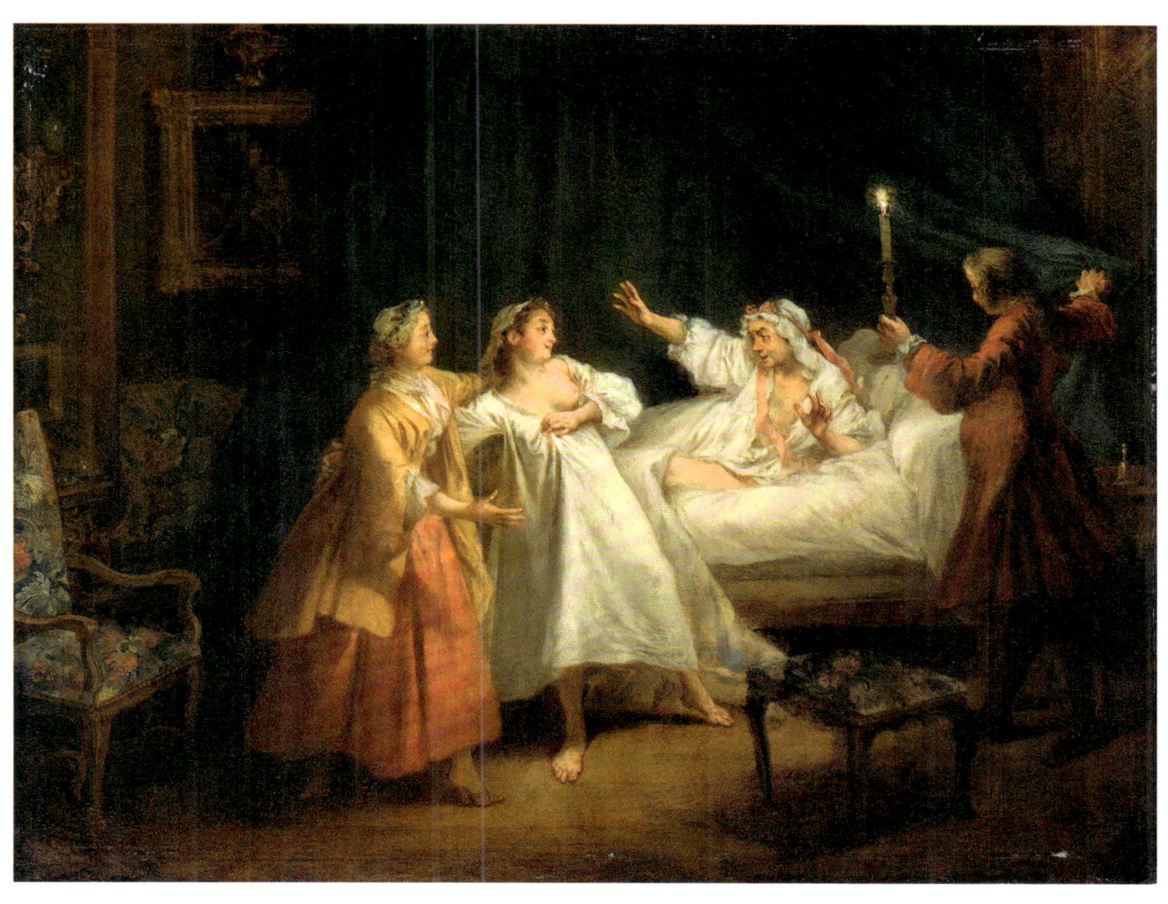

NICOLAS LANCRET   *The Gascon punished (La Fontaine, Contes)*   1738

BETWEEN THE SHEETS

CORA GILROY-WARE AND TEMI ODUMOSU

William Hogarth's *The Discovery* 1743

I saw an opening in Ovid. In the rosy light I chased him in and out of glades. I met Cyclops and Venus and kind old lovers turned to oak and linden trees. Stealing a glimpse round Niobe's shoulder, I felt the lurch of the east wind and realised then that there was so much more to find. So I swore to Ovid I'd be back. But now I see you've claimed him. You've made him your co-conspirator, pouring his words into that blank, unloving mould.

As far as we know, William Hogarth never portrayed a scene from Ovid's *Metamorphoses*.[1] Twenty-four years after his death, however, one of his previously unpublished private prints, *The Discovery*, was reproduced by notable collector and engraver Samuel Ireland, accompanied with a caption from the ceaselessly popular Roman poem. First produced in 1743 for the amusement of a small group of friends, the work depicts four smartly dressed men gathered round a four-poster bed, which serves as a stage, an event, and the scene of an unwieldy transformation. The bed's curtains have been drawn to reveal a woman whose legs and lower torso are enveloped in layers of creased sheets. She reaches out a hand to stroke the chin of one of the men. This gesture, this touch, is the central focus of the bodily drama. To the left, one man holding a candle points to what is happening; another points to the woman's body. On the right, the fourth figure supports the man being stroked. Their bodies are in conversation, working in concert, exchanging meanings.

The woman is Black, African or Afro-Caribbean; put another way, she is made visible as a racialised subject. Who is she? Why is she here? What does she tell us? Her physical pose, in this bed, surrounded by four White men, is oddly perpendicular: an L-shape, suggesting that she has the ability to balance on the side of her left hip without the support of her arm, while holding her upper body straight. She slightly floats in the space between the other figures, an awkward Venus – not as delicately drawn as the goddess in Botticelli's *Venus and Mars*, but still carrying this classical repertoire in articulation.

What is the work that Black Venus is being called on to do? What is foretold by her cross-hatched figuration as ink on paper? Once the engraver scratches their design into copper, a commitment is sealed. The image is made. The desire to impress … express … is no longer just imagining. Through effort, image becomes matter.

The print's title leads to an interpretation of the expression on the central man's face as one of surprise, yet its emotional tenor remains ambiguous.[2] For, what does it mean to receive this woman's touch and attention? And what is really being 'discovered'? The supporting man is tugging at the central man's coat, which we could read as a reminder, or a warning, an implication that he needs reining in. But the saying goes that to ride on a person's coat-tails is to benefit from their success, and the slight smile on his face suggests that the figure who tugs might want in on the action, as if his own curious desire for the woman is blocked by the man in between. This is one of several suggestive details that mark this print as playful and intimate, a joke between 'boys'.

The Discovery is visually indebted to a painting entitled *The Gascon punished* (p.133) by one of Hogarth's French contemporaries, Nicolas Lancret. Lancret's work depicts another play on identity, showing the final moment in Jean de la Fontaine's bawdy and somewhat convoluted tale of a young man tricked into spending the night with another man, or so he is led to believe. The young man has been caught bragging about his conquest of a local maiden, one of whose friends hears of his lies and devises a plot to humiliate him. She convinces him to spend the night with her own husband, asking him to pretend to be her as a practical joke. The man gives in and, dressed in women's nightclothes, creeps into the bed, believing all throughout the tense and uncomfortable night that he is sleeping next to a man who might pounce on him at any second, thinking him to be his wife. At dawn, the maiden's friend and her husband enter the room and the maiden reveals herself as his bedfellow. She teases him, exposing her naked breast and delighting in the fact that he has unwittingly gotten so close to the body he claimed to have seduced. His humiliation is twofold. Not only is his lie brought to light, but it is also shown just how easily he was manipulated into wearing a woman's dress and – so he thought – sharing a bed with another man.

In *The Discovery*, the joke is on the central man, whose friends have played a trick on him by substituting one of his usual mistresses for a woman with darker skin (the woman that should have been there is, however, still present as a portrait on the wall behind the bed).

It is possible to give a proper name to the man who finds his chin caressed in *The Discovery*. He is a relation of Hogarth's father-in-law James Thornhill – an actor and theatre manager named John Highmore, who was known for his womanising. It has also been suggested that we might identify the woman as an infamous London prostitute named Harriot.[3] But there were other women, Black Londoners just like her, making a dangerous and precarious living in this city at the economic heart of the transatlantic slave trade. In such a context, when does a 'Black Venus' become knowable? When does she come fully into view?[4] By contrast, Highmore's identity is clear, and we understand that Hogarth sought to poke fun at him by calling attention to his licentious ways.

Hogarth's work is underpinned by several cultural references that address the intended viewer: White, male, anglophone, literate, culturally affluent, and including both Highmore and the artist. To tune into these worldviews and sensibilities is also to confront the attitudes provoked by the presence of African and African-descendant people in Britain during the eighteenth century. In visual culture, and especially humorous imagery, Black women appear as an index for taboo colonial 'pleasures' and privileges, physically exaggerated to contrast with European beauty norms, and/or typecast as sex workers. This is a particularly troubling dimension of the xenophobia and contempt which typified jokes about a whole range of foreigners. Englishmen depicted as choosing or fraternising with the Black woman were thus having their tastes called into question. Hogarth's in-joke relies on a reductive racial imaginary, and he uses this Black woman's presence to add friction and risk to the scene, her very presence in Highmore's nocturnal antics being 'symbolic of illicit desire'.[5]

After the artist's death, his wife Jane insisted that the original copperplate was destroyed.[6] However, despite attempts to suppress the image, Hogarth's private interests eventually became public; the boisterous mockery between notable friends, and the implication of intimacies with foreign women beyond the printed page, were now exposed. Due to Samuel Ireland's attentiveness to the artist's oeuvre, *The Discovery* resurfaced and came back into circulation. When published for enthusiasts in 1788, Ireland's re-engraving was contextualised with lines from Book 11 of *Metamorphoses*, in which Apollo punishes the raven by turning his plumage from snow-white to black. 'Qui color albus erat, nunc est contrarius albo': Who was once white, is now white's opposite.

For the unknowable, a moment to pause; a critical quietness for the stories slipped through cracks in the ledger. Stories ossified by classical inflections. The then and the now do not need to be mutually exclusive. We can travel in between what was intended and what could be. We can decide to recondition a pose or a gesture or a sleight of hand. Whose hand? … We can disrupt this 'continuous/discontinuous thing'.[7]

Samuel Ireland's addition of a phrase from Ovid, however, layers the scene with other possible meanings. It suggests that not only is the woman's blackness an issue but that also, and perhaps more disturbingly, she is not what (or where) she is supposed to be. Caution about appearances filtered through many aspects of eighteenth-century life, and humour was often the space where pretences and misrecognitions were punctured. Even in the more serious-minded realm of high culture, a palpable tension arose when outsider influences flouted epidermal expectations. Roughly thirty years after *The Discovery* was first engraved, and about a decade before Ireland's second version of the print, a young woman across the (Black) Atlantic was making a name for herself as a writer of classical poetry: something that she, a West African female captured as a child and brought to America, was not supposed (or even legally allowed) to be. Phillis Wheatley's short epic based on Book VI of Ovid's *Metamorphoses* appeared in 1773.[8] Part translation and part appropriation of the ancient author, Wheatley's poem describes the fate of Niobe, the queenly mother punished for her hubris.

> *She did not hate the woman in the bed. Within those sheets she saw a tree with gleaming fruits, heavy orbs somewhere between ripe fig and the memory of mango. She smelled perfume and set out to bring the woman home. But halfway up the mountain she saw Niobe painting while her babies turned to stone.*

For Wheatley, poetry, and especially classical poetry, provided a means of insisting that she was more than, in the words of June Jordan, 'bed bait'.[9] Her earliest readers were amazed, enraptured, confused and indignant, some accusing her of blindly imitating Alexander Pope.[10] When she came to England to recite her poems, she drew curious crowds but was also mocked for her speaking accent.[11] The woman in *The Discovery* is a figuration of what Wheatley was contending with and writing against. Long after her death in 1784, Wheatley continued to unsettle readers by refusing to conform to an abstract stereotype; twentieth-century critics expressed disappointment that her verse had 'almost nothing distinctively racial in it'.[12] Both during her lifetime and beyond, she enigmatically transformed stigma through writing that charted a path of emergent possibilities, an autonomous metamorphosis.

HIGH LIFE

The theatres, marketplaces and pleasure gardens of the eighteenth-century city created opportunities for the classes and sexes to mix as never before. At the same time, in drawing rooms and ballrooms the life of the elite was glimpsed and reported, in the press and in literary form, far more extensively than before. In these public and semi-public spaces there was a more fluid sense of identity than had prevailed within the rituals and physical divisions of the old, aristocratic world. This is evoked in visual representations by the blurred distinctions between performance and reality. In portraits and narrative pictures an exchange of glances, a pet or still-life detail could suggest subtexts and ironies. The delicious handling of paint and evocation of rich textiles and consumables, the glittering ceramics, silver and exposed flesh, were all meant to engage the senses and stimulate knowing, ironic ways of interpreting these scenes.

In France, Watteau developed the genre of the *fêtes galantes* – a genteel garden or parkland scene where the interplay between reality and fantasy, the theatrical and the everyday, was suggestively played out. This playful imagery became influential around Europe, as artists and artworks travelled. Watteau visited England towards the end of his short life; Hogarth's narrative series *Marriage A-la-Mode* self-consciously evokes French art and style. The virtuosic treatment of still-life details running through the series, perhaps most appealingly in the breakfast setting of *The Tête à Tête*, were intended to delight and entice. Hogarth was already painting like Chardin in the 1730s, and in 1743 met the artist in Paris when he was tracking down fine engravers to reproduce *Marriage A-la-Mode*. But whereas the delicate genre paintings of the French artist were contemplative objects, Hogarth's series was a hard-hitting story of greed, self-delusion and immorality.

The elements of erotic play and satire in eighteenth-century pictures of high life underpinned a generally flattering self-image for Europe's wealthy classes. But as Hogarth exposed, there were also faultlines that could contradict the claims to enlightenment and glamour, exposing more tense relationships. In many of his paintings there are glances between characters, or a subservient figure who fixes our gaze, which seem to offer a subversive, alternative interpretation of the scene. But this is not just true of pictures by Hogarth; something of the kind also surfaces occasionally in the work of other artists as well. In some instances there is the glimpse, even, of suppressed or marginalised subjectivities, of same-sex desire or of resistance to the dominant hierarchies of gender, race and class.

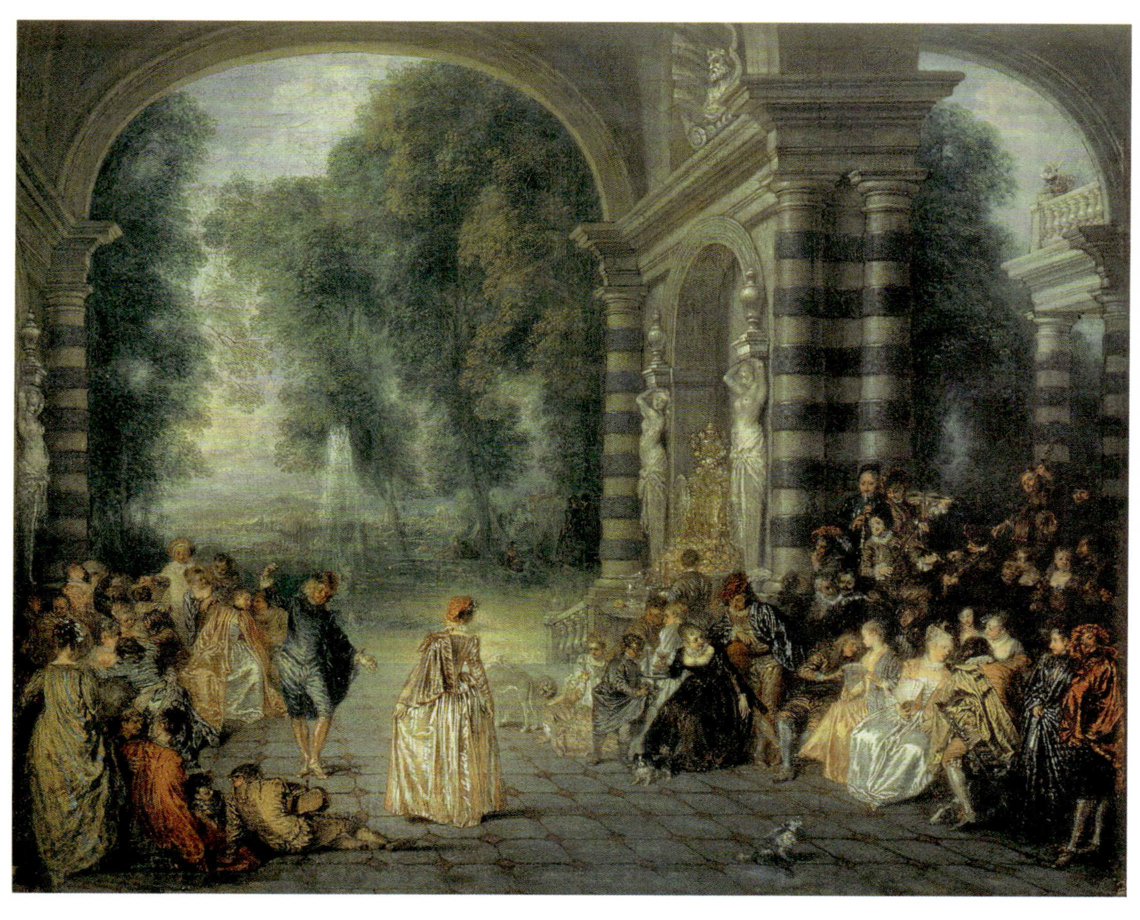

JEAN-ANTOINE WATTEAU   *The Pleasures of the Ball*   c.1715–17

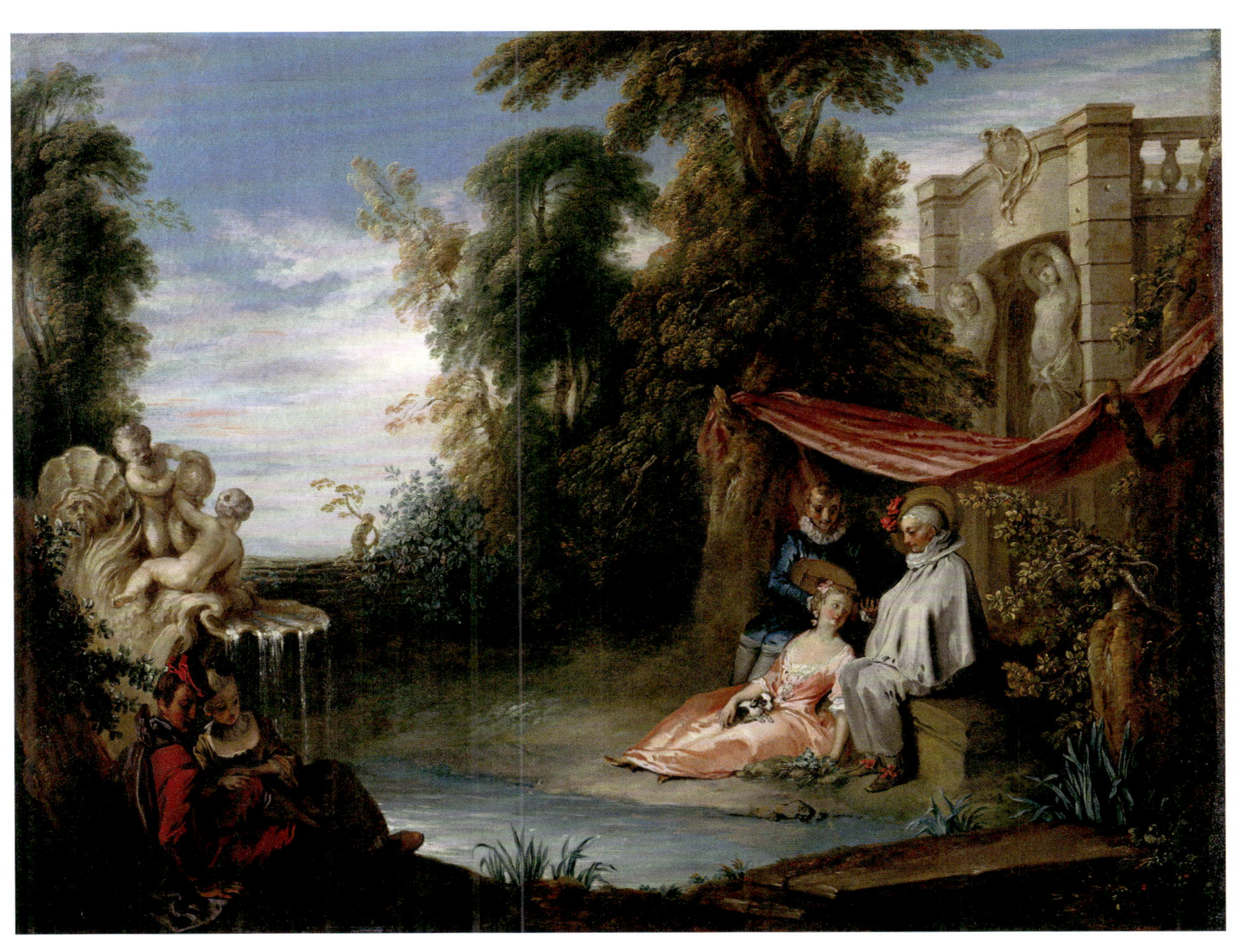

PHILIP MERCIER *Comedians by a Fountain* C.1735

If *fêtes galantes* blurred distinctions between theatre and reality, here the distinction between amorous play and sexual violence is also unclear. The picture seems to combine placid portraiture, illegible allegory and threat in a way which has yet to be sufficiently explained. It exposes the ambiguities that prevailed in the mixed genres of eighteenth-century painting.

Nicolas Lancret   *Group Portrait in a Landscape with Amorous Couple*   c.1737

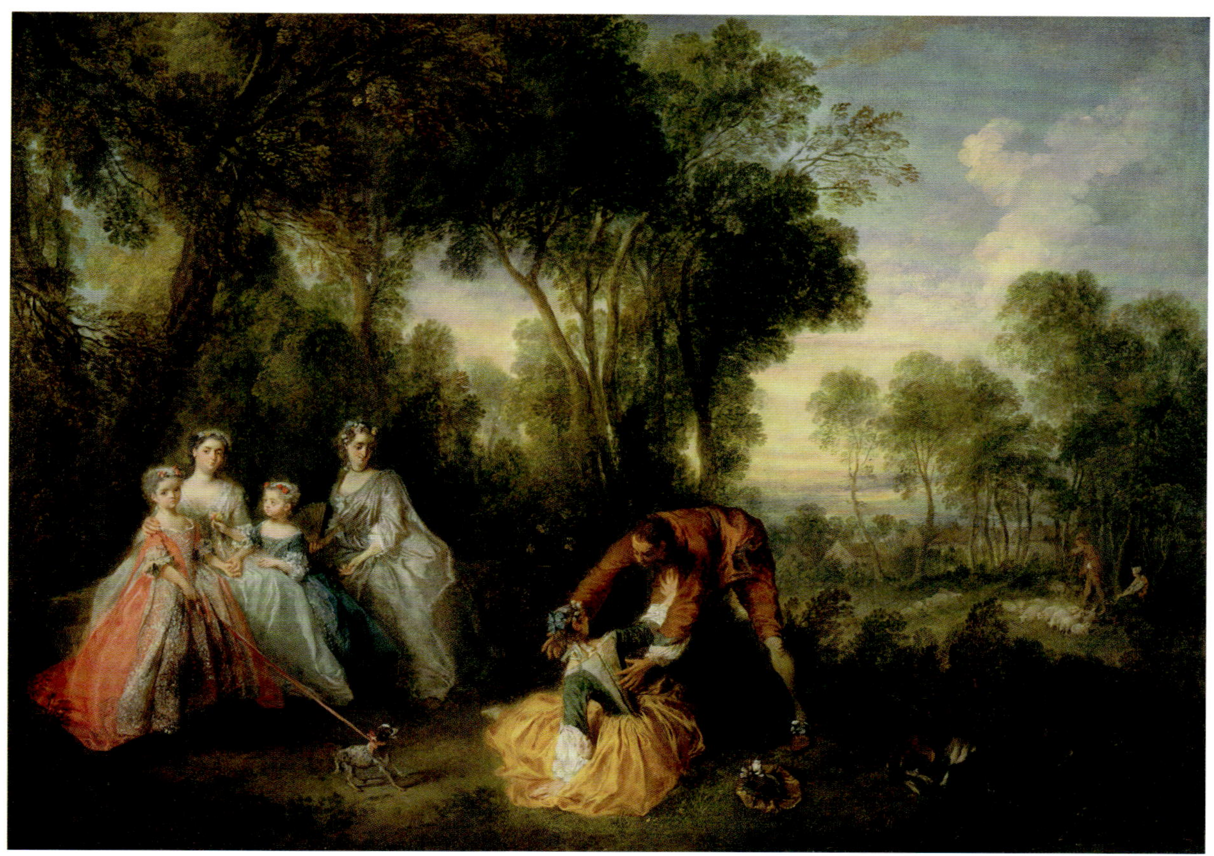

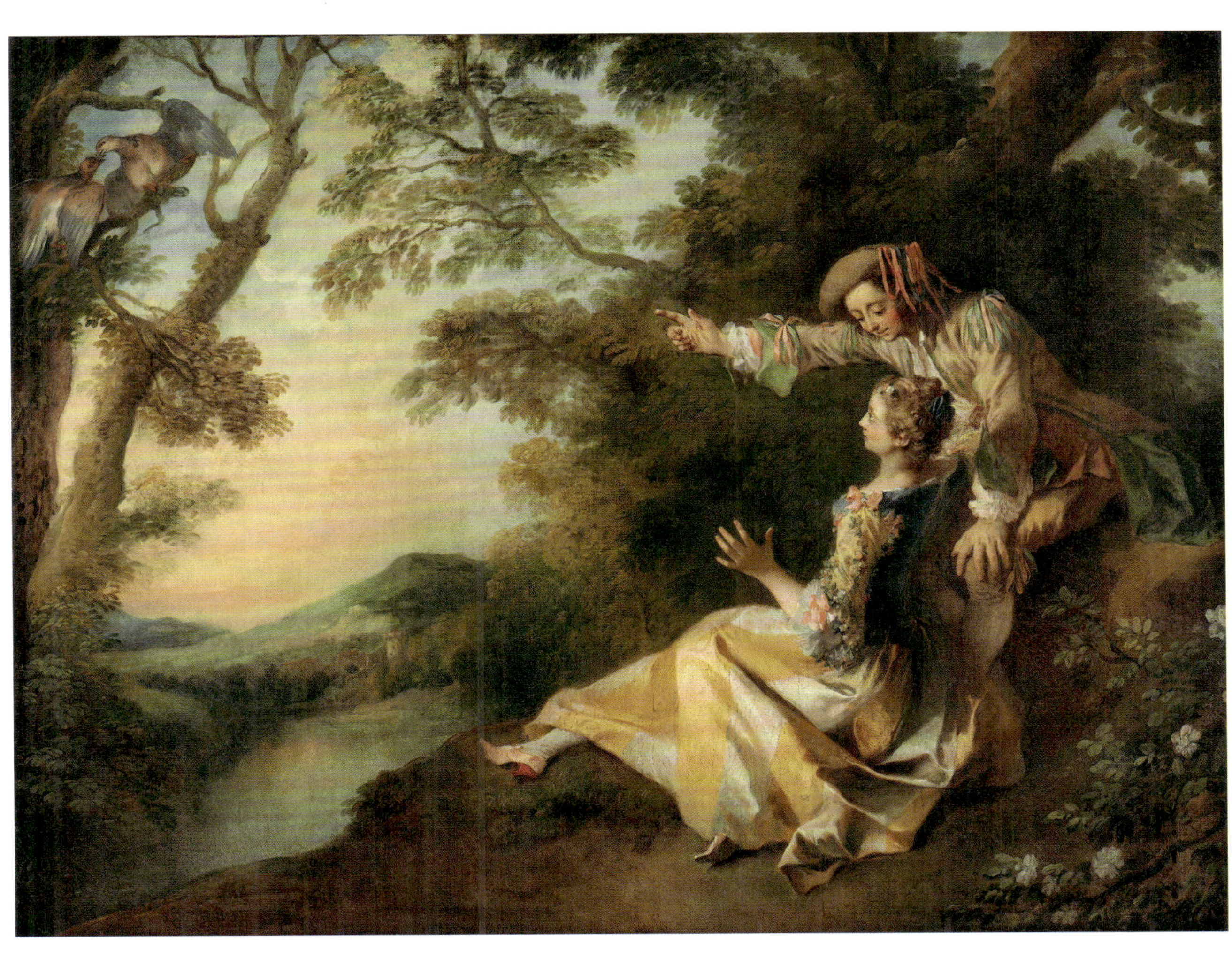

NICOLAS LANCRET *Lovers in a Landscape (The Turtle Doves)* c.1720–30

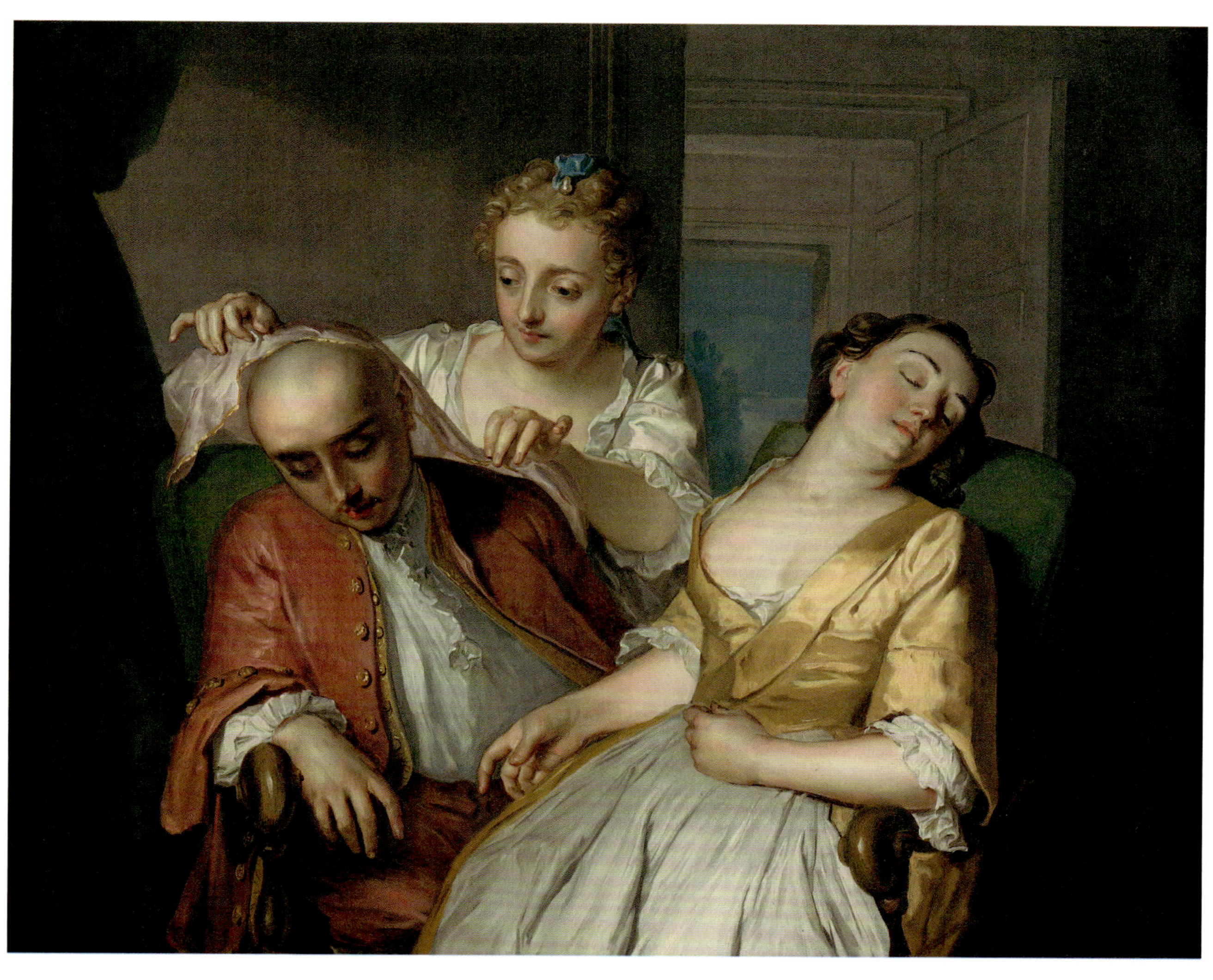

  PHILIP MERCIER *A Scene from 'The Careless Husband'* 1738

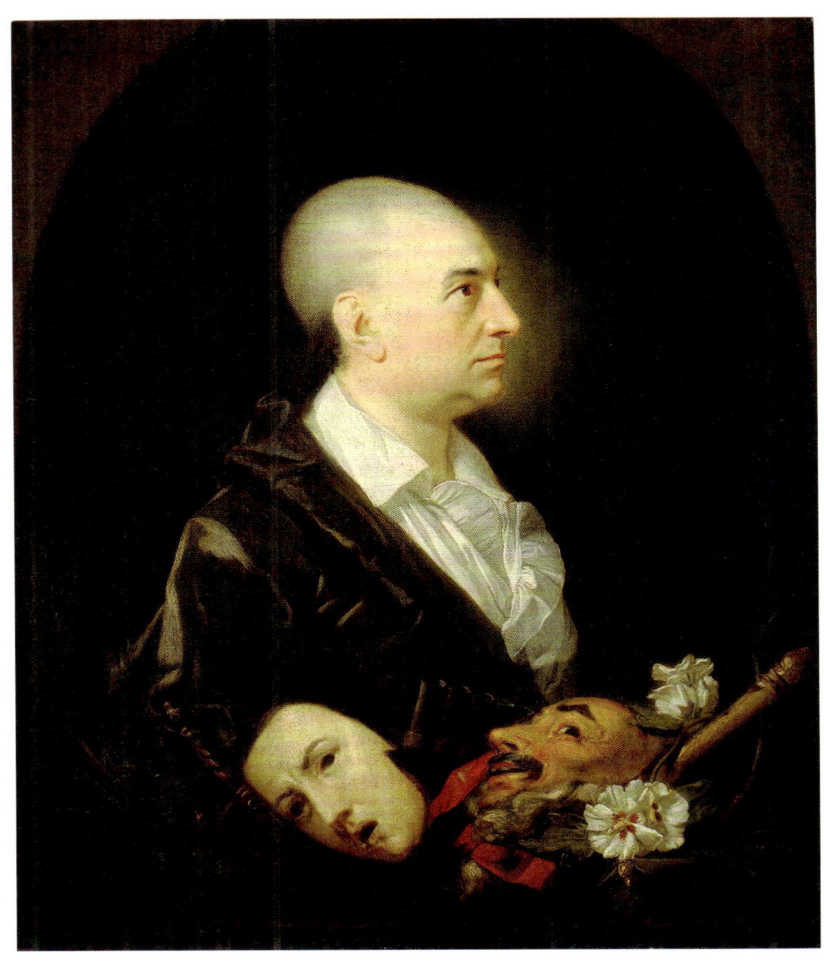

JOHAN ZOFFANY *David Garrick* 1762–3

It was common for men to wear wigs in eighteenth-century polite society. Underneath, the head was normally shaved for hygienic reasons. Uncovering the bald head had erotic or violent undertones, making Garrick's choice to be shown wigless confrontational and striking.

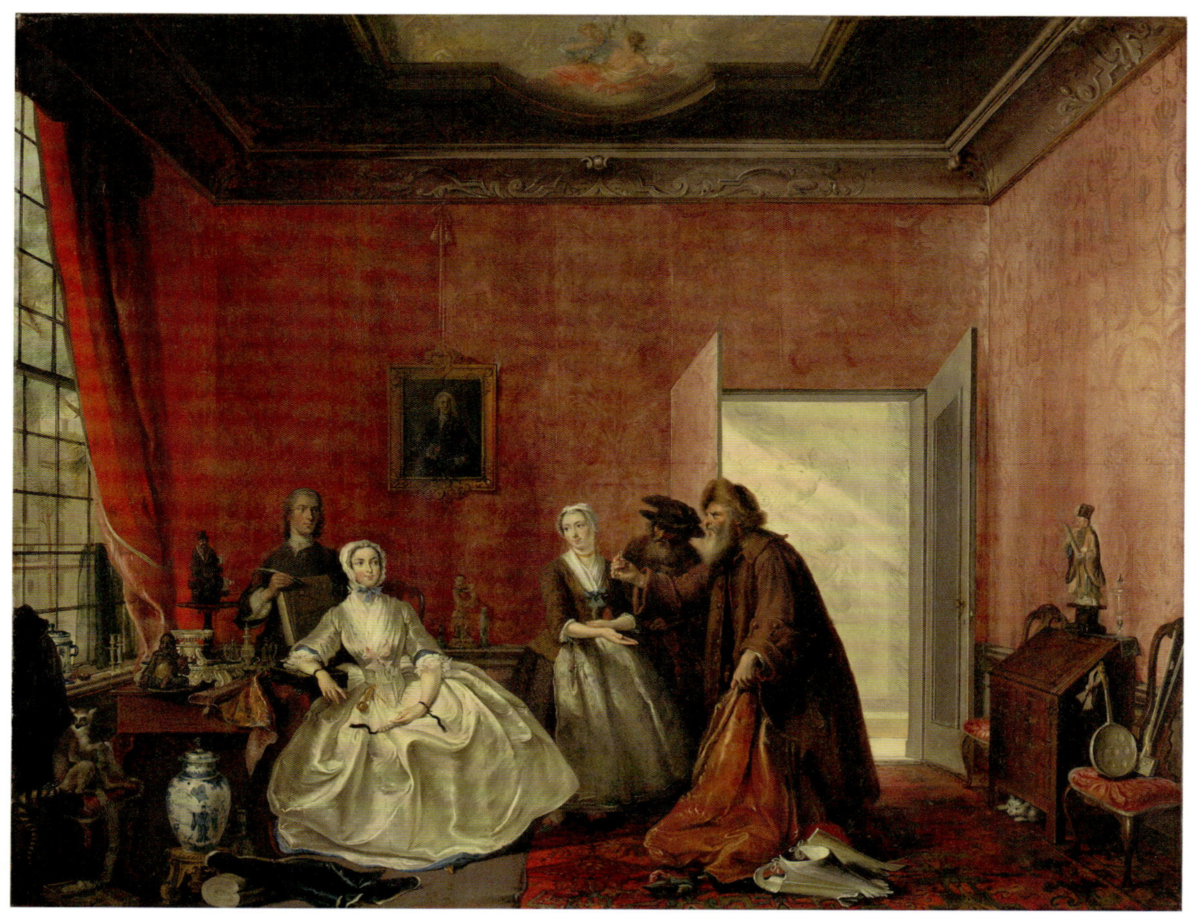

CORNELIS TROOST *Johanna and the Jewish Merchants* 1741

Like Hogarth, Troost weaves together social types, allusion and blunt humour, which might include straightforward ethnic and gender stereotypes, notably of Jewish characters, as in *Johanna and the Jewish Merchants*. In *The Lost Sentry* a genteel young man relays a message to his lover at the window by addressing the guard in the doorway. The sentry is dressed in theatrical Harlequin costume with a woman's dress and lace cap, and has a blackened face with racist implications.

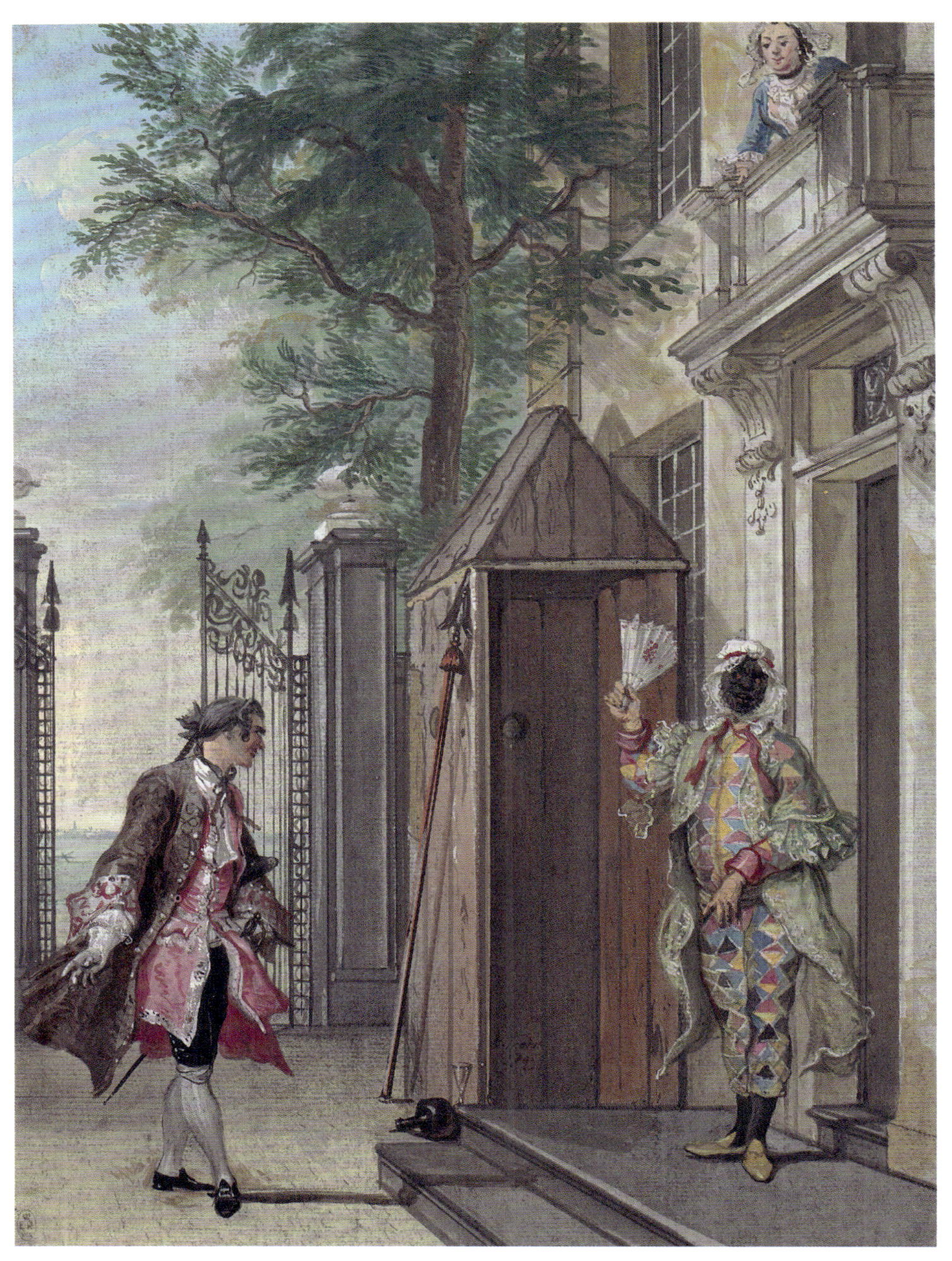

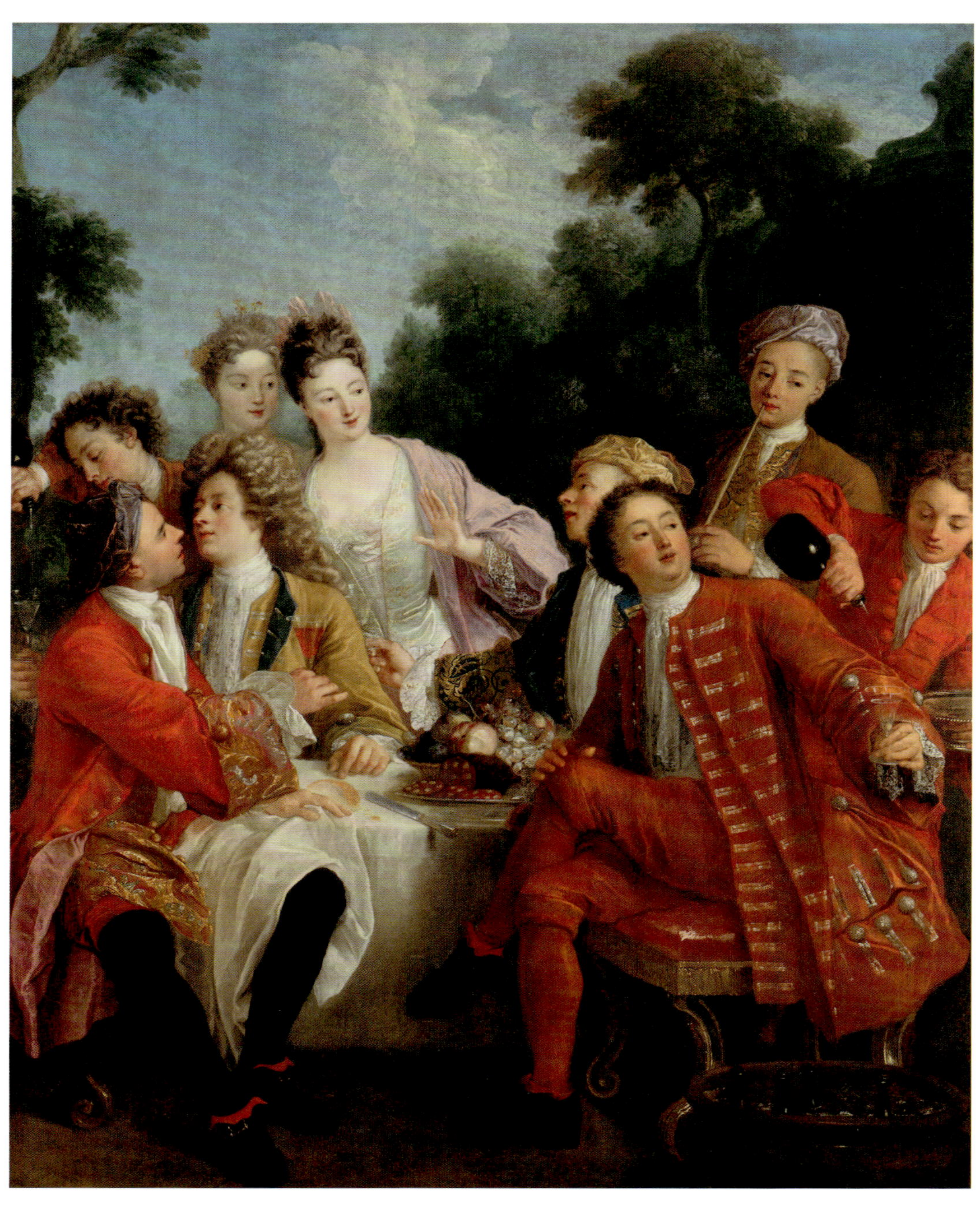

UNKNOWN ARTIST, FRENCH SCHOOL   *The Hunting Lunch*   1710–15

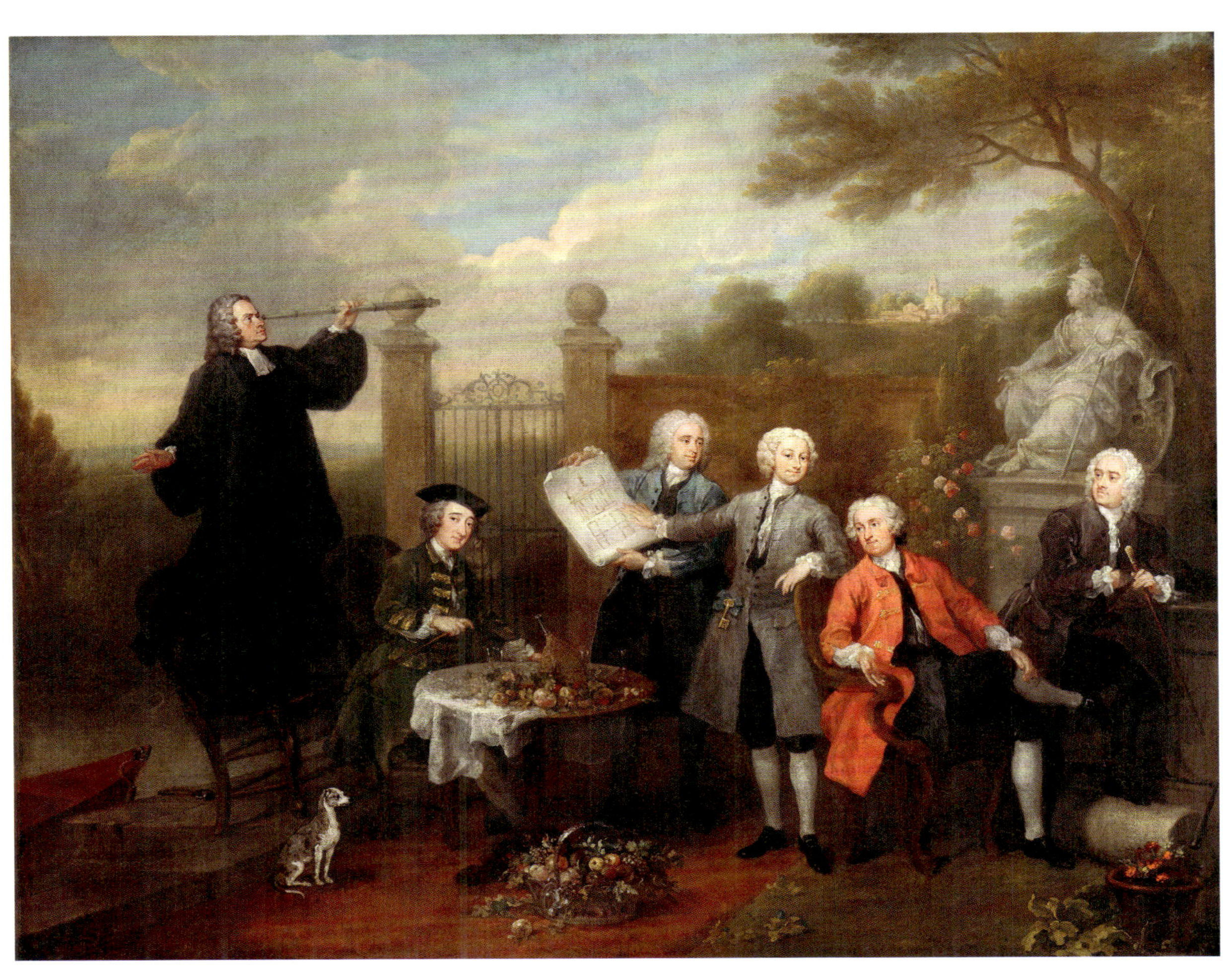

WILLIAM HOGARTH   *The Hervey Conversation Piece*   1738–40

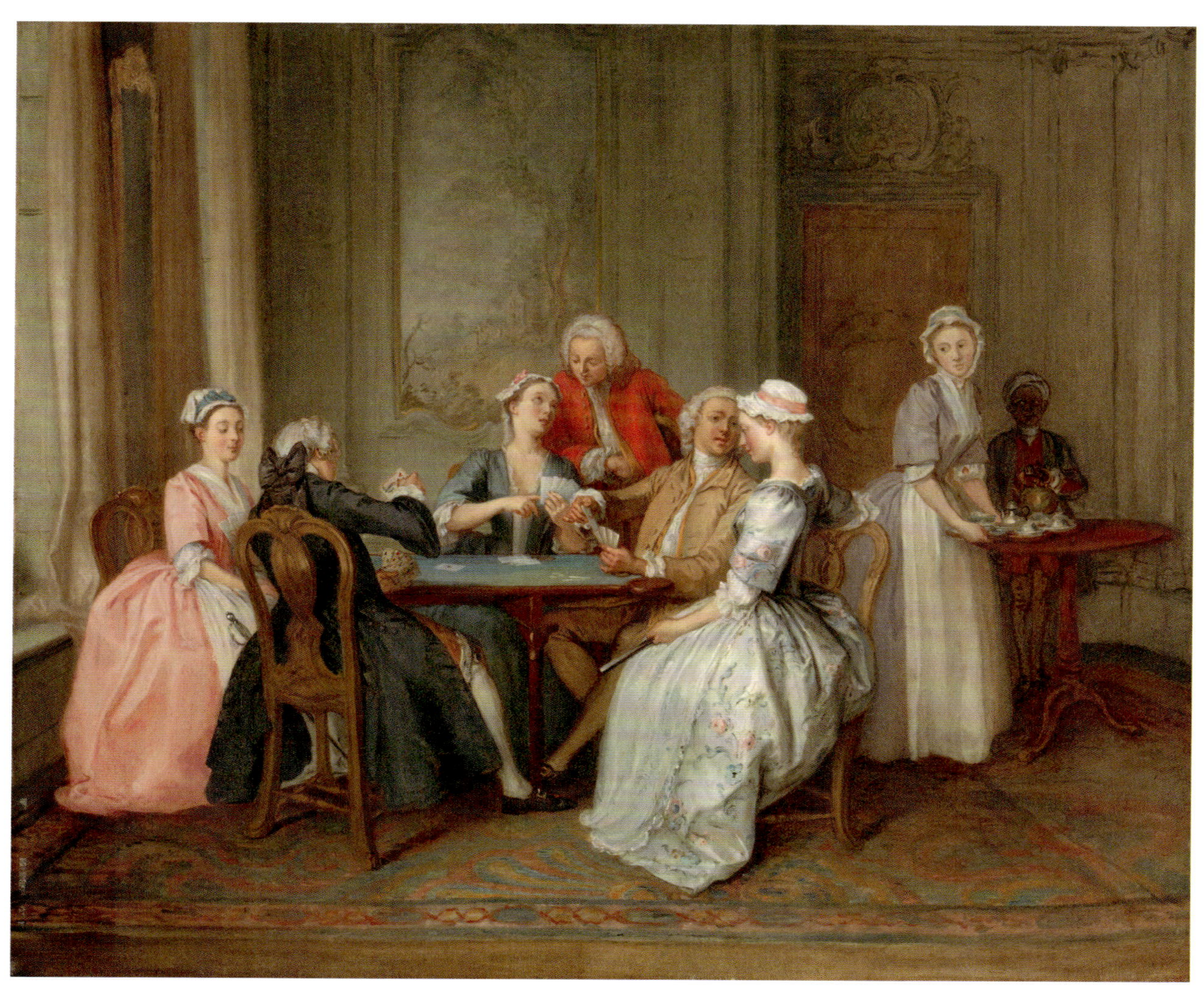

HUBERT FRANÇOIS GRAVELOT   *A Game of Quadrille*   c.1740

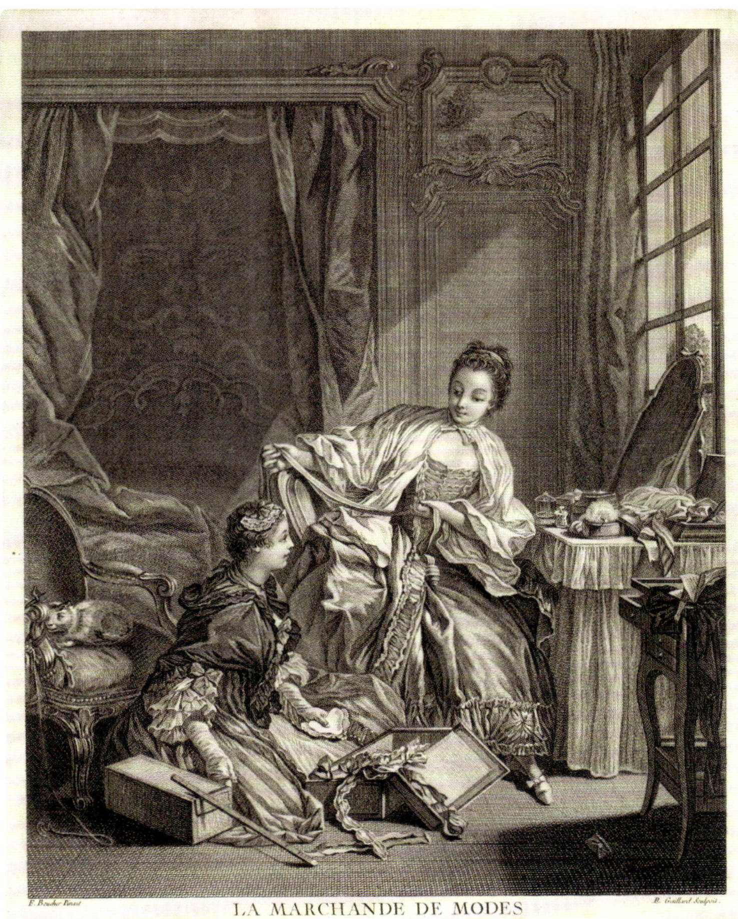
F. Boucher Pinxit
R. Gaillard Sculpsit.
LA MARCHANDE DE MODES
Les Dieux ont pris plaisir à vous rendre parfaite,
Et ces vains ornemens qu'à tort vous empruntez,
Ne Servent qu'à cacher de réelles beautés;
Quitez donc pour toujours, Philis, votre toilette.
Voulez-vous exciter les plus vives ardeurs?
A vos aimables loix soumettre tous les cœurs,
Ainsi qu'en l'âge d'Or sans fard et sans parure,
Montrez-vous dans l'état de la simple nature.
Tiré du cabinet de Mr. Brousseau Capitaine des Gardes de la Ville.
A Paris chez l'Auteur Rue St. Jacques au dessus des Jacobins, entre un Perruquier et une Lingere.

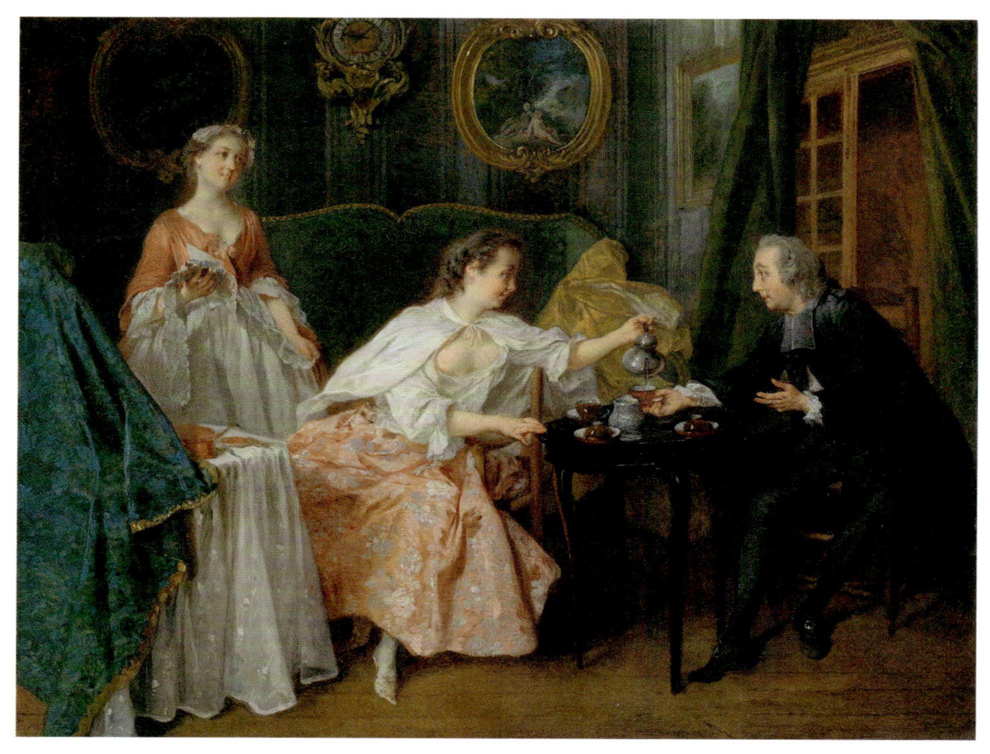

NICOLAS LANCRET   *The Four Times of Day: Morning*   by 1739

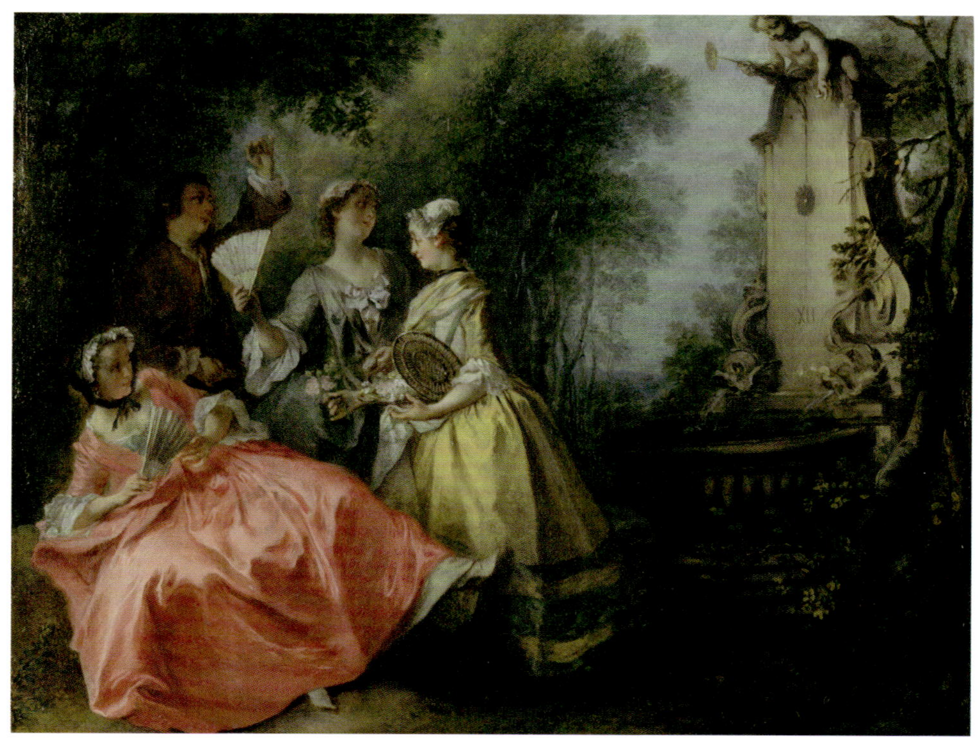

    NICOLAS LANCRET   *The Four Times of Day: Midday*   1739–41

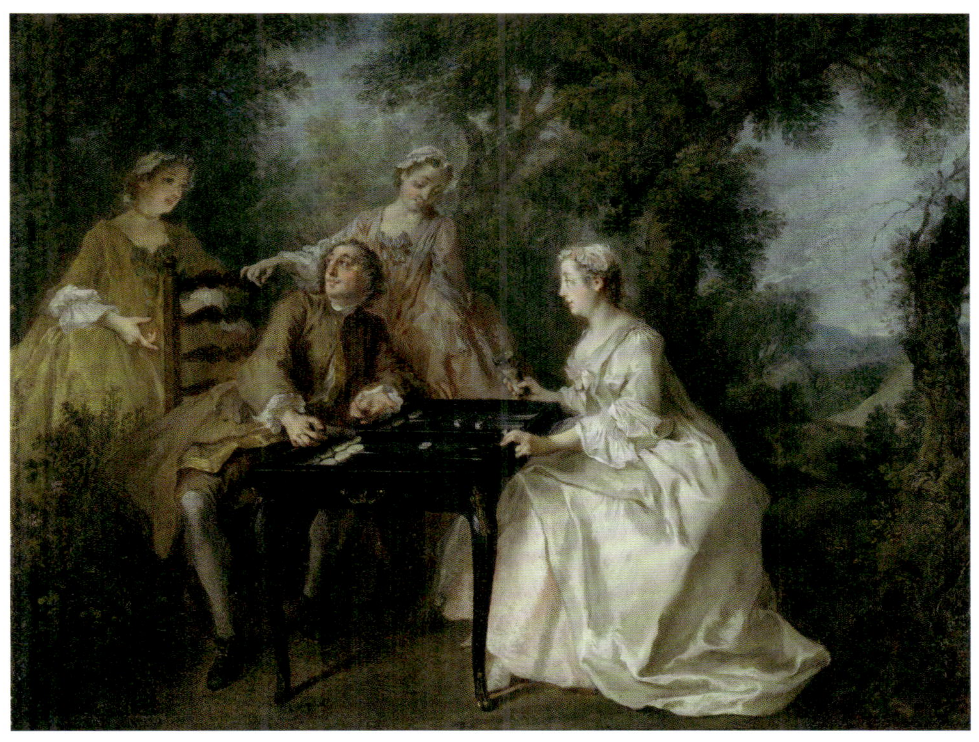

NICOLAS LANCRET   *The Four Times of Day: Afternoon*   1739–41

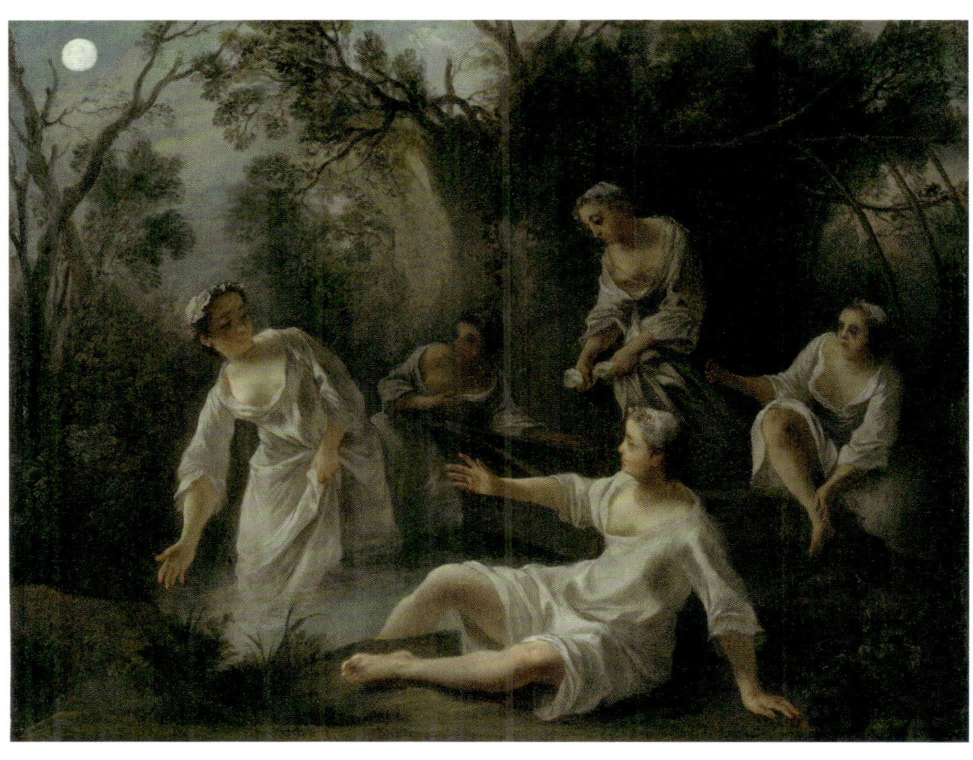

NICOLAS LANCRET   *The Four Times of Day: Evening*   1739–41

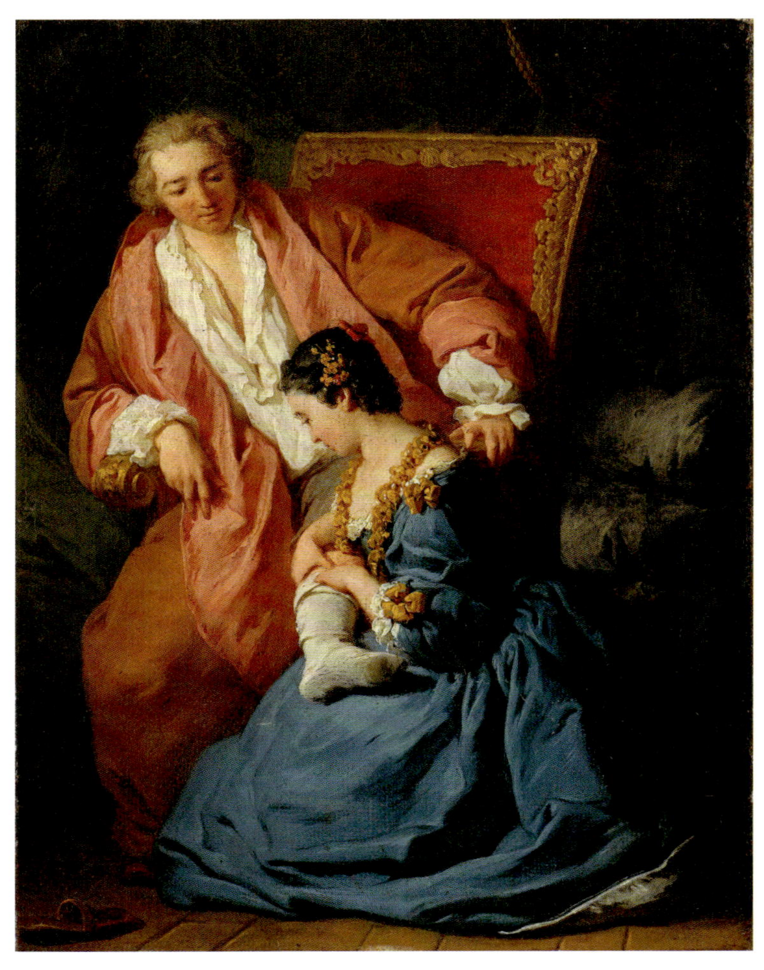

PIERRE SUBLEYRAS   *The Amorous Courtesan,
from a tale by Jean de la Fontaine*   c.1735

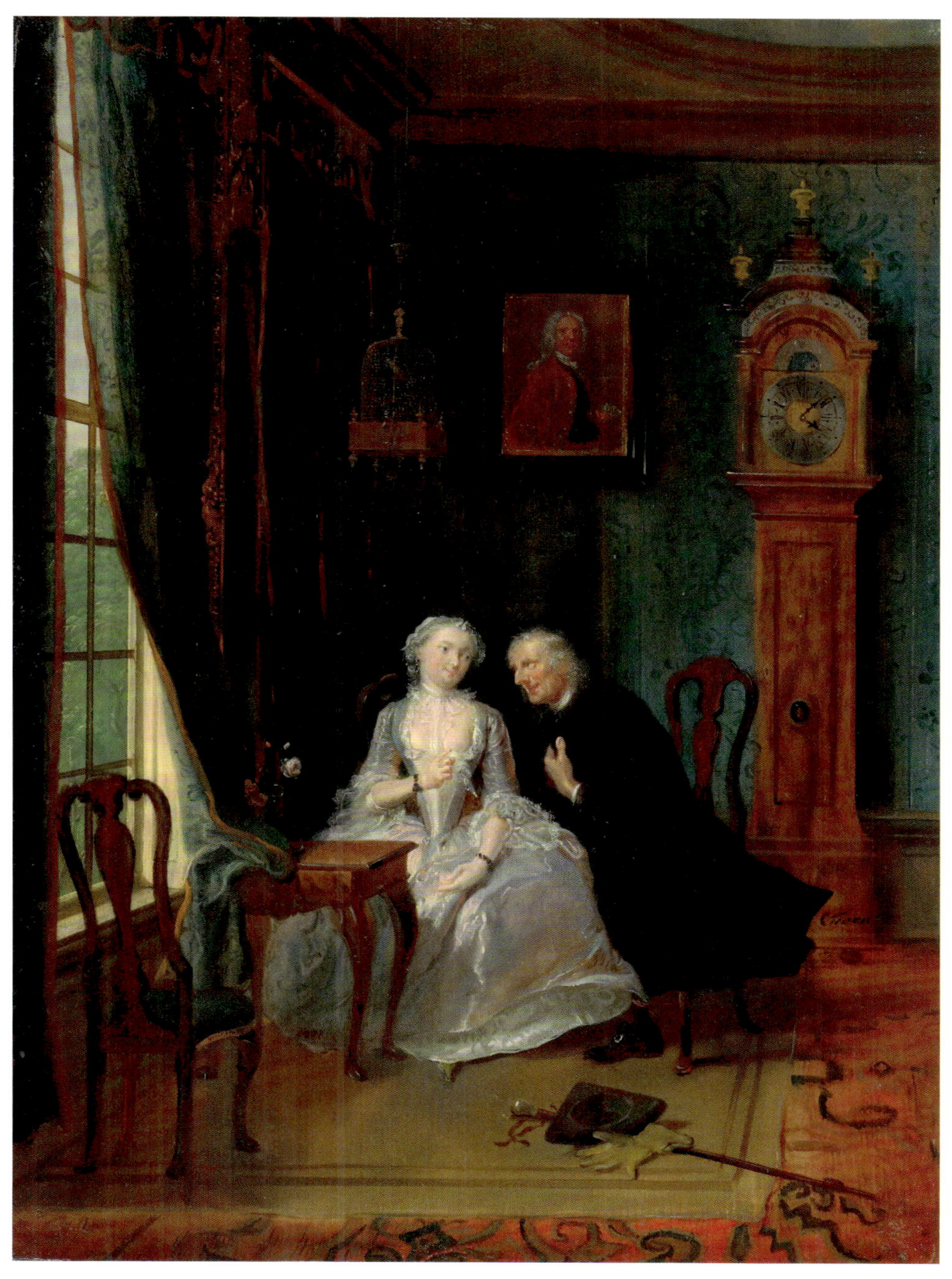

CORNELIS TROOST   *Unseemly Love, perhaps a scene of the Widower Joost with Lucia,*
2nd scene from the play 'De wanhebbelijke liefde' by C.J. van der Lijn   1720–50

PERFORMING FURNITURE

SONIA E. BARRETT

I perform furniture and find that Hogarth affirms my work.

In Georgian England, people started to gender furniture in a binary way. All types of furnishings are classed as feminine or masculine, with the feminine being 'more diminutive'.[1] The tea table, for instance, is classed as essentially feminine.

I think that during this period furniture becomes raced as well as gendered – but race is not as clearly articulated. If the curvaceous table or chair is female, that female is often also brown, and is made of a tree that began life, and grew up, in the Caribbean. And most of the furniture in Hogarth's work is indeed brown, curvaceous and from the Tropics.

Brown femininity has long been understood as supporting White femininity.[2] Their femininity is scaffolded. In Hogarth's work, furniture tells all. It depicts the real order (or disorder). When brown furniture actually physically tips, it 'tells' of the moral fall of a White person. The brown scaffolding of decorum has fallen down.

In *Marriage A-la-Mode, The Tête à Tête* (p.161) depicts a woman taking tea for one, ignoring her husband. She brings disparate men together – not to improve society, as in other works by Hogarth, but for illicit sexual liaisons that damage society. Front and centre of this scene is a brown chair on its back, the set of its feet echoing the couple's feet. This position, legs in the air, is probably how the wife positioned herself with the hastily departed music master, or how the husband positioned the young girl whose cap is carelessly stuffed in his pocket. The tipping chair in the background alerts us to another complicit person.

In *Before* and *After* (pp.170–1), dressing tables tip and fall, their mirrors smashing when their owner gets undressed out of wedlock. Tables are abused to distract from the inappropriateness of a woman's behaviour. But the upset table is, in and of itself, a travesty of polite femininity in Georgian England, so one impropriety distracts from another.

Can we write the labour of Black women abroad back into the picture via a mahogany chair tipped on its back? Black women's original on-her-back labour (birthing the next generation of slaves) is the source of all the depicted wealth that will be progressively squandered or increased in these paintings in the first place. If we see mahogany standing in for Black bodies, this puts the many Black people who served and supported Georgian England in other countries back into the picture as a kind of objectified support.[3]

Of his own work, Hogarth writes:

my picture is my stage and men and women my players, who by means of certain actions and gestures are to exhibit a dumb show[4]

But in addition to his players, Hogarth lets the 'dumb' speak, again and again. Animals and furniture 'tell' the viewer in his paintings as much as (sometimes more than) any man or woman. Most of his story is told in the 'dumb' blank spaces in between the tableaux, where we have to imagine the progression between the scenes.

Over and over, Hogarth uses the performance of furniture to point to inappropriate behaviour. Hogarth is not a quick read, if you ask of each painting what the chair or table says you will probably get to the crux of things soonest – as an artist I listen to furniture all the time, so for me Hogarth just makes sense.

Individuals using things as furniture when they are not 'actually' furniture is a quick pointer to trouble. A coffin is used as a table in *Industry and Idleness* 1747, Plate 3, and *A Harlot's Progress* 1733, Plate 6 (p.101), two engravings where things are awry; a British ship's figure-head vaunting victory over the French is used as a chair in another problematic scene (*An Election II: Canvassing for Votes* 1754–5). In *The Cholmondeley Family* 1732, the children's need for instruction is shown by their misuse of furniture (p.181).

Hogarth uses 'foreign' furnishings to crowd scenes of inappropriate behaviour. Furniture imported from Asia and the Middle East, such as sofas, are spaces of explicitly illicit sexual encounters and voyeurism all at once – although furniture made from tropical trees and shipped around the Empire is of course not foreign but quintessentially British. Shelves heave with foreign collectables that point out their owners' 'bad taste'.

The poorest Georgians, on the other hand, are without furniture or a room to call their own – in *Cruelty in Perfection* 1751 they only have the locking 'deal box' to their name. The tipping and upturning of this box is the furniture performance of the poor. In his 'Progress', Hogarth's harlot has a curvaceous brown table to push over with her indolent foot but later, as she dies impoverished, it is a plain table that is upturned and the contents of her trunk box are ransacked (pp.99–101).[5] This underlines her moral fall. Similarly, in *The Arrest*, the rake's lover loses the contents of her deal box when she comes to his aid by using her hard-earned money to settle his debts (p.109).

Even when upright, the way a table is set enables it to 'voice' impropriety. Chardin's work *The White Tablecloth* (p.160) shows a hastily set table but this is as nothing compared to the carelessness of Hogarth's immorally 'unset' tables. Food is often on the floor and not the table;[6] plates tumble from tables and mix with chamber pots on the floor. In a time where many people were hungry, without even chamber pots and definitely without servants to empty them, this is an extreme image. In *An Election Entertainment* 1754 Hogarth even pulls the tablecloth from Abraham van Beyeren's Dutch still-life portraits of a table, *Still Life with Jug and Lobster* c.1670, painting the same still life dumped on the floor. Plates are polished and actually set on the table, only to be danced upon by naked women, known as 'Posture Molls', so we can glimpse their genitals in the plate's reflection (p.109).[7] Beds also 'speak': the beds of degenerates are broken, or have a large knot (not) in their curtains.[8]

The tables and chairs are like those Black subjects who, while usually supporting the 'decorum' of White people, can be toppled at whim to distract from the inappropriate behaviour of those same White people.[9] This is like modern day 'othering'. Today when the footballer Marcus Rashford's function as a social reformer is questioned, some write he should stay in his place and serve as intended on the sports field.[10] People of a certain class should, like furniture, know their purpose and not attempt to fulfil roles other than those assigned to them; their proper function remains to stand and serve as they were designed to do. In terms of furniture, this requires a chair to remain a chair and the sitter to use the chair as it is intended. In terms of people, this is class obedience on the back of a napkin.

Perhaps this is the essence of Britishness – this, and the visible delight Hogarth sometimes takes in thwarting those rules. Brown furniture tumbles everywhere, reflecting poorly on the human figures who should use them as intended and sit appropriately. But importantly, sitting itself is never questioned. Appropriate, respectful sitting is a quick pause from eager, inexhaustible, virtuous productive industry, as exemplified by George Arnold, who appears to sit down briefly, just in from business, hat still in hand, and is likely to be off again in a minute (p.191).[11] This is the 'correct' performance of the chair. Hogarth demonstrates this himself when he sits and goes at his painting (p.67).[12]

Without tables and chairs, polite conversation is impossible. The brutishness of the street scenes relates in part to the lack of furnished places to withdraw to, to rest and converse undisturbed. The ideal model is offered by the distant country houses in so many paintings.[13] All the activities the Manor separates out are jumbled in the life of the street, which is at once dining room, toilet and even bedchamber, all without tables, chairs or beds.[14] The exception is *Beer Street* 1751 (p.80) – the instructional opposite of debauched *Gin Lane* 1751 (p.81) – where all is well with the world and there is actually a table in use on the pavement.

Furniture is not just a product of the British Empire. It can stand in for its structures, making them visible. Hogarth gives that furniture a chance to speak, letting it stand and enable polite society, or letting it tip, flagging up a debauched society. Ironically, the undepicted horrors of Empire abroad supply and enable these exemplary places of decorum at home. Furniture is the very scaffolding of deportment.

Perhaps what we learn following the lives of the corrupt and corrupted is that inhumanity begins at home. Even as Hogarth struggles to articulate what British art really is when it's at home, it is clear 'home' is often in disarray. Social commentators have calculated that in Hogarth's time 'one woman in five was involved in some manner in the sex industry with as many as 62,500 sex workers of various types in London'.[15] The Foundling Hospital, built to house 600 abandoned children, actually housed 6,233 children. From 1758 to 1759 it admitted 1,469 children, while 2,264 died in its care.[16] The worst practices of the Empire were perhaps not a response to what lay beyond these isles, but rather a development of some of the stories already within them – stories that Hogarth shared over and over again.

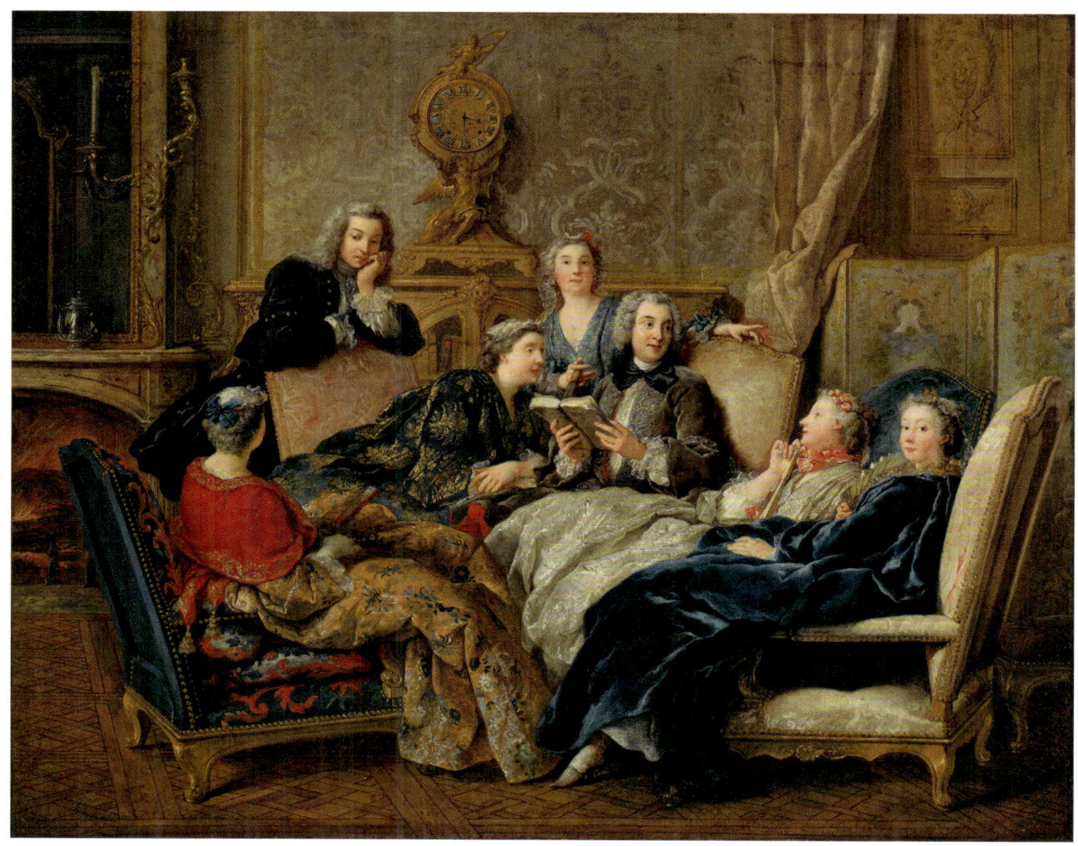

JEAN-FRANÇOIS DE TROY *Reading from Molière* c.1728

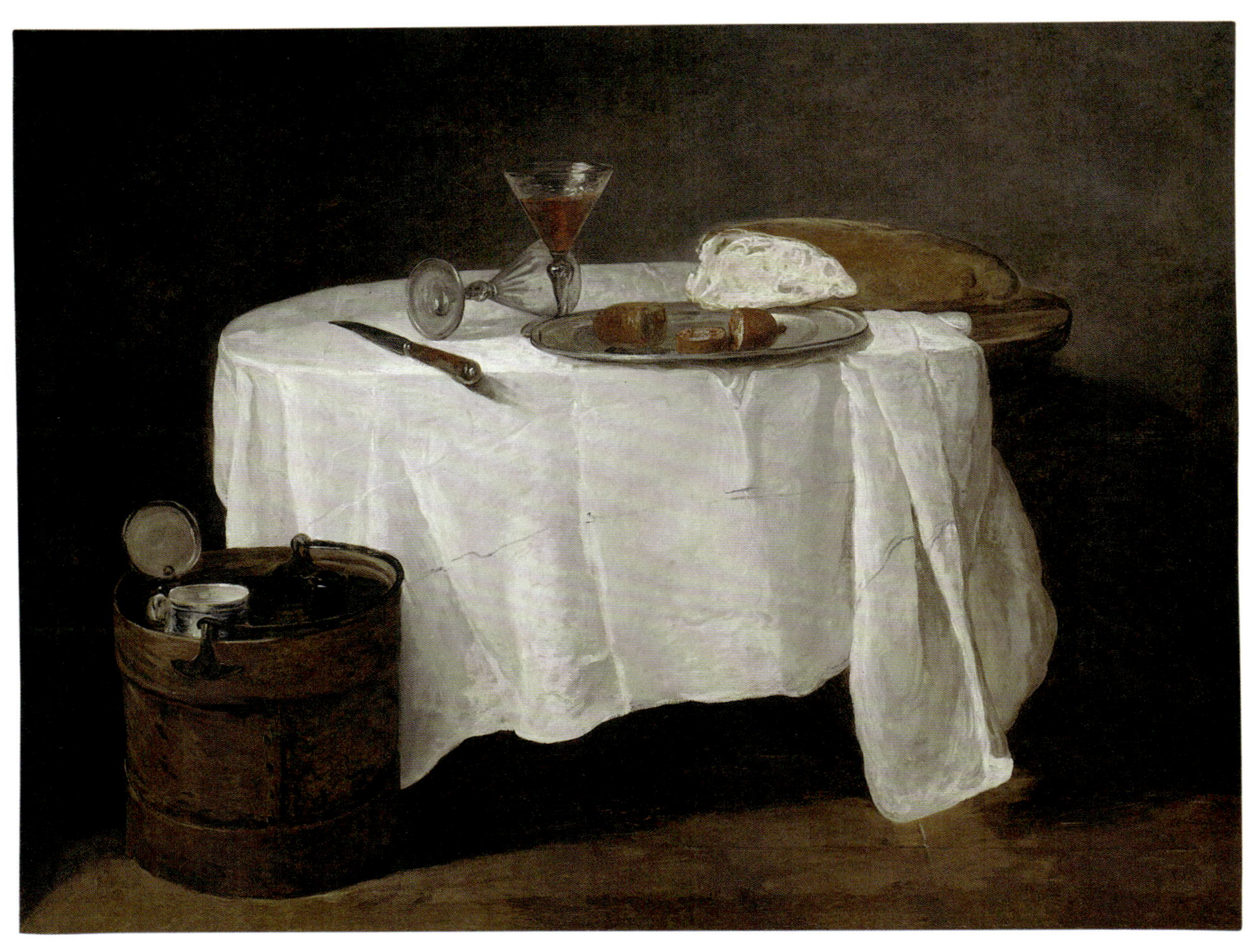

JEAN-SIMÉON CHARDIN   *The White Tablecloth*   1731/2

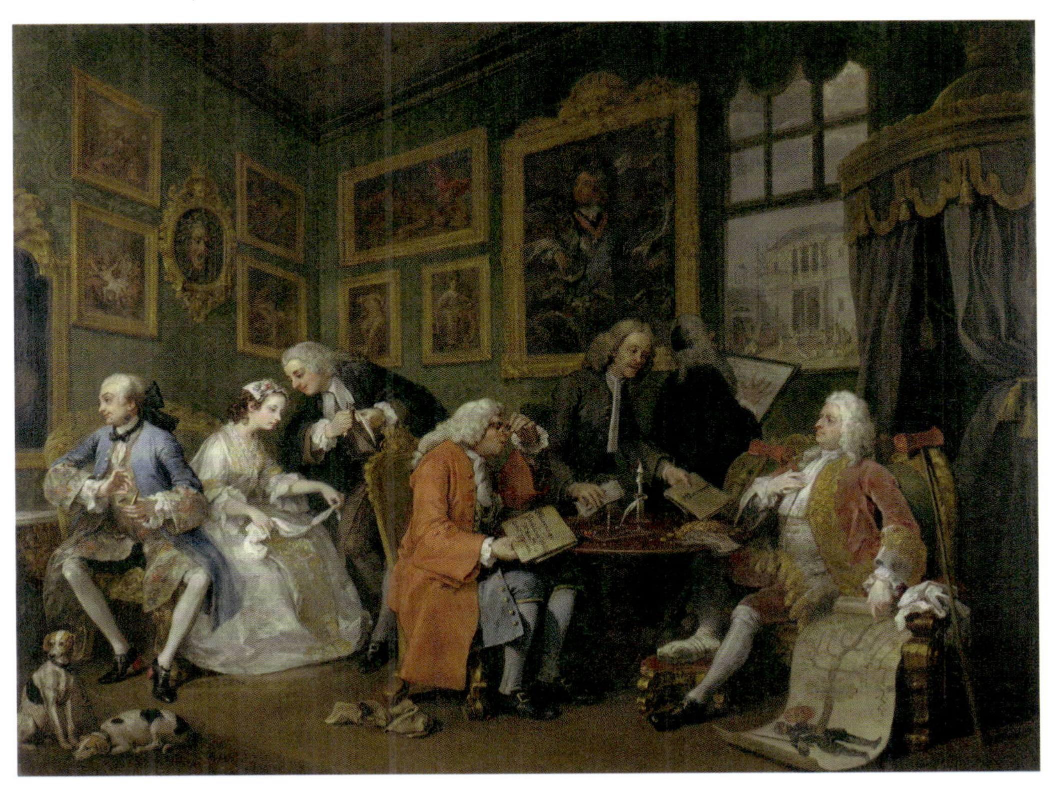

WILLIAM HOGARTH   *Marriage A-la-Mode: 1, The Marriage Settlement*   c.1743

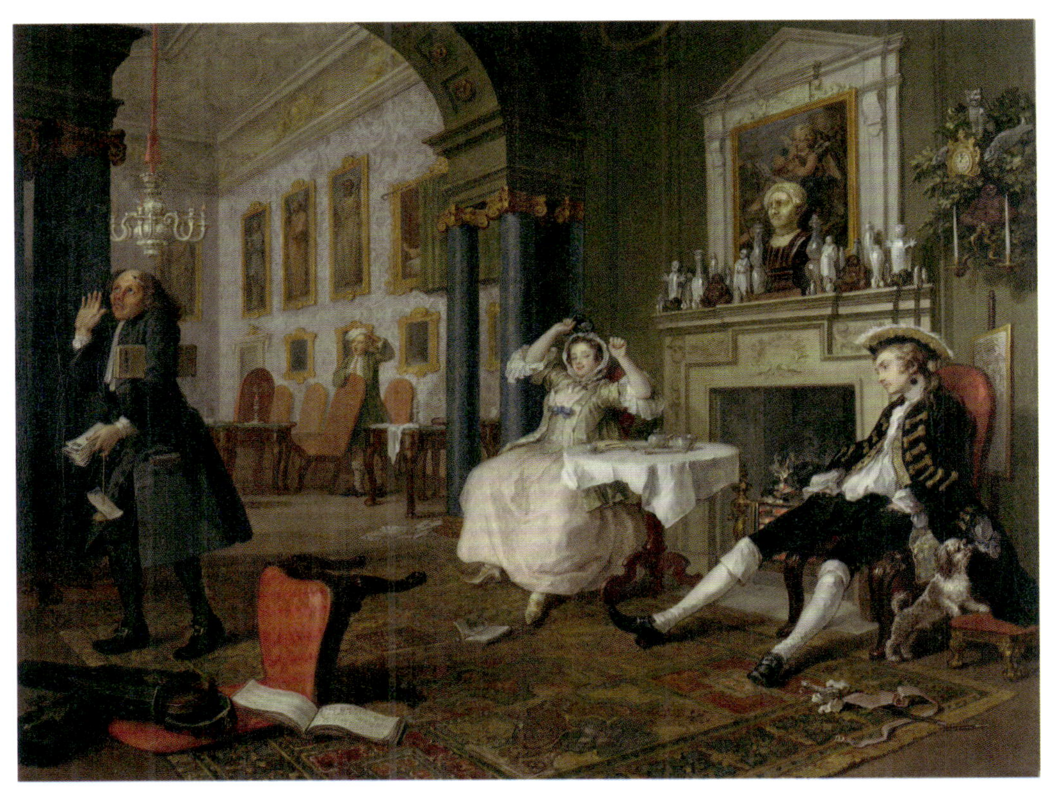

WILLIAM HOGARTH   *Marriage A-la-Mode: 2, The Tête à Tête*   c.1743

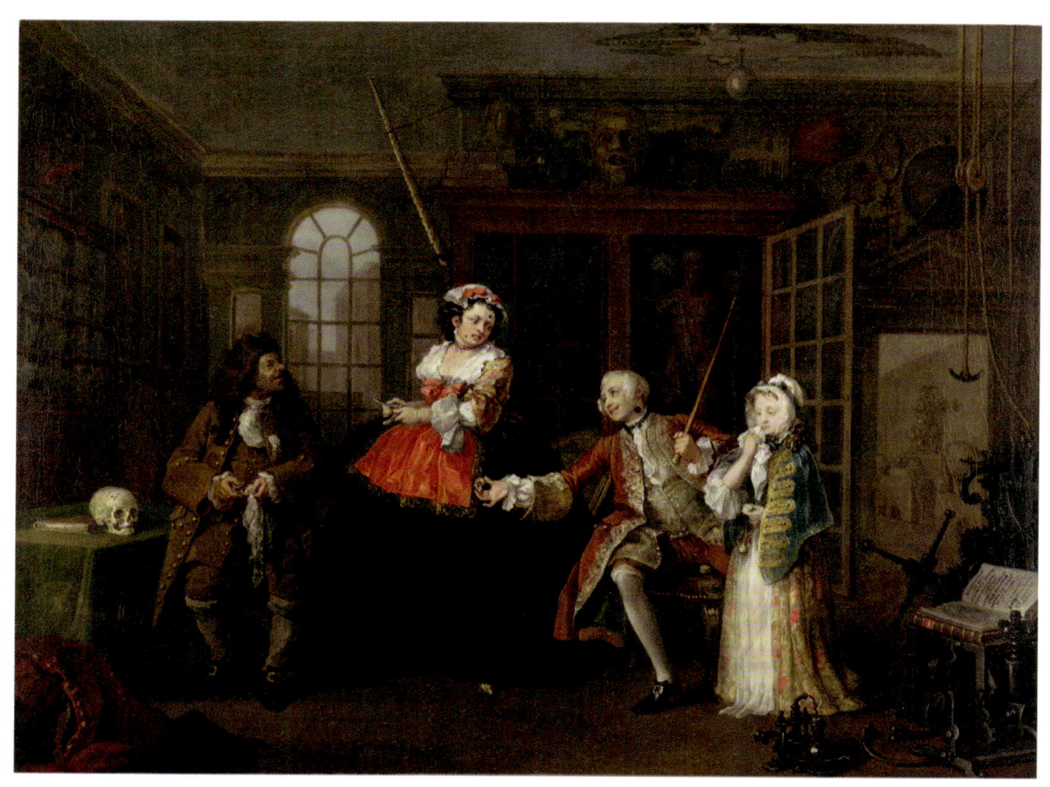

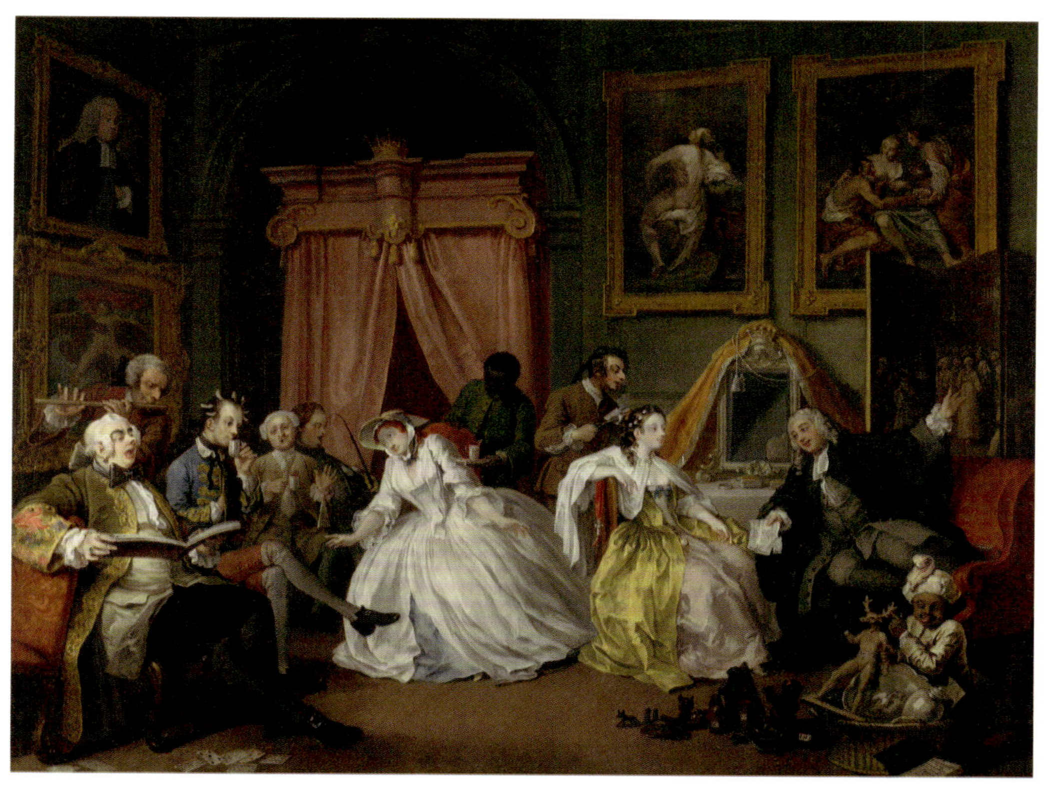

162

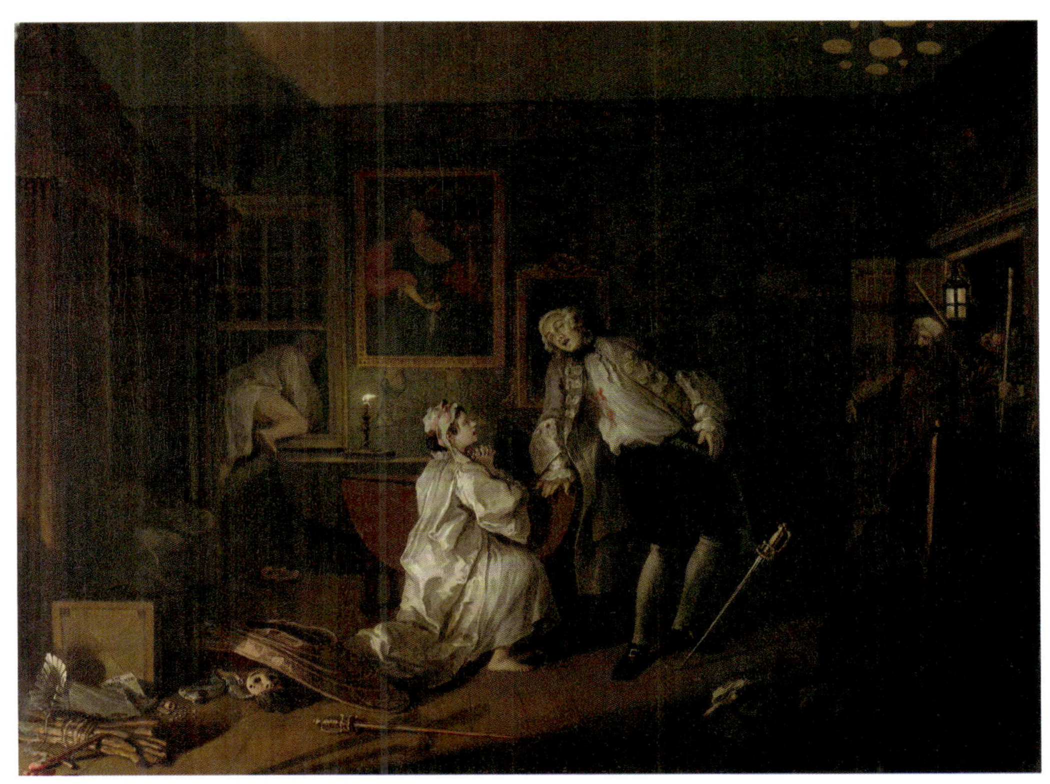

WILLIAM HOGARTH   *Marriage A-la-Mode: 5, The Bagnio*   c.1743

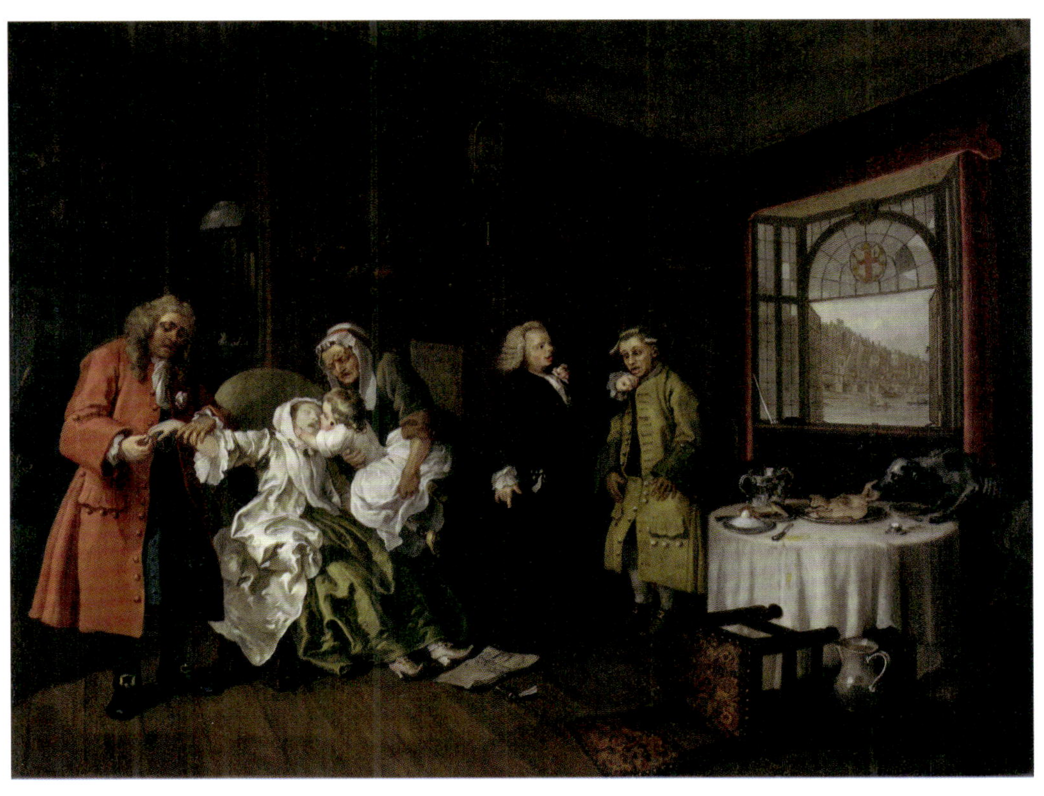

WILLIAM HOGARTH   *Marriage A-la-Mode: 6, The Lady's Death*   c.1743

A FASHIONABLE MARRIAGE

LUBAINA HIMID

My name is Oumar and I am a butler-cum-manservant from Mali. However, my main function is to make this unimportant aristocratic household look exceptionally wealthy. I'm funny and love to make people laugh – a dangerous hobby, but frankly I don't really care. I'm not particularly good looking and my hair could be better but no one notices; they either think I'm ugly because of the colour of my skin or they fall for me because of, yes, the colour of my skin. I know how to be charming, it's my job to be decorative.

I woke up even earlier this morning than usual to help my fellow invisibles prepare for the hilarious and sordid little morning party my mistress the Countess has insisted on staging. She of course slept until late, soft and pink and sugary, wrapped in the fat arms of her lover Silvertongue the Lawyer. They imagine themselves to be a powerful pair, contriving to meet at luxurious parties and then sleeping together while her idiot of a husband is away – somehow believing that they are untouchable. The old nursemaid Anna looked after the little baby girl in the nursery as usual.

The Countess treats me with disdain almost all of the time, but she loves the way that I can be a delightful African Gentleman when she needs me to take that role. To her I am simply a black body rippling with exotic otherness. I know it never occurs to her that although I am bound to end up in a gutter someday soon, abandoned for a Chinese servant or a fancy dog or luscious plant, I am in reality totally aware of her strategy to have, take and keep or get rid of whatever she wants in an attempt to satisfy her quite phenomenal appetite for sex.

Silvertongue is pretty brutal but exceptionally lazy, rarely spotted working very hard, but fantastically smart when it comes to finding women who adore him.

The invitees to our breakfast gathering (including you) pale into insignificance next to the guest of honour, the Castrato Carestini. He must have cost a fortune to hire, but how brilliant of the Countess to use his amazing high notes and charismatic personality to distract everyone away from the intense heat and smell that filled the bedroom this morning.

This great singer usefully attracts the silliest of fans.

I'm rather good at making a very smooth and strong hot chocolate drink – yes, what a hilarious joke. This morning my mistress insisted

I must use all her ideas about my powers of Black masculinity to fool the Eager Listener – wriggling, open-mouthed, all dressed up in frilly white – into feeling that she is the centre of attention, equally attractive to the Italian Castrato and the African slave servant, so I made her a cup of the stuff and she never took her eyes off Carestini or her hands off me.

My adorable little compatriot who is pretending to sit quietly looking pretty in exchange for sweets and fancy pink clothes is actually the cleverest person in the room. The Boy can sing and of course he can dance, but what you might not realise is that he can read and write and understands a little too much for someone so young about politics, strategy and sexual deceit. He constantly makes fun of Silvertongue, mocking his imagined sexual prowess. We work together and spend an inordinate amount of time laughing. We know however that this family is doomed, ruined by boredom and greed. But we will fall before they do and we can never hope to recover.

Let me tell you more about that shower of hopeless hangers-on you came in with, pretending to care about the songs and the perfect notes. They are simply calculating who may be (or may soon become) the most important person in this room. They feel privileged, especially the particularly nervous man, sipping another cup of my chocolate, who is so desperate to be associated with fame and celebrity that he has been to the hairdressers and dressed himself in a rather elegant outfit.

Speaking of hairdressers, imagine how painful it is that I have to live in the same freezing quarters as that vicious little Hairdresser without whom the Countess would be lost. He is constantly competing with me in some misguided attempt to be more of a man than me. It has to be admitted though that he is quite a spectacular craftsman when it comes to the sculptural possibilities of hair; follicles are his friends.

That tiresome self-centred pair of Country Bumpkins were of course bored and mucked about, singing along and making ridiculous remarks about noses, toes and penises all through the morning's entertainment. Frankly neither of them should ever have been invited; they were only here because they are a bit stupid, take up space, know a number of important moneyed people and incidentally are distantly related to the Countess's cousin. Someone said that the older richer one was married to The Eager Listener, I'm not sure.

As for the Old Flautist sweetly playing his expensive instrument to accompany the Castrato – oh, what a clever fellow, making money in so many ways: blowing into that flute and seducing, cajoling, influencing and managing the careers of artistes all over London.

*

The butler Oumar can be bitter, I know, but you must forgive him. He has a tendency to do as he is told and then regret it later. I like him

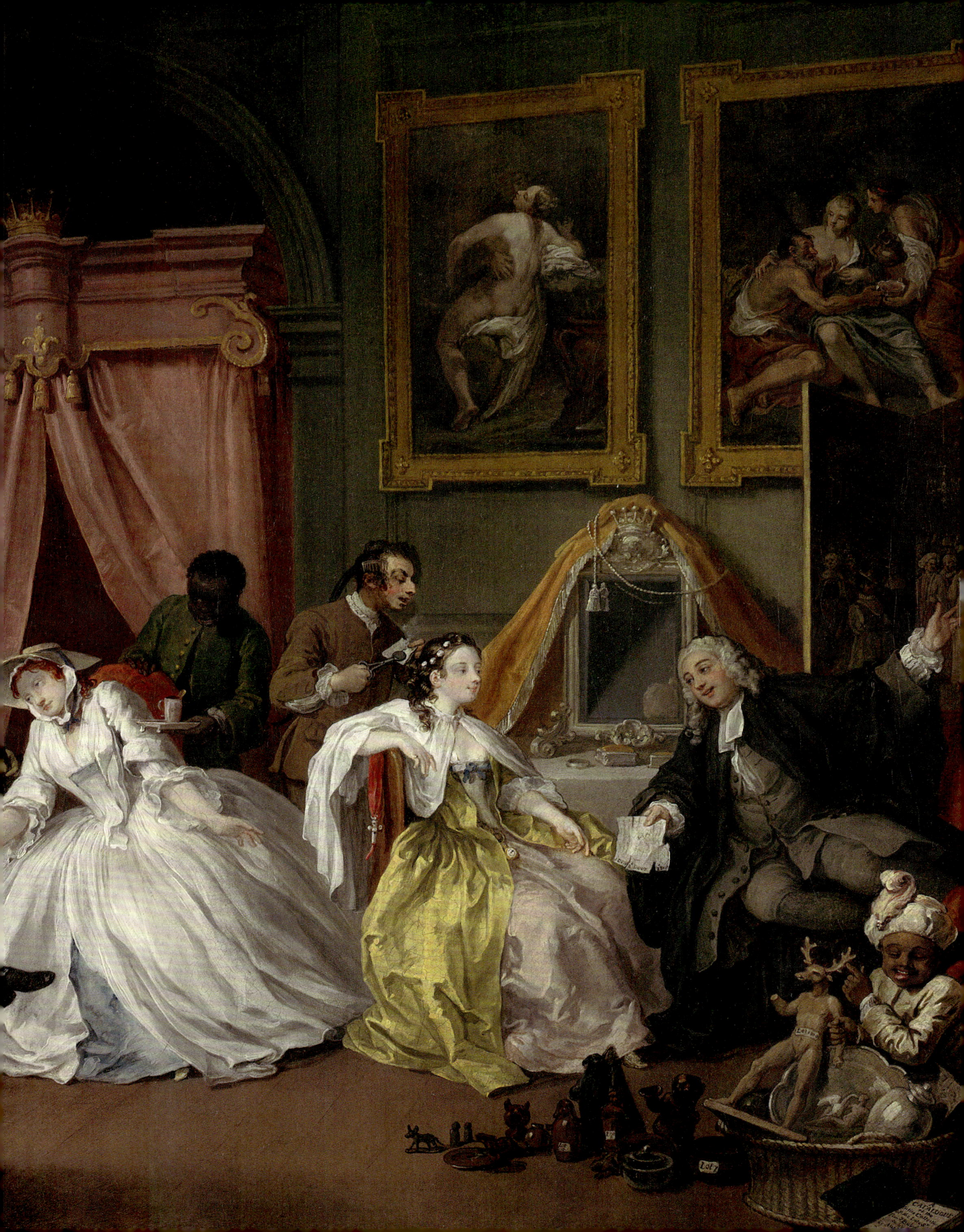

and we look out for each other but he is old-fashioned and can only cope with the problems that are right in front of him, which is useful because I cannot be bothered with the minute details of each moment. I am better at thinking ahead, working out what we can learn from the events which have already happened.

My name is Adeban, but I am known as Sam or The Boy. I try to look as pretty as possible and do my job of smiling and playing with toys and sometimes even play with the baby, but always signifying wealth as efficiently as I can; mine is a waiting game. I wasted time at the party this morning playing about with some lewd-looking rubbish bought from an auction: a doll that's supposed to be Acteon the peeping Tom and other stuff you could use for all sorts of fun in the bedroom. Sitting about and pretending to find this tat funny gave me time to assess the situation and better still to listen to some incredible singing – what a voice that Castrato has, I love it! Once men like Oumar have finished feeling that being sycophantic and amusing is useful, our time will come.

I have my eye on the lawyer Silvertongue and do a fairly good job of pretending to like him when he calls on my mistress. I deliver messages for him and arrange secret meetings for him with continental bankers and dealers in collectables. He won't last long, though; anyone can see that he has the air and bravado of a killer.

That damn Hairdresser, her valet de chambre, is a menace too. He and his friends are the kind of thugs who look fine and well-dressed, but on dark nights and wet afternoons in London they beat up Black men as a competitive sport or for casual exercise. He is a brilliant hair sculptor, mind you. Astonishing finesse with ribbons and curls.

The Countess loves her baby girl when she is in the room with us all, but the little thing is no golden ticket to staying in this marriage à la mode. She is on a dangerous voyage, I know she has been bored for years and met Silvertongue at her wedding, but she is a woman (powerless) and she has to be careful. The Earl was never interested in her really, he found his mistresses more exciting and had a touch of the pox before he was married. He will catch her out soon enough, when he thinks it suits him to expose her. When he does, everything is bound to unravel, even for him.

It will certainly be curtains for me and Oumar too, unless we can work out a way of getting ourselves sold off before the auction, to some other wealthy idiot, before the boxes of ornaments, before the rooms full of old-fashioned furniture, before the endless bad paintings and way before the buckets full of flashy jewels. I'm working on it.

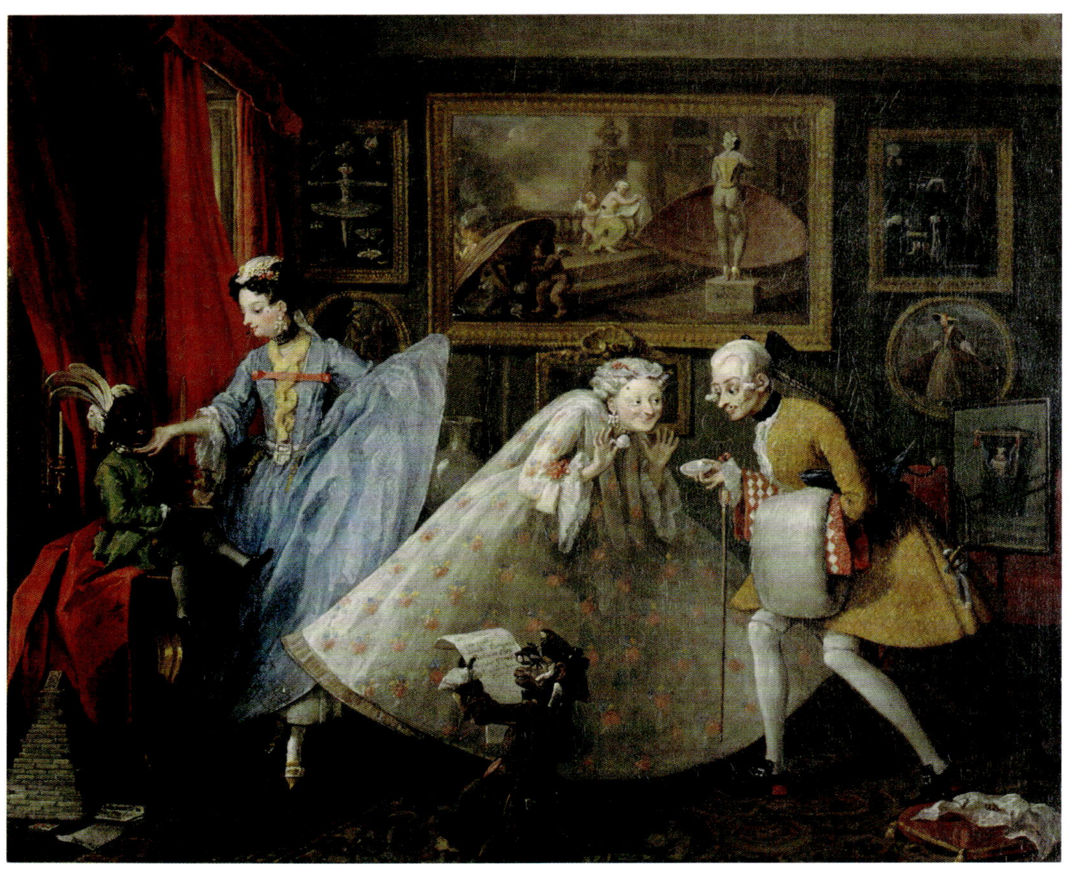

Both *Taste in High Life* and *The Lady's Last Stake* satirise contemporary fashionable life, picturing luxurious materials and artefacts with a painterly eloquence that parallels French paintings of high society. *The Lady's Last Stake* draws on a play by Colley Cibber of the same title (1708); it shows an aristocratic woman who has lost her fortune through gambling and is contemplating the young soldier's offer to enter one last bet risking the restoration of her wealth against an obligation to become his lover.

 Taste in High Life is a much blunter image, bordering on caricature. It lampoons the self-delusion of the rich, presenting an array of Turkish and Chinese imported goods and textiles that are meant, from a western perspective, to be seen as grotesque or trivial. The monkey dressed as a servant in the foreground is intended to be compared with both the 'Frenchified' and 'effeminate' connoisseur holding a tiny piece of china, and, in an overtly racist way, the Black page boy seated to the left.

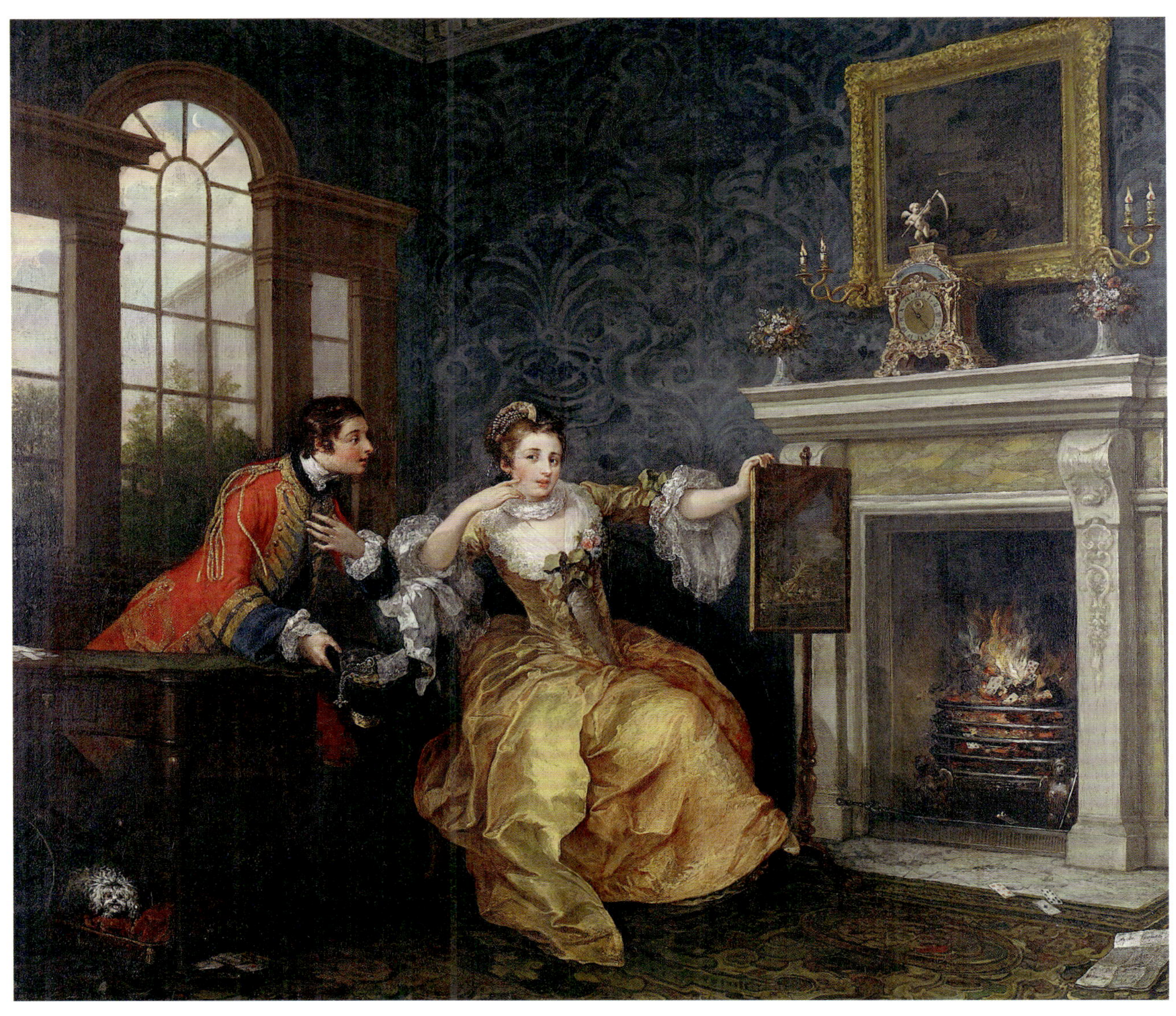

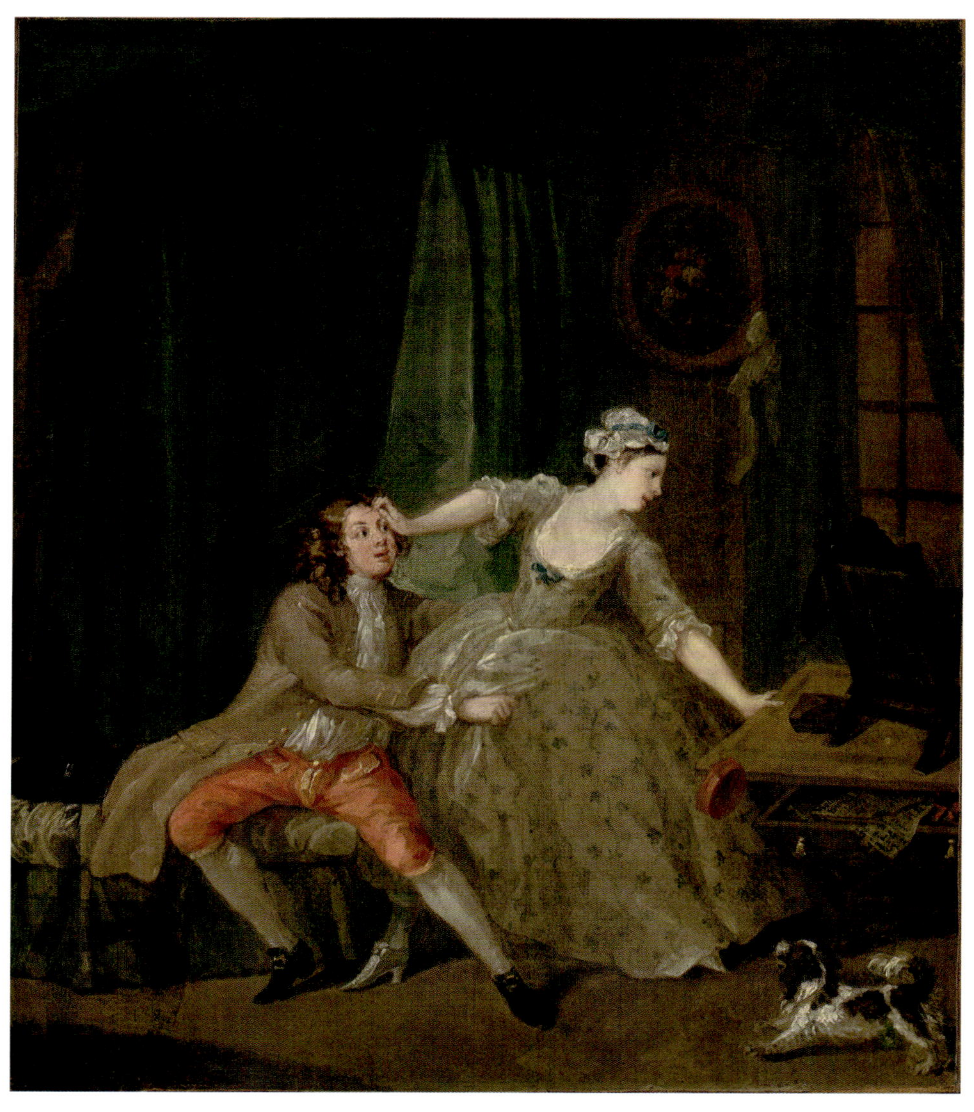

WILLIAM HOGARTH   *Before*   1730–1

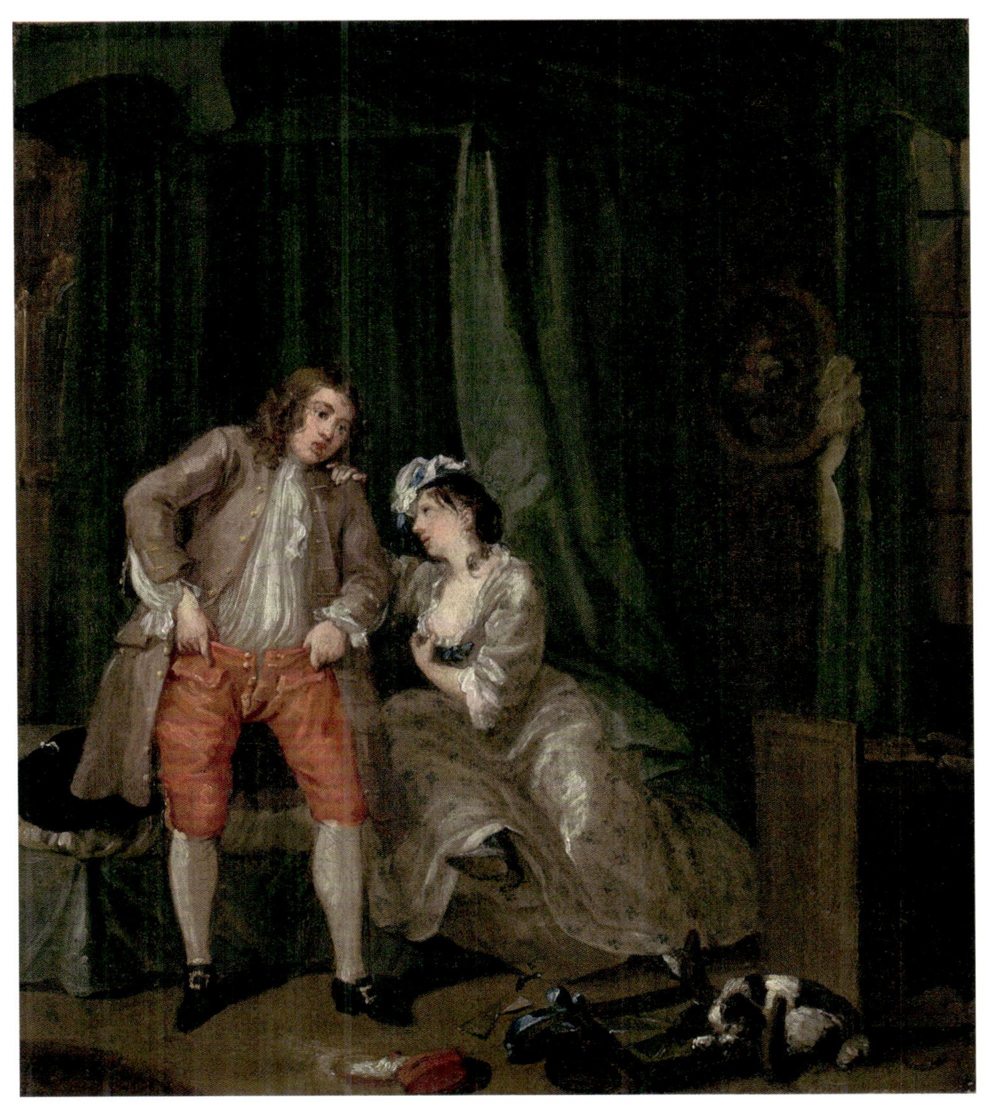

WILLIAM HOGARTH   *After*   1730–1

SEXUALITY AND SEDUCTION

MEREDITH GAMER

In 1730 or so, William Hogarth painted a pair of works known as *Before* and *After*, which depict the prelude to and aftermath of a sexual encounter (p.173). In *Before*, a foppishly dressed young man courts a pretty young woman in the clearing of a wood. He daintily professes his affections, whilst sliding one leg indecorously between her skirts; she replies with a coquettish turn of head, but seems not at all opposed to his advances. In *After*, the couple appears again, this time locked in a sweaty embrace, their faces flushed, hair and clothes in disarray. The apples that have fallen from the lady's white apron (a none-too-subtle allusion to sexual innocence) suggest that something has been lost – most likely, her virginity. But if that's the case, it seems not to have been taken by force so much as willingly given.

Around the same time, Hogarth produced another version of the same theme, allegedly 'at the particular request of a certain vicious nobleman'.[1] Much is different about this second set (pp.170–1). The scene has moved indoors, to a less 'natural' setting, and the nature of the encounter has changed as well. In *Before*, the man, his gold-trimmed trousers bulging visibly at the crotch, grabs the woman's skirts as she twists violently away. With one hand, she claws at his face; with the other, she overturns a nearby dressing table and mirror, which come crashing to the floor. *After* finds them both subdued: he in a stunned, postcoital stupor, she gazing imploringly up at him, though exactly why is left unclear. Is she begging his discretion or – perhaps more plausibly, given the way she suggestively fingers her low décolletage – inviting him to another round?

In all four paintings, Hogarth approaches his central subject matter – heterosexual sex – with an explicitness that is unusual for his period. In early eighteenth-century France, scenes of seduction often featured in a category of picture known as the *fête galante*, in which richly attired men and women are typically shown mingling in lush garden settings (p.140). Rarely do such works make reference to the fact of or potential for sexual violence, except in the most understated of ways. For example, in Jean-Antoine Watteau's *Le Faux Pas* (The Misstep) 1716–18, a seated woman fends off the embrace of an eager

"

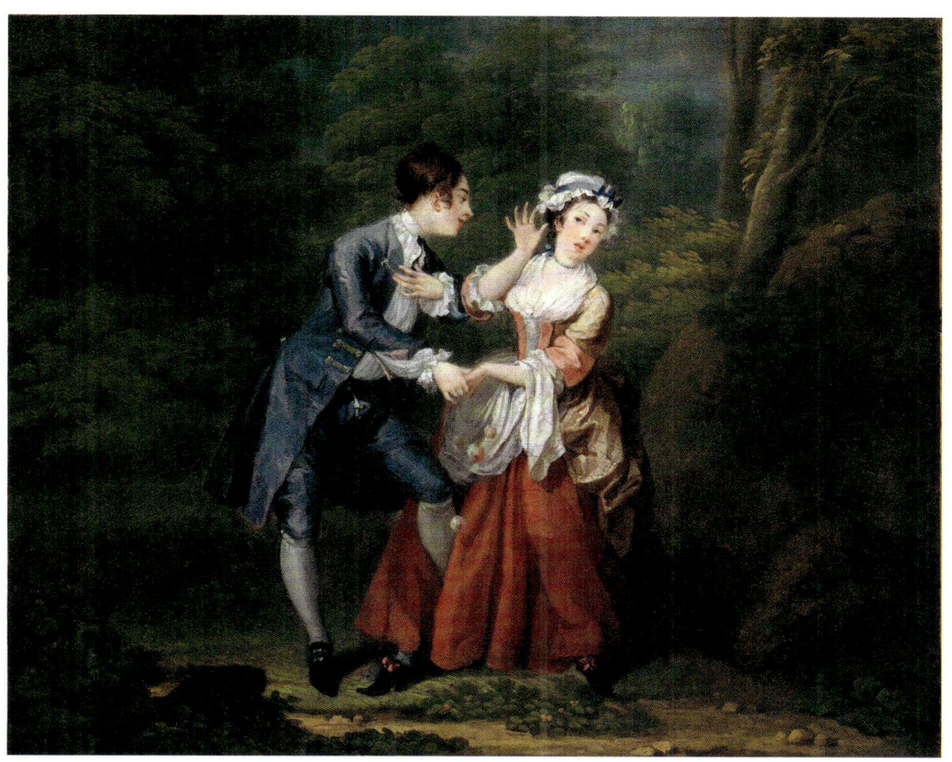

WILLIAM HOGARTH   *Before*   c.1730–1

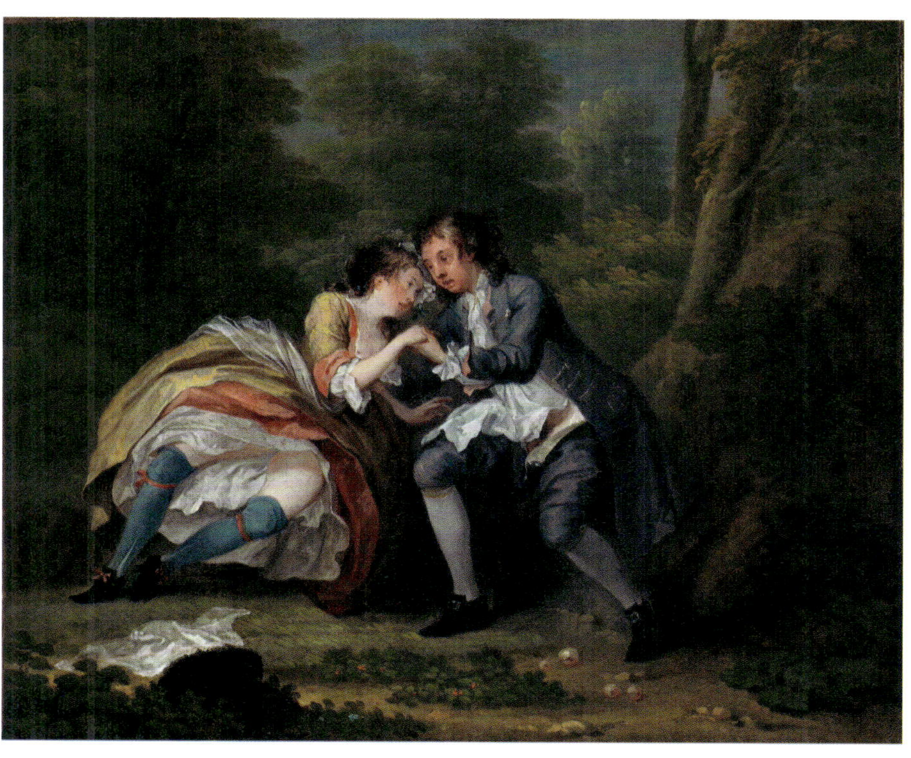

WILLIAM HOGARTH   *After*   c.1730–1

suitor, whose swollen red hand pulls tight at the small of her back (p.175).[2] Nicolas Lancret's enigmatic and evasively titled *Group Portrait in a Landscape with Amorous Couple* c.1737 hinges on a more overt instance of refusal (p.142). Yet even these compositions leave much to our imagination. In neither do we see the facial expression of the resisting woman, nor do we know what the ultimate outcome of her resistance will be.

Hogarth, by contrast, plays out the scenarios he sets up to their logical conclusions. In doing so, he offers two distinct portraits of relations between the sexes: one that appears consensual and mutually gratifying, and another in which force and coercion are patently at play. In the first pair of paintings, we are invited to share in the pleasures the lovers enjoy, most directly, through the titillating glimpses the artist gives of their near-exposed genitalia in *After* (remarkably, he not only pictures the woman's creamy pink thighs, but also the man's limp cock and dark pubic hair, which peek out from behind his dishevelled clothes). The nature of our pleasure in the second set – if there is pleasure to be had at all – is of a darker kind, for it comes, inevitably, at the woman's expense. What we are looking at in this *Before* appears quite clearly to be a scene of rape, a term which began to acquire its modern meaning in the very years these works were painted.[3] The fact that, in *After*, the woman may be interpreted as having been aroused by her assault may be surprising and disturbing to us today. But in the context of dominant eighteenth-century ideas about female sexuality, it made a troubling kind of sense. Ovid's famous dictum in *Ars Amatoria* (The Art of Love) that 'force is pleasing to girls' remained a commonplace of the era, and it was routinely used to justify and even glorify what were, in fact, acts of sexual aggression.[4]

Indeed, such acts are implied and alluded to throughout Hogarth's oeuvre. We need only think of Moll Hackabout in *A Harlot's Progress* 1733, who falls prey to the infamous rake and rapist, Colonel Francis Charteris, in the very first plate of the series (p.99); the unfortunate Sarah Young in *A Rake's Progress* 1734, whom Tom Rakewell seduces with promises of marriage and then jilts as soon as he comes into his inheritance (p.108); or, more unfortunate still, the maidservant Ann Gill in *The Four Stages of Cruelty* 1751, whom Tom Nero not only seduces but savagely murders, after making her his accomplice in a ruthless crime. Most disquieting of all, perhaps, is the young girl in the third scene of *Marriage A-la-Mode, The Inspection* c.1743, who dabs at a sore on her mouth, an early symptom of syphilis; the clear implication is that she has been sold into the sexual service of the series' debauched protagonist, Lord Squanderfield, who sits proprietarily beside her (p.162).[5]

And yet, in other instances, Hogarth represents his female subjects not as sexual victims, but instead – and more interestingly – as sexual agents in their own right. In many eighteenth-century artworks, including Philip Mercier's *A Scene from 'The Careless Husband'* 1738 (p.144), women appear simply as passive and vulnerable objects of a desirous male gaze. Not so in Hogarth's art. Look, for example, at the voluptuous stretch of the young wife in *Marriage A-la-Mode*, back from a night of extramarital indiscretions (p.161); or at the decidedly ambiguous expression of the aristocratic lady in *The Lady's Last Stake* 1759 as she contemplates the possibility of an illicit affair with the dashing officer beside her (p.169). Or look back, for that matter, at the coy maiden in the first of Hogarth's *Before* paintings, as she sizes up her potential lover with a sly, sidelong glance. These are women who are awake and alert to their own sexual appetites, and who have a mind to satisfy them. No doubt, such sexualised figures must have been pleasing to Hogarth himself, and to his many male patrons and buyers. But plenty of women saw his pictures, too – and they could draw their own conclusions.

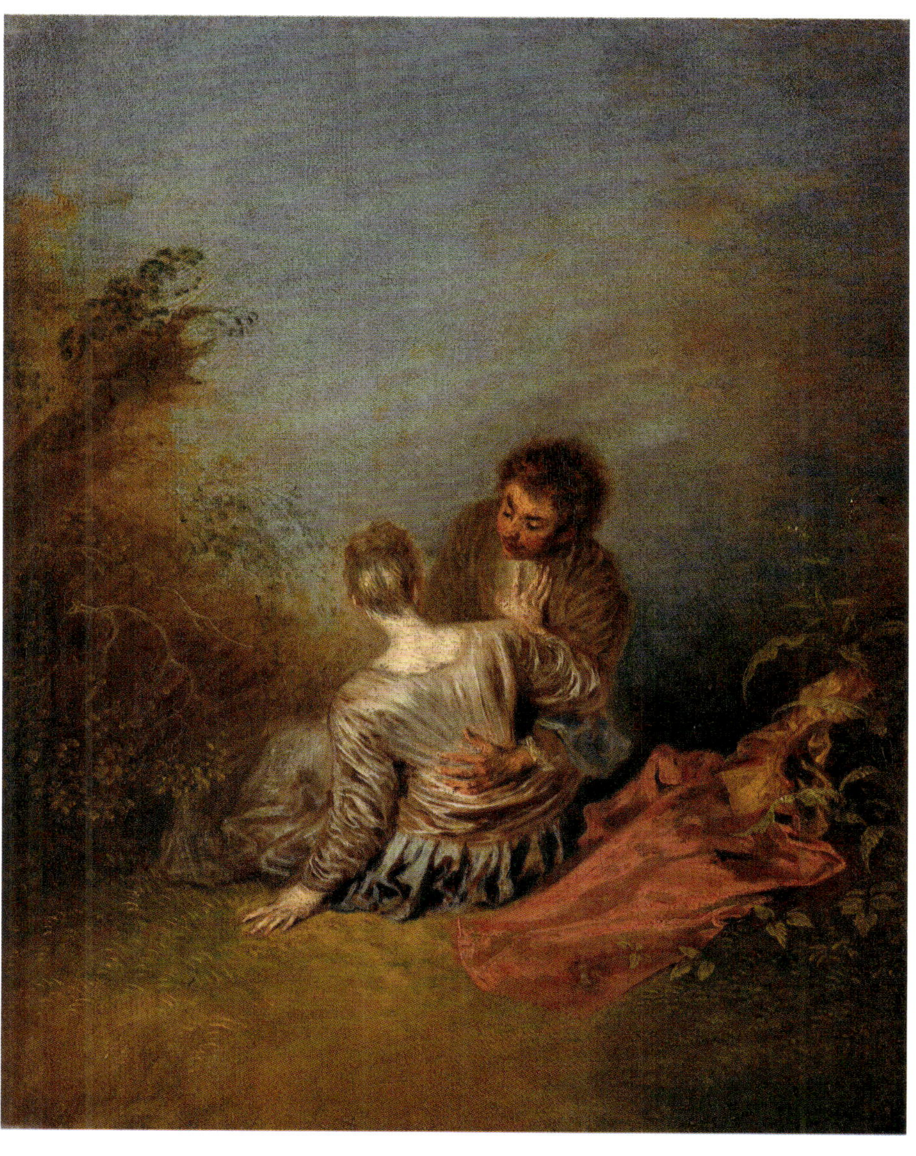

THE NEW
EUROPEANS

Portrait painting was the most dependable source of income for artists across eighteenth-century Europe. It had traditionally involved soliciting the support of state, monarchy and aristocracy, who alone could afford to pay for flattering self-images. The resulting portraits followed quite firmly established formulae, making the sitter's status, and supposed personal qualities, immediately legible to those in the know.

As the century progressed, however, a wider range of people commissioned portraits and the character of portraiture changed. Instead of the rigid hierarchies of status and stiff poses of earlier images, there was a new emphasis upon individuality, informality and ease. While this led to greater pictorial variety, the way these pictures communicated ideas about status and identity arguably became less definite and less immediately legible. Sometimes these images seem to test distinctions of class, gender and race. They can seem to speak subjectively across the centuries to give a glimpse of possibilities for alternative histories and identities, but in ways which can feel inscrutable or open to interpretation.

Many of the artworks reproduced in this book speak to the emergence of new ideas about society and the individual. These are visible in the way cities and communities are shown, in the stories they tell and the social types they present. The images assembled in this section focus more intently on historical individuals. In their frank expressions, casual poses and apparent realism, many of these images seem to address us directly.

Hogarth's portraits of his sisters (pp.196–7) are tokens of familial affection, but also offer an image of commercially independent women whose important presence in London's burgeoning economy has often been overlooked. His picture of the actor David Garrick and his wife, the Austrian dancer Eva-Maria Veigel, presents a flamboyantly relaxed idea of creative partnership. His striking portrait of Mary Edwards, one of his most extraordinary single images, gives a lively presentation of intellectual independence and cultural agency.

But artists in France, the Netherlands and elsewhere were simultaneously exploring a far more diverse and individualistic sense of portraiture, which could make visible – even in the handling of paint or marble – the new sense of personal freedom that was emerging in mid-eighteenth-century Europe. These are images which speak loudly of the ethos of individuality that remains influential in the western world today. But these same qualities may help to disguise how dependent modernising Europe was upon global commerce, exploitation and social injustice. These new Europeans were being characterised by artists in emphatically individualistic terms, in ways which we may still find engaging. But by being themselves they were participating in the daunting rise of western individualism and the economic and imperial power which sustained it, and whose contradictions, creativity and destructive force have shaped the world we live in.

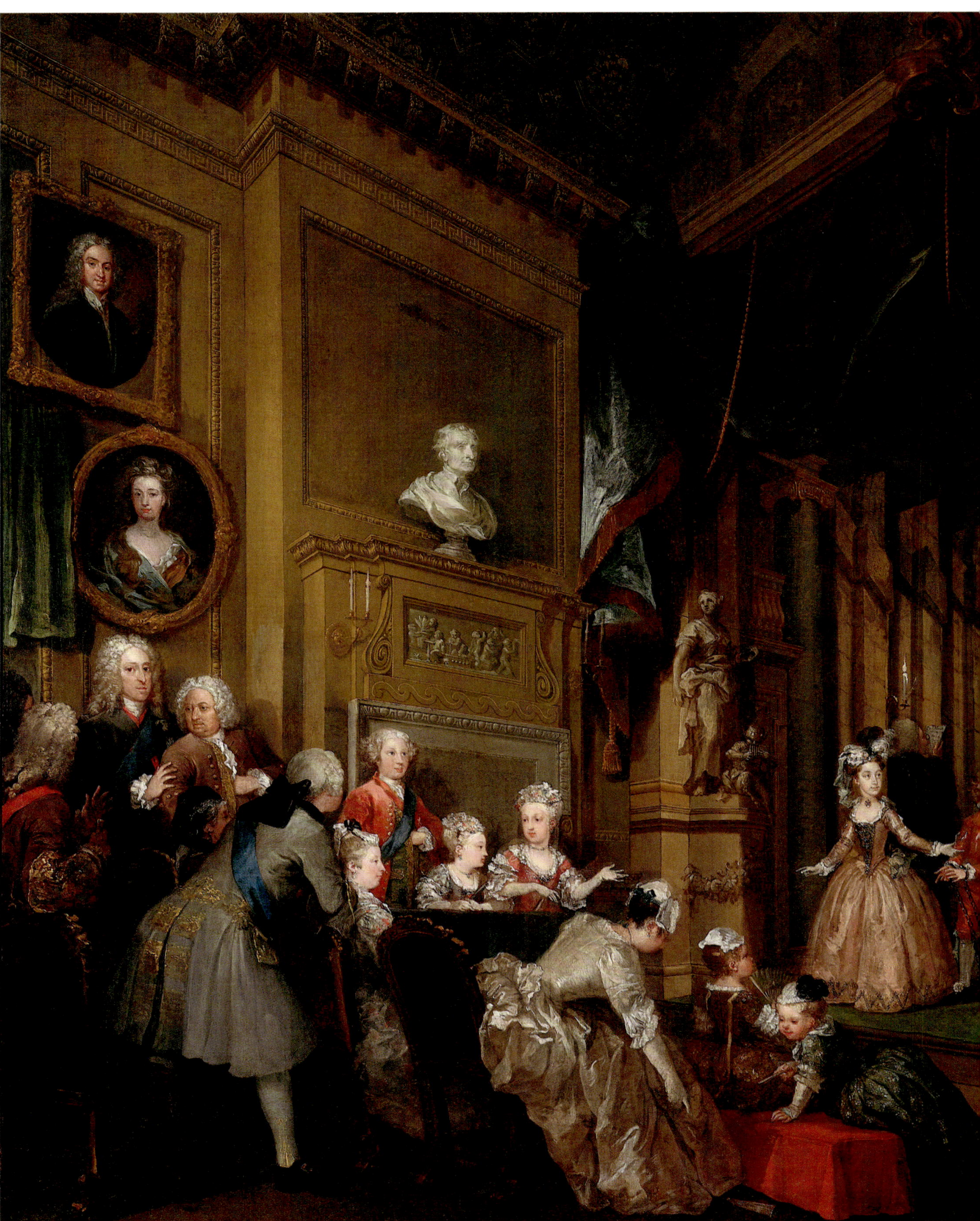

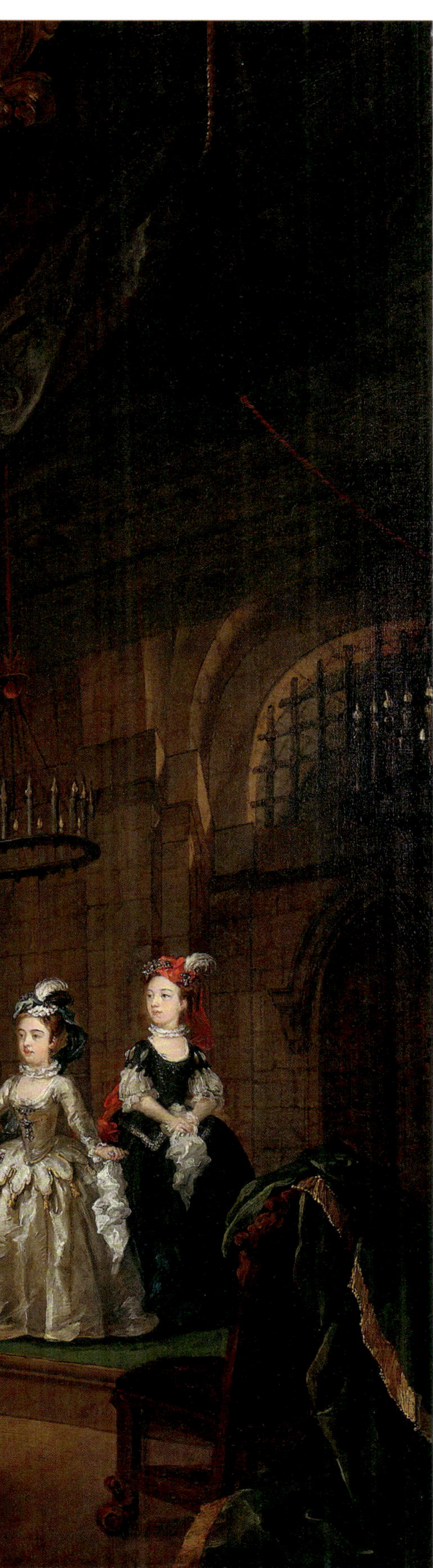

*A Performance of 'The Indian Emperor or
The Conquest of Mexico by the Spaniards'*   c.1732–5

Reality and theatre, the local and the global, mix and
blur in Hogarth's most ambitious 'conversation
piece'. In the household of John Conduitt, Master of
the Mint, children perform John Dryden's *The Indian
Emperor* (1665), which deals thematically with the
Spanish conquest of Mexico.

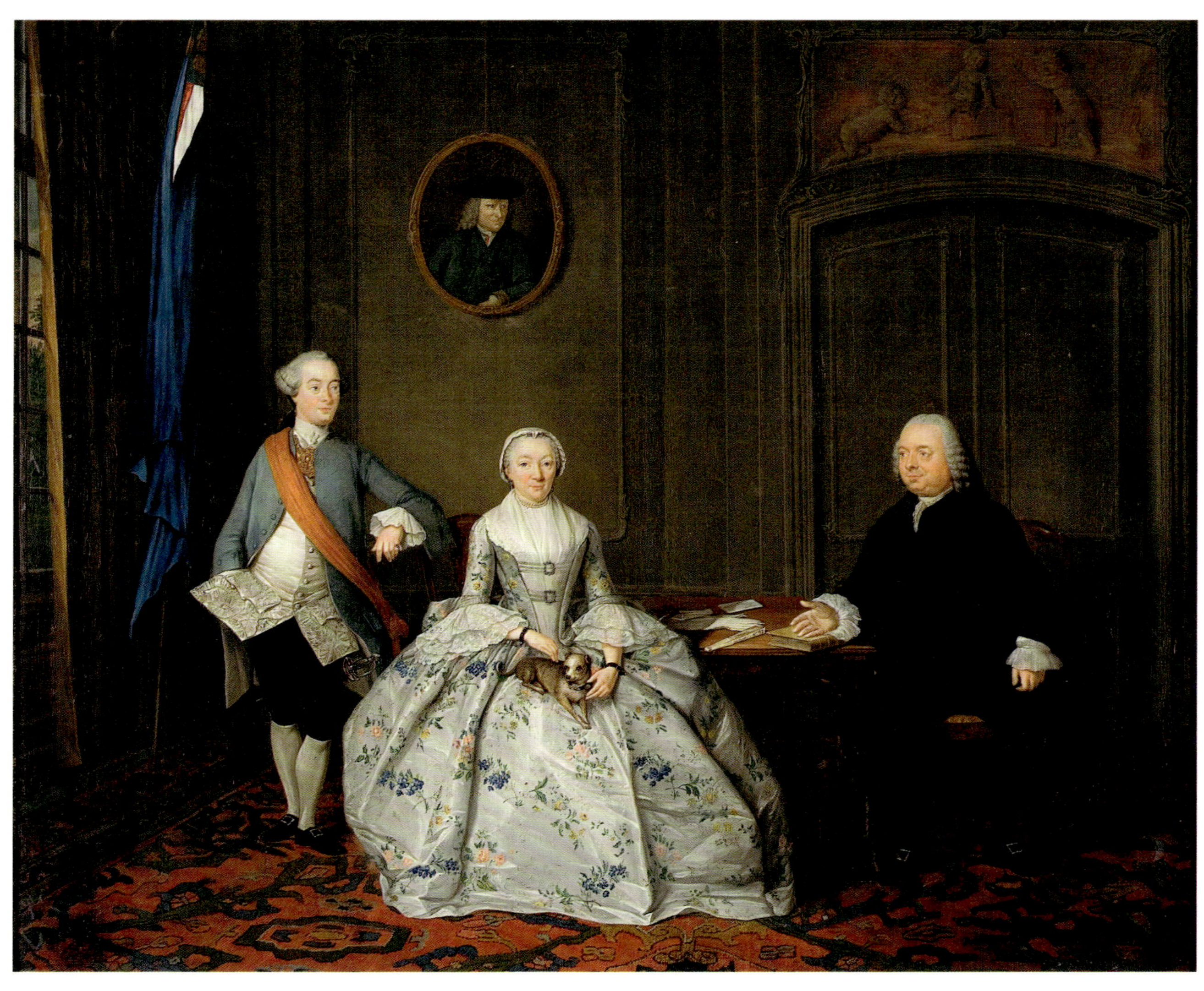

TIBOUT REGTERS   *Portrait of the Van den Broeck family*   c.1760

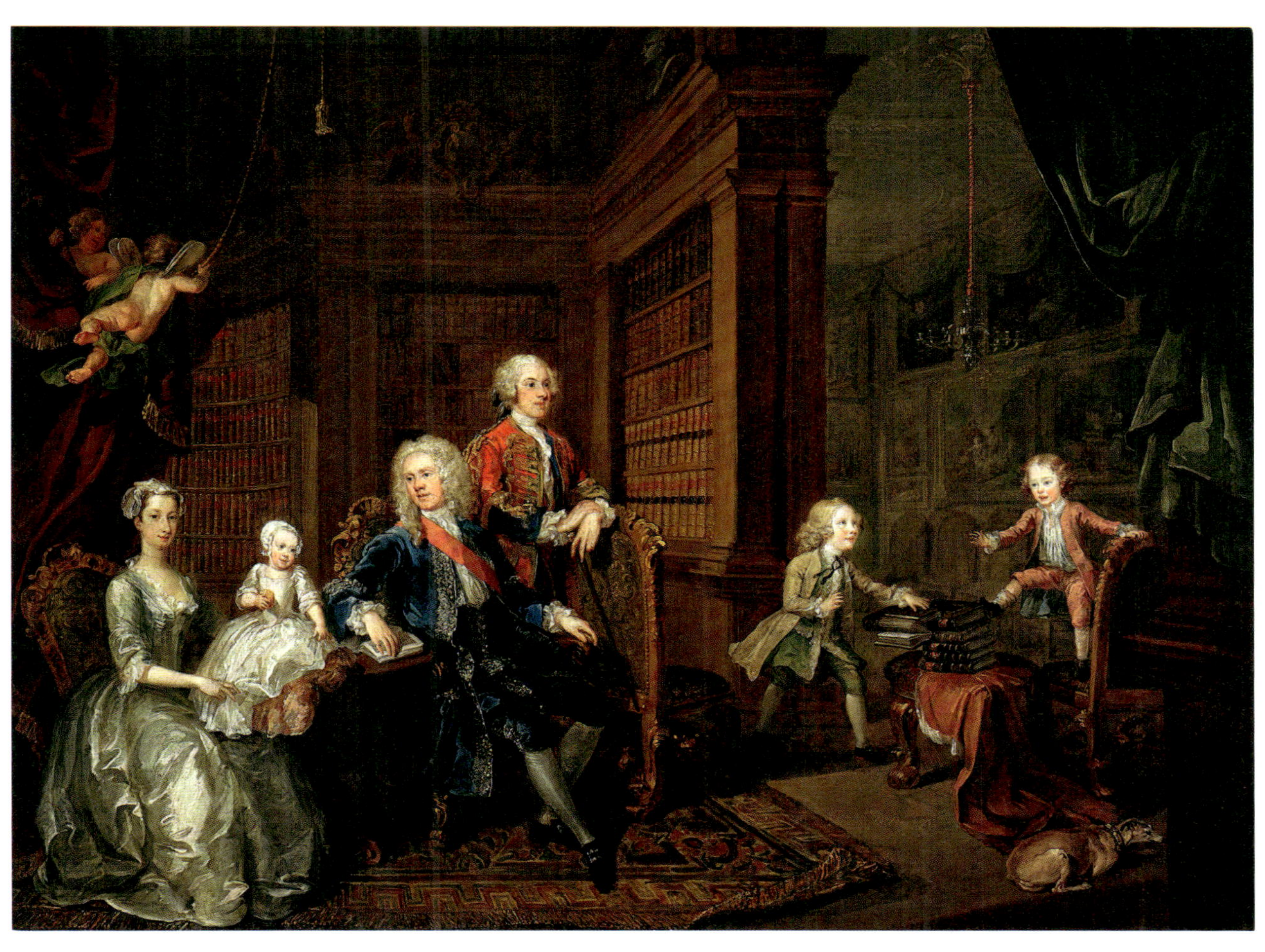

181

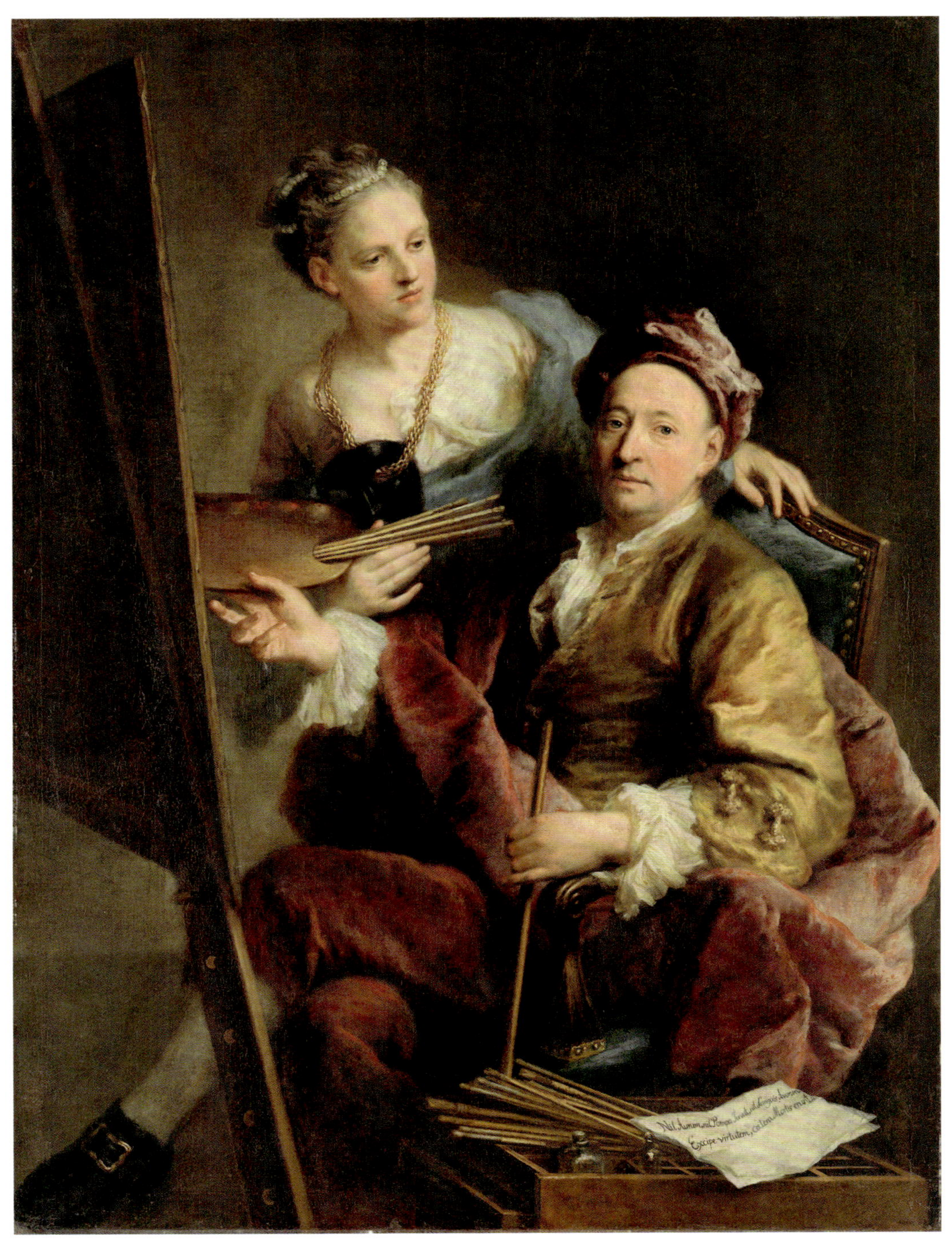

GEORG DESMARÉES *The Artist with his Daughter Antonia* 1760

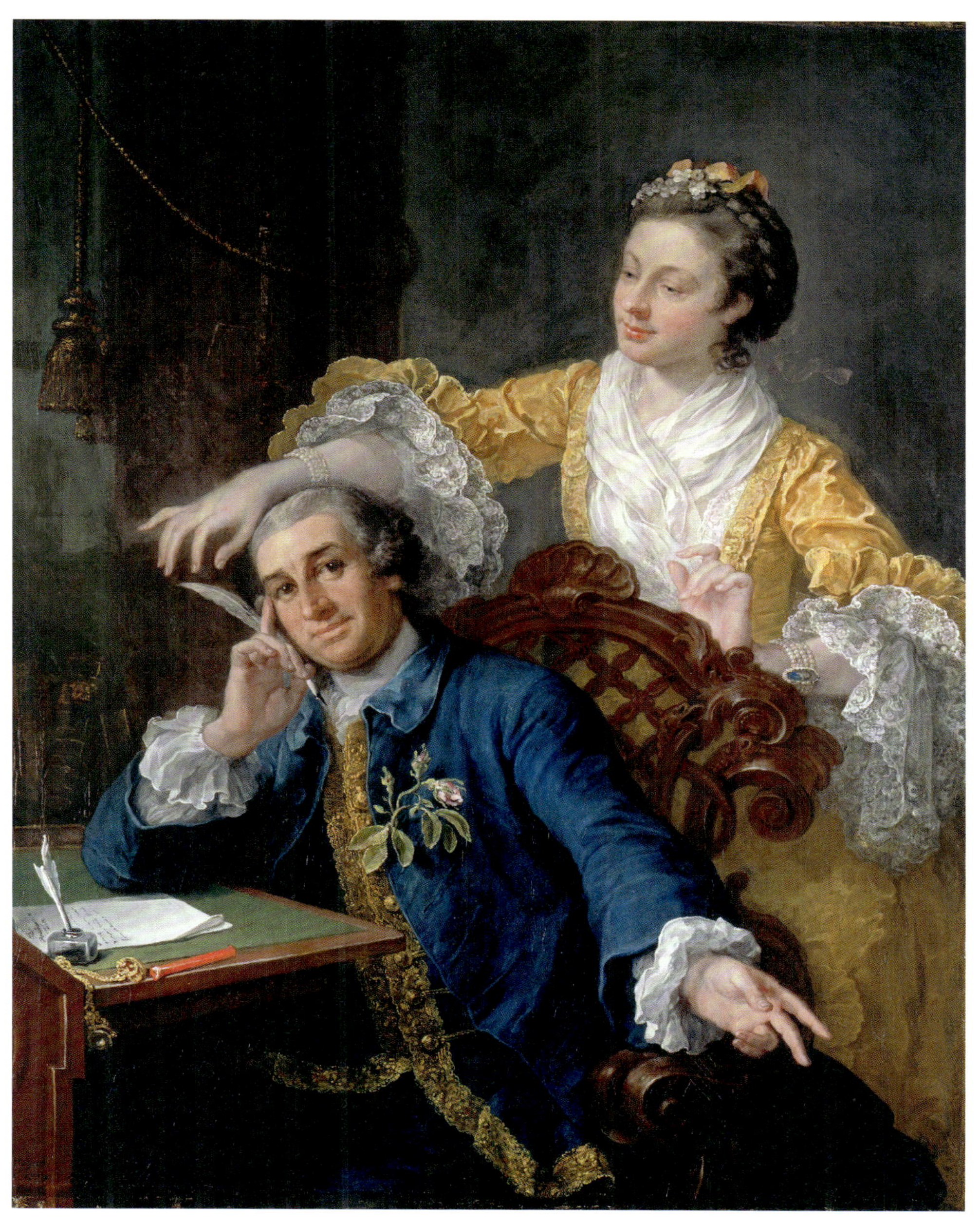

WILLIAM HOGARTH   *David Garrick with his Wife Eva-Maria Veigel*   c.1757–64

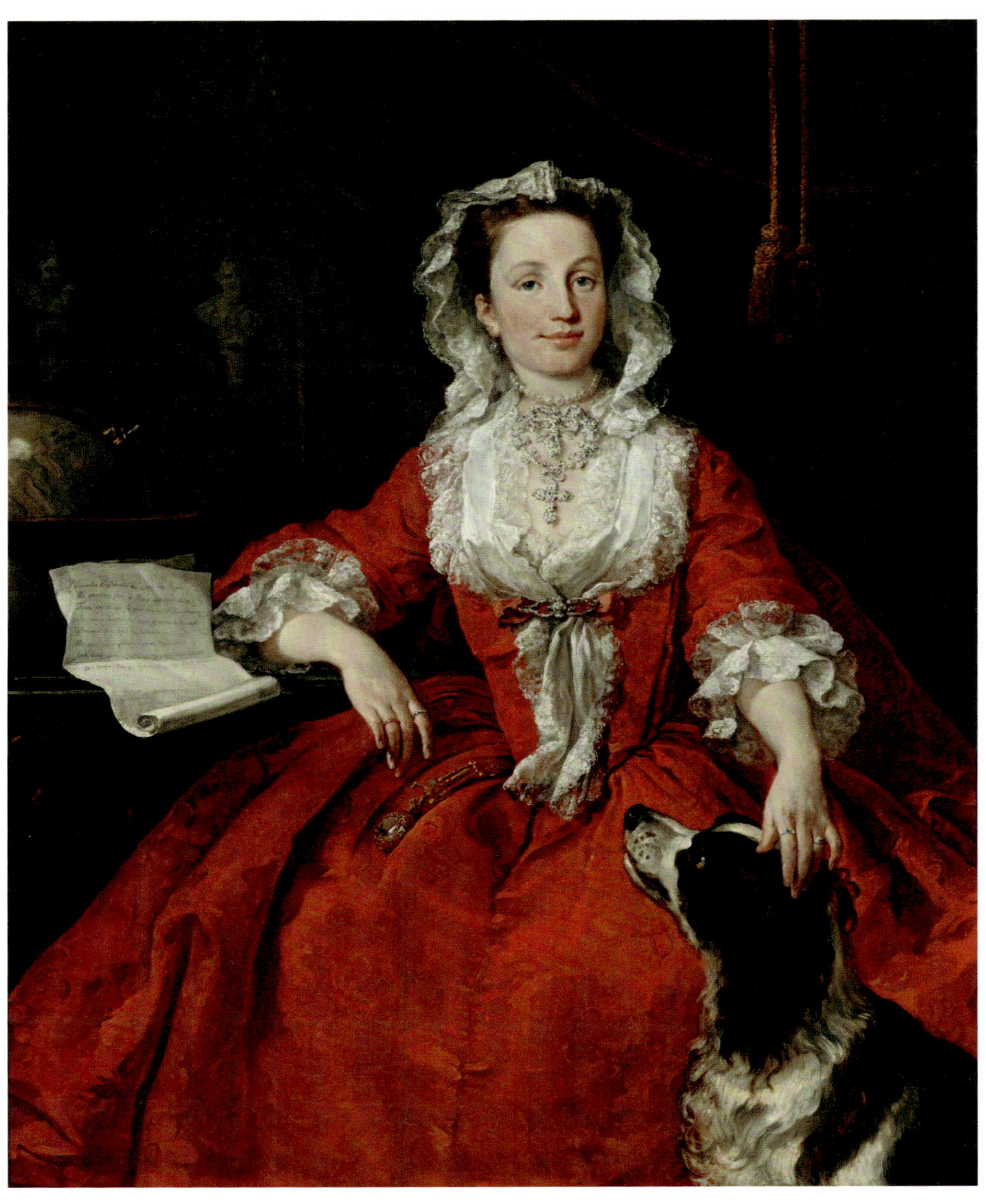

184

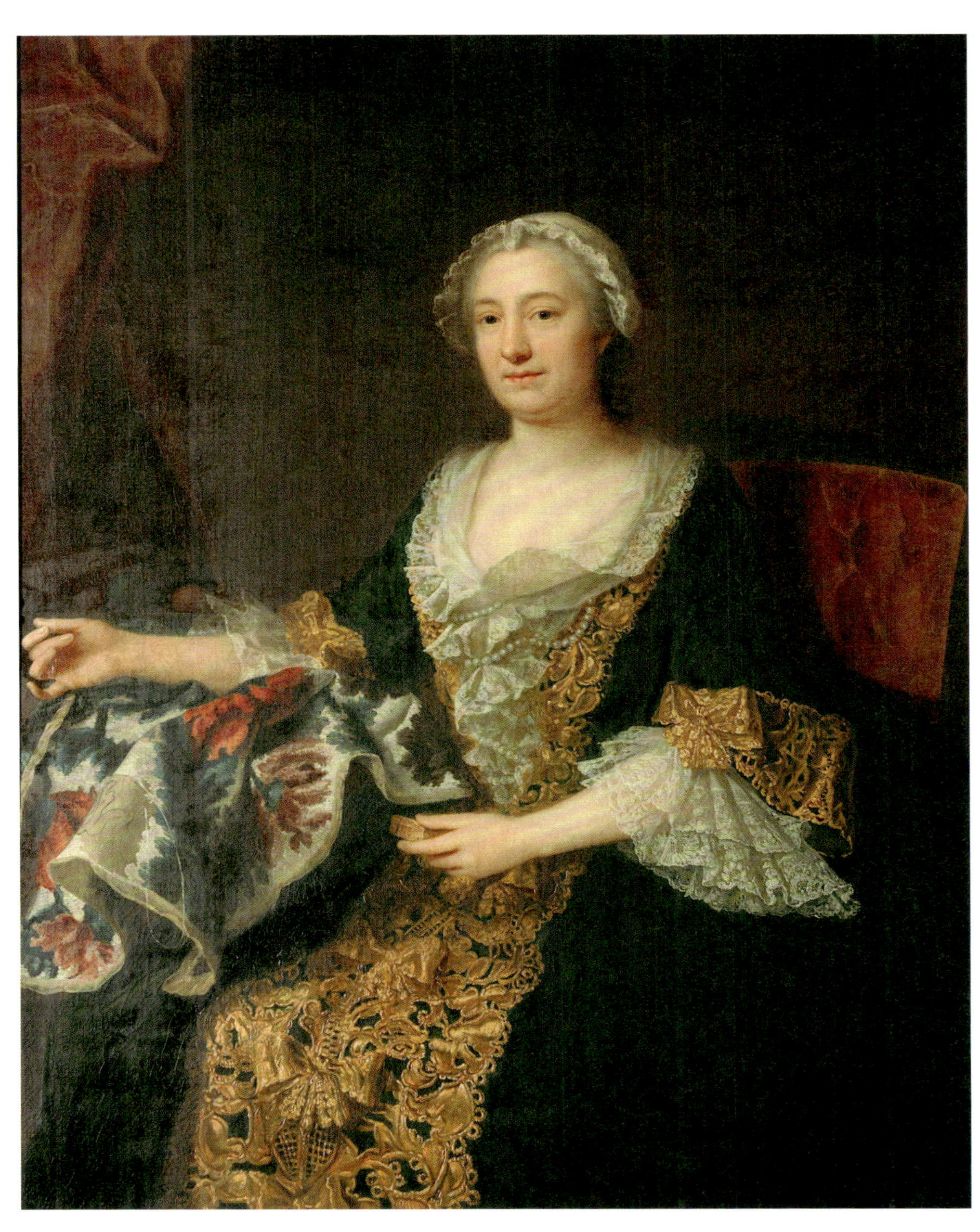

JACQUES-ANDRÉ-JOSEPH AVED
The Marquise de Castellane with Her Embroidery   1743

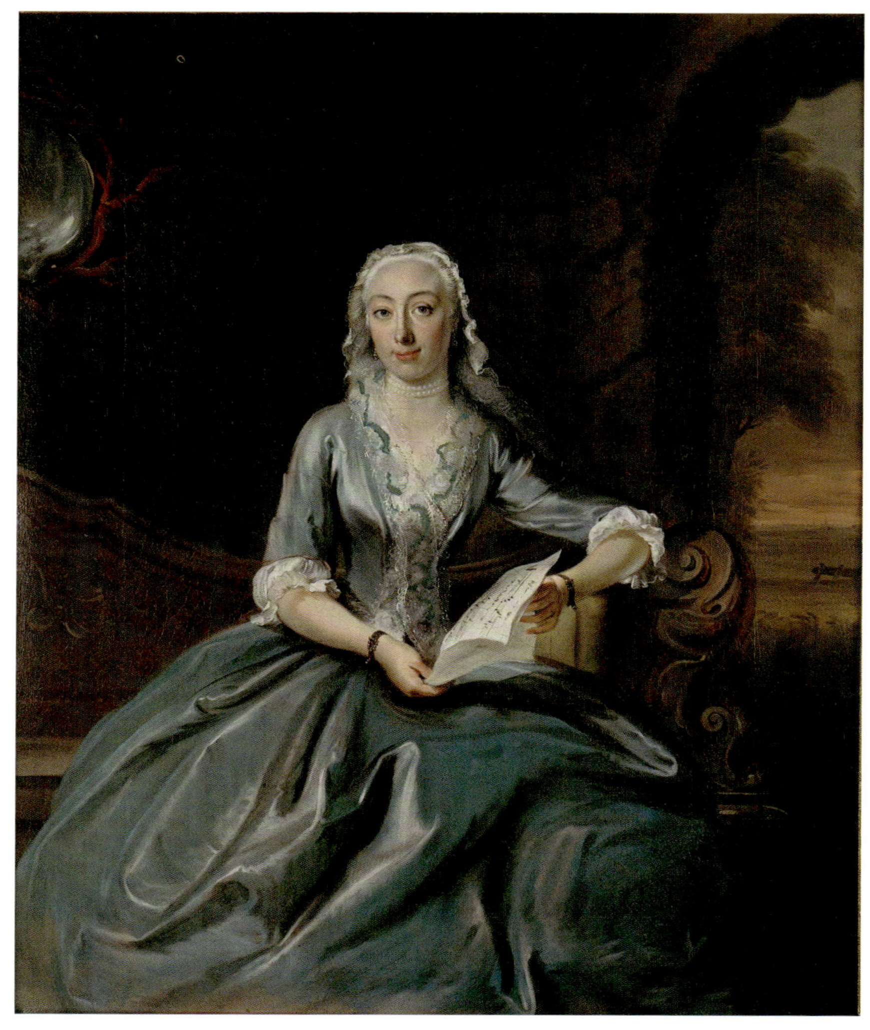

CORNELIS TROOST   *Portrait of a Lady*   1741

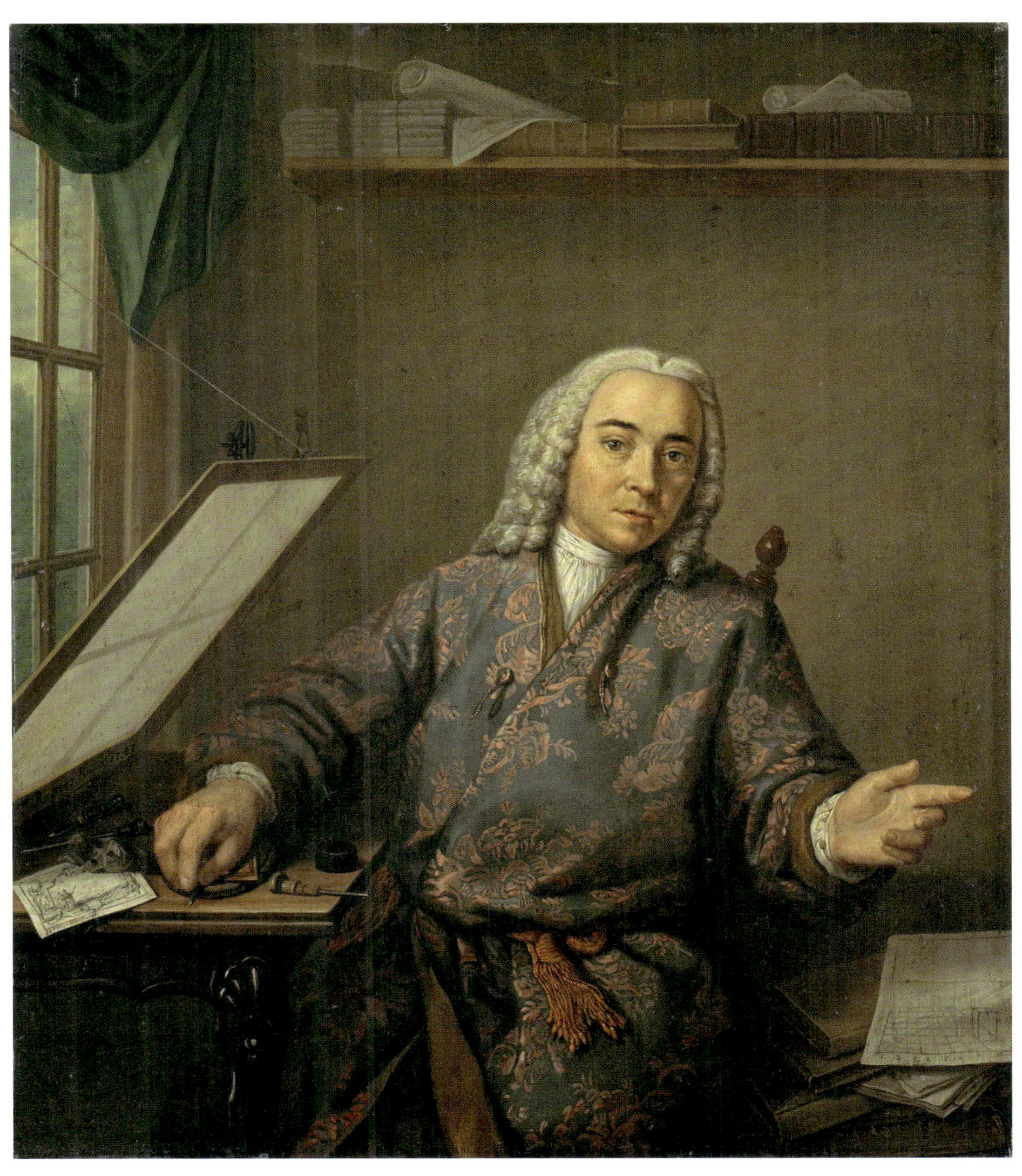

TIBOUT REGTERS   *Portrait of the engraver Jan Casper Philips*   1747

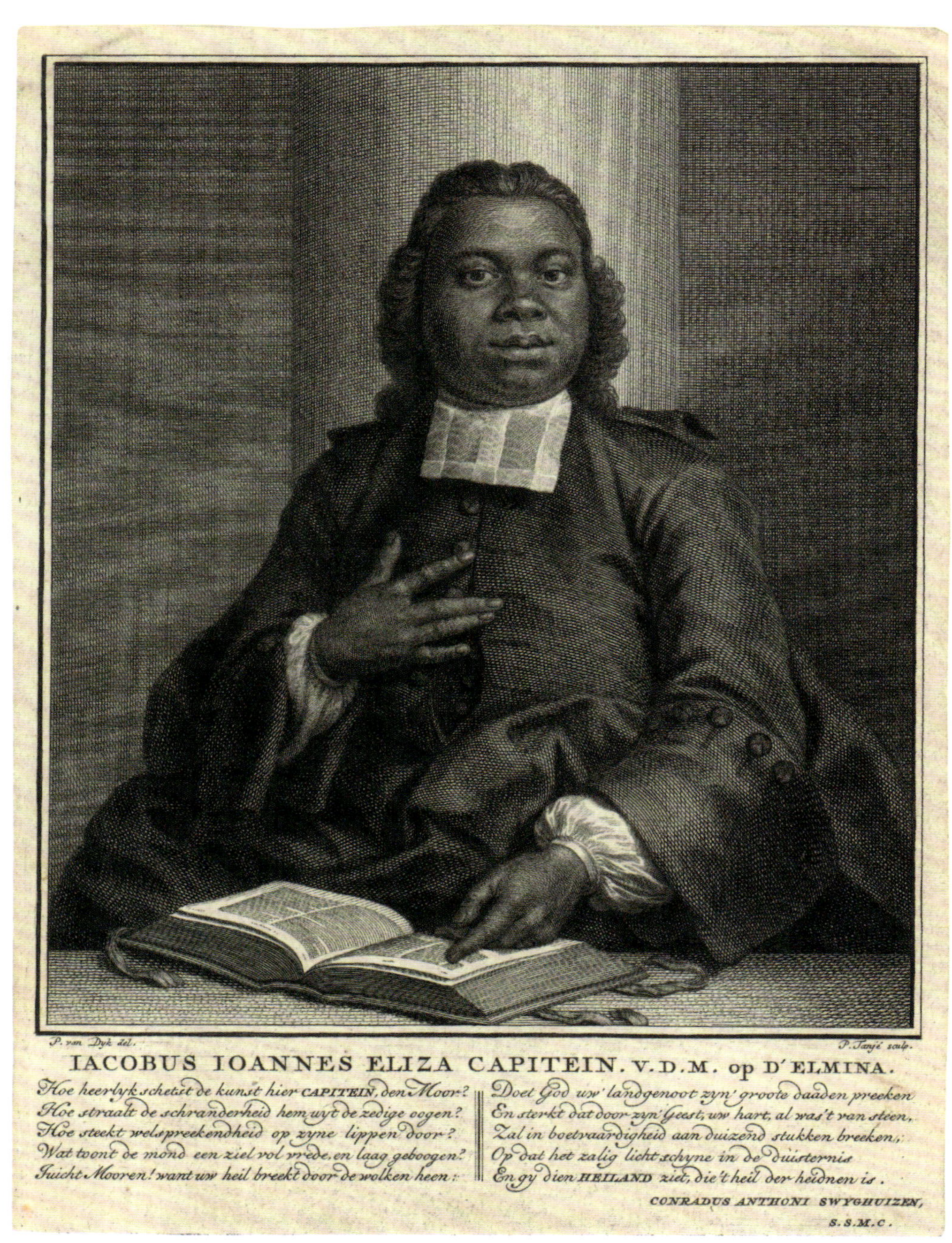

PIETER TANJÉ AFTER PHILIP VAN DIJK
Portrait of Pastor Jacobus Elisa Capitein   1742

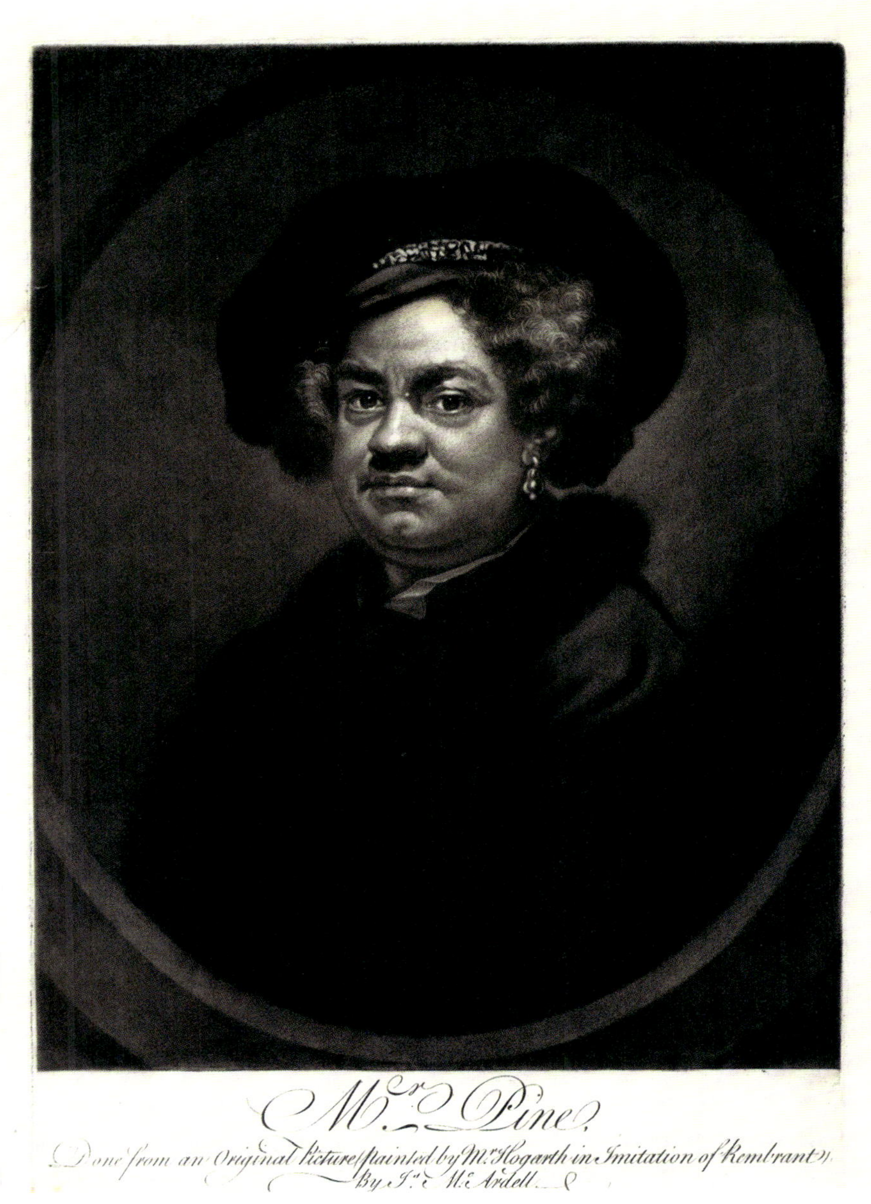

JAMES MACARDELL AFTER WILLIAM HOGARTH *John Pine* c.1756

Hogarth's portrait of his friend, the engraver John Pine – who also featured as the friar in *The Gate of Calais* (p.57) – adopts the direct, dramatically lit style of Rembrandt. From at least the late nineteenth century Pine was being identified as of African descent, especially within the literature of Freemasonry which claimed him as a pioneer 'Black Mason'. Modern art historical literature has been dismissive of these claims, despite the lack of any evidence for or against it. This attitude is, in itself, telling, for it is entirely possible that he could have had African heritage: by the mid-eighteenth century there were thousands of Black people in London, perhaps 1–3 per cent of the overall population of 650,000.

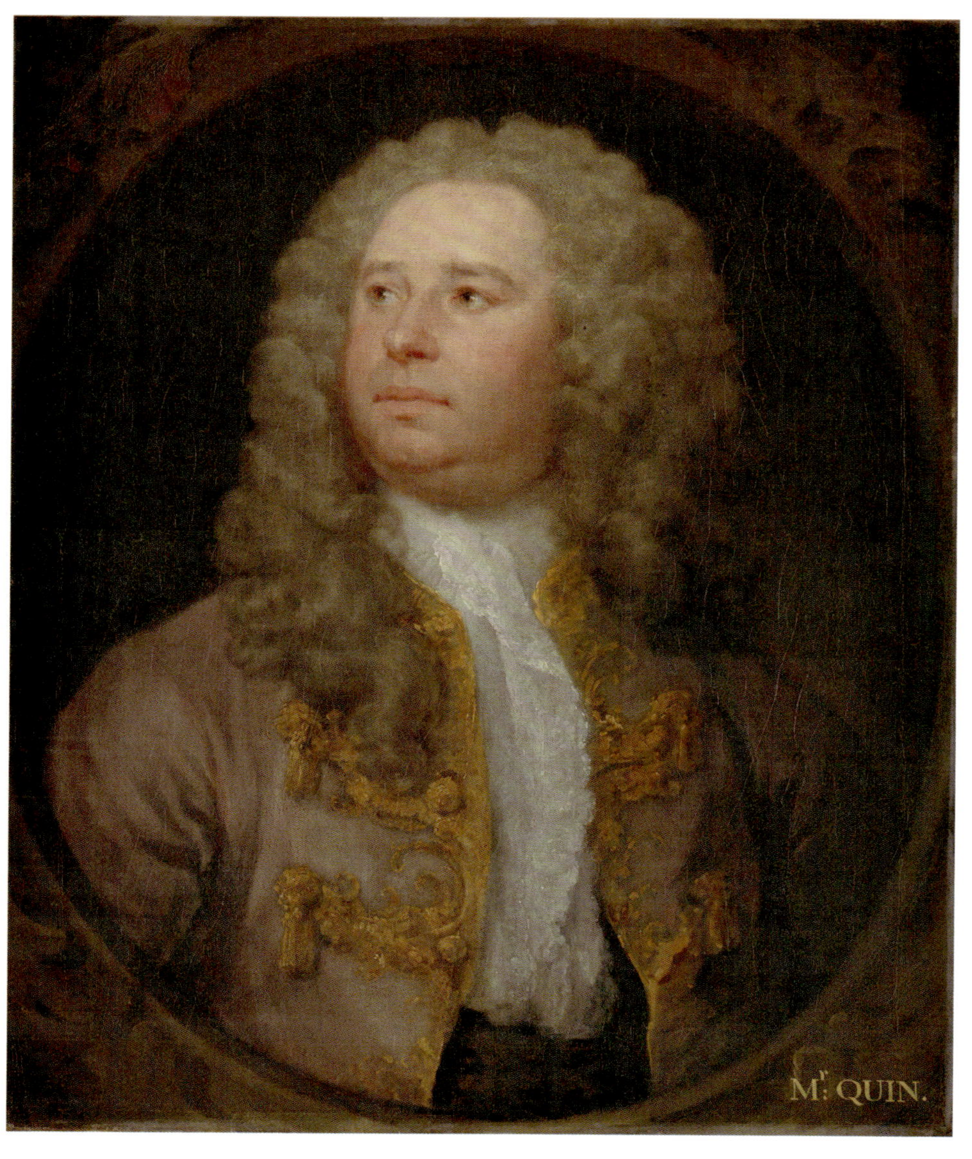

WILLIAM HOGARTH   *James Quin, Actor*   c.1739

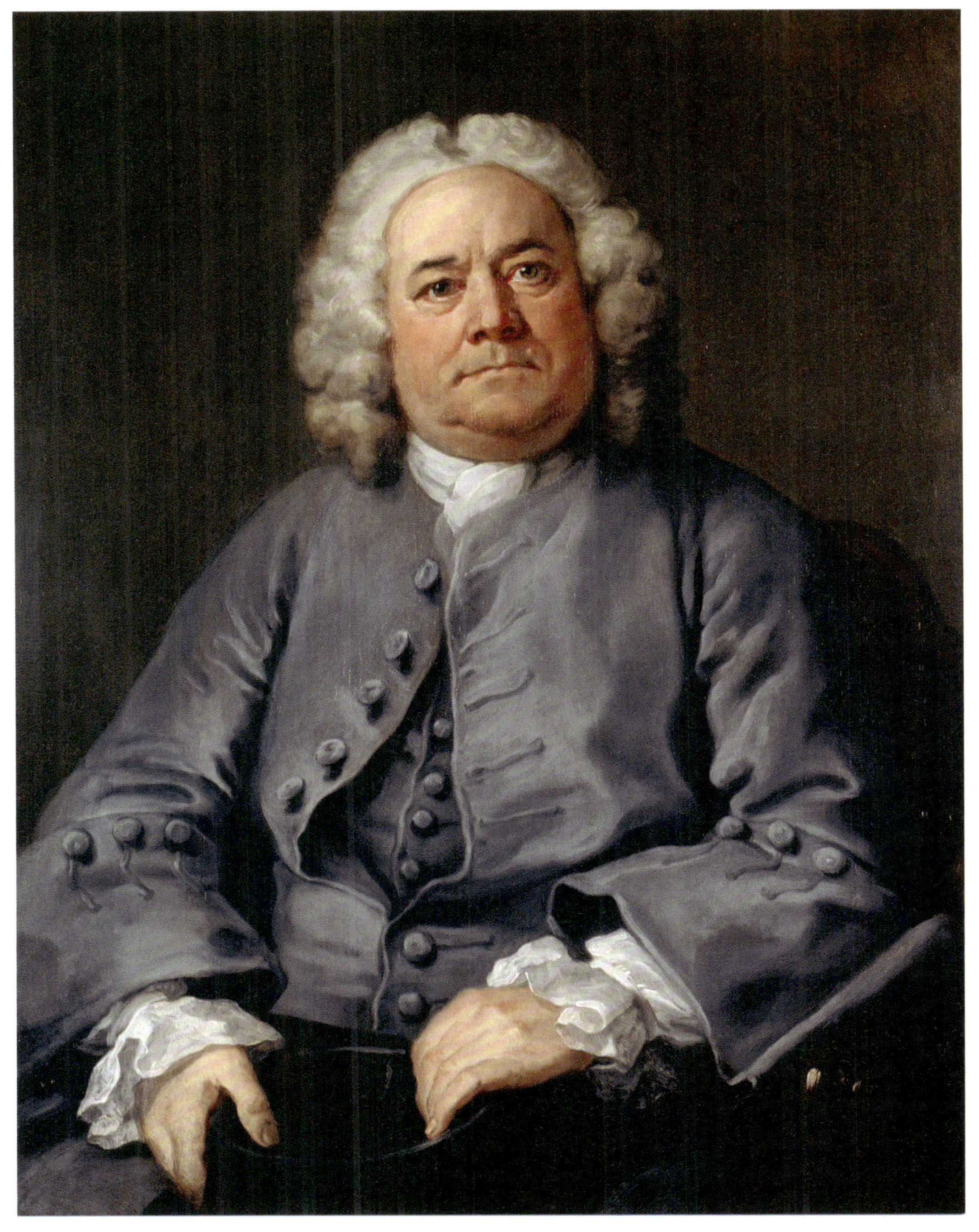

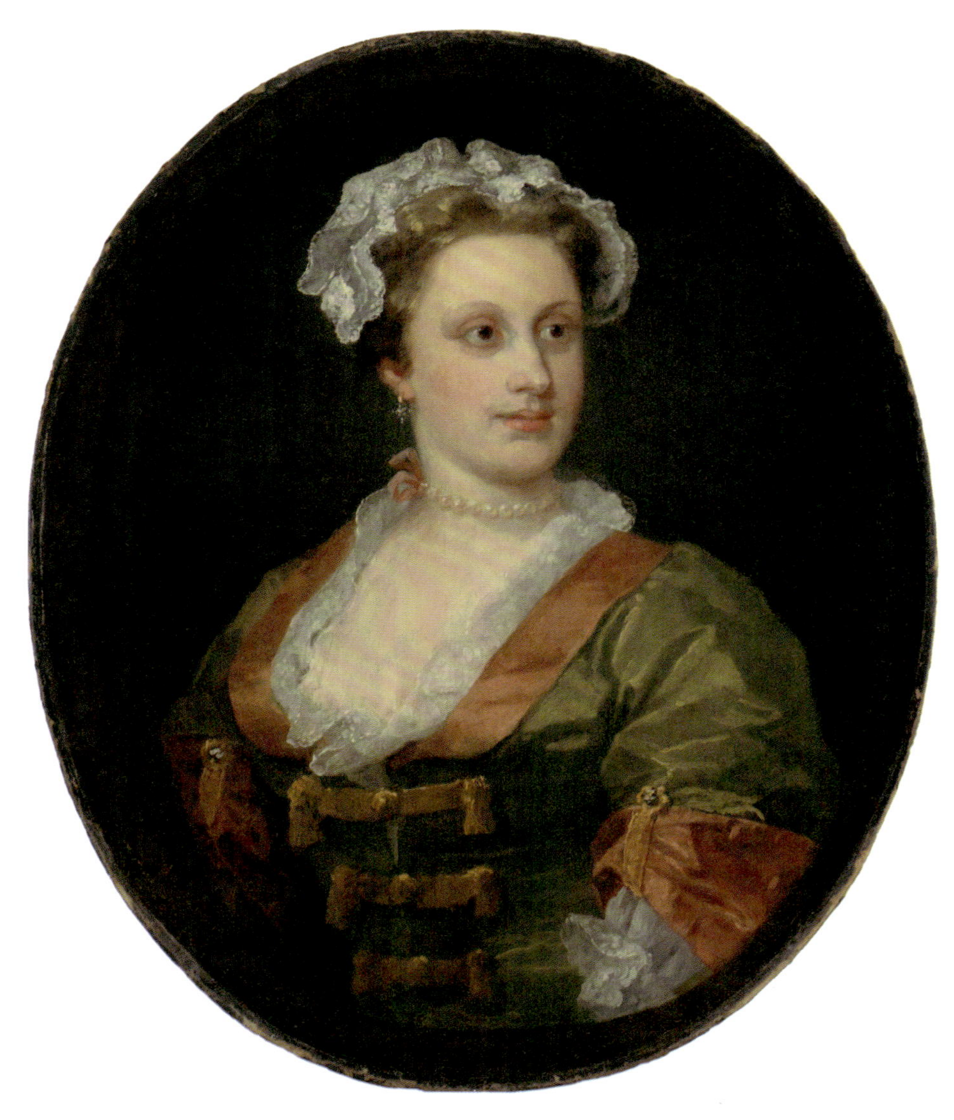

192 WILLIAM HOGARTH *Lavinia Fenton, Duchess of Bolton* c.1740–50

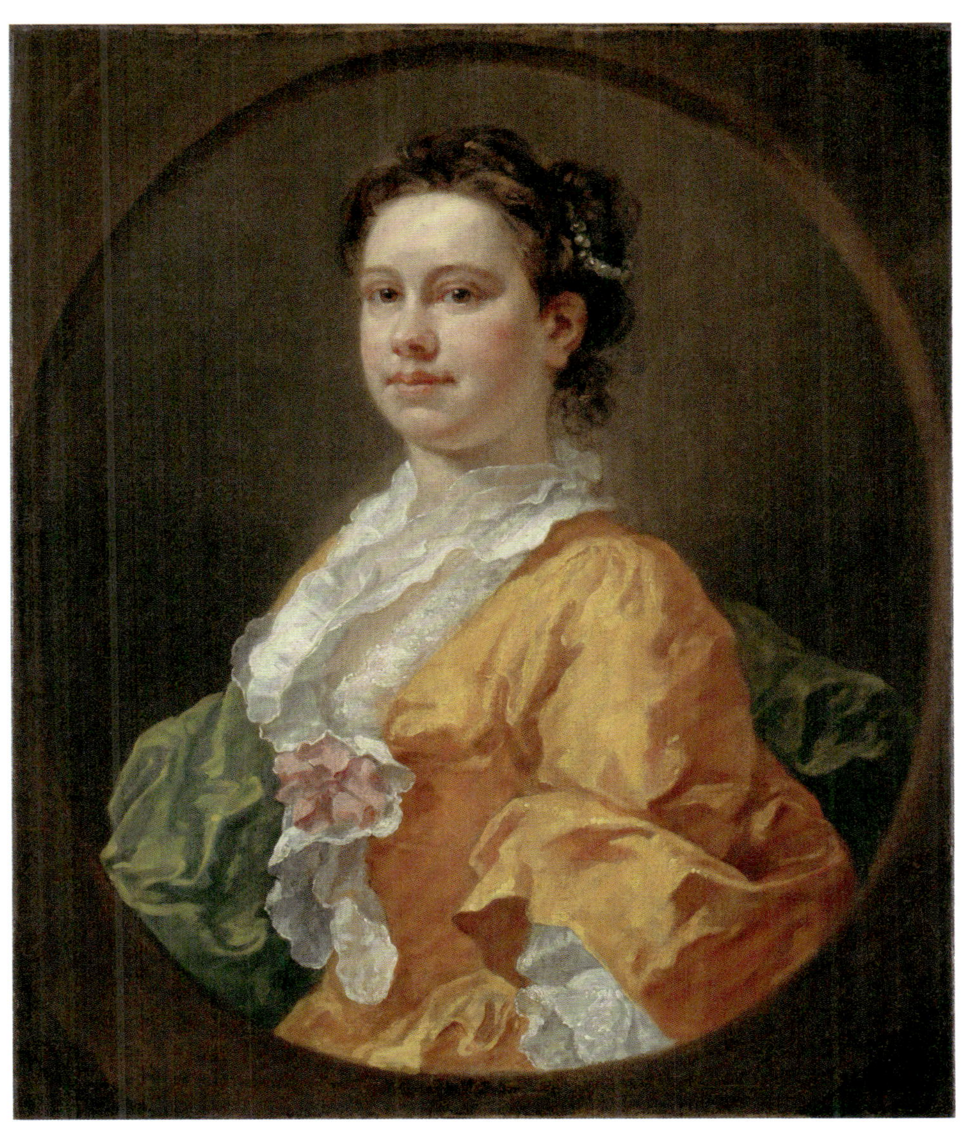

WILLIAM HOGARTH   *Mrs Salter*   1741

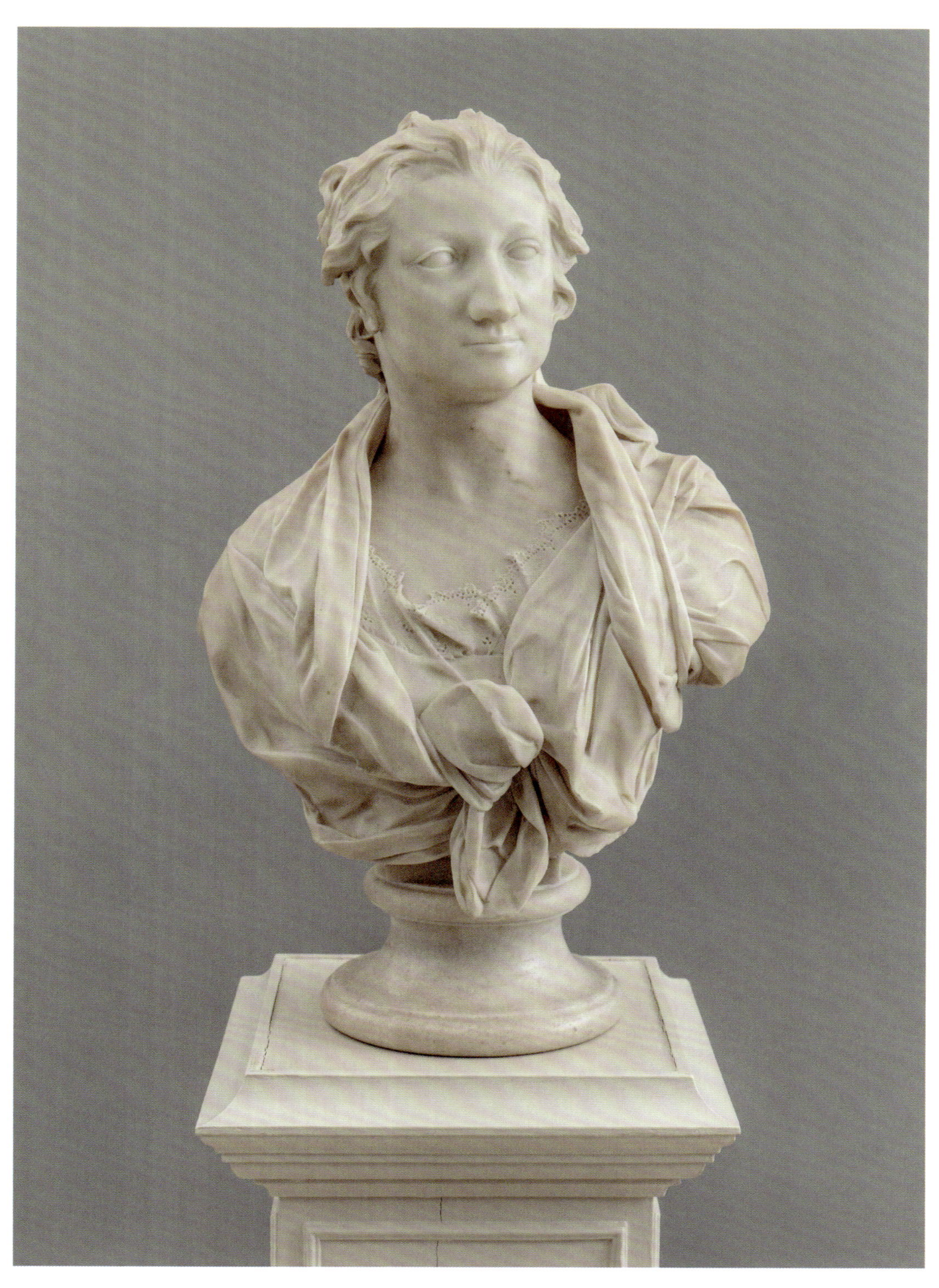

LOUIS FRANÇOIS ROUBILIAC
Arabella, née Bates, wife of George Aufrere   1748

194

WILLIAM HOGARTH
Portrait of Elizabeth Betts, Mrs Benjamin Hoadly   1741

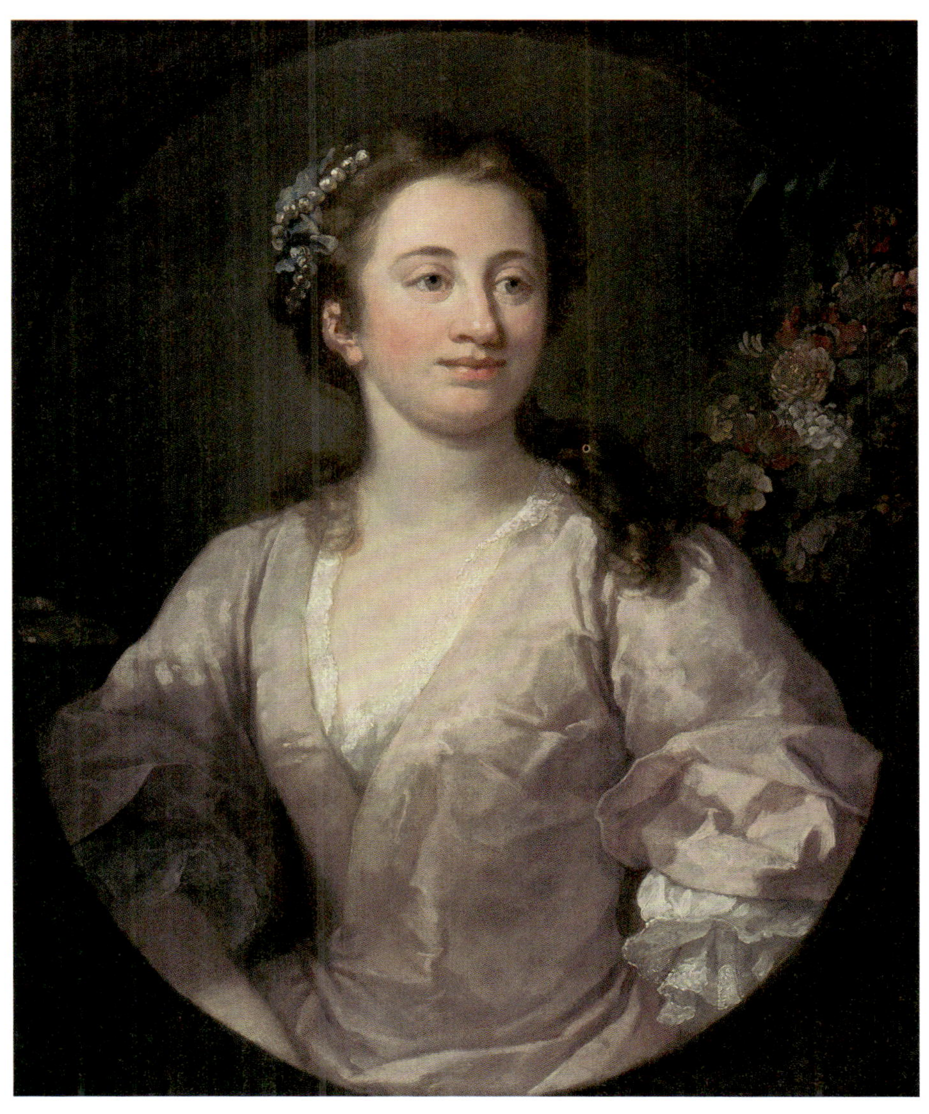

195

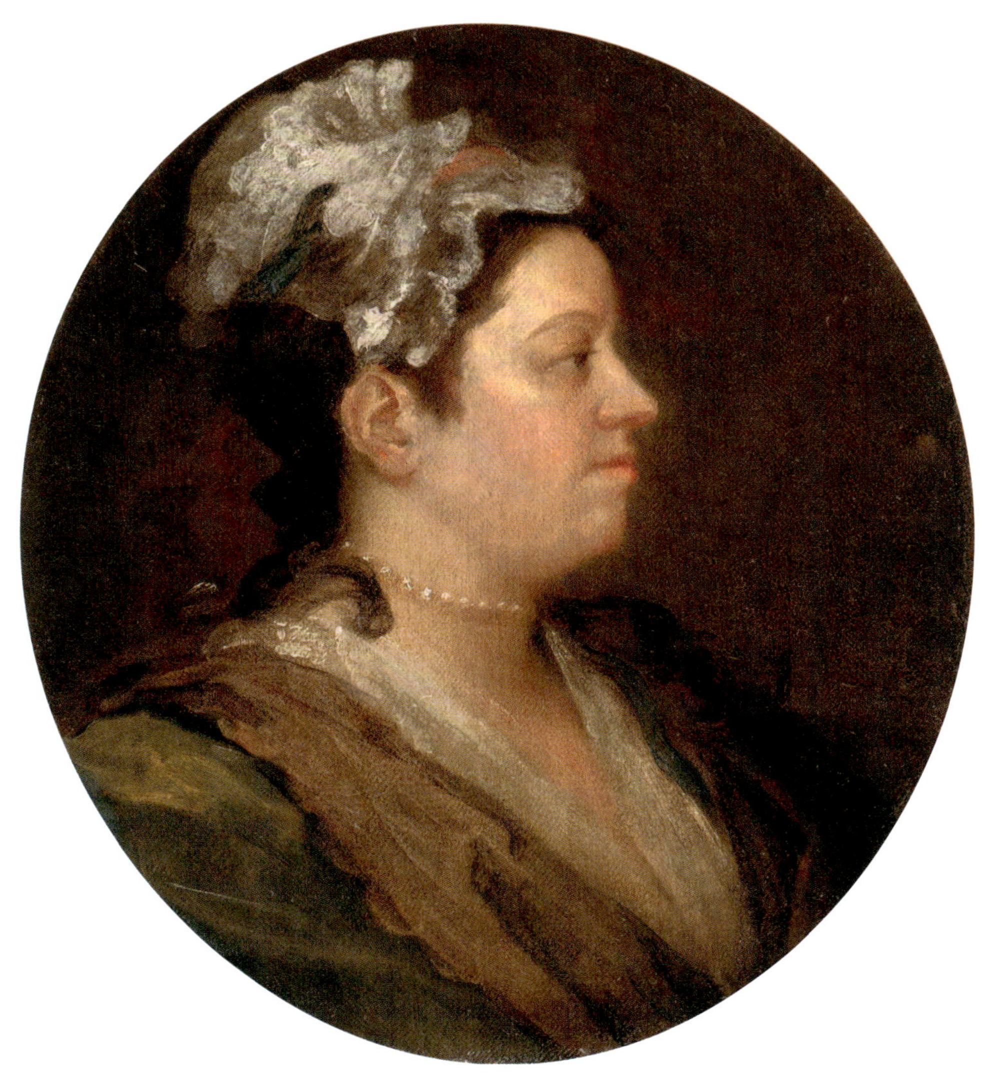

  WILLIAM HOGARTH *Mary Hogarth* c.1740

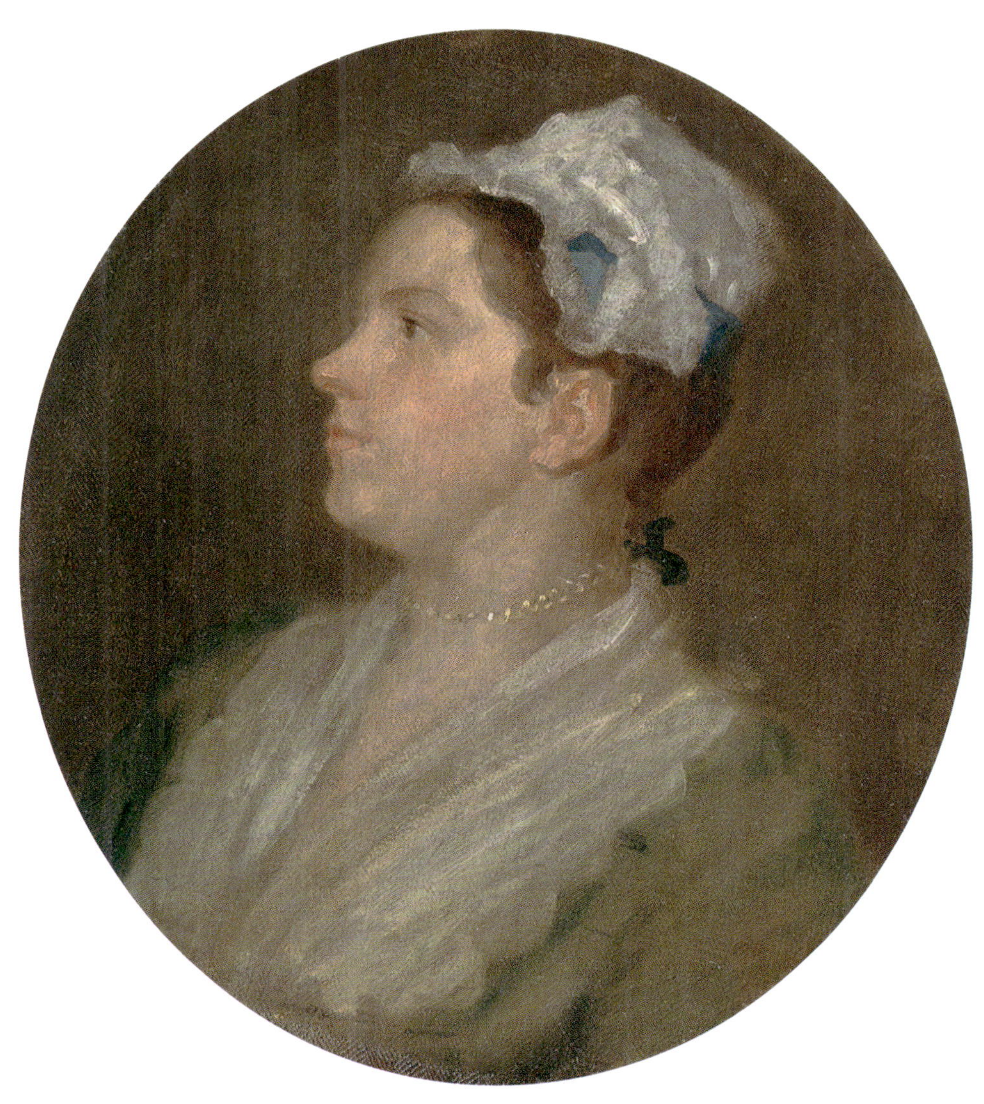

WILLIAM HOGARTH *Anne Hogarth* c.1740

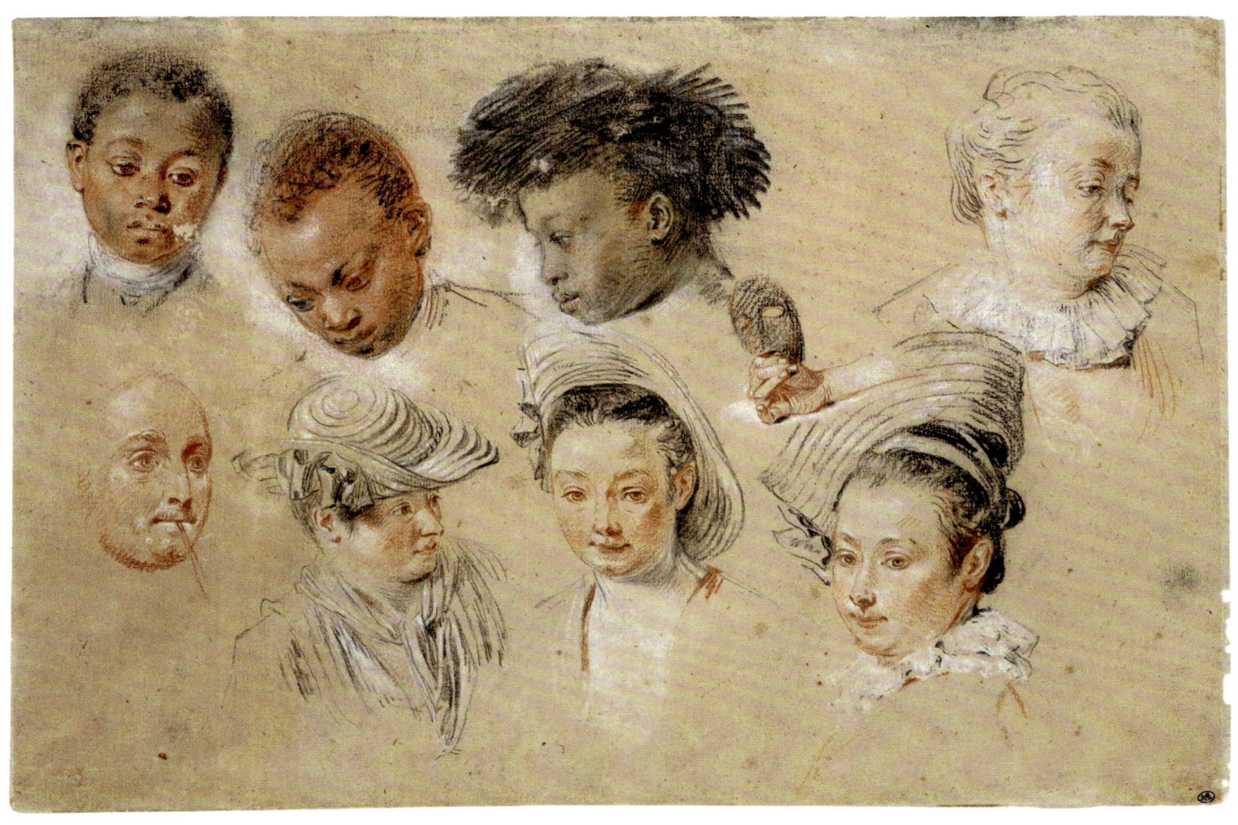

JEAN-ANTOINE WATTEAU *Eight Studies of Heads* c.1715–16

The forms of naturalistic representation which came to prevail in portraiture and genre painting in the mid-eighteenth century might appear to give pictorial life to a wider range of subjectivities: in the case of Hogarth's famous portrait of his servants, the working-class. But the picture may have served as a kind of advertisement for his skills as a portraitist, and whatever new sense of egalitarianism may have arisen at this point within culture, the economic and social divisions that underpinned society arguably only deepened, with divisive effect. In this respect, that Watteau's drawn studies have been counted among Hogarth's pictorial sources may be revealing. Such apparently informal studies seem to suggest a new spirit of individualism, but inequities of race and social status persisted alongside the new philosophies and aesthetics of personal freedom in Europe.

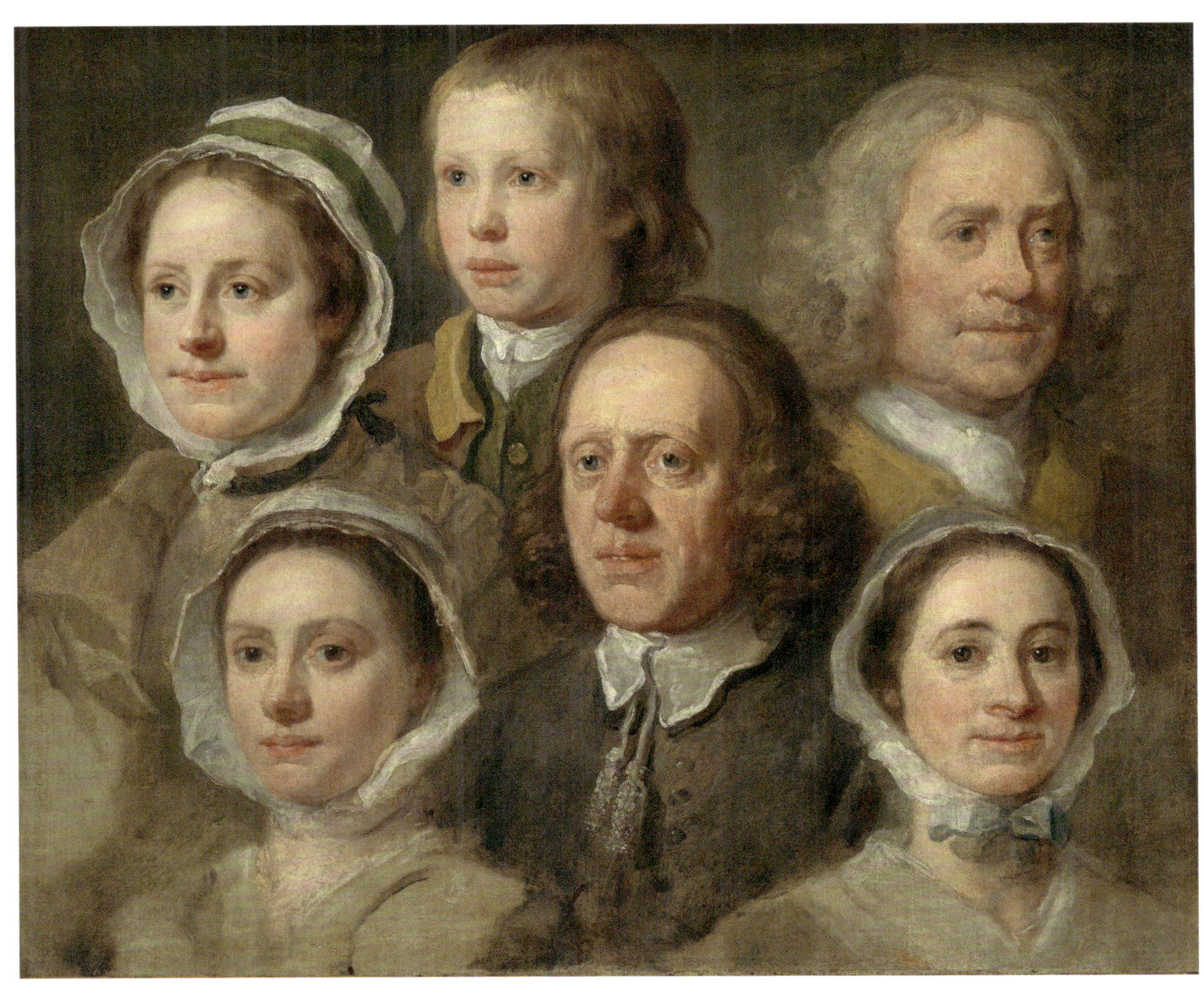 WILLIAM HOGARTH *Heads of Six of Hogarth's Servants* c.1750–5

ARTIST BIOGRAPHIES

JACQUES AUTREAU
1657–1745

Much of Jacques Autreau's biography remains obscure and somewhat anecdotal. The poet Rousseau's claim that he was 'always drunk' and his reputation as a misanthrope have proved enduring. Born in Paris, the son of a wine merchant, he is first mentioned as a master painter residing at Quai de l'Horloge in 1686. His known works include portraits and conversation pieces, some of which feature members of the literary circles he appears to have moved in. From 1717, he exchanged paintbrush for pen, writing comedies, operas and ballets, most of which were performed at the Théâtre-Italien and generally well received. But neither Autreau's painting nor writing seems to have been financially rewarding. He appealed for admittance to the Hospice des Incurables, Paris in 1737, where he spent the rest of his life. He died in 1745, aged eighty-eight.

JACQUES-ANDRÉ-JOSEPH AVED
1702–66

Though born in northern France to Flemish parents, Aved grew up in Amsterdam and, by sixteen, was peddling drawings at fairs across the Netherlands. After short spells in the Amsterdam studios of the French painters Bernard Picart and François Boitard, he left for Paris in 1721. There he trained under the fashionable portraitist Alexis-Simon Belle, but soon established himself independently. His portraiture was praised for its realism and psychological penetration, showing the influence of Dutch art and, perhaps, his friendship with Chardin. He was accepted into the Académie Royale in 1734 and gained the prestigious position of painter to the king in 1744. While mostly based in Paris, he also worked in Brussels around 1738–40 and in The Hague from 1750 to 1751. Later, Aved also became renowned as a connoisseur, amassing an important personal art collection. He spent the rest of his life in Paris and died on 4 March 1766.

EDMÉ BOUCHARDON
1698–1762

Bouchardon was born in Chaumont-en-Bassigny, Haute Marne, and trained first with his father, then with the sculptor Coustou the Younger in Paris. In 1722 Bouchardon won the prestigious Prix de Rome, an award to study in the Italian city. He spent nine years in Rome, his classicising style bringing him fame and commissions, especially among papal circles and British aristocrats. Returning to Paris, he continued to be highly regarded: he was accepted into the Académie in 1735 and was appointed sculptor to the King. He was also a prolific and talented draughtsman, a reputation he cultivated by exhibiting his red chalk drawings and through his engravings. His sculptural work was slow and painstaking, though, with many designs remaining unrealised and the rest of his career taken up with only a few important commissions. His last major work was an equestrian statue of Louis xv, begun in 1748 but left unfinished at his death in July 1762.

FRANÇOIS BOUCHER
1703–70

Born in Paris, François Boucher was probably first taught by his father, before briefly studying with the history painter François Le Moyne. In 1723 he won the Prix de Rome, but did not go to Italy until 1728, raising the funds himself through book illustrations and printmaking. Returning to Paris in 1731, he became one of the most fashionable artists of the day. His sumptuously painted mythological and pastoral subjects were particularly celebrated, but he also made highly successful designs for porcelain, tapestry and various theatre productions, while the circulation of prints after his work ensured his international fame. He was the favourite painter of Mme Pompadour, winning numerous royal commissions and, in 1765, he was appointed first painter to the king and director of the Académie Royale. Nevertheless, as tastes changed, his art was later criticised for being artificial, frivolous and morally corrupt. With his eyesight failing, he died in Paris in May 1770.

GERRIT DE BROEN II
1692–1774

De Broen was from a family of engravers living and working in Amsterdam. Born in 1692, he no doubt learned his profession through his father, also Gerrit, and his uncle, Johannes. Working independently from around 1719, he registered as a burgher of the city in 1732. At this point, his profession was recorded as 'plate cutter', though alongside engraving and etching, he also turned his hand to draughtsmanship, cartography, bookselling and publishing. He is perhaps best known for his highly detailed map of Amsterdam, which went through several editions. He is not known to have travelled outside the city and died in Amsterdam in December 1774.

GIOVANNI ANTONIO CANAL
(KNOWN AS CANALETTO)
1697–1768

Born in Venice, Canaletto initially trained with his father who specialised in theatrical scenery. He visited Rome around 1719 and seems to have been inspired to paint his surroundings. Back in Venice, his evocative views of that city established his reputation, particularly among foreign tourists. Joseph Smith, an English merchant, became an important patron and his principal agent. In 1740–1, Canaletto toured the Brenta and mainland Italy, making studies for new subjects and engravings. The popularity of his work among British collectors probably prompted his journey to England in 1746, where he stayed for the next decade bar short visits back to Venice. Concentrating on English views, especially of London, his landscapes helped raise the status of the genre there. Returning to Venice, he was finally elected to the painting academy in 1763 and remained in the city until his death in April 1768.

JEAN-SIMÉON CHARDIN
1699–1779

Unlike many of his contemporaries who travelled widely, Chardin spent his entire life in Paris. From a well-to-do artisan family, he began his career painting street signs and details in other artists' work. In 1728 he gained public recognition when he exhibited his paintings at the open-air Exposition de la jeunesse, on Place Dauphine. This prompted his admittance into the Académie Royale as a still-life painter. In the 1730s, however, he turned to genre painting, characterised by his careful observation and finessed handling of paint. These solemn, everyday scenes were highly regarded and sought after by collectors across Europe. Additionally, from 1738, engravings brought his art to a still wider audience. He returned to still-life subjects after 1751 and later, possibly because of his deteriorating eyesight, he began working in pastels. He died in his apartment in the Louvre in December 1779.

ERNST LUDWIG CREITE
active c.1728–65

Little is known about the German-Dutch printmaker Ernst Ludwig Creite. He trained in Braunschweig, in north-central Germany, but spent his entire career in the Hague, in the Netherlands. Active from around 1728 to 1765, he engraved a range of subjects from portraits, book illustrations, floral pictures, and, notably, a copy of Hogarth's *Midnight Modern Conversation* for the international market.

GIUSEPPE MARIA CRESPI
1665–1747

Crespi was born in Bologna, where he spent most of his career. His distinctive style was developed through studying the Italian masters, first in Bologna and then as he travelled to Parma, Urbino, Pesaro and Venice in the late 1680s. By 1700 he had established his reputation and among his most important patrons was Ferdinando de' Medici, Grand Prince of Tuscany. He visited the court in Florence several times, including a longer stay of eight months in 1709. During this time, he was most active in genre painting, producing innovative contemporary narratives and vivid scenes of everyday life. Returning to Bologna, he helped found the Accademia Clementina in 1710. Despite his success, from the late 1720s he became increasingly reclusive and mainly received religious commissions. In 1745 he suffered a stroke and was left blind for the last two years of his life.

JEAN DELAGRIVE
1689–1757

Born in Sedan in north-east France, Jean Delagrive was initially ordained as a Lazarist priest. Soon after, he was sent to Kraków in Poland where he taught philosophy. Upon his return to Paris in 1714, he left the priesthood, instead choosing to study geography, drawing and engraving, and the techniques of surveying and triangulation. His attainment of these skills was reflected in the new map of Paris he produced in 1728, followed by a map of the Seine in 1733, and a map of Paris's environs in 1740, among others. He was subsequently appointed as Official Geographer of the City of Paris, helped measure the meridian through the Paris Observatory in 1733, and was elected as a fellow of the Royal Society in London in 1734. He continued his cartographic projects until his death in Paris in April 1757.

GEORG DESMARÉES
1697–1776

Desmarées was born in Gimo, Sweden, and was trained by his maternal uncle, the Dutch-Swedish painter Martin van Meytens II, in Stockholm from 1710. In 1724 he left to continue his training abroad, first in Amsterdam, then in Nuremberg and lastly in Venice (travelling via Augsburg, Munich, Innsbruck and Rome). Returning to Bavaria in 1728, he settled in Munich and was appointed court painter to Prince-Elector Charles VII. As well as painting for the Ancestral Gallery at the Munich Residenz, he soon became established as a leading portraitist. In 1742 he visited Frankfurt and in 1745 went to Bonn, where he stayed for four years working for Prince-Bishop Clemens August of Cologne. With Munich remaining his main residence, he also spent time at the Kassel court in 1752, before returning to Bonn again in 1753, and making brief trips to Würzburg and Mainz. He died in Munich in October 1776.

RENÉ GAILLARD
1719–90

The engraver René Gaillard spent his entire career living and working in Paris. There is some uncertainty about his early years, but it is thought he was born in 1719 and trained with his fellow Parisian, the engraver Jacques-Philippe Le Bas. He was primarily a reproductive printmaker and is best known today for his engravings after paintings by the acclaimed portraitist Hyacinthe Rigaud, the fashionable François Boucher, and the genre painter Jean-Baptiste Greuze. He died in Paris in April 1790.

HUBERT FRANÇOIS GRAVELOT
(FORMERLY BOURGUIGNON)
1699–1773

The Parisian Gravelot did not immediately take up art professionally. Educated at the Collège des Quatre Nations in Paris, he was briefly employed by the ambassador to Rome (though he didn't actually go further than Lyon), before pursuing business in the French colony of Haiti. Returning penniless in 1729, he began his artistic training in Paris with Jean Restout the Younger and then with François Boucher. By 1733 Gravelot was in London where his French rococo style proved influential. A talented draughtsman and engraver, he became the leading book illustrator of the day and produced numerous designs for items as wide-ranging as fans and watches. He was also at the heart of London's artistic community and taught at St Martin's Lane Academy. However, the rise of anti-French sentiment in England after 1745 led Gravelot to return to Paris, where he remained until his death in April 1773.

JOHN GREENWOOD
1727–92

Of English heritage, Greenwood was born in Boston in British America. He was apprenticed to the heraldic painter and engraver Thomas Johnston at fifteen, but by 1747 had turned his attention to portraiture. In late 1752 he left for Suriname, then a Dutch colony, and remained there for the next five years. Only *Sea Captains* survives from this period, but his notebooks reveal he was occupied with portrait commissions and with documenting his surroundings, including visiting the plantations. Next, he travelled to Amsterdam where he trained in mezzotint printing, continued his portrait practice, and began dealing in old masters. Five years later he moved again, travelling to London (via Paris) in 1763. In England he was most successful as an art dealer and auctioneer, claiming to have brought over 15,000 paintings into the city. Perhaps his most notable sale was that of Hogarth's studio contents in 1790. He died while on a visit to Margate in 1792.

ANTONIO GUARDI
1699–1760

From an Italian family of artists, Guardi was born in Vienna but moved to Venice as an infant. It is thought he took over the family studio in Venice in 1716, but he is also recorded in Vienna in 1719, indicating that he may have trained in Austria. Little more is known until 1730, when he began copying paintings by Venetian masters for Johann Matthias von der Schulenburg, Field Marshal of the Venetian Armies and a notable art collector. Alongside this, he also received portrait commissions from the local nobility and for religious subjects from churches in northern Italy. Later, his brother-in-law, the painter Giovanni Battista Tiepolo, nominated him as a founding member of the Accademia di Belle Arti in Venice. Guardi died in 1760. His posthumous reputation has been overshadowed by his younger brother, the famed view-painter Francesco Guardi, with whose paintings his own art has often been confused.

FRANCIS HAYMAN
1708–76

Born in Exeter, by the age of ten Hayman was in London and apprenticed to the Devonian history painter Robert Browne. His first independent work was as a scenery painter for London theatres, including Drury Lane, during the 1730s. By the 1740s he had turned to portraiture, conversation pieces and history painting, as well as book illustration. Perhaps his most notable achievement was a series of decorative paintings for the supper-boxes at Vauxhall Pleasure Gardens, first unveiled in 1742. Hayman was a central figure in the St Martin's Lane circle, and in 1748 accompanied Hogarth on his visit to France. He took an active role in founding both the Society of Artists in 1761, and in the Royal Academy in 1768. These activities distracted from his art, however, and in later life ill health made painting difficult. He died in February 1776 and is buried in Soho.

WILLIAM HOGARTH
1697–1764

Hogarth was born in London and resided in the city all his life. He initially trained as an engraver, but broke off his apprenticeship early to set up independently in 1720. At this time, he also began studying painting, soon becoming known for his lively conversation pieces. But it was *A Harlot's Progress* that launched him into fame in 1732, followed next by *A Rake's Progress*. These series established his international reputation, but they were also widely plagiarised, prompting Hogarth's campaign for the Engraver's Copyright Act in 1735. During the 1740s Hogarth made two trips to France: the first to secure the best engravers in Paris for *Marriage A-la-Mode* in 1743, the second in 1748 when he was arrested as a spy in Calais (memorialised in *The Gate of Calais)*. In 1753 he published his aesthetic theories in *The Analysis of Beauty* and was appointed Serjeant Painter to the King in 1757. In later years, however, he was also widely criticised, and became increasingly isolated before his death in October 1764.

ÉTIENNE JEAURAT
1699–1789

From Vermenton in north-central France, Jeaurat was orphaned at an early age and moved to Paris where his elder brother, the engraver Edmé Jeaurat, entrusted his care to the painter Nicolas Vleughels. When Vleughels was appointed director of the Académie de France in Rome in 1724 he took Étienne with him. In Italy Étienne made studies of everyday life, but also began painting history subjects, which brought him considerable success. Returning to Paris he was received into the Académie Royale in 1733, becoming a professor in 1743 and chancellor in 1781. He was also appointed Keeper of the King's Paintings at Versailles in 1767, a position he held until his death in 1789. Jeaurat retained his interest in urban, everyday subjects, and today is best known for vividly portraying Parisian street life. These pictures reveal the influence on him of Hogarth's prints.

NICOLAS LANCRET
1690–1743

The Parisian Nicolas Lancret initially trained as an engraver. By 1708, however, he had taken up painting and was studying at the Académie Royale. He then trained with the French artist Claude Gillot, perhaps revealing his intention to specialise in *fêtes galantes* (playful figures in parkland settings). He was greatly inspired by Watteau's paintings, and so it is unsurprising that when he was received into the Académie in 1719, like Watteau it was as a painter of *galanteries*. Following Watteau's death in 1721 and Gillot's in 1722, Lancret emerged as the leading genre painter of the day and enjoyed considerable success. He received royal patronage and his work became better known through popular prints. His *galanteries* gained distinction for their lively colouring, their playful portrayal of upper-class pastimes, and their imaginative exploration of allegory and portraiture. His death in 1743 did nothing to diminish the popularity of his paintings, which continued to be collected throughout Europe.

JEAN-ÉTIENNE LIOTARD
1702–89

The peripatetic Liotard was born in Geneva to Huguenot parents and initially trained as a miniaturist. He moved to Paris in 1723 to continue his training, then, in 1736, departed for Italy, where he began specialising in pastels. In Florence he met the British aristocrat William Ponsonby, whom he joined on an extended Grand Tour to the Levant. Having arrived in Constantinople in 1738, Liotard spent four years making portraits of British and European expatriates, but also numerous studies of his surroundings. These local subjects informed later pictures that reflected and contributed to European fantasies of the Ottoman Empire. Liotard also adopted the local dress and customary long beard, deliberately cultivating an 'exotic' appearance to increase his European celebrity, earning him the nickname 'The Turk'. After Constantinople he spent ten months in Moldavia, before travelling to Vienna in 1743. Achieving great success, Liotard travelled next to Venice, then Germany, settling in Paris in 1746 for seven years. From there he visited

England in 1753–5 (later returning in 1773–4), and travelled to the Netherlands in 1755, before settling in Geneva in 1758. He spent most of his later life there, exploring still life and genre subjects as well as publishing a treatise on painting. He continued to work until two years before his death in June 1789.

PIETRO LONGHI
1700/2–85

Born in Venice, the son of a goldsmith, Longhi first studied drawing with his father, before training with the history painter Antonio Balestra. He may also have studied with Crespi in Bologna but this remains uncertain (the affinity between both artists' scenes of contemporary life has been widely noted). Much of Longhi's early career is undocumented, but by the 1730s he was painting small-scale genre subjects and, by 1737, was a member of the Venetian painters' guild. He gained success as the leading painter of everyday Venetian life, producing images notable for their quiet simplicity, careful observation and light irony or humour. Contemporaries praised the novelty and realism of his pictures, which gained further popularity through engravings. He later became a founding member of the Accademia dei Pittori in 1756, where he taught the life class until 1780. He died at his home in Venice in May 1785.

JAMES MACARDELL
1727/8–65

MacArdell was born in Dublin and trained in the workshop of the Irish engraver John Brooks. In early 1746 Brooks moved to London, taking his best assistants with him, including MacArdell. It was not long before MacArdell was working independently, and by 1754 he was established in Covent Garden, publishing and selling his own work. An interest in the theatre led him to engrave a number of actors in character, notably David Garrick, and he was employed by leading artists of the day to reproduce their paintings, including Thomas Hudson, Allan Ramsay and Sir Joshua Reynolds (who famously claimed he would be 'immortalised' by MacArdell's prints). Widely recognised as the best mezzotint engraver in London, he became one of the original directors of the Society of Artists of Great Britain

at its incorporation in 1765. He died in June the same year, aged just thirty-seven.

PHILIP MERCIER
1689?–1760

The son of a Huguenot tapestry-weaver, Mercier was born in Berlin and began his training at the city's painting academy under the French artist Antoine Pesne. He continued his studies in France and Italy, before arriving in England around 1715/16 with a recommendation from the royal court in Hanover. Settling in London, Mercier played an important role in bringing French influences to British painting, especially in his art's inspiration from Watteau (early in his career he made prints – and perhaps forgeries – after Watteau's work). He was also instrumental in developing the conversation piece in Britain, and later the fancy picture (depicting everyday scenes, but with a storytelling or imaginative, and often sentimental, element). By 1739 he moved to York where he stayed until 1751 – apart from visits to Ireland in 1747 and Scotland in 1750 – and had a successful portrait practice. He is recorded in Portugal in 1752 but returned to London where he remained until his death in July 1760.

JOHN PINE
1690–1756

Pine was born in London, where he remained throughout his life – apart from possibly training in the Amsterdam studio of the French engraver-printseller Bernard Picart some time before 1719. He became well-established in the London art world and highly regarded as an engraver, as well as working as a publisher and print- and map-seller. Pine was an active member of the St Martin's Lane circle of artists and closely associated with Hogarth, notably petitioning for Hogarth's Copyright Act of 1735 and appearing as the monk in *The Gate of Calais* 1748, from which arose his nickname of 'Friar Pine'. During his career, Pine held prestigious positions including engraver to the Masonic Grand Lodge and Bluemantle Pursuivant at the College of Arms, and undertook such famed projects as collaborating on the Rocque map of London in 1746. He died in London in May 1756.

JAN PUNT
1711–79

The Amsterdammer, Jan Punt enjoyed a remarkably varied career. After training with the engraver Adolf van der Laan, and perhaps with the painter Jacob de Wit, he worked as a printmaker, painter and art dealer from around 1731. While his engravings were mainly book illustrations or reproductions of pictures by his contemporaries, he also painted portraits, history subjects and decorative schemes, and from 1765 was a member of the Amsterdam Guild of St Luke. Alongside this he maintained a successful career as an actor, best known for his recitations on stage. He spent most of his life in Amsterdam, apart from a period in Rotterdam around 1773–7, and died in his hometown in December 1779.

TIBOUT REGTERS
1710–68

Regters spent his entire career as a successful portraitist in the Netherlands. Born in Dordrecht, he trained with the now little-known painters Ten Hage in Arnhem and Meijers in Rotterdam, before finishing his studies with Jan Maurits Quinkhard in Amsterdam. Settling permanently in Amsterdam, he established himself as an independent artist from around 1740. He is perhaps best known for the small-scale group portraits he began painting from the late 1740s onwards. Characterised by the seemingly relaxed arrangement and poses of the figures, as well as his inspiration from genre painting, these reflect the development of the conversation piece in the northern Netherlands. Besides conversation pieces and individual portraits, he also painted a few genre scenes of markets and some mythological subjects (although none of the latter survive). He died in Amsterdam in January 1768.

MARCO RICCI
1676–1729

The Italian landscape painter Marco Ricci initially studied with his uncle, Sebastiano Ricci, in Venice. Details of his early career remain uncertain, but he reputedly killed a gondolier and fled to Spalato (present-day Split, Croatia) for four years. By 1705, though, he was seemingly working in Milan, then in Florence and, possibly, Rome. In 1708, he travelled to London (via the Low Countries) with the painter Giovanni Antonio Pellegrini. Staying for nearly two years, he collaborated on decorative schemes for patrons' houses and on stage scenery, as well as painting popular landscapes. After a brief return to Venice, he was back in London in winter 1711/12, bringing Sebastiano with him. Four years later, both he and his uncle were back in Venice, returning via the Netherlands and Paris. From then until his death in January 1729, Ricci was highly active in Venice: continuing to collaborate with Sebastiano, painting stage scenery, developing new imaginary and atmospheric landscapes, and exploring gouache and printmaking.

JEAN ROCQUE
c.1704–62

Before his first published work in 1734, little is known of the map-maker Jean Rocque. Born into a Huguenot family in France (which later settled in Geneva), he probably arrived in England around 1709. He maintained close links to the Huguenot community in London throughout his career and often published works with bilingual titles. By the late 1730s he had begun an ambitious career as a cartographer: he is best known for the large-scale maps and plans he produced of towns and counties based on his own land surveys, including London in 1746 (engraved by John Pine), Bristol, Exeter and Dublin – which perhaps prompted his stay in Ireland between 1753 and 1756. These projects could be financially precarious and protracted, though, and Rocque maintained a successful business alongside this, publishing numerous general maps and atlases. From 1751 he was based in the Strand, the centre of London's map trade, and his business continued even after his death in January 1762, run by his enterprising widow Mary Ann Rocque.

LOUIS FRANÇOIS ROUBILIAC
1702–62

The French sculptor Louis François Roubiliac spent almost his entire career in England. Born in Lyon, it is thought he trained with the sculptors Balthasar Permoser in Dresden and Nicolas Coustou in Paris. Settling in London in 1730, he made his name with a full-length statue of the German composer George Frideric Handel for Vauxhall Gardens in 1738. This typifies the invention, lively naturalism and vivid characterisation so admired in Roubiliac's sculpture. During the 1730s and 1740s he mostly worked as a portrait sculptor, making busts of writers, thinkers and artists. These reveal the creative circles he moved in, notably those around St Martin's Lane Academy where he taught. In 1752 he visited Rome with fellow artists, including Francis Hayman. In this later period, he also worked on ambitious monuments, bringing new drama and animation to the genre. Despite his success and high status among contemporaries, after a long illness he died in debt in January 1762.

ANDRÉ ROUQUET
1701–59

The son of Huguenots, Rouquet was born in Geneva and trained as an enamellist there. Moving to London during the 1720s, he soon established his reputation as a painter of enamel portrait miniatures, which were fashionable in Britain at this time. He is perhaps better known for his writings on art, however, notably his explanation of Hogarth's prints for foreign audiences (the two artists were close friends) and his highly successful commentary on English art, *L'Etat des arts, en Angleterre,* published in 1755 in both French and English. Having maintained links with the Continent throughout his time in London, he settled in Paris in 1753 where he exhibited regularly, received a royal commission, and was elected to the Académie Royale. In later years however, his mental health deteriorated severely and he died in an asylum in December 1759.

PAUL SANDBY
c.1730/1–1809

Born in Nottingham, Sandby probably learnt to draw from his elder brother, Thomas. From 1747, and over the next five years, he worked as a draughtsman to the military survey of the Scottish Highlands. Settling in London after this, he continued to explore and exhibit landscape subjects in oil and watercolour. He did venture into caricature in 1753, though, satirising Hogarth's *Analysis of Beauty.* Sandby helped raise the appreciation of watercolour and was active in the London art world, becoming a founding member of the Royal Academy and chief drawing master at the Royal Military Academy in Woolwich. During the 1770s he made several tours of Wales, printing his scenic views from these in aquatint, a technique he pioneered. His later landscapes became increasingly imaginary, perhaps because travel became harder as he got older. By the time of his death, in November 1809, he was struggling with poor health and eyesight, as well as financial difficulties.

ANDREA SOLDI
c.1703–71

Little is known of Soldi's early life. He was born in Florence and spent time working in the Levant, where he was patronised by British merchants working in Aleppo and Constantinople. On their recommendation, he settled in England in 1736 and initially enjoyed considerable success. His portraiture was distinctive for its lively theatricality and proved popular, especially among the nobility. In 1744, however, his extravagant lifestyle caught up with him and he spent time in debtors' prison. His career never fully recovered after this: the social standing of his sitters declined, and his portraits became more restrained and sober in response to changing tastes. He may have worked in Scotland from 1756 to 1757, and during the 1760s he exhibited in London. By 1771, though, he was forced to apply for poor relief from the Royal Academy and he died in the same year, his funeral supposedly paid for by Sir Joshua Reynolds.

PIERRE SUBLEYRAS
1699–1749

From Saint-Gilles-du-Gard in the south of France, Subleyras first trained with his father before entering the studio of the painter Antoine Rivalz in Toulouse in 1717. Following this, in 1726 he moved to Paris where he studied at the Académie Royale and won the Prix de Rome the following year. This coveted award gave him the opportunity to study in the Italian capital, where he arrived in 1728. His studies were extended until 1735, and ultimately he settled permanently in Rome (despite invitations to the royal courts in Dresden and Madrid). He established himself within the city's artistic and intellectual circles, gaining success as a portraitist and as an accomplished draughtsman and printmaker. He was most famed, though, for his religious paintings and received several major commissions from Rome's ecclesiastical circles. He suffered from ill health, however, and died aged forty-nine from tuberculosis.

PIETER TANJÉ
1706–61

Born in Bolsward, in the northern Netherlands, Tanjé initially worked on the barge service running between his hometown and Amsterdam but spent his spare time engraving tobacco boxes. Pursuing this interest further, he began training as an engraver with Jacob Folkema in Amsterdam in 1730, as well as attending the city's art academy. He then spent some time as an assistant to the printmaker Frans de Bakker, before working independently. He remained in Amsterdam until his death in June 1761, and had a considerable output, mostly of prints after works by other artists. These included portraits, book illustrations and vignettes, and, notably, genre scenes by Cornelis Troost.

CORNELIS TROOST
1696–1750

The Dutchman Cornelis Troost spent his entire life residing and working in Amsterdam. It was not until 1723 that he took up painting, when he began studying with the portraitist Arnold Boonen. Prior to this, Troost had worked as an actor at Amsterdam's Schouwburg Theatre and he retained an interest in the stage throughout his life. While he began mainly painting portraits, he soon gained success painting conversation pieces and, increasingly, theatrical subjects and comical genre scenes. These reveal his keen observation of the world around him and his humour, qualities that have seen Troost frequently dubbed the 'Dutch Hogarth'. He also developed a distinctive technique, using pastel with gouache and watercolour. During the 1740s he also depicted numerous military scenes, especially off-duty soldiers. He died in March 1750, and soon after his pictures were copied as prints, becoming popular throughout the Netherlands and abroad.

JEAN-FRANÇOIS DE TROY
1679–1752

The Parisian Jean-François de Troy came from a family of painters, and was first taught by his father, François, a well-regarded portraitist. He then studied at the Académie Royale (where his father was professor), before travelling to Rome in 1699 to complete his artistic education, including visits to Florence and Pisa. Returning to Paris in 1706, he became one of the leading painters of his day: he was accepted into the Académie, he received prestigious royal commissions at Versailles and Fontainebleau, later becoming first painter to the king, and he produced a popular series of designs for the Gobelins tapestry manufactory. Today, he is best known for his inventive *tableaux de mode,* depicting the fashions, manners and pastimes of French high society. In 1738 he was appointed director of the Académie de France in Rome, a position he held until 1751. He died there shortly after, in January 1752.

LODOVICO UGHI
[dates unknown]

Very little is known about Lodovico Ughi except for his role in making the first and largest map of Venice to be based upon accurate field studies in 1729 (pp.46–7). This was a collaborative project, but Ughi was the cartographer and perhaps engraver of the map portion. It seems likely that he may have trained in Venice as, by the eighteenth century, it had become an important centre for printing and mapmaking.

PHILIP VAN DIJK
1680/3–1753

Van Dijk is thought to have been born in either Amsterdam in 1680 or in Oud-Beijerland in 1683. By 1696, though, he was in Amsterdam and apprenticed to the painter Arnold Boonen, later moving to Rotterdam and then, in 1708, to Middleburg, the capital of the province Zeeland and an important centre of the Dutch slave trade. Staying for ten years, he gained great success as a portraitist and painted many prominent Zeelanders (he seems to have maintained links to the city throughout his career). He finally settled in The Hague in 1718, working as

an art dealer and painter for an elite clientele. This included William VIII, Landgrave of Hesse-Kassel, and in 1725 he was appointed court painter, visiting the Kassel court the same year, and again in 1736, the latter followed by a visit to Amsterdam in 1737. Back in The Hague, he continued to receive commissions until his death in February 1753.

GEORGE VERTUE
1684–1756

The engraver George Vertue lived and worked in his native London. He began his artistic training in 1697, probably with the French silversmith Blaise Genton, before apprenticing with the Flemish engraver Michael Vandergucht between 1702 and 1709. Setting up independently, Vertue embarked upon a successful, remarkably prolific and varied career: he made prints after paintings, designed and engraved numerous book illustrations and frontispieces, undertook prestigious private commissions and was a successful publisher. In 1717 he became official engraver to the Society of Antiquaries, taking an active role in its scholarly activities and responsibility for engraving and printing all images published by the society. This was all alongside his project to write a history of British art. Begun in 1712, this work occupied the rest of his life, as he travelled around the country and compiled the numerous notebooks for which he is best remembered today. Despite suffering from ill health, he continued to work until his death in July 1756.

JEAN-ANTOINE WATTEAU
1684–1721

Watteau was born in Valenciennes, in northern France, but the region's recent secession from the Spanish Netherlands meant he was often regarded as Flemish. In 1702 he left for Paris, where he worked as a copyist before studying with the theatrical painter Claude Gillot from 1705, and then with the decorative painter Claude Audran III. Aside from a visit to Valenciennes in 1709, Watteau remained in Paris, developing his personal style and painting characters from the *commedia dell'arte.* He especially gained success for his playful pictures of elegant groups in parkland or garden settings, which blurred the line between fantasy and reality – as his acceptance into the Académie Royale as a painter of *fêtes galantes* shows. Perhaps restless or drawn by new opportunities – or because he wanted to consult with the respected doctor Richard Mead – Watteau moved to London in 1719. However, his health continued to deteriorate, and he returned to Paris in 1720; he died the following year of tuberculosis, aged thirty-six.

JOHAN ZOFFANY
1733–1810

Born near Frankfurt am Main, Zoffany began studying painting in Regensburg before moving to Rome, aged seventeen, to pursue an artistic career. By the late 1750s he was already receiving independent commissions, notably from the court at Trier. In 1760, attracted by the city's artistic opportunities, he journeyed to London where he settled. Though he initially struggled to establish himself, his novel theatrical paintings and lively conversation pieces brought success; he enjoyed the royal family's patronage and became a founding member of the Royal Academy in 1769. Still highly regarded, the summer of 1772 took him to Florence, and from there to Vienna, only returning to London in 1779, where he found artistic tastes had changed in his absence. This probably prompted his move to India in 1783, where he made his fortune working for employees of Britain's East India Company and local Indian rulers in Calcutta and Lucknow. Returning to London six years later, he seems to have stopped painting in 1800, perhaps because of ill health, and he died in November 1810.

NOTES

PREFACE

1. See Mark Hallett, 'Hogarth and Europe', blog post 8 December 2014, https://www.paul-mellon-centre.ac.uk/about/news/hogarth-and-europe/page/27.

2. Francis Klingender, *Hogarth and English Caricature,* 1944; Frederick Antal, *Hogarth and his Place in European Art,* London 1962.

3. Lawrence Gowing, *Hogarth*, exh. cat. Tate Gallery, London 1971.

4. Ronald Paulson, *Emblem and Expression: Meaning in English Art of the Eighteenth Century,* London 1975 and *Popular and Polite Art in the Age of Hogarth and Fielding*, Notre Dame and London 1979.

5. Key works include: David Bindman, *Hogarth*, London 1981; David Dabydeen, *Hogarth's Blacks: Images of Blacks in Eighteenth Century English Art*, Manchester 1987; David Solkin, *Painting for Money: The Visual Arts and the Public Sphere in Eighteenth-century England*, New Haven and London 1993; Frédéric Ogée ed., *The Dumb Show: Image and Society in the Works of William Hogarth*, Oxford 1997; Marcia Pointon, *William Hogarth's Sigismunda in Focus*, London 2000; David Bindman, Frédéric Ogée and Peter Wagner eds., *Hogarth: Representing Nature's Machine*, Manchester 2001; Bernadette Fort and Angela Rosenthal eds., *The Other Hogarth: Aesthetics of Difference*, Princeton and Oxford 2001.

6. Including: Felicity A. Nussbaum ed., *The Global Eighteenth Century*, Baltimore and London 2003; David T. Gies and Cynthia Wall eds., *The Eighteenth Centuries: Global Networks of Enlightenment*, Charlottesville and London 2018; Michael Elia Yonan and Stacey Sloboda eds., *Eighteenth-century Art Worlds: Global and Local Geographies of Art*, London 2019; Bärbel Czennia and Greg Clingham eds., *Oriental Networks: Culture, Commerce, and Communication in the Long Eighteenth Century*, Lewisberg 2021. See also Dorothy Price and Catherine Grant eds., 'Decolonizing Art History', *Art History* (February 2020), https://onlinelibrary.wiley.com/doi/epdf/10.1111/1467-8365.12490.

PAINTING MODERN LIFE, MAKING THE MODERN WORLD

1. See Katelyn D. Crawford, 'Painting New England in the Dutch West Indies: John Greenwood's *Sea Captains Carousing in Surinam*', in David T. Gies and Cynthia Wall (eds.), *The Eighteenth Centuries: Global Networks of Enlightenment*, Charlottesville, VA and London 2018, pp.187–9.

2. See David Dabydeen's seminal *Hogarth's Blacks: Images of Blacks in Eighteenth Century English Art,* Athens, GA 1987, and cf. Catherine Molineux, 'Hogarth's Fashionable Slaves: Moral Corruption in Eighteenth-Century London', *ELH*, vol.72, no.2, Summer 2005, pp.495–520; Sara D. Schotland, 'Africans as Objects: Hogarth's Complex Portrayal of Exploitation', *Journal of African American Studies*, vol.13, no.2, 2009, pp.147–63.

3. The descent of the painting through a Rhode Island family, who also provided identifications for some of the figures, has led to the reasonable argument that this was commissioned by one of them. However, the picture's character and format would make it likely to be a tavern decoration, at least initially, perhaps removed as a memento, rather than a commission as such. See Robert W. Kenny, 'Sea Captains Carousing in Surinam', *Rhode Island History*, vol.36, no.4, Nov. 1964, pp.107–17.

4. For more on this subject see James Walvin, *Slavery in Small Things: Slavery and Modern Cultural Habits*, 2017

5. Brown University, 'Slavery and Justice Report' 2007, pp.10–11, https://www.brown.edu/Research/Slavery_Justice/documents/SlaveryAndJustice.pdf (accessed 18 March 2021).

6. National Trust, London, catalogue file, ICK.P.31.

7. John Gage, *The History and Antiquities of Suffolk*, London 1838, p.308.

8. Michelle Lespes, 'Le Peintre Jacques Aved (1702–1766) et La Maison de Riqueti-Mirabeau', *Provence Historique*, no.229, 2007, pp.235–56 (p.244, ill.p.245); catalogue file, Manchester City Art Gallery.

9. In 1938, the art historian C.H. Collins Baker suggested 'none of the drawing looks to me quite slick enough for French accomplishment. This leaves you with all sorts of marginal French

school stuff, for example Swedish, to guess in': Catalogue file, Manchester City Art Gallery, letter of 28 Dec. 1938. The art dealer Alec Martin similarly doubted it was French as well, 'but could suggest no name': reported in a letter by Lawrence Haward, 30 Nov. 1938 also at the Gallery. For the recent identification of artist and sitter see Marion Richards, 'The mystery of Jacques Aved and a French revolutionary's grandmother', Art UK, 16 Jan. 2019, https://artuk.org/discover/stories/the-mystery-of-jacques-aved-and-a-french-revolutionarys-grandmother (accessed 17 March 2021).

10. Lespes 2007, p.244; Robin Simon, *Hogarth, France and British Art: The Rise of the Arts in 18th-Century Britain*, London 2007, pp.27–36.

11. Honoré Gabriel Riquetti, *Memoirs of Mirabeau: Biographical, Literary, and Political,* vol.1, London 1835.

12. See Loïc Charles and Paul Cheney, 'The Colonial Machine Dismantled: Knowledge and Empire in the French Atlantic', *Past & Present,* no.219, May 2013, pp.127–63; Pernille Røge, *Economistes and the Reinvention of Empire: France in the Americas and Africa, c.1750–1802,* Cambridge 2019, p.10.

13. Our thanks to fashion historian Aileen Ribeiro for her analysis of the Marquise's appearance, clothing and activity, communicated 9 Sept. 2020.

14. Aileen E. Ribeiro, *Clothing Art: The Visual Culture of Fashion, 1600–1914,* New Haven and London 2017, pp.107, 133–56.

15. An audit of the original and early owners of the paintings by Hogarth represented in the book indicated that a quarter could be identified as benefitting directly from slave ownership or the slave trade, or were involved in the military or in trading companies furthering British imperial interests.

16. Arthur Murphy, *The Works of Henry Fielding, Esq. with an Essay on his Life and Genius,* new edn., 10 vols., London 1806, vol.5, p.13.

17. Frédéric Ogée and Olivier Meslay, 'William Hogarth and Modernity', in *Hogarth*, exh. cat., Tate Britain, London 2006, pp.24–5; Frédéric Ogée, 'The Pleasure of Progress: Hogarth and the Pictorial Sequence', in *Hogarth: Place and Progress*, exh. cat., Sir John Soane's Museum, London 2019, p.36.

18. Ogée and Meslay 2006, pp.23–5.

19. John Brewer, *The Pleasures of the Imagination: English Culture in the Eighteenth Century*, 2nd edn, London and New York 2013, pp.77–8.

20. Robin Simon has considered this parallel development in some detail. See Simon 2007, pp.27–36.

21. Elizabeth Einberg, *William Hogarth: A Complete Catalogue of the Paintings,* New Haven 2016, pp.245–6.

22. Ibid., pp.246–8.

23. Ribeiro 2007, p.168.

24. Robin Simon points to the complexity of this relationship (and the closeness of Hogarth's portrait of Mary Edwards to those by Aved). Simon 2007, pp.41–7.

25. Capitein's life has been discussed in relation to the Dutch transatlantic slave trade in Olivette Otele, *African Europeans: An Untold History,* London 2020, pp.67–80.

26. For discussion of Capitein's theology and pro-slavery in the Netherlands, see David Kofi Amponsah, 'Christian Slavery, Colonialism, and Violence: The Life and Writings of an African Ex-Slave, 1717–47', *Journal of Africana Religions*, vol.1, no.4, 2013, pp.431–57.

27. See also Christine Levecq, 'Jacobus Capitein: Dutch Calvinist and Black Cosmopolitan', *Research in African Literatures*, vol.44, no.4, Winter 2013, pp.145–66.

28. Frederick Antal, 'Hogarth and his Borrowings', *Art Bulletin*, no.29, March 1947, pp.36–48, and *Hogarth and his Place in European Art*, London 1962; F.D. Klingender, *Hogarth and English Caricature*, London 1944. See Simon 2007, pp.2–3, and David Bindman, 'Hogarth: The People's Artist?' in *Hogarth: Place and Progress*, exh. cat., Sir John Soane's Museum, 2019, p.31.

29. See, for instance, Joachim Möller (ed.), *Hogarth in Context: Ten Essays and a Bibliography*, Marburg 1996, and Werner Busch, *Englishness: Beiträge zur englischen Kunst des 18. Jahrhunderts von Hogarth bis Romney*, Berlin and Munich 2010. For a recent study deepening our understanding of the continental cultural heritage of Hogarth's art, see Kate Grandjouan, 'Refugees, Patriotism, and Hogarth's *The Gate of Calais* (1748)', *Studies in Ethnicity and Nationalism*, vol.20, no.3, 2020, pp.287–303.

30. Stephen Greenblatt et al., *Cultural Mobility: A Manifesto*, Cambridge 2010, p.242.

LONDON

1. Ralph Hyde, 'Portraying London Mid-Century – Jean Rocque and the Brothers Buck', in *London 1753*, exh. cat., The British Museum, London 2003, p.30.

2. Pamela Sharpe, 'Population and Society 1700–1840', in Peter Clark (ed.), *The Cambridge Urban History of Britain*, Vol.2: 1540–1840, Cambridge 2008, pp.491–528.

3. John Pine and Jean Rocque, *A proposal, by Jean Rocque, surveyor, and John Pine, engraver, for engraving and printing, by subscription, a new, accurate, and comprehensive plan of the cities of London and Westminster, and borough of Southwark*, London 24 October 1740, p.1.

4. *The Quiet Conquest*: *The Huguenots 1685 to 1985*, exh. cat., Museum of London, London 1985; *Rococo*: *Art and Design in Hogarth's England*, exh. cat., Victoria and Albert Museum, London 1984, pp.27–33.

5. Elizabeth McKellar, *Landscapes of London: The City, the Country, and the Suburbs 1660–1840*, New Haven and London 2013; and Elizabeth McKellar, *The Birth of Modern London: the Development and Design of the City, 1660–1720*, Manchester 1999.

6. These included Thomas Chippendale, John Channon, William Vile and John Cobb, William and John Linnell, Matthias Lock, Thomas Johnson and William Hallett.

7. Ilaria Bignamini, 'Art Institutions in London, 1689–1768: A Study of Clubs and Academies', *The Volume of the Walpole Society*, no.54, 1988, pp.95–124; Rica Jones, 'The Artist's Training and Techniques', in *Manners and Morals: Hogarth and British Painting 1700–1760*, exh. cat., Tate Gallery, London 1987, pp.19–22; Martin Postle, 'The St. Martin's Lane Academy: True and False Records', *Apollo*, vol.132, no.353, July 1991, pp.33–8.

8. Susan Sloman, 'Pine, John (1690–1756)', *Oxford Dictionary of National Biography*, Oxford 2008, https://doi.org/10.1093/ref:odnb/22293 (accessed 6 April 2021).

9. Timothy Clayton, 'Bickham, George (c.1704–1771)', *Oxford Dictionary of National Biography*, Oxford 2008, https://doi.org/10.1093/ref:odnb/2352 (accessed 6 April 2021); Mark Hallett, *The Spectacle of Difference: Graphic Satire in the Age of Hogarth*, New Haven and London 1999, pp.131–67.

10. London house museums included those of Hans Sloane, Richard Mead, William Hunter, the Earl of Burlington, the Duchess of Northumberland, and the Duke of Richmond, who also opened his collection of plaster casts and antique statuary to students of William Shipley's drawing academy.

11. David Coke and Alan Borg, *Vauxhall Gardens: A History*, New Haven and London 2011, pp.85–137; David Solkin, *Art in Britain 1660–1815*, New Haven and London 2015, pp.99–102.

12. David Bindman and Malcolm Baker, *Roubiliac and the Eighteenth-Century Monument: Sculpture as Theatre*, New Haven and London 1995; Malcolm Baker, *Figured in Marble: The Making and Viewing of Eighteenth-Century Sculpture*, Los Angeles 2000.

13. Solkin 2015, pp.102–4; Jacob Simon, 'Picture Frames at the Foundling Museum, London', National Portrait Gallery 2006, https://www.npg.org.uk/research/programmes/the-art-of-the-picture-frame/guides-foundling-museum.php (accessed 6 April 2021); Jacqueline Riding, '"The mere relation of the sufferings of others": Highmore, History Painting and the Foundling Hospital', *Art History*, vol.35, no.3, June 2012, pp.522–53.

14. Anne Puetz, 'Art and Fancy: The Intersection of Art and Design in Mid-Eighteenth-Century London', *RIHA Journal*, Special Issue, 2014, pp.1–35.

15. Timothy Clayton, *The English Print, 1688–1802*, New Haven and London 1997.

16. Robin Simon, *Hogarth, France, and British Art: The Rise of the Arts in 18th Century Britain*, London 2007.

17. Hans Hammelmann and T.S.R. Boase, *Book Illustrators in Eighteenth-Century England*, New Haven and London 1975, pp.38–46; Hallett 1999, pp.145–51.

AMSTERDAM

I am grateful to Thijs de Raedt for his careful reading of the first draft of this text.

1. This urban expansion is discussed in Jaap Evert Abrahamse, *De grote uitleg van Amsterdam – Stadsontwikkeling in de zeventiende eeuw*, Amsterdam 2010.

2. See Bert Gerlagh, 'Zwevend boven daken en pleinen: Amsterdam in vogelvlucht', *Ons Amsterdam*, 16 Oct. 2002, https://onsamsterdam.nl/zwevend-boven-daken-en-pleinen-0.

3. Clé Lesger, 'De locatie van het Amsterdamse winkelbedrijf in de achttiende eeuw', *Tijdschrift voor Sociale en Economische Geschiedenis*, no.4, 2007, pp.35–70; Clé Lesger, 'Waar het volk is, is de nering: bewinkelingspatroon en winkelarchitectuur in Amsterdam, circa 1550–1850', *Bulletin KNOB*, vol.114, no.2, 2015, pp.65–83; C.M. Lesger, *Shopping Spaces and the Urban Landscape in Early Modern Amsterdam, 1550–1850*, Amsterdam 2020. For markets, see https://www.theobakker.net/pdf/markten.pdf (accessed 14 March 2021).

4. Maarten Hell, *De Amsterdamse herberg 1450–1800: Geestrijk centrum van het openbare leven*, Nijmegen 2017.

5. For the 1720 speculative scandal, see C.H. Slechte, 'Een noodlottig jaar voor veel zotte en wijze', *De Rotterdamse windhandel van 1720*, The Hague 1982 and Maarten Hell, '"Afgaand getij" en woelige baren. Amsterdam in de achttiende eeuw', in *Kijk Amsterdam 1700–1800. De mooiste stadsgezichten*, exh. cat., Stadsarchief Amsterdam, 2017, pp.10–19.

6. *De Geschiedenis van het Nederlandse koffiehuis*, https://isgeschiedenis.nl/nieuws/de-geschiedenis-van-het-nederlandse-koffiehuis (accessed 14 March 2021).

7. Edwin Buijsen and J.W. Niemeijer, *Cornelis Troost and the Theatre of his Time. Plays of the 18th Century*, exh. cat., Mauritshuis, The Hague, 1993.

8. Some examples of eighteenth-century painted theatrical scenery have survived in print form; see: Wiebe Hoogendoorn, *Setting the Scene: The Amsterdam Stage in Pictures, 1665–1772*, Houten 2012. For De Lairesse, see Alain Roy, *Gerard de Lairesse (1640–1711)*, Paris 1992; J. Beltman, P. Knolle and Q. van der Meer Mohr (eds.), *Eindelijk! De Lairesse. Klassieke schoonheid in de Gouden Eeuw*, exh. cat., Rijksmuseum Twenthe, Enschede 2016; *Journal of Historians of Netherlandish Art*, vol.12, no.1, Winter 2020 (special issue on Gerard de Lairesse), https://jhna.org/issues/vol-12-1-2020.

9. See D.J. Balfoort, *Het muziekleven in Nederland in de 17de en 18de eeuw*, The Hague 1981.

10. See Rudolf Rasch, 'Operatroepen in Amsterdam, 1750–1763', *De Achttiende Eeuw*, no.29, 1997, pp.169–90 and the literature cited there.

11. André Hanou, 'Dutch periodicals from 1697 to 1721. An imitation of the English?', in *Studies on Voltaire and the Eighteenth Century*, no.199, 1981, pp.187–204.

12. Johan van Gool, *De Nieuwe Schouburg der Nederlantsche Kunstschilders en Schilderessen: (…)*, vol.2, The Hague 1751, p.251.

13. See Frans Grijzenhout, *Cornelis Troost, NELRI*, Bloemendaal 1993, pp.61–7 and Frans Grijzenhout, 'Hogarth in Holland', in *Ekkehard Mai, Holland nach Rembrandt: Zur niederländischen Kunst zwischen 1670 und 1750*, Cologne, Weimar and Vienna 2006, pp.89–90.

14. For Dutch painting of the late seventeenth and early eighteenth century see, amongst others, W. Loos, G. Jansen and W. Kloek, *Het galante tijdperk. Schilderijen uit de collectie van het Rijksmuseum, 1700–1800*, Amsterdam and Zwolle 1995; R. Baarsen et al., *Netherlandish Art in the Rijksmuseum*, Vol.3: 1700–1800, Amsterdam and Zwolle 2006; *De kroon op het werk. Hollandse schilderkunst 1670–1750*, exh. cat., Wallraf-Richartz-Museum, Cologne, Dordrechts Museum, Dordrecht and Museumlandschaft Hessen Kassel 2006; Mai 2006.

15. Paul Knolle and Everhard Korthals Altes (eds.), *Nicolaas Verkolje (1673–1746). De fluwelen hand*, Zwolle and Enschede 2011.

16. See Rudi Ekkart, *Tibout Regters (1710–1768), schilder van portretten en conversatiestukken*, Leiden 2006.

17. For Troost see, amongst others, J.W. Niemeijer, *Cornelis Troost 1696–1750*, Assen 1973; Grijzenhout 1993 (see n.13 above); Paul Knolle and Robert-Jan te Rijdt, *Cornelis Troost uit het Koninklijk Oudheidkundig Genootschap*, Enschede 2008.

18. See, for instance, *De wereld binnen handbereik. Nederlandse kunst- en rariteitenverzamelingen, 1585–1735*, exh. cat., Amsterdams Historisch Museum, Amsterdam 1992, and *Kijk Amsterdam 1700–1800. De mooiste stadsgezichten*, exh. cat., Stadsarchief Amsterdam, 2017. There were forty private collections in Amsterdam at the beginning of the eighteenth century that could be visited on invitation or payment of an entry fee (Hell, '"Afgaand getij" en woelige baren', p.17).

19. Art collecting in the Netherlands in this period is dealt with in Michiel C. Plomp, *Hartstochtelijk verzameld. 18de-eeuwse Hollandse verzamelaars en hun collecties*, Paris and Bussum 2001, and *Hartstochtelijk verzameld. 18de-eeuwse Hollandse verzamelaars en hun collecties*, exh. cat., Teylers Museum, Haarlem 2001, amongst others.

20. Boudewijn Bakker, *Amsterdam in the Eighteenth Century*, trans. Patricia Wardle and Gillian Downing, Delft 1969.

21. Paul Knolle, 'De Amsterdamse stadstekenacademie, een 18de-eeuwse "oefenschool" voor modeltekenaars', *Nederlands Kunsthistorisch Jaarboek*, no.30, 1979, pp.1–41. These speeches – particularly the ones given by the timber merchant, academy director and art collector Cornelis Ploos van Amstel, as well as the issues he addressed – are discussed in Paul Knolle, 'Cornelis Ploos van Amstel als pleitbezorger van de "Hollandse" iconografie', *Oud Holland*, vol.98, no.1, 1984, pp.43–52, and Paul Knolle, 'An asset to art. The purchase of Italian drawings by Teyler's Foundation in 1790 and the context of art theory in the Netherlands', in Ellinoor Bergvelt and Debora Meijers (eds.), *Teyler's Foundation in Haarlem and its 'Book and Art Room' of 1779. A Key Moment in the History of a Learned Institution*, Leiden and Boston 2020, pp.168–89.

PARIS

1. Nathalie Heinich, *Du peintre à l'artiste: artisans et académiciens à l'âge classique*, Paris 1993; Katie Scott, 'Hierarchy, Liberty and Order: Languages of Art and Institutional Conflict in Paris (1766–1776)', *Oxford Art Journal*, vol.12, no.2, 1989, pp.59–70; Charlotte Guichard, '"Liberal Arts" and "Free Arts" in Paris in the Eighteenth Century: Artists Between the Guild and the Royal Academy', *Revue d'histoire moderne et contemporaine*, vol.49, no.3, 2002–3, pp.54–68.

2. For one of the earliest versions of this narrative, see the Academy's *Mémoires pour servir à l'histoire de l'Académie royale de peinture et de sculpture depuis 1648 jusqu'en 1664*, 1664, ed. Anatole de Montaiglon, 2 vols, Paris 1853.

3. David Bindman, *Hogarth and his Times: Serious Comedy*, Berkeley and Los Angeles 1997, p.203.

4. Jules Guiffrey, 'Logements d'artistes au Louvre', *Nouvelles Archives de l'art français*, 1873, pp.1–221; Hannah Williams, 'Artists and the City: Mapping the Art Worlds of Eighteenth-Century Paris', *Urban History*, vol.46, no.1, 2019, pp.14–17.

5. David Maskill, 'The Neighbor from Hell: André Rouquet's Eviction from the Louvre', *Journal18*, no.2, Fall 2016, http://www.journal18.org/822 (accessed 14 March 2021).

6. All these academicians' addresses are taken from Hannah Williams and Chris Sparks, *Artists in Paris: Mapping the 18th-Century Art World*, www.artistsinparis.org (accessed 14 March 2021).

7. Marianne Grivel, *Le commerce de l'estampe au XVIIe siècle*, Geneva 1986, pp.59–62.

8. Williams 2019, pp.17–21.

9. Letter from Jean-Baptiste-Marie Pierre to Comte d'Angiviller, 29 Sept. 1775. See *Correspondance de M. d'Angiviller*, ed. Marc Furcy-Raynaud, *Nouvelles Archives de l'Art Français*, vol.XXI, 1905, pp.51–2.

10. Jules Guiffrey, *Histoire de l'Académie de Saint Luc*, Paris 1915, pp.170, 408.

11. Demachy's engagement with Paris has been explored in *Le témoin méconnu: Pierre-Antoine Demachy, 1723–1807*, exh. cat., Musée Lambinet, Versailles 2014.

12. On Bouchardon's drawings of street-sellers, see Katie Scott, 'Edmé Bouchardon's "Cris de Paris": crying food in early modern Paris', *Word and Image*, vol.29, no.1, 2013, pp.59–91.

VENICE

1. Cristina Cortese, 'Pietro Longhi, Giuseppe Wagner a Giambattista Remondini', *Lettere artistiche del Settecento veneziano*, vol.1, 2002, pp.379–414.

2. Philip L. Sohm, 'Pietro Longhi and Carlo Goldini: Relations between Painting and Theater', *Zeitschrift für Kunstgeschichte*, vol.45, no.3, 1982, p.259 (translation my own).

3. For Venice as a Grand Tour city, see Bruce Redford, *Venice & the Grand Tour*, New Haven and London 1996.

4. Martin Folkes, 'Journey from Venice to Rome', Oxford, Bodleian Library, MS Eng. Misc. C.444, fol 2.

5. *Rosalba Carriera: Lettere, diari, frammenti*, ed. Bernardina Sani, 2 vols., Florence 1985.

6. McSwiny's correspondence has recently been published. See ed. T.D. Llewellyn, 'Owen McSwiny's letters, 1720–1744', *Lettere artistiche del Settecento veneziano*, vol.4, 2009.

7. 'The Notebooks of George Vertue, vol.III', *The Walpole Society*, vol.22, 1933/34, p.75.

8. Ronald Paulson, *Hogarth: High Art and Low, 1732–1750*, vol.2, Cambridge 1991, pp.77–81.

'THE DUTCH HOGARTH': CORNELIS TROOST

1. Frans Grijzenhout, *Cornelis Troost, NELRI*, Bloemendaal 1993, pp.26–7 and *Kopstukken: Amsterdammers geportretteerd 1600–1800*, exh. cat., Amsterdam Museum 2002, p.146. See also Cornelis Joannes de Bruyn Kops, 'Aanwinsten in de gedeeltelijk gereorganiseerde afdeling 18de en 19de eeuwse schilderkunst', *Bulletin van het Rijksmuseum*, vol.22, 1974, p.20.

2. Elizabeth Einberg and Judy Egerton, *The Age of Hogarth: British Painters Born 1675–1709*, London 1988, pp.110–14.

3. Elizabeth Einberg, *William Hogarth: a complete catalogue of the paintings*, London 2016, pp.113–15, no.65.

4. Einberg and Egerton 1988, pp.110–14.

5. Troost made another self-portrait (Mauritshuis, The Hague, inv. no. 194) for the important collector Jeronimus Tonneman, who was also the first owner of the painting of *Johanna and the Jewish Merchants* discussed below. See *Cornelis Troost en het Theater: Tonelen van de 18de eeuw/Cornelis Troost and the Theatre of his Time: Plays of the 18th Century*, exh. cat., Mauritshuis, The Hague 1993, pp.31–3, no.1, and *The Age of Elegance: Paintings from the Rijksmuseum in Amsterdam, 1700–1800*, exh. cat., Rijksmuseum, Amsterdam 1995, p.46, no.14. For the engravings of the self-portrait see J.W. Niemeijer, *Cornelis Troost 1696–1750*, Assen 1973, pp.156–7, no.5S.

6. Einberg and Egerton 1988, pp.110–14.

7. Niemeijer 1973, p.114.

8. Niemeijer 1973, pp.77–8.

9. *The Age of Elegance* 1995, p.46, no.14.

10. Niemeijer 1973, pp.113–14.

11. A figure in Hogarth's *Midnight Modern Conversation* was used in the fourth pastel in the famous NELRI series (1739–40), one of Troost's masterpieces (Mauritshuis, The Hague): see Grijzenhout 1993, pp.82–4. For Troost's interest in foreign art and examples of borrowings, see Niemeijer 1973, pp.67–82 and *Cornelis Troost en het Theater*, 1993, p.20, pp.48–9, no.9, pp.66–7, no.18.

12. Niemeijer 1973, pp.79 and 304, no.525T; Grijzenhout 1993, p.87.

13. Niemeijer 1973, pp.76–9; Grijzenhout 1993, pp.80–7.

POTS IN HOGARTH

1. William Hogarth, *Anecdotes of William Hogarth*, London 1833, p.9.

2. The Chinese attribution is helped by knowing that the painting just pre-dates the very first English porcelain factories; other up-and-running Continental porcelain factories did not manufacture this particular form, which was imported into London in very large quantities.

3. Hogarth's reference appears to be the blanc de Chine 'pagod' – since the 1600s a fashionable mantelpiece staple.

4. Hogarth maintains the porcelain metaphor for Moll's Fall through the remaining four images where the ceramics on display in each descend through to common broken crockery, with another table and its contents completely toppled en route to Moll's wake – in whose bottom right-hand corner the artist places a stoneware Bellarmine bottle with grotesque grinning facial features, a final full stop to Moll's theatrical tragicomedy.

5. Now in the collection of the Foundling Museum, London, under the gaze of Hogarth's great portrait of Thomas Coram.

AN AMERICAN PARTY
IN A DUTCH COLONY

1. *Original Memorandum Book (No.2) of John Greenwood, Artist*, p.113, in the collection of the New-York Historical Society.

2. Ibid., p.105.

3. Alex van Stipriaan, *Surinaams Contrast,* Leiden 1993, p.33.

4. Ibid., p.311.

5. Voltaire, *Candide* (English translation), New York 1918, p.91.

6. John Gabriel Stedman, *The Narrative of a Five Years Expedition against the Revolted Negroes of Surinam*, London 1796.

7. Greenwood, p.122.

8. Johannes Postma, 'Suriname and its Atlantic Connections, 1667–1795', in Johannes Postma and Victor Enthoven (eds.), *Riches from Atlantic Commerce: Dutch Transatlantic Trade and Shipping, 1585–1817*, Leiden 2003, pp.300–5.

9. NL-HaNA (Dutch National Archives), Suriname Society, inv. no.202, entry 9 Dec. 1752.

10. For Greenwood's time in Suriname, see also Katelyn D. Crawford, 'Painting New England in the Dutch West Indies: John Greenwood's *Sea Captains Carousing*

in Surinam', in David T. Gies and Cynthia Wall (eds.), *The Eighteenth Centuries: Global Networks of Enlightenment*, Charlottesville, VA and London 2018, pp.178–96.

11. NL-HaNA, Suriname Society, inv. no.204, entry 22 April 1758.

12. Alan Burroughs, *John Greenwood in America, 1745–1752*, Andover, MA 1943, p.51.

BETWEEN THE SHEETS

1. Hogarth did, however, paint a subject associated with Ovid's text: the Greek mythological princess Danaë. Currently untraced, Hogarth's *Danaë* was sold at the 1745 auction of his works. Ronald Paulson notes that the artist may have been 'burlesquing Ovid's story': see Ronald Paulson, *Hogarth,* vol.2, New Brunswick, NJ 1992, p.104. Hogarth's view of Ovid was likely mediated by Titian, whose six compositionally identical paintings of the same mythological figure were widely known during the artist's lifetime.

2. The ambiguity of the print is discussed in Temi Odumosu, *Africans in English Caricature 1769–1819: Black Jokes White Humour*, London and Turnhout 2017, pp.99–100.

3. Felicity A. Nussbaum makes this claim in *The Limits of the Human: Fictions of Anomaly, Race and Gender in the Long Eighteenth Century*, Cambridge 2003, p.164.

4. See Saidiya V. Hartman, 'Venus in Two Acts', *Small Axe: A Journal of Criticism*, no.26, 2008, pp.1–14.

5. Odumosu 2017, p.103.

6. Samuel Ireland, *Graphic Illustrations of Hogarth*, London 1794, p.112.

7. Édouard Glissant, *Poetics of Relation* (trans. Betsy Wing), Ann Arbor 2010, p.7.

8. Phillis Wheatley, *Poems on Various Subjects Religious and Moral*, Albany 1793, pp.72–81. This volume was first published in London in 1773.

9. June Jordan, 'The Difficult Miracle of Black Poetry in America: Something like a sonnet for Phillis Wheatley', *Poetry Foundation*, https://www.poetryfoundation.org/articles/68628/the-difficult-miracle-of-black-poetry-in-america (accessed 14 March 2021). For insight into Wheatley's deployment of classicism to assert her humanity, see 'Part I: New Manifestations of Classicism in the Poetry of Phillis Wheatley' in John C. Shields and Eric D. Lamore, *New Essays on Phillis Wheatley*, Knoxville, TN 2011, pp.3–111.

10. For a discussion of Wheatley and Pope, see Patrick Mosely, 'Empowerment Through Classicism in Phillis Wheatley's *Ode to Neptune*' in Shields and Lamore 2011, pp.95–110.

11. John Hunter and Richard Owen, *Essays and Observations on Natural History, Anatomy, Physiology, Psychology, and Geology*, vol.1, London 1861, pp.183–4.

12. This is a quotation from Benjamin Brawley's *The Negro Genius: a New Appraisal of the American Negro in Literature and the Fine Arts*, New York 1966, p.19.

PERFORMING FURNITURE

1. Furniture design manuals were a key new source of explicitly gendered language around objects. In 1762, Thomas Chippendale and Ince and Mayhew both published catalogues that gendered furniture. See Amanda Vickery, *Behind Closed Doors: At Home in Georgian England*, New Haven and London 2009.

2. See William Blake's *Europe Supported by Africa and America* 1796. This point was also reiterated by Sokari Douglas Camp's sculpture *Europe Supported by Africa and America* 2015.

3. Whilst David Dabydeen and Lubaina Himid have started the critical work of voicing Black people who are, so to speak, in the picture, I am interested in the traces of all those Black people who lie outside it, labouring elsewhere.

4. William Hogarth, *Anecdotes of William Hogarth*, London 1833, p.9.

5. *A Harlot's Progress*, Plate 5.

6. *Sir Francis Dashwood at his Devotions* c.1750s; *The Four Times of Day: Noon* 1738; *A Harlot's Progress*, Plate 5 and Plate 6.

7. *A Rake's Progress*, Plate 3. See Dan Cruickshank, *The Secret History of Georgian London*, London 2009, p.93.

8. See *Industry and Idleness*, Plate 7 and *A Rake's Progress*, Plate 7 respectively.

9. *A Harlot's Progress*, Plate 2.

10. In June 2020, the Manchester United footballer Marcus Rashford campaigned for free school meals for UK children during school holidays. Brendan Clarke-Smith, MP for Bassetlaw, responded by saying that footballers should stay footballers and leave politics to politicians, condemning Rashford's actions as mere 'celebrity virtue-signalling on Twitter by proxy'. Clarke-Smith described Rashford's intervention into the political arena as 'nationalising children' (Matthew

Stead, 'Rashford is driving football as a vehicle for societal change', *Football 365*, 26 October 2020, https://www.football365 .com/news/opinion-rashford-driving -football-vehicle-for-change-politics). A few months later, it was reported:

> [...] the BBC will not consider [Rashford] as a candidate for this year's Sports Personality of the Year (SPOTY) award, which it says must be given for achievements on the field, not for involvement in matters off it.

Before this announcement the bookies had made him an outstanding favourite for SPOTY (Alan Hubbard, 'Food for thought as Rashford plays political football and wrong-foots British Government', *Inside the Games*, 27 October 2020, https://www.insidethegames.biz/articles /1100071/alan-hubbard-rashford)

A footballer, it seems, is to be recognised only for their personality *in their place* on the sports field and not *out of their place* in the arenas of politics or social action (which is then somehow not relevant to their personality).

11. *George Arnold* c.1738–40. See also *William Jones* 1740.

12. *Self-Portrait of William Hogarth Painting the Comic Muse* 1757–8.

13. Many works of this period make use of this convention; see, for example, *The Jones Family* c.1730.

14. *The Four Times of Day: Night* and *Morning* 1738.

15. Cruickshank 2009, p.xi.

16. Ibid., p.268.

SEXUALITY AND SEDUCTION

I would like to thank Susannah Blair and Zoë Dostal for their valuable comments on a draft of this text.

1. John Nichols, *Biographical Anecdotes of William Hogarth; with a catalogue of his works chronologically arranged; and occasional remarks. The Third Edition, Enlarged and Corrected*, London 1782, p.233.

Hogarth translated this second set of *Before* and *After* paintings into engravings, which he published in 1736. For further information about and analysis of the *Before* and *After* paintings and prints, see Elizabeth Einberg, *William Hogarth: A Complete Catalogue of the Paintings*, New Haven 2016, pp.78–80, nos.39–42; *Hogarth*, exh. cat., Tate Britain, London 2006, pp.76–9, nos.40–2; and Ronald Paulson, *Hogarth's Graphic Works*, 3rd revised edn, London 1989, pp.99–100, nos.141–2. As Einberg notes, it is not absolutely clear which set Hogarth painted first, though it is most often presumed to be the outdoor pair (see pp.80, nos.41–2).

2. For a discussion of this painting and 'the refusal' theme in the *fête galante* genre more generally, see Mary Vidal, *Watteau's Painted Conversations: Art, Literature, and Talk in Seventeenth- and Eighteenth-Century France*, New Haven 1992, pp.113–18. My thanks to David Pullins for sharing his expertise on this topic.

3. Toni Bowers, *Force or Fraud: British Seduction Stories and the Problem of Resistance, 1660–1760*, Oxford 2011, pp.4–8, 11–20. According to Nathan Bailey, author of *Dictionarium Britannicum. Or a More Compleat Universal Etymological English Dictionary Than Any Extant*, rape meant 'a Ravishing, or forcible Violation of the Chastity of a Woman' (London 1730, unpag.). The *Oxford English Dictionary* defines its chief current meaning as 'the act of forced, non-consenting, or illegal sexual intercourse with another person'.

4. Bowers 2011, p.11.

5. The history of child sex trafficking in eighteenth-century Britain remains largely unstudied; however, court records offer ample evidence of sexual assault and rape committed against young girls in the period. See, for example, Esther Snell, 'Trials in Print: Narratives of Rape Trials in the Proceedings of the Old Bailey', in David Lemmings (ed.), *Crime, Courtrooms, and the Public Sphere in Britain, 1700–1850*, Farnham 2013, pp.23–41.

EXHIBITED WORKS

The works are listed chronologically by artist.

Measurements of artworks are given in centimetres, height before width and depth.

JACQUES AUTREAU
1657–1745

The Wine Drinkers, or The poet Piron (1689–1773) at table with his friends Vadé and Collé 1747
Les Buveurs de vin. Ou: Le poète Piron (1689–1773) à table avec ses amis Vadé et Collé
Oil paint on canvas
54.5 × 66.5
Paris, Musée du Louvre, Department of Paintings
RF 2440 [p.114]

JACQUES-ANDRÉ-JOSEPH AVED
1702–66

The Marquise de Castellane with Her Embroidery 1743
Oil paint on canvas
127.5 × 101.9
Manchester Art Gallery
1904.1 [p.185]

GERRIT DE BROEN II
1692–1774

Amsterdam 1720–30
Tot Amsterdam
Copperplate engraving on paper 96.7 × 117.5
The British Library
Maps K. Top. 106.56 [pp.30–1]

GIOVANNI ANTONIO CANAL (KNOWN AS CANALETTO)
1697–1768

The Grand Walk, Vauxhall Gardens c.1751
Oil paint on canvas
51 × 76
Compton Verney Art Gallery & Park
CVCSC:0355.s [p.76]

The Interior of the Rotunda, Ranelagh c.1751
Oil paint on canvas 51 × 76
Compton Verney Art Gallery & Park
CVCSC:0356.s [p.77]

JEAN-SIMÉON CHARDIN
1699–1779

The White Tablecloth 1731/2
Oil paint on canvas
96.8 × 123.5
The Art Institute of Chicago, Mr. and Mrs. Lewis Larned Coburn Memorial Collection
1944.699 [p.160]

Still-life: The Kitchen Table c.1733–4
Oil paint on canvas
40.6 × 32.4
National Galleries of Scotland. Purchased 1908
NG 959 [p.56]

The Governess c.1738
La gouvernante
Oil paint on canvas 72.5 × 65
National Trust Collections, Tatton Park (The Egerton Collection)
NT 1298184 [p.88]

GIUSEPPE MARIA CRESPI
1665–1747

The Flea 1707–9
La pulce
Oil paint on copper 46.3 × 34
Gallerie degli Uffizi
In.1890 no.1408 [p.98]

Courtyard Scene c.1710–15
Oil paint on canvas 76 × 90
Pinacoteca Nazionale di Bologna
415 [p.94]

A Woman Looking for Fleas c.1715–20
Oil paint on canvas 49.5 × 37.8
The Henry Barber Trust, the Barber Institute of Fine Arts, University of Birmingham
65.3 [p.89]

JEAN DELAGRIVE
1689–1757

New map of Paris and its Suburbs 1728
Nouveau plan de Paris et de ses Faubourgs
Engraving on paper
154.5 × 184
The British Library
Maps S.T.P.185 [pp.38–9]

GEORG DESMARÉES
1697–1776

The Artist with his Daughter Antonia 1760
Der Künstler und seiner Tochter
Oil paint on canvas
159 × 118
Bayerische Staatsgemäldesammlungen München – Alte Pinakothek
Inv.42 [p.182]

RENÉ GAILLARD
c.1719–90
AFTER
FRANÇOIS BOUCHER
1703–70

The Modiste c.1755
Le Marchande de Modes
Engraving on paper
38.4 × 27.2
Victoria and Albert Museum, London
E.361-1905 [p.151]

HUBERT FRANÇOIS GRAVELOT
1699–1773

A Game of Quadrille c.1740
Oil paint on canvas
63.5 × 76.2
Yale Center for British Art, Paul Mellon Fund, in honor of Brian Allen, Director of Studies, Paul Mellon Centre for Studies in British Art (1993–2012)
B2011.34 [p.150]

HUBERT FRANÇOIS GRAVELOT
1699–1773
WITH
JEAN-ÉTIENNE LIOTARD
1702–89
AND POSSIBLY
FRANCIS HAYMAN
1708–76

The Hon. Mrs Constantine Phipps (1722–1780) being led to greet her Brother, Captain the Hon. Augustus Hervey, later 3rd Earl of Bristol (1724–1779) 1750
Oil paint on canvas
99.1 × 124.5
National Trust Collections, Ickworth (The Bristol Collection [acquired through the National Land Fund and transferred to The National Trust in 1956])
NT 851727 [p.16]

JOHN GREENWOOD
1727–92

Sea Captains Carousing in Surinam c.1752–8
Oil paint on bed ticking
95.9 × 190.5
Saint Louis Art Museum, Museum Purchase
256.1948 [pp.15, 126–7]

ANTONIO GUARDI
1699–1760

The Sala Grande of the Ridotto, Palazzo Dandolo, San Moise 1755–60
Oil paint on canvas
50 × 85
The Syndics of the Fitzwilliam Museum, University of Cambridge
PD.1-1980 [p.93]

WILLIAM HOGARTH
1697–1764

Before 1730–1
Oil paint on canvas 40 × 33.7
The J. Paul Getty Museum,
Los Angeles
78.PA.204 [p.170]

After 1730–1
Oil paint on canvas
39.4 × 33.7
The J. Paul Getty Museum,
Los Angeles
78.PA.205 [p.171]

*A Scene from 'The Beggar's
Opera' VI* 1731
Oil paint on canvas
57.2 × 76.2
Tate. Purchased 1909
[p.78]

The Cholmondeley Family 1732
Oil paint on canvas 185 × 225
Private collection
[p.181]

A Harlot's Progress, plate 1 1732
Etching and engraving
on paper 32 × 38
Andrew Edmunds, London
[p.99]

A Harlot's Progress, plate 2 1732
Etching and engraving
on paper 32 × 38
Andrew Edmunds, London
[p.99]

A Harlot's Progress, plate 3 1732
Etching and engraving
on paper 32 × 38
Andrew Edmunds, London
[p.100]

A Harlot's Progress, plate 4 1732
Etching and engraving
on paper 32 × 38
Andrew Edmunds, London
[p.100]

A Harlot's Progress, plate 5 1732
Etching and engraving on
paper 32 × 38
Andrew Edmunds, London
[p.101]

A Harlot's Progress, plate 6 1732
Etching and engraving
on paper 32 × 38
Andrew Edmunds, London
[p.101]

*A Performance of 'The Indian
Emperor or The Conquest
of Mexico by the Spaniards'*
c.1732–5
Oil paint on canvas
131 × 146.7
Private collection
[pp.178–9]

*A Midnight Modern
Conversation* 1733
Etching and engraving
on paper 34.5 × 47
Andrew Edmunds, London

*A Midnight Modern
Conversation* 1733
Etching and engraving
printed in red on paper
35.9 × 48.4
The Royal Collection /
HM Queen Elizabeth II
RCIN 811532 [p.122]

Southwark Fair 1733
Oil paint on canvas
120.7 × 151.1
Cincinnati Art Museum,
The Edwin and Virginia
Irwin Memorial
1983.138 [pp.72–3]

The Distressed Poet c.1733–5
Oil paint on canvas
65.9 × 79.1
Lent by Birmingham
Museums Trust on behalf
of Birmingham City Council
1934P500 [p.68]

*Sir Francis Dashwood
at his Devotions* c.1733–9
Oil paint on canvas
120 × 80.7
Private collection
[p.118]

*A Rake's Progress I:
The Heir* 1734
Oil paint on canvas 62.2 × 75
By courtesy of the Trustees
of Sir John Soane's Museum,
London
SM P40 [p.108]

*A Rake's Progress II:
The Levée* 1734
Oil paint on canvas 63 × 75.5
By courtesy of the Trustees
of Sir John Soane's Museum,
London
SM P41 [p.108]

*A Rake's Progress III:
The Orgy* 1734
Oil paint on canvas
62.5 × 75.2
By courtesy of the Trustees
of Sir John Soane's Museum,
London
SM P42 [p.109]

*A Rake's Progress IV:
The Arrest* 1734
Oil paint on canvas
62.5 × 75.2
By courtesy of the Trustees
of Sir John Soane's Museum,
London
SM P43 [p.109]

*A Rake's Progress V:
The Marriage* 1734
Oil paint on canvas
62.2 × 75.2
By courtesy of the Trustees
of Sir John Soane's Museum,
London
SM P44 [p.110]

*A Rake's Progress VI:
The Gaming House* 1734
Oil paint on canvas
62.5 × 75.5
By courtesy of the Trustees
of Sir John Soane's Museum,
London
SM P45 [p.110]

*A Rake's Progress VII:
The Prison* 1734
Oil paint on canvas 63 × 75.5
By courtesy of the Trustees
of Sir John Soane's Museum,
London
SM P46 [p.111]

*A Rake's Progress VIII:
The Madhouse* 1734
Oil paint on canvas
62.5 × 75.2
By courtesy of the Trustees
of Sir John Soane's Museum,
London
SM P47 [p.111]

*The Times of Day:
Morning* 1738
Etching and engraving
on paper 48.7 × 39.2
Andrew Edmunds, London
[p.82]

The Times of Day: Noon 1738
Etching and engraving
on paper 48.6 × 40.2
Andrew Edmunds, London
[p.82]

The Times of Day: Evening
1738
Etching and engraving
on paper with B. Baron
48.8 × 40.2
Andrew Edmunds, London
[p.82]

The Times of Day: Night 1738
Etching and engraving
on paper 48.6 × 40.2
Andrew Edmunds, London
[p.82]

A Night Encounter c.1738–9
Oil paint on canvas 62 × 75
Private collection
[p.120]

*The Hervey Conversation
Piece* 1738–40
Oil paint on canvas
101.6 × 127
National Trust Collections,
Ickworth (The Bristol
Collection (acquired through
the National Land Fund and
transferred to The National
Trust in 1956))
NT 851983 [p.149]

Charity in the Cellar 1739
Oil paint on canvas
99 × 124.5
Private collector, London
[p.121]

James Quin, Actor c.1739
Oil paint on canvas
76 × 62.2
Tate. Purchased 1904
[p.190]

Anne Hogarth c.1740
Oil paint on canvas
46.7 × 41.6
Yale Center for British Art,
Paul Mellon Fund
B2002.2.1 [p.197]

Mary Hogarth c.1740
Oil paint on canvas
46.7 × 41.6
Yale Center for British Art,
Paul Mellon Fund
B2002.2.2 [p.196]

George Arnold, Esq. c.1740–5
Oil paint on canvas
90.5 × 70.8
The Syndics of the
Fitzwilliam Museum,
University of Cambridge
21 [p.191]

*Lavinia Fenton, Duchess
of Bolton* c.1740–50
Oil paint on canvas
73.7 × 58.4
Tate. Purchased 1884
[p.192]

Mrs Salter 1741
Oil paint on canvas
76.2 × 63.5
Tate. Purchased 1898
[p.193]

*Portrait of Elizabeth Betts,
Mrs Benjamin Hoadly* 1741
Oil paint on canvas 76 × 63.5
York Museums Trust (York
Art Gallery). Purchased with
the aid of grants from the
Heritage Lottery Fund, the
Victoria and Albert Museum
Purchase Grant Fund, The
Art Fund, York Civic Trust
and the Friends of York
Art Gallery in their fiftieth
anniversary year, 1998
YORAG: 1485 [p.195]

The Enraged Musician 1741
Etching and engraving
on paper 39.2 × 44.9
Andrew Edmunds, London

Miss Mary Edwards 1742
Oil paint on canvas
126.4 × 101.3
The Frick Collection,
New York. Henry Clay
Frick Bequest
1914.1.75 [pp.19, 184]

Taste in High Life 1742
Oil paint on canvas 63 × 75
Private collection
[p.168]

*Captain Lord George Graham,
1715–47, in his Cabin* 1742–4
Oil paint on canvas
68.5 × 88.9
National Maritime Museum,
Greenwich, London,
Caird Collection
BHC2720 [p.115]

*Marriage A-la-Mode: 1,
The Marriage Settlement*
c.1743
Oil paint on canvas
69.9 × 90.8
The National Gallery,
London. Bought, 1824
NG113 [p.161]

*Marriage A-la-Mode: 2,
The Tête à Tête* c.1743
Oil paint on canvas
69.9 × 90.8
The National Gallery,
London. Bought, 1824
NG114 [p.161]

*Marriage A-la-Mode: 3,
The Inspection* c.1743
Oil paint on canvas
69.9 × 90.8
The National Gallery,
London. Bought, 1824
NG115 [p.162]

*Marriage A-la-Mode: 4,
The Toilette* c.1743
Oil paint on canvas
70.5 × 90.8
The National Gallery,
London. Bought, 1824
NG116 [pp.162, 166]

*Marriage A-la-Mode: 5,
The Bagnio* c.1743
Oil paint on canvas
70.5 × 90.8
The National Gallery,
London. Bought, 1824
NG117 [p.163]

*Marriage A-la-Mode: 6,
The Lady's Death* c.1743
Oil paint on canvas
69.9 × 90.8
The National Gallery,
London. Bought, 1824
NG118 [p.163]

*Qui color albus erat,
nunc est contrarius albo.
'The Discovery'* 1743
Etching on paper
20.4 × 22.6
The Royal Collection /
HM Queen Elizabeth II
RCIN 812362 [p.132]

The Painter and his Pug 1745
Oil paint on canvas 90 × 69.9
Tate. Purchased 1824
[pp.2, 58]

Simon, Lord Lovat 1746
Etching and engraving
on paper 37.3 × 24.6
Andrew Edmunds, London

*O the Roast Beef of Old
England ('The Gate of Calais')*
1748
Oil paint on canvas
78.8 × 94.5
Tate. Presented by the
Duke of Westminster 1895
[p.57]

*The March of the Guards
to Finchley* 1749–50
Oil paint on canvas
100.3 × 133.3
The Foundling Museum,
London
2005.4
[pp.74–5]

*Heads of Six of Hogarth's
Servants* c.1750–5
Oil paint on canvas 63 × 75.5
Tate. Purchased 1892
[p.199]

Gin Lane 1751
Etching and engraving
on paper 38 × 32.1
Andrew Edmunds, London
[p.81]

Beer Street (first state) 1751
Etching and engraving
on paper 39 × 32.6
Andrew Edmunds, London
[p.80]

*Francis Matthew Schutz
in Bed* c.1755–60
Oil paint on canvas
63 × 75.5
Norfolk Museums Service
(Norwich Castle Museum
and Art Gallery). Purchased
with assistance from the
National Heritage Memorial
Fund, V&A Purchase
Grant Fund, Art Fund
(with a contribution from
the Wolfson Foundation),
Pilgrim Trust, Esmée
Fairbairn Charitable
Trust, Friends of Norwich
Museums, J. Paul Getty
Charitable Trust, PF
Charitable Trust, Norfolk
County Council 1990
NWHCM: 1990.130 [p.119]

*Self-portrait Painting the
Comic Muse* c.1757–8
Oil paint on canvas
45.1 × 42.5
National Portrait Gallery,
London. Purchased, 1869
NPG 289 [p.67]

*David Garrick with his Wife
Eva-Maria Veigel* c.1757–64
Oil paint on canvas
132.7 × 104.2
The Royal Collection /
HM Queen Elizabeth II
RCIN 405682 [p.183]

The Cockpit (or Pit Ticket) 1759
Etching and engraving
on paper 31.8 × 38.5
Andrew Edmunds, London
[p.116]

The Lady's Last Stake 1759
Oil paint on canvas
91.4 × 105.4
Collection Albright-Knox Art
Gallery, Buffalo, New York.
Gift of Seymour H. Knox,
Jr., 1945
1945:2.1 [p.169]

John Wilkes Esq. 1763
Etching and engraving
on paper 35.5 × 22.9
Andrew Edmunds, London

ÉTIENNE JEAURAT
1699–1789

Arrest by the Watch 1743
Oil paint on canvas 53 × 63
Madresfield Estate, England
[p.83]

*Removal of the Effects
of a Painter* 1743
Le Déménagement du Peintre
Oil paint on canvas 53 × 63
Madresfield Estate, England
[p.85]

*Scene in the Streets
of Paris* 1743
Oil paint on canvas 53 × 63
Madresfield Estate, England
[p.85]

*The Market 'Des Innocents',
Paris* 1743
Oil paint on canvas 53 × 63
Madresfield Estate, England
[p.84]

The Place Maubert, Paris 1743
Oil paint on canvas 53 × 63
Madresfield Estate, England
[p.84]

*Interior of the Artist's
Studio* 1755
Oil paint on canvas
117.5 × 88.7
Ferens Art Gallery:
Hull Museums
KINCM:2005.5079 [p.69]

NICOLAS LANCRET
1690–1743

*Lovers in a Landscape
(The Turtle Doves)* c.1720–30
Oil paint on canvas
76.5 × 98.5
The Henry Barber Trust, the
Barber Institute of Fine Arts,
University of Birmingham
37.10 [p.143]

*Group Portrait in a Landscape
with Amorous Couple* c.1737
Oil paint on canvas 68 × 86
Krannert Art Museum,
University of Illinois
Urbana-Champaign,
Museum Purchase
through the Ellnora
D. Krannert Fund
1967.3.5 [p.142]

*The Gascon punished
(La Fontaine, Contes)* 1738
Le Gascon puni
(La Fontaine, Contes)
Oil paint on copper 28 × 36
Paris, Musée du Louvre,
Department of Paintings
MI 1074 [p.133]

*The Four Times of Day:
Morning* by 1739
Oil paint on copper
28.3 × 36.4
National Gallery, London.
Bequeathed by Sir Bernard
Eckstein, 1948
NG5867 [p.152]

*The Four Times of Day:
Midday* 1739–41
Oil paint on copper
28.6 × 36.9
National Gallery, London.
Bequeathed by Sir Bernard
Eckstein, 1948
NG5868 [p.152]

*The Four Times of Day:
Afternoon* 1739–41
Oil paint on copper
28.8 × 36.7
National Gallery, London.
Bequeathed by Sir Bernard
Eckstein, 1948
NG5869 [p.153]

*The Four Times of Day:
Evening* 1739–41
Oil paint on copper
28.8 × 36.8
National Gallery, London.
Bequeathed by Sir Bernard
Eckstein, 1948
NG5870 [p.153]

PIETRO LONGHI
1700/2–1785

The Painter in His Studio
c.1741–4
Oil paint on canvas 41 × 53.3
The J. Paul Getty Museum,
Los Angeles, Purchased in
part with funds realised from
the sale of paintings donated
by Burton Frederickson and
William Garred
2011.20 [p.68]

The Dance c.1750
Oil paint on canvas
61.6 × 49.5
The Art Institute of Chicago,
Charles H. and Mary F.S.
Worcester Collection
1932.52 [p.95]

The Tooth Puller 1746–52
Oil paint on canvas 50 × 62
Pinacoteca di Brera, Milano
2085 [p.92]

JAMES MACARDELL
1727/8–65
AFTER
WILLIAM HOGARTH
1697–1764

John Pine c.1756
Mezzotint on paper
29 × 22.2
Museum of Freemasonry,
London
GBR 1991 P 10/32/22
[p.189]

MEISSEN
PORCELAIN
FACTORY

*Plate featuring scene II of
Hogarth's 'A Harlot's Progress'*
c.1740
Hard-paste porcelain,
painted in enamels and
gilded 25 × 25
Victoria and Albert Museum,
London
C.240-1923 [p.102]

PHILIP MERCIER
1689?–1760

Comedians by a Fountain
c.1735
Oil paint on canvas
71.3 × 91.8
The Royal Collection /
HM Queen Elizabeth II
RCIN 401328 [p.141]

*A Scene from 'The Careless
Husband'* 1738
Oil paint on canvas
100.3 × 124.5
York Museums Trust
(York Art Gallery)
YORAG: 1179 [p.144]

JAN PUNT
1711–79
AND
PIETER TANJÉ
1706–61
AFTER
CORNELIS TROOST
1696–1750

*Guardhouse of Dutch
Officers* 1754
Corps de Garde van
Hollandsche Officiers
Engraving on paper
38.6 × 51
Collection Rijksmuseum
Twenthe, Enschede (NL)
3134 [p.116]

TIBOUT REGTERS
1710–68

*Portrait of the Engraver
Jan Casper Philips* 1747
Oil paint on panel
35 × 30
Rijksmuseum
SK-A-2671 [p.187]

*Portrait of the Van den Broeck
family* c.1760
Portret van de familie
Van den Broeck
Oil paint on canvas 86 × 103
Collection Rijksmuseum
Twenthe, Enschede (NL).
Loan Family Van Katwijk
BR3049 [p.180]

MARCO RICCI
1676–1729

Rehearsal of an opera c.1709
Oil paint on canvas
48.3 × 55.9
Yale Center for British Art,
Paul Mellon Collection
B1981.25.523 [p.79]

Rehearsal of an opera c.1709
Oil paint on canvas
46.4 × 57.8
Yale Center for British Art,
Paul Mellon Collection
B1981.25.524 [p.79]

JEAN ROCQUE
c.1704–62
AND
JOHN PINE
1690–1756

*A Plan of the Cities of London
and Westminster, and Borough
of Southwark; with the
contiguous buildings* 1746
Engraving on paper
204.2 × 386.5
The British Library
Maps* 3480 (293)
[pp.22–3]

LOUIS FRANÇOIS
ROUBILIAC
1702–62

William Hogarth c.1741
Terracotta bust 74 × 48
National Portrait Gallery,
London. Puchased, 1861
NPG 121 [p.64]

*Arabella, née Bates,
wife of George Aufrere* 1748
Marble 69 × 44 × 25
Private collection
8515 [p.194]

ANDRÉ ROUQUET
1701–59

William Hogarth c.1740–5
Enamel on copper 4.5 × 3.7
National Portrait Gallery,
London. Purchased, 1984
NPG 5717 [p.64]

PAUL SANDBY
c.1730/1–1809

*London Cries: A Tinker
and His Wife* c.1759
Wash, graphite and
watercolour on paper
19.4 × 14.3
Yale Center for British Art,
Paul Mellon Collection
B1975.3.220

*London Cries: Last Dying
Speech and Confession* c.1759
Watercolour over graphite
on paper 17.5 × 14.3
Yale Center for British Art,
Paul Mellon Collection
B1975.3.225 [p.86]

*London Cries: A Girl with
a Basket of Oranges* c.1759
Watercolour on paper
18.8 × 17.1
Yale Center for British Art,
Paul Mellon Collection
B1975.3.223 [p.86]

ANDREA SOLDI
c.1703–71

Louis François Roubiliac 1751
Oil paint on canvas 97.5 × 83
Dulwich Picture Gallery,
London
DPG603 [p.65]

PIERRE SUBLEYRAS
1699–1749

*The Amorous Courtesan,
from a tale by Jean de
la Fontaine* c.1735
La Courtisane amoureuse
d'après un conte de
Jean de la Fontaine
Oil paint on canvas
30 × 23
Paris, Musée du Louvre,
Department of Paintings
RF 1985-80 [p.154]

PIETER TANJÉ
1706–61 AFTER
PHILIP VAN DIJK
1680/3–1753

*Portrait of Pastor Jacobus
Elisa Capitein* 1742
Portret van predikant
Jacobus Elisa Capitein
Etching on paper 24.2 × 18.1
Rijksmuseum. Gift of
Mrs Brandt, Amsterdam
and Mrs Brandt, Amsterdam
RP-P-1903-A-23405 [p.188]

CORNELIS TROOST
1696–1750

*Unseemly Love, perhaps a
scene of the Widower Joost
with Lucia, 2nd scene from the
play 'De wanhebbelijke liefde'
by C.J. van der Lijn* 1720–50
Oil paint on panel
45.4 × 33.6
Rijksmuseum
SK-A-4099 [p.155]

Self-portrait 1739
Oil paint on canvas 103 × 83
Rijksmuseum. Purchased
with the support of the
Verniging Rembrandt and
the Stichting tot Bevordering
van de Belangen van het
Rijksmuseum
SK-A-4225 [p.59]

*Misled: The Ambassador of the
Rascals Exposes himself from
the Window of 't Bokki Tavern
in the Harlemmerhout*
c.1739–50
Oil paint on canvas 157 × 104
Rijksmuseum
SK-A-4089 [p.91]

*Johanna and the Jewish
Merchants* 1741
Oil paint on panel 68.5 × 86
Rijksmuseum. Gift of
Mr and Mrs Leopold
Siemens-Ruyter, Blaricum
SK-A-4209 [p.146]

Portrait of a Lady 1741
Oil paint on canvas 69 × 57
York Museums Trust (York
Art Gallery). Presented by
F.D. Lycett Green through
The Art Fund, 1955
YORAG: 786 [p.186]

The Lost Sentry, tenth scene 1745
De Verloren Schildwacht
Watercolour and gouache
over graphite on paper
33.6 × 24.7
The Royal Collection /
HM Queen Elizabeth II
RCIN 912858 [p.147]

Guardroom Scene 1747
Oil paint on canvas
83.5 × 122.5
Mauritshuis, Den Haag,
on long-term loan from the
Friends of the Mauritshuis
Foundation, since 1980
1034 [p.117]

LODOVICO UGHI

*Iconographic Representation
of the City of Venice* 1729
Iconografica Rappresentatione
Della Inclitta Città Di Venezia
Copperplate engraving
on paper 153.6 × 210
The British Library
Maps K. Top. 78.63.8
TAB END [pp.46–7]

UNKNOWN ARTIST
AFTER
WILLIAM HOGARTH
1697–1764

*A Midnight Modern
Conversation* c.1732
Oil paint on canvas
76.2 × 163.8
Yale Center for British Art,
Paul Mellon Collection
B1981.25.351 [pp.12, 124–5]

*Punchbowl decorated with
a depiction of Hogarth's
'A Midnight Modern
Conversation'* c.1775
Porcelain with coloured
enamel 23 × 53.5
Chen Art Gallery,
Torrance CA USA
PO-199 [pp.104–5]

*Punchbowl featuring Hogarth's
'A Midnight Modern
Conversation'* 1780s
Chinese export porcelain
22.5 × 53.5
KODE Art Museums and
Composer Homes, Norway
VK.01153 [p.123]

UNKNOWN ARTIST,
FRENCH SCHOOL

The Hunting Lunch 1710–15
Le Goûter de chasse
Oil paint on canvas
251.6 × 203.2
Musée des Beaux-Arts,
Orléans
Inv.553 [p.148]

GEORGE VERTUE
1684–1756
AND
WILLIAM HOGARTH
1697–1764

*The Reverend Mr Benjamin
Hoadly, BD* 1704–16
Engraving with annotations
in ink and gouache on paper
35.5 × 28
The Royal Collection /
HM Queen Elizabeth II
RCIN 812477 [p.120]

JEAN-ANTOINE
WATTEAU
1684–1721

The Pleasures of the Ball
c.1715–17
Les Plaisirs du Bal
Oil paint on canvas
52.5 × 65.2
Dulwich Picture Gallery,
London
DPG156 [p.140]

JOHAN ZOFFANY
1733–1810

David Garrick 1762–3
Oil paint on canvas
75.2 × 62.7
The Ashmolean Museum,
University of Oxford.
Accepted by HM Government
in lieu of Inheritance
Tax from the estate of
Mrs Joan Cecily Conway
and allocated to the
Ashmolean Museum, 1999
WA 1999.10 [p.145]

WORKS ILLUSTRATED
BUT NOT EXHIBITED

GIOVANNI
ANTONIO CANAL
(KNOWN AS
CANALETTO)
1697–1768

The Feast Day of Saint Roch
1735
Oil paint on canvas
47.7 × 199.4
National Gallery, London
[p.50]

ROSALBA CARRIERA
1673–1757

*Gustavus Hamilton, 2nd
Viscount Boyne, in Masquerade
Costume* 1730–1
Pastel on paper 56.5 × 42.9
The Metropolitan Museum
of Art, New York. Purchase,
George Delacorte Fund Gift,
in memory of George T.
Delacorte Jr., and Gwynne
Andrews, Victor Wilbour
Memorial, and Marquand
Funds, 2002
[p.53]

ERNST LUDWIG
CREITE
1728–1765
AFTER
WILLIAM HOGARTH
1697–1764

*A Midnight Modern
Conversation* 1733–50
Engraving on paper
35.5 × 26.2
The British Museum
Cc,2.105 [p.122]

PIERRE-ANTOINE
DEMACHY
1723–1807

*View of the Colonnade
of the Louvre* 1772
Oil paint on canvas
49.8 × 73.5
Musée du Louvre, Paris
[p.43]

THOMAS
GAINSBOROUGH
1727–88

Ignatius Sancho 1768
Oil paint on canvas
73.7 × 62.2
National Gallery of Canada,
Ottawa
[p.21]

WILLIAM HOGARTH
1697–1764

Self-Portrait c.1735
Oil paint on canvas
54.6 × 50.8
Yale Center for British Art,
Paul Mellon Collection
[p.62]

Before c.1730–1
Oil paint on canvas
36.5 × 44.8
Fitzwilliam Museum,
Cambridge
[p.173]

After c.1730–1
Oil paint on canvas
37 × 44.6
Fitzwilliam Museum,
Cambridge
[p.173]

DOROTHY MERCIER

Tradecard c.1750
(acquired by
Sarah Banks 1791)
Etching on paper
25.3 × 14.9
The British Museum
[p.29]

CORNELIS PRONK
1691–1759 fl.1735–68

*The Town Hall and Weighhouse
on Dam Square* 1743
Ink on paper 16.8 × 24.7
Stadsarchief Amsterdam,
Collectie Atlas Splitberger
[p.36]

GABRIEL-JACQUES
DE SAINT-AUBIN
1724–80

A Street Show in Paris 1760
Oil paint on canvas
80 × 64.1
National Gallery, London
[p.44]

THOMAS SANDBY

A View of St. Martin's Court
c.1765
Pen, ink and watercolour
on paper 17.8 × 18.7
The Lewis Walpole Library
c/o Lowell Lisbon &
Jonny Yarker Ltd
[p.26]

HERMANUS PETRUS
SCHOUTEN
1747–1822

*Picture Sale at the Oudezijds
Herenlogement* 1771
Watercolour and ink
on paper 27.7 × 26.4
The British Museum
[p.34]

CORNELIS TROOST
1696–1750

*False Virtue Discovered:
the discovery of Volkert
in the basket* 1735
Oil paint on canvas
105 × 82.2
Collection Rijksmuseum
Twenthe, Enschede (NL).
This work was recovered
from Germany after
the Second World War,
was placed under the
management of the Dutch
State and is awaiting the
restitution to the rightful
owners or their heirs.
[p.90]

*False Virtue Discovered:
the feigned sadness of
Geertruy* 1745
Oil paint on canvas
105 × 82
Collection Rijksmuseum
Twenthe, Enschede (NL).
Pending restitution to
the rightful owner.
[p.90]

REINIER VINKELES
1741–1816

*Drawing after a nude model
in the City Drawing Academy
in the Leidsepoort* 1764
Engraving 34.9 × 49.3
Stadsarchief Amsterdam,
Collectie Atlas Splitberger
[p.37]

JEAN-ANTOINE
WATTEAU
1684–1721

The Misstep 1716–18
Oil paint on canvas
40 × 31
Musée du Louvre, Paris
[p.175]

Eight Studies of Heads
c.1715–16
Chalk on paper
26.7 × 39.7
Musée du Louvre, Paris
[p.198]

ANTON MARIA
ZANNETTI THE ELDER
1680–1767

*A Self-portrait in carnival
costume, sketching* c.1740
Pen and ink 28.5 × 20.4
Royal Collection
RCIN 907419 [p.52]

*The Court Room at the
Foundling Museum*
The Foundling Museum,
London
[p.28]

CREDITS

Collection Albright-Knox Art Gallery, Buffalo, New York; Gift of Seymour H. Knox, Jr., 1945 (1945:2.1). Photo: Brenda Bieger for Albright-Knox Art Gallery, Buffalo, New York 169

The Art Institute of Chicago 95, 160

© Ashmolean Museum 145

Collection Atlas Splitgerber 36–7

© The Henry Barber Trust, The Barber Institute of Fine Arts, University of Birmingham 89, 143

Photo by Birmingham Museums Trust, licensed under CC0 68 bottom

© British Library Board / Maps* 3480 (293) 22–4; / Maps K. Top. 106.56 30–2; / Maps S.T.P.185 38–40; / Maps K. Top. 78.63.8 TAB. END. 46–8

Cincinnati Art Museum, The Edwin and Virginia Irwin Memorial, 1983.138 72–3

© Compton Verney / Bridgeman Images 76–7

Photo © Christie's Images / Bridgeman Images 104–5

© Dulwich Picture Gallery / Bridgeman Images 65, 140

Andrew Edmunds 81, 99–101; / Photography by Prudence Cuming 80, 82, 116 top

Ferens Art Gallery: Hull Museums 69

© Fitzwilliam Museum, Cambridge 93, 173, 191

Photographer: Sybille Forster. Munich, Alte Pinakothek Muenchen – Bayerische Staatsgemaeldesammlungen. © 2021. Photo Scala, Florence / bpk, Bildagentur fuer Kunst, Kultur und Geschichte, Berlin 182

Dag Fosse / KODE 123

© The Foundling Museum, London 74–5

Copyright The Frick Collection 19, 184

Photography by Mike Hayward 118, 120 top

Houghton Hall archives 181

The J. Paul Getty Museum, Los Angeles 68 top, 170–1

Courtesy of Krannert Art Museum, University of Illinois Urbana-Champaign 142

The Lewis Walpole Library c/o Lowell Libson & Jonny Yarker Ltd 26

© Manchester Art Gallery / Bridgeman Images 185

Mauritshuis, The Hague. On long-term loan from the Friends of the Mauritshuis Foundation, since 1980 117

© The Metropolitan Museum of Art, New York 53

By permission of the Ministry of Culture – National Art Gallery of Bologna 94

© Museum of Freemasonry, London 189

© National Gallery, London 44, 50, 152–3, 161–3, 166

National Gallery of Canada, Ottawa. Photo: NGC 21

National Galleries of Scotland. Purchased 1908 56

© National Maritime Museum, Greenwich, London 115

© National Portrait Gallery, London 64, 67

© National Trust Images 16, 149; / John Hammond 88

Norfolk Museums Service (Norwich Castle Museum & Art Gallery) 119

Orléans, Musée des Beaux-arts © François Lauginie 148

©Pinacoteca di Brera, Milano 92

Private collection 178–9

Private collection / John Bodkin of Dawkins Colour 159

Private Collection / Source: Historic England Archive 168

Rijksmuseum, Amsterdam 59, 91, 188

Collection Rijksmuseum Twenthe, Enschede (photography R. Klein Gotink) 90, 116 bottom; / Bruikleen Rijksmuseum Amsterdam (photography R. Klein Gotink) 146, 155; / Bruikleen Familie van Katwijk (photography R. Klein Gotink) 180; / Bruikleen Rijksmuseum Amsterdam (photography Rijksmuseum Amsterdam) 187

Photo © RMN-Grand Palais / Daniel Arnaudet 66

Photo © RMN-Grand Palais (musée du Louvre) / Jean-Gilles Berizzi 133, 198; / Stéphane Maréchalle 43; / Franck Raux 154, 175; / Michel Urtado 114

Royal Collection Trust / © Her Majesty Queen Elizabeth II 2021 52, 120 bottom, 122 top, 132, 141, 147, 183

Saint Louis Art Museum, Museum Purchase 256:1948 15, 126–7

© 2021. Photo Scala, Florence 98

© Sir John Soane's Museum, London 108–11

© Tate, 2021 / Oliver Cowling 199; / Oliver Cowling and Sam Day 83–5; / Oliver Cowling and Joe Humphrys 121; / Lucy Dawkins front cover, 2, 57–8; / Lucy Dawkins and Joe Humphrys 194; / Joe Humphrys 78, 190, 192–3

© The Trustees of The British Museum 29, 34, 87, 122 bottom

© Victoria and Albert Museum, London 102, 151

Steve Vidler / Alamy Stock Photo 28

Yale Center for British Art, Paul Mellon Collection 12, 62, 79, 86, 124–5, 196–7; / Yale Center for British Art, Paul Mellon Fund, in honour of Brian Allen, Director of Studies, Paul Mellon Centre for Studies in British Art (1993–2012) 150

York Museums Trust (York Art Gallery) 144, 186, 195

SUPPORTING TATE

Tate relies on a large number of supporters – individuals, Tate Patrons, International Council, Acquisitions Committees, foundations, companies and public sector sources – to enable it to deliver its programme of activities, both on and off its gallery sites. This support is essential in order for Tate to acquire works of art for the Collection, run education, outreach and exhibition programmes, care for the Collection in storage and enable art to be displayed, both digitally and physically, inside and outside Tate.

Please contact us at:

Development Office
Tate
Millbank
London SWIP 4RG

Tel: +44 (0)20 7887 4900
Fax: +44 (0)20 7887 8098

Tate Americas Foundation
520 West 27 Street Unit 404
New York, NY 10001
USA

Tel: 001 212 643 2818
Fax: 001 212 643 1001

Donations, no matter the size, are gratefully received, either to support particular areas of interest, or to contribute to general activity costs.

LEGACIES

A legacy to Tate may take the form of a residual share of an estate, a specific cash sum, or an item of property such as a work of art. Legacies to Tate are free of inheritance tax and help to secure a strong future for the Collection and galleries. For further information please contact the Development Office.

OFFERS IN LIEU OF TAX

Inheritance Tax can be satisfied by transferring to the Government a work of art of outstanding importance. In this case the amount of tax is reduced. It can be made a condition of the offer that the work of art is allocated to Tate. Please contact us for details.

TATE MEMBERS

Tate Members enjoy unlimited free admission throughout the year to all exhibitions at Tate, as well as a number of other benefits such as exclusive use of our Members' Rooms and a free annual subscription to *Tate Etc*. Whilst enjoying the exclusive privileges of membership, members also help secure Tate's position at the very heart of British and modern art. Members support actively contributes towards new purchases of important art, ensuring that Tate's collection continues to be relevant and comprehensive, as well as funding projects in London, Liverpool and St Ives that increase access and understanding for everyone.

TATE PATRONS

Tate Patrons share a passion for art and are committed to supporting Tate on an annual basis. The Patrons help enable the acquisition of works across Tate's broad collecting remit and support the staging of major exhibitions in the galleries. They also give their support to vital conservation, learning and research projects. The scheme provides a forum for Patrons to share their interest in art and meet curators, artists and one another in an enjoyable environment through a regular programme of events. These events take place both at Tate and beyond and encompass curator-led exhibition tours, visits to artists' studios and private collections, art trips both in the UK and abroad, and access to art fairs. The scheme welcomes supporters from outside the UK, giving the programme a truly international scope.

CORPORATE MEMBERSHIP

Corporate Membership at Tate offers companies opportunities for corporate entertaining and the chance for a wide variety of employee benefits. These include special private views, special access to paying exhibitions, out-of-hours visits and tours, invitations to VIP events and talks at members' offices.

CORPORATE INVESTMENT

Tate has developed a range of imaginative partnerships with the corporate sector, ranging from international interpretation and exhibition programmes to local outreach and staff development programmes. We are particularly known for high-profile business to business marketing initiatives and employee benefit packages. Please contact the Corporate Partnerships team for further details.

CHARITY DETAILS

The Tate Gallery is an exempt charity; the Museums & Galleries Act 1992 added the Tate Gallery to the list of exempt charities defined in the 1960 Charities Act. Tate Foundation is a registered charity (number 1085314).

TATE AMERICAS FOUNDATION

Tate Americas Foundation is an independent charity based in New York that supports the work of Tate in the United Kingdom. It receives full tax exempt status from the IRS under section 501(c)(3) allowing United States taxpayers to receive tax deductions on gifts towards annual membership programmes, exhibitions, scholarship and capital projects. For more information please contact the Tate Americas Foundation office.

This information is correct as of the beginning of April 2021

Šejla Kamerić
Peter and Maria Kellner
J. Patrick Kennedy and
    Patricia A. Kennedy
Ku-lim Kim
Jack Kirkland
David Knaus
Evgenij Kozlov and
    Hannelore Fobo
Samuel H. Kress
    Foundation
David Kronn
Lachaise Foundation
The Estate of Sheila
    Lanyon
Fondation Walter &
    Nicole LeBlanc
Agnès and Edward
    Lee Acquisition Fund
Edward Lee in memory
    of Agnès Lee
Legacy Trust UK
Kiyoko Lerner
Ruben Levi
Lévy Gorvy Gallery
The Linbury Trust
James Lindon
The London Community
    Foundation
LUMA Foundation
Lyndsey Ingram Ltd
Kathleen Madden and
    Paul Frantz
Kim Manocherian
The Manton Foundation
The Estate of Sir Edwin
    Manton
Matt's Gallery
Lord McAlpine of
    West Green
David McDermott and
    Peter McGough
The Estate of Kenneth
    McGowan
The Mead Family
    Foundation
The Andrew W.
    Mellon Foundation
The Estate of Ana
    Mendieta
Helen Mignano
Naomi Milgrom AC
Greg Miller
Victoria Miro
Ronald Moody Trust
Henry Moore Foundation
Mottahedan Family
National Heritage
    Memorial Fund
The National Lottery
    Heritage Fund
The National Trust
Mike Nelson
New Carlsberg
    Foundation
Hermann Nitsch and
    Nitsch Foundation
Simon Nixon and family
Mike and Sukey Novogratz
Reine and Boris Okuliar
Open Hand

Ordnance Survey
Outset Contemporary
    Art Fund
Pace Gallery
Yukiko Pajot
Maureen Paley
Midge and Simon Palley
Veronique Parke
Martin Parr
Paul Mellon Centre for
    Studies in British Art
Estate of Carl-Henning
    Pedersen
Yana and Stephen Peel
Catherine Petitgas
Patricia Phelps de Cisneros
The Stanley Picker Trust
The Pivovarov Family
The Porthmeor Fund
David W. Posnett, OBE
John and Joyce Price
Fiona Rae, in honour
    of Sir Nicholas Serota
Joanna Rajkowska and
    l'étrangère
Michael Rakowitz
Priya Rath & Vishrut Jain
The Rennie Foundation
Marsha Ribeiro
Dianne Roberts
Ms Erica Roberts
The Roman Family
    Collection
The Estate of Eugene and
    Penelope Rosenberg
Dr Ian Rothery
The Rothschild Foundation
Kristin Rey and Michael
    Rubel
Roland Rudd
The Estate of
    Simon Sainsbury
Gillian and Simon
    Salama-Caro
Jean and Melanie Salata
John Schaeffer
Karsten Schubert
Jake and Hélène
    Marie Shafran
Jack Shear
Philippa Simpson
The Estate of Sylvia Sleigh
Matthew Slotover and
    Emily King
Jay Smith and Laura Rapp
Wendy Smith
Rimma Solod-Iankilevski
Lord Stevenson of
    Coddenham, CBE
Emile Stipp
Mercedes and Ian
    Stoutzker
Maria Sukkar
Mr Patrick Sun
The Sunpride Foundation
SUPERFLEX
Beth Swofford
Tamares Real Estate
    Holdings, Inc. in
    collaboration with the
    Zabludowicz Collection

Nicolas Tate
Tate 1897 Circle
Tate Africa Acquisitions
    Committee
Tate Americas Foundation
Tate Asia-Pacific
    Acquisitions Committee
Tate European Collection
    Circle
Tate International Council
Tate Latin American
    Acquisitions Committee
Tate Members
Tate Middle East North
    Africa Acquisitions
    Committee
Tate North American
    Acquisition Committee
Tate Patrons
Tate Photography
    Acquisitions Committee
Tate Russia and Eastern
    Europe Acquisitions
    Committee
Tate South Asia
    Acquisitions Committee
Tavolozza Foundation
Teiger Foundation
Dr Andreas Teoh
Terra Foundation
    for American Art
The Estate of Mr
    Nicholas Themans
Thomas Dane Gallery
Imants Tillers and
    Michael Nelson
    Jagamara
Russell Tovey
Francois Trausch, in
    memory of Caroline
    Trausch
Bill and Ruth True
Luc Tuymans
Lance Uggla
V-A-C Foundation
The Estate of Miguel Angel
    Vidal and The Ungallery
Mercedes Vilardell
John Virtue and Ali and
    Michael Hue-Williams,
    in memory of Karsten
    Schubert
Estate of Branko Vlahović
Marie-Louise von
    Motesiczky Charitable
    Trust
Wagner Foundation
Anne Walmsley
Peter Warwick
Michael Werner, in honour
    of Sir Nicholas Serota
Emma Whitaker
White Cube Ltd
Rachel Whiteread
Jane and Michael Wilson
The Michael G. and C.
    Jane Wilson 2007 Trust
The Lord Leonard and
    Lady Estelle Wolfson
    Foundation
Zhang Xiaogang

Qiao Zhibing, in honour
    of Gregor Muir
Fernando Zobel de Ayala
Roman Zubal
*and those who wish to
remain anonymous*